Kevin S. McCurley   Claus Dieter Ziegler   (Eds.)

Advances in Cryptology
1981 – 1997

Electronic Proceedings and Index of the
CRYPTO and EUROCRYPT Conferences
1981 – 1997

Springer

Series Editors

Gerhard Goos, Karlsruhe University, Germany
Juris Hartmanis, Cornell University, NY, USA
Jan van Leeuwen, Utrecht University, The Netherlands

Volume Editors

Kevin S. McCurley
IBM Almaden Research Center
650 Harry Road, San Jose, CA 95120, USA
E-mail: mccurley@almaden.ibm.com

Claus Dieter Ziegler
Fachinformationszentrum Karlsruhe, Abteilung Mathematik und Informatik
Franklinstrasse 11, D-10587 Berlin, Germany
E-mail: cdz@zblmath.fiz-karlsruhe.de

Cataloging-in-Publication data applied for

Die Deutsche Bibliothek - CIP-Einheitsaufnahme

Advances in cryptology : 1981 - 1997 ; electronic proceedings and index of the
Crypto and Eurocrypt Conferences 1981 - 1997 / Kevin S. McCurley ; Claus Dieter
Ziegler (ed.). - Berlin ; Heidelberg ; New York ; Barcelona ; Hong Kong ;
London ; Milan ; Paris ; Singapore ; Tokyo : Springer, 1999
  (Lecture notes in computer science ; Vol. 1440)
  ISBN 3-540-65069-5

CR Subject Classification (1991): E.3, G.2.1, D.4.6, K.6.5, F.2.1-2, C.2, J.1

ISSN 0302-9743
ISBN 3-540-65069-5 Springer-Verlag Berlin Heidelberg New York

© Springer-Verlag Berlin Heidelberg 1998
Printed in Germany

Typesetting: Camera-ready by author
SPIN 10638017   06/3142 – 5 4 3 2 1 0   Printed on acid-free paper

Lecture Notes in Computer Science 1440

Edited by G. Goos, J. Hartmanis and J. van Leeuwen

Springer

Berlin
Heidelberg
New York
Barcelona
Hong Kong
London
Milan
Paris
Singapore
Tokyo

Table of Contents

Foreword

About Cryptology

It is now widely perceived that we are experiencing an information revolution whose effects will ultimately be as pervasive and profound as was brought by the industrial revolution of the last century. From the beginning of time, information has been an important asset for humans. In the early days of human existence, the mere knowledge of where to most easily gather food was the difference between life and death. Throughout history, information has provided the means for winning wars, making fortunes, and shaping history. The underlying theme of the information revolution is that we continue to find new ways to use information. These new uses for information serve to highlight our need to protect different aspects of information.

Cryptology may be broadly defined as the scientific study of adversarial information protection. Cryptology has traditionally dealt with the confidentiality of information, but innovation in using information produces new requirements for protection of that information. Some are longstanding and fundamental - how do we guarantee that information is "authentic"? How do we guarantee that information is timely? How can we produce bits that have the same properties as "money"? Each of these questions has been grappled with in the cryptologic research community.

History of the IACR

Cryptography has a long and illustrious history, but relatively little published scientific literature existed prior to the mid 1970s, when public key cryptography was discovered and interest was sparked in the scientific study of information protection. The early 1980's saw a number of conferences on the subject of cryptography, including the first conference held in Santa Barbara in 1981, organized by Alan Gersho of UCSB. This was followed in 1982 by the CRYPTO '82 conference. A report on this conference was published by David Kahn in Cryptologia the following year:

> "At the initiative of David Chaum the organizer of CRYPTO '82, some attendees met the last day to begin organizing what they

tentatively called an International Association for Cryptologic Research. Its main functions would be (1) to coordinate meetings on cryptology as to time, place and program and in some cases to run them, and (2) to publish a bulletin to give notice of conferences and of cryptologic sessions other conferences. Members of the organizing committee are Chaum; Henry J. Beker of RACAL-Comsec Ltd. in Salisbury, England; Whitfield Diffie of BNR in Palo Alto, California; Robert R. Jueneman of Satellite Business Systems in McLean, Virginia; Ernest F. Brickell of Sandia National Laboratories in Albuquerque, New Mexico; Stephen Kent of Bolt, Beranek & Newman in Cambridge, Massachusetts; and David Kahn of Great Neck, New York, an editor of Cryptologia."

CRYPTO '83 then became the first conference officially sponsored by IACR. From these early beginnings, IACR has grown to be a scientific organization with over a thousand members worldwide, representing over 65 countries. IACR now sponsors two conferences each year, called CRYPTO and EUROCRYPT. CRYPTO is held each year in August at the University of California in Santa Barbara, USA. EUROCRYPT is held each spring in a different location in Europe. IACR will also begin sponsorship of the Asiacrypt conference in 2000.

Proceedings of CRYPTO and EUROCRYPT

The work published here includes the proceedings of all conferences that have been organized by the International Association for Cryptologic Research since 1983. In addition, material from a few other conferences that spawned IACR is included:

- proceedings of CRYPTO '81. These were first published as a technical report by the University of California, Santa Barbara, and have had only very limited circulation prior to this volume. In addition, it was previously published in SIGACT News in 1983.
- proceedings of the 1982 predecessor to EUROCRYPT. The IACR was in the process of being formed at that time, but there was already an intent among many of the organizers for this to be the first in a series of European conferences on cryptology organized by IACR. The '82 conference was not originally called EUROCRYPT, but is now generally referred to as EUROCRYPT '82.
- proceedings of Crypto '82 and '83. These were originally published by Plenum Publishing. As of the time of this writing (mid-1998), the proceedings of Crypto '83 are no longer available in print.
- abstracts from EUROCRYPT '86. This volume was only distributed to conference attendees.

EUROCRYPT '86 and CRYPTO '81 had no formal proceedings, and the material included here consists mostly of abstracts. In fact, over time it is possible to detect a noticeable change in the tone of papers in all of these volumes, from early publication of "Extended Abstracts" to more carefully refereed high quality papers.

The proceedings of both CRYPTO and EUROCRYPT have been published by Springer-Verlag since 1984 in the series "Lecture Notes in Computer Science". Prior to 1994, authors submitted abstracts that were distributed to attendees at the conference, and these abstracts were then refined and published as a formal proceedings at a later date. (an exception was made at EUROCRYPT '86). Beginning with CRYPTO '94, proceedings of EUROCRYPT and CRYPTO have been available at the conference.

The Evolution of Cryptology Research

The work published here represents the majority of the important research work that has been published by the open cryptologic research community during the last fifteen years. In spite of the great work that has been done, there are still huge gaps in our knowledge of information protection. I hope that the republication of these proceedings will stimulate further research in the field and I thank Springer-Verlag for supporting the initiative to produce them.

Looking at how the field has evolved over the years, there are some noticeable trends. The ones that are most noticeable to this author are the following:

Complexity-based reasoning on security

The first mention that I am aware of involving reasoning about security based on what an adversary could *compute* appeared in Shannon's seminal paper of 1948. Once Diffie and Hellman published their paper on public key cryptography, we were presented with concrete constructions that led to a huge body of work on complexity-based reasoning on security. In recent years some of the work in complexity-based security has incorporated some of the original ideas of Shannon on information-theoretic security. In spite of the considerable progress that has been made, I would argue that the field is still not closed, because some of the assumptions we are required to make in order to prove reasonable security are still questionable. Moreover, computing is fundamentally about resource management, and in spite of Moore's law, there continue to be increasing demands for processing speed, storage, and communication. The constructions that we have today may have considerable room for improvement, both in their security and their practicality.

Environmental Attacks and Protocols

I use the term "environmental attacks" to include things such as fault analysis, timing attacks, and power analysis. Each of these has been demonstrated to pose a serious hazard in real world applications, and also serves to highlight several defects in our abstract modeling of security. First is the fact that our models of computers fail to take into account all aspects of their physical instantiation. Looking at a computer as a "black box" provides an elegant abstraction, but in practice the box exists in three dimensional space, manipulates energy, and produces ancillary outputs. Future models of computers and security may emerge to describe these phenomena. The second deficiency in our understanding has to do with the fact that true security requires analysis of protocols instead of serial algorithms. If we include parallel and distributed algorithms, then the difference between a protocol and an algorithm is that an algorithm *may* involve multiple parties, but a protocol always does. When reasoning about security, there are always at least two parties: the adversary and the participant. Any analysis that fails to address the capabilities of an adversary to affect the outputs is doomed to failure.

Linear and Differential Cryptanalysis

Linear and Differential cryptanalysis have emerged as the most effective general techniques available for attacking practical ciphers. At the same time, progress has been made in designing ciphers that are resistant to these attacks.

New Applications

Cryptology is no longer restricted to the study of only encryption and confidentiality. As new uses of information emerge, they bring with them new requirements for information. As a result, we have seen discussion of cryptographic constructions for electronic cash, timestamping, program checking, intellectual property protection, etc. Each of these applications raises whole new areas for investigation.

It is ironic that the publication of this CDROM itself raises interesting and serious issues in the protection of information, since the information age is changing the very foundation of what it means to "publish". Some have argued that electronic publishing raises serious concerns about the mechanism for archiving scientific work for the ages. Others have argued that the role of traditional publishers is threatened by the information age. Some publishers are concerned that their ability to make a living is threatened by electronic distribution of information, since bits are easily copied and the meaning of traditional copyrights are evolving. Nevertheless, Springer-Verlag has taken the lead in developing technologies that offer new capabilities for the use of information.

Some Statistics

I close this section with some statistics and trivia about the body of literature. This collection contains 1285 individual papers, by a total of 854 authors. In what follows, we use a shorthand notation for references. For example, a reference of the form c90-323 refers to a paper in CRYPTO '90 starting on page 323, and e91-14 refers to a paper in EUROCRYPT '91 starting on page 14.

Most Authors on a Single Paper

The following papers have the most co-authors.

10 authors c83-171, Davio, M., Desmedt, Y., Fosseprez, M., Govaerts, R., Hulsbosch, J., Neutjens, P., Piret, P., Quisquater, J. J., Vandewalle, J. and Wouters, P., Analytical characteristics of the DES

7 authors c88-37, Ben-Or, M., Goldreich, O., Goldwasser, S., Hastad, J., Kilian, J., Micali, S. and Rogaway, P., Everything provable is provable in zero-knowledge

7 authors c91-44, Bird, R., Gopal, I., Herzberg, A., Janson, P., Kutten, S., Molva, R. and Yung, M., Systematic design of two-party authentication protocols

7 authors e92-194, Desmedt, Y., Landrock, P., Lenstra, A. K., McCurley, K. S., Odlyzko, A. M., Rueppel, R. A. and Smid, M. E., The Eurocrypt '92 Controversial Issue: Trapdoor Primes and Moduli

6 authors e89-267, Vandewalle, J., Chaum, D., Fumy, W., Jansen, C. J. A., Landrock, P. and Roelofsen, G., A European call for cryptographic algorithms: RIPE; Race Integrity Primitives Evaluation

6 authors e91-547, Preneel, B., Chaum, D., Fumy, W., Jansen, C. J. A., Landrock, P. and Roelofsen, G., Race Integrity Primitives Evaluation

6 authors c92-471, Blundo, C., De Santis, A., Herzberg, A., Kutten, S., Vaccaro, U. and Yung, M., Perfectly-secure key distribution for dynamic conferences

5 authors c96-329, Hughes, R. J., Luther, G. G., Morgan, G. L., Peterson, C. G. and Simmons, C., Quantum Cryptography over Underground Optical Fibers

5 authors c81-154, Diffie, W., Klein, M., Dertouzos, M. L., Gleason, A. and Smith, D., Panel Discussion: National Security and Commercial Security: Division of Responsibility

5 authors c84-144, Davio, M., Desmedt, Y., Goubert, J., Hoornaert, F. and Quisquater, J. J., Efficient hardware and software implementations for the DES

5 authors e85-43, Vandewalle, J., Govaerts, R., De Becker, W., Decroos, M. and Speybrouck, G., Implementation study of public key cryptography protection in an existing electronic mail and document handling system.

5 authors c85-3, Estes, D., Adleman, L. M., Kompella, K., McCurley, K. S. and Miller, G. L., Breaking the Ong-Schnorr-Shamir signature scheme for quadratic number fields

5 authors c86-277, Orton, G. A., Roy, M. P., Scott, P. A., Peppard, L. E. and Tavares, S. E., VLSI implementation of public-key encryption algorithms

5 authors c88-297, Abadi, M., Allender, E., Broder, A., Feigenbaum, J. and Hemachandra, L. A., On generating solved instances of computational problems

5 authors e89-294, Chaum, D., den Boer, B., van Heyst, E., Mjoelsnes, S. F. and Steenbeek, A., Efficient offline electronic checks (extended abstract)

5 authors e90-161, Preneel, B., Van Leekwijck, W., Van Linden, L., Govaerts, R. and Vandewalle, J., Propagation characteristics of Boolean functions

5 authors e90-253, Bennett, C. H., Bessette, F., Brassard, G., Salvail, L. and Smolin, J., Experimental quantum cryptography

5 authors e90-465, Guillou, L. C., Quisquater, J. J., Walker, M., Landrock, P. and Shaer, C., Precautions taken against various potential attacks in ISO/IEC DIS 9796

5 authors e92-356, Biehl, I., Buchmann, J. A., Meyer, B., Thiel, C. and Thiel, C., Tools for proving zero knowledge

5 authors c92-215, Dwork, C., Feige, U., Kilian, J., Naor, M. and Safra, M., Low communication 2-prover zero-knowledge proofs for NP

5 authors e93-126, Kurosawa, K., Okada, K., Sakano, K., Ogata, W. and Tsujii, S., Nonperfect secret sharing schemes and matroids

5 authors e94-433, Charnes, C., O'Connor, L., Pieprzyk, J., Safavi-Naini, R. and Zheng, Y., Comments on Soviet encryption algorithm

5 authors c94-150, Blundo, C., De Santis, A., Di Crescenzo, G., Gaggia, A. Giorgio and Vaccaro, U., Multi-secret sharing schemes

Most Papers by a Single Author

The following authors have the most papers published in the series:

Chaum, D. (38) c81-138, c82-199, c83-153, c83-387, c84-432, c84-481, e85-241, c85-18, c85-192, c86-49, c86-118, c86-195, c86-200, e87-127, e87-227, c87-87, c87-156, c87-462, e88-177, c88-319, e89-267, e89-288, e89-294, c89-212, c89-591, e90-458, c90-189, c90-206, e91-96, e91-257, e91-547, e91-554, c91-470, e92-390, c92-1, c92-89, e93-344, e94-86

Desmedt, Y. (34) c83-171, e84-62, e84-142, c84-144, c84-147, c84-359, c85-42, c85-516, c85-537, e86-17, c86-111, c86-459, c87-21, c87-120, e88-23, e88-183, c88-375, e89-75, e89-122, c89-6, c89-307, e90-1, e90-11, c90-169, c90-177, e91-81, e91-205, c91-457, e92-25, e92-194, c92-549, e94-275, e95-147, e96-107

Yung, M. (30) c84-439, c85-128, c87-40, c87-135, e89-3, e89-192, e89-196, e90-412, c90-94, c90-177, c90-366, e91-205, c91-44, c92-196, c92-442, c92-471, e93-267, e94-67, c95-222, c95-287, c95-339, e96-72, c96-89, c96-186, e97-62, e97-280, e97-450, c97-31, c97-264, c97-440

Kilian, J. (16) c88-2, c88-37, c89-498, c89-545, c90-62, c90-313, c90-378, c91-225, c92-215, c93-319, c94-341, c94-411, e95-393, c95-208, c95-311, c96-252

Vandewalle, J. (16) c83-171, e85-43, e86-20, e87-109, e87-287, e88-257, e89-267, c89-154, e90-161, e91-141, e93-159, c93-175, c93-224, c93-368, c96-298, e97-348

Pedersen, T. P. (16) c88-583, c90-189, e91-221, e91-522, c91-129, e92-366, e92-390, c92-15, c92-89, e93-329, c93-250, e94-140, e94-171, e95-39, e96-237, e96-372

Stinson, D. R. (15) c86-418, c87-330, c87-355, e88-51, c88-564, c90-242, c91-62, c91-74, e92-1, c92-168, e94-35, c94-247, c96-16, c96-387, e97-409

Goldwasser, S. (15) c82-211, c84-276, c84-289, c85-448, c88-37, c89-194, c89-498, c89-589, c89-604, c90-77, c92-228, c94-216, c97-105, c97-112, c97-277

Govaerts, R. (14) c83-171, e85-43, e86-20, e87-109, e88-257, c89-154, e90-161, e91-141, e93-159, c93-175, c93-224, c93-368, c96-298, e97-348

Massey, J. L. (14) e82-289, e84-74, e86-35, e87-3, e87-237, e89-382, c89-100, e90-389, e91-17, e92-55, c92-540, c94-332, e95-24, c96-358

Zheng, Y. (13) e89-412, c89-461, c90-285, c92-292, e93-181, c93-49, e94-299, e94-376, e94-433, c94-383, e95-274, e96-294, c97-165

De Santis, A. (13) c87-52, c88-269, e90-46, e90-412, c90-366, c91-101, e92-1, c92-148, c92-471, e93-118, c93-73, c93-110, c94-150

Pfitzmann, B. (13) e89-373, e89-690, e90-441, c91-338, c91-470, e92-153, c92-15, c93-250, e94-332, e95-121, e96-84, e97-88, e97-480

Beaver, D. (12) c89-560, c89-589, c90-62, c90-326, c91-377, c91-420, e92-285, e92-307, e93-424, c95-97, e96-119, c97-75

Krawczyk, H. (12) c88-146, c89-113, c89-138, c93-22, c93-136, c94-129, e95-301, c95-339, e96-354, c96-1, c96-157, c97-132

Stern, J. (12) e89-173, e90-313, c91-204, e93-50, c93-13, c93-435, c94-164, c94-202, e96-245, e96-387, e97-27, c97-198

Golic, J. D. (12) e90-487, e91-160, e91-527, e92-113, e92-124, e92-472, e94-230, e95-248, e96-268, e97-226, e97-239, c97-499

Naor, M. (12) c88-319, c89-128, c92-139, c92-196, c92-215, c93-355, c93-480, e94-1, c94-234, c94-257, c97-90, c97-322

Knudsen, L. R. (11) c92-497, c92-566, e93-286, e94-410, e94-419, c95-274, e96-224, e96-237, c96-216, e97-1, c97-485

Peralta, R. (11) e84-379, e85-62, c85-87, e86-15, c86-200, c87-128, e89-75, c89-507, e90-11, c92-324, e96-131

Rogaway, P. (11) c88-37, c90-62, c91-392, c93-232, e94-92, c94-341, c95-15, c95-29, e96-399, c96-252, c97-470

Kurosawa, K. (11) e90-374, c90-339, e93-126, e93-248, e93-461, c94-140, e95-289, c95-410, e96-200, e97-409, e97-434

Yacobi, Y. (11) e87-117, c87-418, c87-429, c89-344, e90-222, c90-268, c90-639, e91-498, e92-208, e92-458, c95-197

Beth, T. (11) e82-1, e84-88, c86-302, e87-25, e88-77, e89-533, e90-189, c90-169, e91-316, e93-65, c94-318

Program Committee Service

Serving on a program committee is a time consuming task, and often results in little recognition from the community. The following people have served on at least five program committees:

- Odlyzko, Andrew (10)
- Rivest, Ronald (9)
- Schnorr, Claus (7)
- Massey, James L. (7)
- Beth, Thomas (7)
- Berson, Thomas (7)
- Rueppel, Rainer (6)
- Desmedt, Yvo (6)
- Davies, Donald W. (6)
- Damgård, Ivan (6)
- Brickell, Ernest (6)
- Simmons, Gustavus J. (5)
- Quisquater, Jean-Jacques (5)
- Okamoto, Tatsuaki (5)
- Maurer, Ueli (5)
- Ingemarsson, Ingemar (5)
- Feigenbaum, Joan (5)
- Diffie, Whitfield (5)
- Denning, Dorothy (5)
- Chaum, David (5)
- Beker, Henry (5)

A complete list of program committees is included in this collection.

Kevin S. McCurley
IBM Almaden Research Center
September 1998

Preface

One of the challenges of embracing the information age is to enhance and carry forward the enormous amount of information that is archived in paper format. In this collection we have collected together the 14692 pages of information from the 32 volumes of conference proceedings of CRYPTO and EUROCRYPT. In addition, we have derived textual information that can be used to index and search this archive.

Compressing this much information onto a single CDROM required significant effort, but it was felt that this would enhance the usability of the collection with current technology. As a rough estimate we might assume that one printed volume of cryptology proceedings contains in the average about 460 pages. If we assume that a volume of 460 pages is 3.5 centimeters thick, one has to store 1.12 meters of paper proceedings. Suppose one page of a proceedings volume contains in the average 380 words or, including punctuation, 2500 characters (e.g. one page of volume 963 of LNCS contains 482 words or 3200 characters in the average whereas volume 196 contains only 253 words or 1710 characters per page). In this case we have to store 5.582.960 words or 36.730.000 characters or in computer terms about 40 megabytes if we store it as ASCII text.

Unfortunately, producing such text is nearly impossible, and we have chosen to provide information in the form of PDF files containing images. This is dictated by the content of the volumes, which are predominantly text, but are also mathematical in nature, containing many formulas and mathematical expressions. Over the years the fonts and typefaces changed from typewriter styles to DVI files, and particularly the quality of some early printed source documents is rather poor (especially the proceedings of CRYPTO 81 and EUROCRYPT 86). These factors contribute to a very high error rate for optical character recognition (OCR). Since mathematical content is of no value if the accuracy is compromised, we chose to deliver an electronic product that is as faithful as possible to the original material.

Given that a CDROM has a capacity of approximately 650 MB, this implies that the size of one proceedings page should not be much larger than about 40 KB, in order to leave room for a Keyword Index, an Author Index, the Table of Contents and a search engine for efficient and convenient retrieval of the documents.

By experimentation we learned that 400 dpi is a resolution where the OCR software could be trained to produce reasonable results. One page, scanned with a resolution of 400 dpi, has an average size of 140 KB when stored as 4636x3232 resolution TIF file. The TIF files served as the basis for the OCR process, because we need the text versions to produce indices. Once the TIF images were produced, we used an automatic process to crop white space from the borders, and transformed into PDF files using some of the software in the IBM database of US Patents. We experimented a great deal with different settings to balance the space requirement against the quality of the result. The final process took several days of processing on a personal computer.

Creating a search engine for OCR scanned text is a challenge in itself, from both an algorithmic and software point of view. We experimented with various approaches to this, and Kevin McCurley finally decided to write a Java applet for incorporation into the CDROM. This has several advantages:

- it is integrated into the browsing process of HTML and PDF documents,
- it offers portability across many different platforms, which is particularly important for a scientific audience accustomed to Unix workstations.

Unfortunately Java is still rather slow, consumes substantial memory, and has not yet reached full maturity as a programming language. As a result, we expect that some users may have trouble using the Applet, but perhaps this situation will improve with time.

From an algorithmic point of view, the problem of searching OCR data for keywords is the dual problem of spell checking - in the case of spell checking you assume the dictionary is correct, and compare a possibly incorrect word against the dictionary. In the case of searching OCR data, you assume the errors are in the dictionary (unless these can be removed by reference to a dictionary appropriate to the context), and look for occurences of the (presumably correct) search words in your approximate data. A great deal of work has been done in this field in the last few years, but we decided to adopt a simple approach for the applet. The method used by the applet is simply to check each string that is an edit distance of at most one from the target string, and see whether it appears in the text. For this purpose we use a hash table to locate all references to a given string. Note that if this method would not scale well to allow an edit distance of two, since the complexity of the algorithm is exponential in the maximal edit distance d.

In addition, we encountered further questions concerning quality control:

- How can corrupted or irregularly cropped pages be detected sytematically without having to go through all 14692 images by hand?
- How can completeness be ensured?
- How can be ensured that no contribution and no author were missed for the automatically produced Table of Contents and the Author Index?

We are satisfied that our process properly addressed the third point, but the first two remain a concern. When working with the CDROM you will certainly find errors, rough patches, and deficiencies. We invite you to tell us about them and send us suggestions for improvements. Any further information that we can provide to enhance the usability of this CD will be placed at the IACR web site (`http://www.iacr.org/cd/`).

The process of creating this work has been a collaboration between several people. We would like to particularly thank Andy Clark, Alfred Hofmann, Thomas Berson, Whitfield Diffie, Joan Feigenbaum, Bart Preneel, Tom Griffin, Jason Zien, Sridhar Rajagopalan, and our student workers. Although a curious series of accidents during this project delayed the publication, we are quite satisfied that the result will be of use to the research community.

Claus Dieter Ziegler
Kevin S. McCurley
September 1998

Part I: Conference Contents

ADVANCES IN CRYPTOGRAPHY

Allen Gersho, Editor

A Report on CRYPTO 81

ECE Rept No 82-04

CRYPTO 81

IEEE Workshop on Communications Security

held at

University of California, Santa Barbara

August 24-26, 1981

August 20, 1982
Department of Electrical & Computer Engineering
Santa Barbara, California 93106

Advances in Cryptography

Preface

     This report contains information provided by the authors about the papers presented at CRYPTO 81. In some cases only abstracts were available, in a few cases essentially complete papers have been included, and in most cases an extended abstract or summary is provided. The Table of Contents gives the complete program with the original titles. In a few papers, the authors have provided closely related material with different titles.

     This report is more an afterthought than a proceedings. The success of the workshop motivated considerable interest in making available some form of record of the event. The report was prepared for the participants of the workshop and for the use of the National Science Foundation whose support was of tremendous value by providing travel funds for several participants who would not otherwise have been able to attend.

Allen Gersho, Editor

CRYPTO 81

was sponsored by

The Data and Computer Communications Committees
of the
IEEE Communications Society

with the cooperation of the
Dept. of Electrical and Computer Engineering
University of California, Santa Barbara

The workshop was supported in part by the
National Science Foundation
Award No. ECS81-17145

Organizing Committee

Chairman: Allen Gersho (Univ. Calif., Santa Barbara)
Committee Members:
        Leonard Adleman (Univ. Southern Calif.)
        Whitfield Diffie (BNR)
        Martin Hellman (Stanford)
        Richard Kemmerer (Univ. Calif., Santa Barbara)
        Alan Konheim (IBM)
        Raymond Pickholtz (George Washington Univ.)
        Brian Schanning (Mitre)
        Gus Simmons (Sandia)
        Stephen Weinstein (American Express)

CRYPTO '81 Table of Contents

Lecture Notes in Computer Science

Edited by G. Goos and J. Hartmanis

149

Cryptography

Proceedings of the Workshop on Cryptography
Burg Feuerstein, Germany, March 29 – April 2, 1982

Edited by Thomas Beth

Springer-Verlag
Berlin Heidelberg New York 1983

Preface

This book contains the proceedings of a workshop on cryptography that took place from March 29th to April 2nd , 1982 , at Burg Feuerstein in the lovely surroundings of the Fränkische Schweiz near Erlangen.

Burg Feuerstein is an extensive estate run by the diocese of Bamberg. It serves many purposes , mainly of social character.

Our workshop on cryptography , however , proved to be in the best traditions of these grounds , since the `Burg´ is not a genuine castle : it was built in the early 1940´s as a camouflaged center for communications engineering emphasizing crypto- graphic research . The unintended coincidence gives a good opportunity to note the changes that cryptographic research has undergone since then. One of the most remarkable was the fact that there were 76 participants from 14 nations.

This volume contains 26 articles altogether. The introduction is an expository survey for non-specialists and places in context the other 25 papers submitted. These are grouped into 10 sections within which they are arranged with regard to content. The editor has refrained judiciously from judging the significance or consistency of all the results. Together with its rather extensive (doubly linked) bibliography the book could be used as a self-contained text. At the back of the book are a list of participants as well as a list of the talks for which no paper was submitted.

The organizer is indebted to the Deutsche Forschungs - Gemeinschaft and to the Gesellschaft für Informatik for supporting the conference.

The advice given by H.J.Beker (Racal-Comsec,Salisbury) , by H.-R. Schuchmann (Siemens-Forschungslaboratorien,München), and by N.J.A. Sloane (Bell Laboratories, Murray Hill) were of substantial help.

Finally it is a pleasure to thank R.Dierstein (DFVLR Oberpfaffenhofen) for his ex- perienced aid in organizing the workshop.

T.B.

EUROCRYPT '82 Table of Contents

12

ADVANCES IN CRYPTOLOGY

Proceedings of Crypto 82

Edited by
DAVID CHAUM
University of California
Santa Barbara, California

RONALD L. RIVEST
and
ALAN T. SHERMAN
Massachusetts Institute of Technology
Cambridge, Massachusetts

PLENUM PRESS • NEW YORK AND LONDON

Preface

In the opening sentence of their seminal 1976 paper, Diffie and Hellman proclaimed: "We stand today on the brink of a revolution in cryptography."[1] Six years later, we find ourselves in the midst of this revolution, surrounded by an explosion of developments in cryptology.

Cryptology is the art of making and breaking codes and ciphers. More generally, cryptology provides techniques for transmitting information in a private, authenticated, and tamper-proof manner. Cryptology was once the exclusive domain of mathematicians, governments, and military forces. But as computer and communications technologies advance, and as we move toward an electronically interconnected society, more and more people now depend on computer mail, electronic business transactions, and computer data banks. Cryptology has become a vital concern of numerous businesses and individuals. Fortunately, the availability of small, fast, and inexpensive computers has made encryption feasible and economical for many applications.

Organized in response to the growing interest in cryptology, CRYPTO 81 was the first major open conference ever devoted to technical cryptologic research.[2] Its successor, CRYPTO 82, was the largest conference of its kind. Held August 23–25, 1982, CRYPTO 82 attracted over 100 participants, including many leading researchers from all over the world. CRYPTO 82 took place at the University of California at Santa Barbara and was held with the cooperation of the IEEE Communications Society, the IEEE Information Theory Group, and the Department of Computer Science at U. C. Santa Barbara.[3] Compiled as the official record of

---

[1] Whitfield Diffie and Martin E. Hellman, "New Directions in Cryptography," *IEEE Transactions on Information Theory*, IT–22 (November 1976), 644.

[2] Held August 24–26, 1981. CRYPTO 81 took place at the University of California at Santa Barbara. It was sponsored by the IEEE Data and Computer Communications Committees and was supported in part by the National Science Foundation. The CRYPTO 81 proceedings are available as a technical report: Allen Gersho, ed., "Advances in Cryptology: A Report on CRYPTO 81," ECE Report no. 82–04, Department of Electrical and Computer Engineering, U. C. Santa Barbara, Santa Barbara, California 93106.

[3] Additional details about the conference can be found in: David Kahn, "The CRYPTO 82 Conference, Santa Barbara: A Report on a Conference," *Cryptologia*, 7 (January 1983), 1–5.

This volume contains 34 papers that were presented at CRYPTO 82, as well as a paper by Donald W. Davies from CRYPTO 81 that did not appear in the CRYPTO 81 proceedings. Most of these papers appear here in print for the first time. As a unique record of the current state of cryptologic research, *Advances in Cryptology: Proceedings of CRYPTO 82* is an invaluable source of information for anyone intrigued by the recent developments in cryptology. *Advances in Cryptology* is also well suited for use as a supplementary textbook in a course in cryptology.

Reflecting the structure of the conference, the proceedings are arranged in six sections. The first five sections contain the main papers of the conference, organized roughly according to the following themes: algorithms and theory, modes of operation, protocols and transaction security, applications, and cryptanalysis. The sixth section contains abstracts describing results presented at the informal "Rump Session."

Each paper in the five main sections was selected by the program committee from brief abstracts submitted in response to a call for papers. The final papers were not formally refereed, and the authors retain full responsibility for the contents of their papers. Several of the papers are preliminary reports of continuing research.

Section I, "Algorithms and Theory," focuses on specific cryptographic algorithms used to encipher messages and on theoretical foundations for the design of secure algorithms. Many of the papers in this section have a number-theoretic flavor.

Section II, "Modes of Operation," explores two major topics: the security of the Data Encryption Standard (DES) and the use of randomization to increase the security of cryptographic algorithms. For example, papers by Donald W. Davies and Robert J. Jueneman investigate the security of DES when used in output feedback mode. The underlying theme of this section is that the security provided by a cryptographic algorithm is determined in part by the way the algorithm is used.

Section III, "Protocols and Transaction Security," studies how protocols can be used to conduct various business transactions electronically. In particular, protocols are discussed for signing checks, making untraceable payments, and enabling two mutually suspicious parties to sign a contract simultaneously. Methods for proving the correctness of such protocols are also examined in detail.

Section IV, "Applications," treats the key management aspects of a number of cryptographic applications, such as protecting personal data cards, controlling access to local networks, and implementing an electronic notary public. This section also includes a paper by Charles Bennett *et al.* suggesting that quantum mechanics, rather than computational complexity, can form the foundation for certain cryptographic schemes.

Section V, "Cryptanalysis," investigates weaknesses of knapsack ciphers. In what is perhaps the most significant unclassified cryptologic paper of the year, Adi Shamir

CRYPTO 82

A Workshop on the Theory and Application of Cryptographic Techniques

held at the University of California, Santa Barbara

August 23–25, 1982

with the cooperation of
the IEEE Communications Society,
the IEEE Information Theory Group,
and the Department of Computer Science
at the University of California, Santa Barbara

Organizers

David Chaum (UCSB), general chairman

Leonard M. Adleman (USC), program committee

Thomas A. Berson (SYTEK), Hatfield conference coordinator

Dorothy Denning (Purdue), program committee

Whitfield Diffie (BNR), program committee

Paul Eggert (UCSB), treasurer

Allen Gersho (UCSB), program committee

John Gordon (Hatfield Polytechnic), organizing committee

David Kahn (Cryptologia), organizing committee

Richard Kemmerer (UCSB), local arrangements chairman

Stephen Kent (BBN), program committee

John Kowalchuk (MITRE), registration

Ronald L. Rivest (MIT), program committee chairman

Alan T. Sherman (MIT), program committee assistant chairman

Stephen Weinstein (AMEX), organizing committee

CRYPTO '82 Table of Contents

EUROCRYPT '83

EUROCRYPT '83 was held on March 21-25, 1983, at the Invernational Centre for Mechanical Sciences C.I.S.M., in Udine, Italy. No proceedings were every published for the conference, although some presentation materials and a few papers were distributed to attendees.

The organizing committee consisted of Henry Beker (Racal Comsac, Ltd.), Thomas Beth (University of Erlangen), David Chaum (CWI), John Gordon (Hatfield University), Giuseppe Longo (C.I.S.M.), and Fred Piper (Westfield College, University of London). The list of presentations at the conference are given below:

- An Overview, David Kahn
- Management of Encipherment Keys - a Survey, W. Price
- Key Distribution and Key Management, R. Blom
- On Key Management in Complex Communications Networks, O. Horak
- Cryptanalytic Attacks on the Multiplicative Knapsack Cryptosystems, A. Odlyzko
- The Security of Iterative Transformations in the Merkle-Hellman Cryptographic Scheme, Y. Desmedt
- How Linear Algebra can Generalise the Knapsack Public-Key Scheme, J. Vandewalle
- New Results on the Security of the RSA System, A. Shamir
- A New Multiplicative Algorithm over Finite Fields and Its Applicability in Public-Key Cryptography, J. Massey
- Untraceable Payments, D. Chaum
- Digital Signatures Based on One-Way Functions, J. Sattler
- A Cryptographic Scheme for the Privacy of Phone Bills, N. Cot
- Randomness Properties and Linear Equivalence, F. Piper
- On the Evaluation of the Security Offered by a Stream Cipher, A. Bromfield
- A Linear Additive Cipher and Applications, J. Gordon
- On the Design of SP-Networks, F. Ayoub
- Phonetics, Pompino-Marschall
- Scrambling Schemes, H. Beker
- Signal Processing and Fourier Transforms, T. Beth
- Frequency Hopping and Spread Spectrum Techniques, J. Massey
- Security Systems, W. Diffie

ADVANCES IN CRYPTOLOGY
Proceedings of Crypto 83

Edited by
DAVID CHAUM
University of California
Santa Barbara, California

PLENUM PRESS • NEW YORK AND LONDON

Preface

An international community of researchers is now flourishing in the area of cryptology—there was none half-a-dozen years ago. The intrinsic fascination of the field certainly is part of the explanation. Another factor may be that many sense the importance and potential consequences of this work, as we move into the information age. I believe that the various meetings devoted to cryptology over the past few years have contributed quite significantly to the formation of this community, by allowing those in the field to get to know each other and by providing for rapid exchange of ideas.

CRYPTO 83 was once again truly the cryptologic event of the year. Many of the most active participants continue to attend each year, and attendance continues to grow at a healthy rate. The informal and collegial atmosphere and the beach side setting which contribute to the popularity of the event were again supported by flawless weather. The absence of parallel sessions seemed to provide a welcome opportunity to keep abreast of developments in the various areas of activity.

Each session of the meeting organized by the program committee is represented by a section in the present volume. The papers were accepted by the program committee based on abstracts, and appear here without having been otherwise refereed. The last section contains papers presented at the informal rump session. A keyword index and an author index to the papers is provided at the end of the volume.

At CRYPTO 82 I proposed the formation of an International Association for Cryptologic Research to organize meetings and keep its members informed of events in the field. The association has taken the form of a non-profit corporation which held its first business meeting at CRYPTO 83. The attendees elected officers, a newsletter editor was selected, and plans were laid for EUROCRYPT 84 in Paris and CRYPTO 84 in Santa Barbara.

Many thanks are due the authors for their timely submission of papers, and to Ron Rivest and Alan Sherman for all their work in setting up the proceedings of CRYPTO 82.

Santa Barbara, California   D.C.
January 1984

CRYPTO 83

A Workshop on the Theory and Application of Cryptographic Techniques

held at the University of California, Santa Barbara

August 22-24, 1983

Sponsored by

The International Association for Cryptologic Research

Organizers

Alan G. Konheim (UCSB), General Chairman
Neil J.A. Sloane (Bell Labs), Program Chairman
David Chaum (UCSB), Proceedings Editor
Paul Eggert (UCSB), Treasurer
Whitfield Diffie (BNR), Rump Session Chairman
Selim Akl (Queens University)
Henry Beker (Racal Research)
Tom Berson (SYTEK)
Thomas Beth (Universität Erlangen)
Dorothy Denning (SRI International)
Allen Gersho (UCSB)
John Gordon (Cybernation)
Robert Juneman (CSC)
Gus Simmons (Sandia Labs)

CRYPTO '83 Table of Contents

Lecture Notes in Computer Science

Edited by G. Goos and J. Hartmanis

209

Advances in Cryptology

Proceedings of EUROCRYPT 84
A Workshop on the Theory and Application
of Cryptographic Techniques
Paris, France, April 9–11, 1984

Edited by T. Beth, N. Cot and I. Ingemarsson

Springer-Verlag
Berlin Heidelberg New York Tokyo

PREFACE

This book contains the proceedings of EUROCRYPT 84, held in Paris in 1984, April 9-11, at the University of Paris, Sorbonne.

EUROCRYPT is now an annual international European meeting in cryptology, intended primarily for the international community of researchers in this area. EUROCRYPT 84 was following previous meetings held at Burg Feuerstein in 1982 and at Udine in 1983. In fact EUROCRYPT 84 was the first such meeting being organized under IACR (International Association of Cryptology Research). Other sponsors were the well-known French association on cybernetics research called AFCET, the LITP (Laboratoire d'Informatique théorique et de Programmation), which is a laboratory of computer science associated with CNRS, and the department of mathematics and computer science at the University René Descartes, Sorbonne.

EUROCRYPT 84 was very successfull, with about 180 participants from a great variety of foreign countries and close to 50 papers addressing all aspects of cryptology, applied as well as theoretical. It also had a special feature, i.e. a special session on smart cards particularly welcome at the time, since France was then carrying on an ambitious program on smart cards.

EUROCRYPT 84 was a great experience. We like to thank all the sponsors and all the authors for their submission of papers.

Paris, December 1984.

Norbert COT

Editors

Thomas Beth
Department of Statistics and Computer Science
Royal Holloway College, University of London
Egham, Surrey TW20 0EX, United Kingdom

Norbert Cot
U.E.R. Mathématiques, Logique Formelle, Informatique, Université Paris-5
Sorbonne, 75005 Paris, France

Ingemar Ingemarsson
Department of Electrical Engineering, Linköping University
S-58183 Linköping, Sweden

Workshop Organizers

N. Cot, General Chairman
I. Ingemarsson, Program Chairman
H. Groscot, Secretary
S. Akl, Program
H. Beker, Program
T. Beth, Program
D. Chaum, Program
D. Davies, Program
D. Denning, Program
W. Diffie, Program
J. Gordon, Program

S. Harari, Program
J. Lebidois, Program
G. Longo, Program
J. Massey, Program
M. Mignotte, Program
A. Odlyzko, Program
J.J. Quisquater, Program
R. Rivest, Program
C. Schnorr, Program
G. Simmons, Program
M. Martin, Registration

The Workshop was sponsored by
International Association of Cryptographic Research
U.E.R. Mathématiques, Logique Formelle, Informatique
(Université René Descartes, Sorbonne)

EUROCRYPT '84 Table of Contents

Lecture Notes in Computer Science

Edited by G. Goos and J. Hartmanis

196

Advances in Cryptology:
Proceedings of CRYPTO 84

Edited by G. R. Blakley and David Chaum

Springer-Verlag
Berlin Heidelberg New York Tokyo

Preface

Here are some major contributions to the literature on modern cryptography: the papers presented at CRYPTO 84. It is our pleasure to share them with everyone interested in this exciting and growing field.

Each section of this volume corresponds to a session at the meeting. The papers were accepted by the program committee often only on the basis of abstracts, and appear here without having been otherwise refereed. The last section contains papers for some of the impromptu talks given at the traditional rump session. An author index as well as a keyword index, whose entries were mainly supplied by the authors, appear at the end of the volume.

The first two open meetings devoted to modern cryptography were organized independently: one by Allen Gersho during late Summer 1981 in Santa Barbara,[1] and the other by Thomas Beth and Rudiger Dierstein in Germany the following Spring.[2] David Chaum organized a successor to the Santa Barbara meeting the next year,[3] which launched the International Association for Cryptologic Research. The sponsorship of the association has continued the unbroken series of annual Summer CRYPTO meetings in the U.S.[4] and annual Spring EUROCRYPT meetings in Europe.[5,6]

It is our pleasure to thank all those who contributed to making these proceedings possible: the authors, program committee, other organizers of the meeting, IACR officers and directors, and all the attendees.

College Station, Texas   G.R.B.
Amsterdam, the Netherlands   D.C.
March 1985

1. Advances in Cryptology: A Report on CRYPTO 81, Allen Gersho, Ed., UCSB ECE Report no. 82-04, Department of Electrical and Computer Engineering, Santa Barbara CA 93106.
2. Cryptography: Proceedings, Burg Feuerstein 1982, (Lecture Notes in Computer Science; 149) Thomas Beth Ed., Springer-Verlag, Berlin, 1983.
3. Advances in Cryptology: Proceedings of CRYPTO 82, David Chaum, Ronald L. Rivest, and Alan T. Sherman, Eds., Plenum NY, 1983.
4. Advances in Cryptology: Proceedings of CRYPTO 83, David Chaum Ed., Plenum NY, 1984.
5. No proceedings were published for EUROCRYPT 83, which was held in Udine Italy.
6. The proceedings of EUROCRYPT 84, Edited by Norbert Cot, are to appear in Lecture Notes in Computer Science, Springer-Verlag, Berlin.

CRYPTO 84

A Workshop on the Theory and Application of Cryptographic Techniques

held at the University of California, Santa Barbara

August 19-22, 1984

sponsored by

the International Association for Cryptologic Research

Organizers

Thomas A. Berson (Sytek, Inc.), General Chairman
G.R. Blakley (Texas A&M), Program Chairman
Henry Beker (Racal Research), Program
David Chaum (CWI), Proceedings
Dorothy Denning (SRI International), Program
Whitfield Diffie (BNR), Rump Session Chairman
Richard A. Kemmerer (UCSB), Local Arrangements
Ronald L. Rivest (MIT), Program
Miles Smidt (NBS), Program
Joe Tardo (DEC), Show & Tell
Kay G. White (Sytek, Inc.), Registration

CRYPTO '84 Table of Contents

40

Lecture Notes in Computer Science

Edited by G. Goos and J. Hartmanis

219

Advances in Cryptology – EUROCRYPT '85

Proceedings of a Workshop on the
Theory and Application of Cryptographic Techniques
Linz, Austria, April 1985

Edited by Franz Pichler

Springer-Verlag

Preface

The storage, routing and transmission of information, either in the form of digital data or of analog signals, plays a central role in modern society. To ensure that such information is protected from access by unauthorized persons is an important new challenge. The development of the theory and practical techniques needed to meet this challenge is the goal of current cryptological research. This research is highly varied and multidisciplinary. It is concerned with fundamental problems in mathematics and theoretical computer science as well as with the engineering aspects of complex information systems. Cryptology today ranks among the most active and interesting areas of research in both science and engineering.

EUROCRYPT '85 maintained the tradition of the three previous workshops in this series (Paris 1984, Udine 1983, Burg Feuerstein 1982) with its emphasis on recent developments in cryptology, but also made a concerted effort to encompass more traditional topics in cryptology such as shift-register theory and system theory. The many papers on these topics in this volume are witness to the success of this effort.

I am grateful to the speakers and to the authors of the papers in this volume for their contributions to EUROCRYPT '85, and to the Program Committee headed by Professor Thomas Beth, University of London, now University of Karlsruhe, for its labors in putting together a provocative and interesting program. My thanks go also to all the sponsors of EUROCRYPT '85, with a special "Dankeschön" to the International Association for Cryptologic Research for its indispensable support. I hope that this volume, with its cross-section of current research in cryptology, will extend the reach of EUROCRYPT '85 and be a stimulation to its readers of their own research in cryptology.

Franz Pichler
Chairman
EUROCRYPT '85

EUROCRYPT '85 - **Afterthoughts**

Thomas Beth, Program Chairman

Having served as Program Chairman for EUROCRYPT 85, held at Linz (Austria) I think this is a suitable place to compare my a posteriori impressions of this 4th European Meeting on Cryptography with the a priori expectations, most of which - with some modifications of course - made me initially organise the first of these meetings at Burg Feuerstein.
As the field of cryptography is by nature an interdisciplinary one it has proved to be a successful policy to arrange these meetings around a skeleton of survey lectures. This is a fruitful tradition, from which everyone - users and designers, practitioners and theoreticians, speakers and participants have gained largely.

To make a skeleton walk, however, one needs a bit more than a strong backbone.

In these past few years we have witnessed some breakthroughs in cryptography, especially in the field of analysis, e.g. breaking the Merkle-Hellman-Scheme, towards which Ingemarson and Shamir took the first steps at Burg Feuerstein leading to the final general method presented by Brickell at Linz.
Other improvements, e.g. in the question of discrete logarithms by Blake, Mullin, Vanstone, Coppersmith and Odlyzko were equally impressive.

The regular appearance of many other "crypto schemes" and their immediate analysis shows, however, that we are still rather far away from a general theory. Even if we consider this problem optimistically, in my view it is clear that such a general theory would have to incorporate results on

- Complexity
- Protocols
- General Systems

which I count amongst the most difficult fields of research at present.

From research in complexity we urgently need results on lower bounds which would be the basis for an approach to a general theory of data security. The need for such a development has become especially obvious in the area of developing sequential ciphers. After the last few years successful work on designing PN-generators of large linear equivalent, it has now become apparent that other evaluation principles have to be applied. While the work by Yao, Blum, Micali and Goldwasser has shown theoretical instances as to how to proceed, the first two practical analytical results are those presented by Siegenthaler and Rueppel at Linz.
What we are lacking at present are PN-generation methods that are fast, easily implemented and secure in the light of the approaches above.
We are also still urgently waiting for fast implementation of exponentiation algorithms as needed for the RSA-System or the Diffie-Helman Scheme.
With respect to public key systems it should meanwhile have become clear that, although more such systems are strongly sought after, the imitations of the original RSA idea by means of different permutations over possibly different semi-simple algebras is of not much impact, - unless reliable security estimates i.e. lower bounds can be achieved.

VI

The need for these estimates is not only a question of great urgency in the very topic of encryption but also in a general approach towards secure systems. On the one hand the readily proposed rather futuristic general systems models, though intellectually stimulating, are largely pending on the availability of suitable encryption schemes. There is no need to refer again to the inherent dangers of systems based on common sense rather than theorems. On the other hand one has to recognize the ideas coming from non-secrecy cryptography as described by Simmons in his survey lecture on authentication.

Equally important are the engineering aspects as described by Davies and Price in their survey lecture. But again, qualitatively and quantitatively sufficient systems analysis tools are missing.

These tools, if they were available, would be of immediate application in the design of Hierarchical Key Distribution Systems as they are urgently needed in large networks as ISDN, but possibly also in the evaluation of Software Protection Systems. Although some first systems have been presented in Linz, it is my conviction that we are far away from a system that is secure beyond the designed man-machine interface, it has been designed for.
This leads us to the question of new technology in cryptography:

Except for a paper on proposed analog encryption schemes, by Davida, no progress can be reported. Concerning the technology of smart cards improvements w.r.t. to their memory size and mechanical stability have been reported. But the heavy criticism uttered by Simmons and myself at the EUROCRYPT '84 is still valid as the British solution by socalled intelligent token is still in its experimental phase.
I would furthermore have liked to see speculative papers for instance on optical scrambling or encryption for soliton transmission systems, to name a few. Expecially the optical solitons on glass fibres could provide a feasible solution for a socalled quantum crypto system i.e. a system which would detect "information theft".

Coming down to earth again, I would like to point out the large efforts taken internationally towards standardisation. The report by Price on the state of a proposed standard for public key encryption had been followed with great interest.

But with the process of accepting DES as ISO standard being in a rather mature state, I would like to draw the attention to the fact, that when DES was conceived more than a decade ago, it was planned to be a standard for the next 10 to 15 years. It is therefore a surprise to me that in view of the latest releases of computer hardware, there was no general effort made or proposed towards a replacement of DES or should I say "DES Ersatz"?

Remark of the editor: These notes have already appeared immediately after the conference in
IACR NEWSLETTER , June 1985

Editor

Franz Pichler
Institute of Systems Science
Department of Systems Theory and Information Engineering
Johannes Kepler University Linz
A-4040 Linz, Austria

Workshop Organizers

F. Pichler, Chairman
T. Beth, Program Chairman
H. Beker, Program
D. E. Denning, Program
R. Eier, Program
E. Henze, Program
T. Herlestam, Program
O. Horak, Program

I. Ingemarsson, Program
J. L. Massey, Program
Ch. Müller-Schloer, Program
A. Odlyzko, Program
W. L. Price, Program
R. Rivest, Program
G. J. Simmons, Program
E. Draxler, Registration

The Workshop was sponsored by
International Association for Cryptologic Research (IACR)
Austrian Computer Society (OCG)
Austrian Society for Cybernetic Studies (ÖSGK)
Ministry of Science and Research, Vienna, Austria
Johannes Kepler University Linz

EUROCRYPT '85 Table of Contents

Lecture Notes in Computer Science

Edited by G. Goos and J. Hartmanis

218

Advances in Cryptology – CRYPTO '85

Proceedings

Edited by Hugh C. Williams

Springer-Verlag
Berlin Heidelberg New York Tokyo

Preface

In the summer of 1981 Allen Gersho organized the first major open conference ever devoted to cryptologic research. This meeting, Crypto '81, was held at the University of California campus in Santa Barbara. Since then the Crypto' conference has become an annual event. These are the proceedings of the fifth[1] of these conferences, Crypto '85.

Each section of this volume corresponds to a session at the meeting. The papers were accepted by the program committee, sometimes on the basis of an abstract only, and appear here without having been otherwise refereed. The last section contains papers for some of the impromptu talks given at the traditional rump session. Each of these papers was refereed by a single member of the program committee. An author index as well as a keyword index, the entries for which were mainly supplied by the authors, appear at the end of the volume.

Unfortunately, two of the papers accepted for presentation at Crypto '85 could not be included in this book they are:

Unique Extrapolation of Polynomial Recurrences
    J.C. Lagarias and J.A. Reeds (A.T. & T Bell Labs)

Some Cryptographic Applications of Permutation Polynomials and Permutation Functions
    Rupert Nöbauer (Universität für Bildungswissenschaften, Austria)

It is my great pleasure to acknowledge the efforts of all of those who contributed to making these proceedings possible: the authors, program committee, other organizers of the meeting, IACR officers and directors, and all the attendees. I would also like to thank Lynn Montz of Springer-Verlag for her patient assistance in preparing this volume.

Winnipeg, Manitoba, Canada   H.C.W.
January 1986

---

[1]Proceedings of the other Crypto conferences have also been published. The interested reader can find these listed in the preface of <u>Advances in Cryptology 84</u> (the proceedings of Crypto '84), published by Springer-Verlag.

CRYPTO 85

A Conference on the Theory and Application of Cryptographic Techniques

held at the University of California, Santa Barbara,
through the co-operation of the
Computer Science Department

August 18-22, 1985

sponsored by

The International Association for Cryptologic Research

in co-operation with

*The IEEE Computer Society Technical Committee
on Security and Privacy*

Organizers

Ernest F. Brickell (Bell Communications Research), General Chairman
H.C. Williams (University of Manitoba), Program Chairman
Thomas A. Berson (Sytek, Inc.), Program
Joan Boyar (University of Chicago), Program
Donald W. Davies (Data Security Consultant), Program
Oded Goldreich (MIT/Technion), Program
Alan G. Konheim (UCSB), Local Arrangements
Carol Patterson (Sandia Laboratories), Registration
Ron Rivest (MIT), Program
Joe Tardo (DEC), Show and Tell

CRYPTO '85 Table of Contents

54

ABSTRACTS OF PAPERS

EUROCRYPT 86

- o -

*A Workshop on the
Theory and Application of
Cryptographic Techniques*

- o -

*20 - 22 May 1986
Linköping, Sweden*

A Word from the Program Chairman

The Program Committee has worked strenuously to ensure that the papers to be presented at Eurocrypt '86 are both interesting and relevant to the advance of scientific cryptology. All papers were selected from among those submitted -- there are no invited papers this year. Judging from the quantity and quality of the submissions, I would say that cryptology is "alive and well" in Europe.

No Proceedings of Eurocrypt '86 will be published. Participants who have especial interest in some paper are urged to request preprints (if they exist!) directly from the author. The decision to publish only abstracts from Eurocrypt '86 was based partly on the belief that not requiring full papers would encourage contributors to speak about their current and still-evolving research. Another reason for this decision arises from the fact that the International Association for Cryptologic Research (IACR) will soon begin to publish its own scholarly journal. The President of the IACR, Dr. Dorothy E. Denning, will announce the formation of this new journal at Eurocrypt '86. It is hoped that Eurocrypt '86 contributors, who have their full papers now ready or in preparation, will submit these papers to this new journal. It would be nice if "Vol. 1, No. 1" of the first scholarly journal devoted entirely to scientific cryptology were to consist primarily of papers from Eurocrypt '86.

James L. Massey

General chairman:
Ingemar Ingemarsson (S)

Program Committee:
Andrew Glass (CH)
James L. Massey (CH), Chairman
Paul Schöbi (CH)
Othmar Staffelbach (CH)
Thomas Beth (D)
David Chaum (NL)
Christoph G. Günther (CH)
Peter Nyffeler (CH)
Thomas Siegenthaler (CH)
Kjell Owe Widman (CH)
Norbert Cot (F)
Tore Herlestam (S)

Organization:
Jan-Olof Brüer (S)

Conference Secretariat:
Arne Kullbjer (S)
Pia Johansson (S)
Ingrid Nyman (S)

EUROCRYPT '86 Table of Contents

Lecture Notes in Computer Science

Edited by G. Goos and J. Hartmanis

263

A. M. Odlyzko (Ed.)

Advances in Cryptology – CRYPTO '86

Proceedings

Springer-Verlag

Berlin Heidelberg New York London Paris Tokyo

Preface

This book is the proceedings of CRYPTO 86, one in a series of annual conferences devoted to cryptologic research. They have all been held at the University of California at Santa Barbara. The first conference in this series, CRYPTO 81, organized by A. Gersho, did not have a formal proceedings. The proceedings of the following four conferences in this series have been published as:

Advances in Cryptology: Proceedings of Crypto 82, D. Chaum, R. L. Rivest, and A. T. Sherman, eds., Plenum, 1983.

Advances in Cryptology: Proceedings of Crypto 83, D. Chaum, ed., Plenum, 1984.

Advances in Cryptology: Proceedings of CRYPTO 84, G. R. Blakley and D. Chaum, eds., Lecture Notes in Computer Science #196, Springer, 1985.

Advances in Cryptology - CRYPTO '85 Proceedings, H. C. Williams, ed., Lecture Notes in Computer Science #218, Springer, 1986.

A parallel series of conferences is held annually in Europe. The first of these had its proceedings published as

Cryptography: Proceedings, Burg Feuerstein 1982, T. Beth, ed., *Lecture Notes in Computer Science #149*, Springer, 1983.

Eurocrypt 83, held in March of 1983 in Udine, Italy, and Eurocrypt 86, held in May of 1986 in Linköping, Sweden, did not have formal proceedings, while the '84 and '85 conference proceedings have appeared as

Advances in Cryptology: Proceedings of EUROCRYPT 84, T. Beth, N. Cot, and I. Ingemarsson, eds., Lecture Notes in Computer Science #209, Springer, 1985.

VI

Advances in Cryptology - EUROCRYPT '85, F. Pichler, ed., Lecture Notes in Computer Science #219, Springer, 1986.

Papers in this volume are presented in seven sections containing most of the papers presented in the regular program, and a final section based on some of the informal presentations at the "Rump Session" organized by W. Diffie. Several of the regular papers presented at the conference are not included in this volume. There was a special session on integer factorization, and the three papers in that section will be published in journals:

C. Pomerance, J. W. Smith, and R. Tuler, A pipeline architecture for factoring large integers with the quadratic sieve algorithm, SIAM J. Comp. (to appear).

T. R. Caron and R. D. Silverman, Parallel implementation of the quadratic sieve, J. Supercomputing (to appear).

M. C. Wunderlich and H. C. Williams, A parallel version of the continued fraction integer factoring algorithms, J. Supercomputing (to appear).

Also, the paper

J. G. Osborn and J. R. Everhart, A large community key distribution protocol,

was not revised in time for publication.

It is my pleasure to thank all those who make these proceedings possible: the authors, organizers, and all the attendees. Special thanks are due to M. Janssen, Y. Cohen, and the Springer staff for their help in the production of this volume.

Murray Hill, New Jersey   Andrew M. Odlyzko

CRYPTO 86

A Conference on the Theory and Applications of Cryptographic Techniques

held at the University of California, Santa Barbara,
through the cooperation of the
Computer Science Department

August 11-15, 1986

sponsored by:

The International Association for Cryptologic Research

in co-operation with

*The IEEE Computer Society Technical Committee
on Security and Privacy*

Organizers

General Chairman: D. Coppersmith (IBM)

Program Committee: T. A. Berson (Anagram Laboratories)
E. F. Brickell (Bell Communications Research)
S. Goldwasser (MIT)
A. M. Odlyzko (AT&T Bell Laboratories, Chairman)
C. P. Schnorr (U. Frankfurt)

Local Arrangements: O. Egelcioglu (UCSB)

CRYPTO '86 Table of Contents

Lecture Notes in Computer Science

Edited by G. Goos and J. Hartmanis

304

David Chaum Wyn L. Price (Eds.)

Advances in Cryptology – EUROCRYPT '87

Workshop on the Theory and Application
of Cryptographic Techniques
Amsterdam, The Netherlands, April 13–15, 1987
Proceedings

Springer-Verlag
Berlin Heidelberg New York London Paris Tokyo

Preface

1987 marked a major upswing in attendance and contributions for this fifth in the series of Eurocrypt meetings. Response was so great that, to our regret, we were only able to accommodate less than half the submitted papers. Attendance was also up by a healthy margin.

The first two open meetings devoted to modern cryptography were organised independently: one by Allen Gersho during late Summer 1981 in Santa Barbara,[1] and the other by Thomas Beth and Rudiger Dierstein in Germany the following Spring.[2] David Chaum organised a successor to the Santa Barbara meeting the next year,[3] which launched the International Association for Cryptologic Research. The sponsorship of the association has enabled the series of annual Summer CRYPTO meetings in the U.S.[4-7] and annual Spring EUROCRYPT meetings in Europe to be continued unbroken.[8-11]

It is our pleasure to thank all those who contributed to making these proceedings possible: the authors, programme committee, organising committee, IACR officers and directors, and all the attendees.

We were all deeply saddened when we learned that Tore Herlestam, a member of the programme committee, had died unexpectedly. This volume is dedicated to him.

Amsterdam, the Netherlands   D.C.
London, England   W.L.P
January 1988

1. Advances in Cryptology: A Report on CRYPTO 81, Allen Gersho, Ed., UCSB ECE Report no. 82-04, Department of Electrical and Computer Engineering, Santa Barbara CA 93106.
2. Cryptography: Proceedings, Burg Feuerstein 1982 (Lecture Notes in Computer Science; 149), Thomas Beth, Ed., Springer-Verlag, 1983.
3. Advances in Cryptology: Proceedings of CRYPTO 82, David Chaum, Ronald L. Rivest, and Alan T Sherman, Eds., Plenum NY, 1983.
4. Advances in Cryptology: Proceedings of CRYPTO 83, David Chaum, Ed., Plenum NY, 1984.

Editors

David Chaum
Centre for Mathematics and Computer Science (CWI)
Kruislaan 413, 1098 SJ Amsterdam, The Netherlands

Wyn L. Price
National Physical Laboratory
Teddington, Middlesex TW11 OLW, U.K.

Workshop Organizers:

General Chairman: D. Chaum (CWI)

Programme Committee: W. L. Price (NPL), Chairman   T. Herlestam (U. Lund)
                      T. Beth (U. Karlsruhe)   F. Piper (U. London)
                      J.-H. Evertse (CWI)   J. J. Quisquater (Philips)
                      L. Guillou (CCETT)

Organising Committee: J. van de Graaf (CWI)   G. Roelofsen (PTT-DNL)
                      C. J. Jansen (Philips USFA)   J. van Tilburg (PTT-DNL)

The workshop was sponsored by the
International Association for Cryptologic Research
with support from the
Centre for Mathematics and Computer Science (CWI), Amsterdam

EUROCRYPT '87 Table of Contents

Lecture Notes in Computer Science

Edited by G. Goos and J. Hartmanis

293

Carl Pomerance (Ed.)

Advances in Cryptology — CRYPTO '87

Proceedings

Springer-Verlag

Berlin Heidelberg New York London Paris Tokyo

Preface

This book is the proceedings of CRYPTO'87, one in a series of annual conferences devoted to cryptologic research. For citations of proceedings of CRYPTO and Eurocrypt conferences before 1986, see

Advances in Cryptology—CRYPTO'86 Proceedings, A. M. Odlyzko, ed.,
Lecture Notes in Computer Science #263, Springer, 1987.

Papers in this volume are organized into seven sections. The first six sections comprise all of the papers on the regular program, including two papers on the program that unfortunately were not presented at the meeting. The seventh section contains some of the papers presented at the "Rump Session" organized by W. Diffie and also includes a short note by T. R. N. Rao which comments on the paper of R. Struik and J. van Tilburg.

CRYPTO'87 was attended by 170 people representing 19 countries. Responsible not only for the conference as a whole, G. B. Agnew also took care of local arrangements in Santa Barbara. We all owe him a debt of gratitude for his highly successful efforts.

It is my special pleasure to thank my fellow members of the Program Committee: T. A. Berson, E. F. Brickell, A. M. Odlyzko, and G. J. Simmons. They all were most prompt, efficient, and willing to cheerfully compromise on disagreements. My task would have been hopeless without them.

I also would like to thank the authors and attendees who made CRYPTO'87 such a success. Special thanks are due to University of Georgia secretaries D. Byrd and P. Sisk and L. B. Montz at Springer for their help in the production of this volume.

Athens, Georgia   Carl Pomerance

CRYPTO'87

A Conference on the Theory and Applications of Cryptographic Techniques

held at the University of California, Santa Barbara,
through the cooperation of the
Computer Science Department

August 16-20, 1987

sponsored by:

The International Association for Cryptologic Research

in cooperation with

The IEEE Computer Society Technical Committee
On Security and Privacy

ORGANIZERS

General Chairman: G. B. Agnew (U. Waterloo)

Program Committee: T. A. Berson (Anagram Laboratories)
                     E. F. Brickell (Bell Communications Research)
                     A. M. Odlyzko (AT&T Bell Laboratories)
                     C. Pomerance (U. Georgia, Chairman)
                     G. J. Simmons (Sandia National Laboratories)

CRYPTO '87 Table of Contents

Lecture Notes in Computer Science

Edited by G. Goos and J. Hartmanis

330

Christoph G. Günther (Ed.)

Advances in Cryptology – EUROCRYPT '88

Workshop on the Theory and Application
of Cryptographic Techniques
Davos, Switzerland, May 25–27, 1988
Proceedings

PREFACE

The International Association for Cryptologic Research (IACR) organizes two international conferences every year, one in Europe and one in the United States. EUROCRYPT'88, held in the beautiful environment of the Swiss mountains in Davos, was the sixth European conference. The number of contributions and of participants at the meeting has increased substantially, which is an indication of the high interest in cryptography and system security in general.

The interest has not only increased but has also further moved towards authentication, signatures and other protocols. This is easy to understand in view of the urgent needs for such protocols, in particular in connection with open information systems, and in view of the exciting problems in this area. The equally fascinating classical field of secrecy, *i.e.* the theory, design and analysis of stream or block ciphers and of public key cryptosystems, was however also well represented and several significant results were communicated.

The present proceedings contain all contributions which were accepted for presentation. The chapters correspond to the sessions at the conference.

I am grateful to all authors of these contributions for the careful preparation and prompt submission of their papers. On behalf of the General Chairman, it is a pleasure to thank the authors and the members of the Program Committee for having made the conference such an interesting and stimulating meeting. We are indebted to the sponsors for their generous donations and to the members of the Organization Committee, who have so perfectly organized the meeting.

Baden, June 1988   C.G.G.

EUROCRYPT'88

was sponsored by the

International Association for Cryptologic Research (IACR)

General Chairman: James L. Massey, Swiss Federal Institute of Technology,
Zürich, Switzerland
Program Chairman: Ingemar Ingemarsson, Linköping University, Sweden

Organizing Committee:

José Clarinval, Zürich
Christoph G. Günther, Baden
Kirk H. Kirchhofer, Zug
Ueli Maurer, Zürich
Rainer A. Rueppel, Zug
Paul Schoebi, Regensdorf
Thomas Siegenthaler, Zürich
Othmar Staffelbach, Regensdorf

Program Committee:

Rolf Blom, Stockholm
Lennart Brynielsson, Stockholm
Ivan Damgård, Aarhus
Viveke Fåk, Linköping
Tor Helleseth, Bergen
Rolf Johannesson, Lund

The conference was generously supported by

Union Bank of Switzerland, Zürich
Springer-Verlag, Heidelberg and New York
Amstein Walthert Kleiner AG, Zürich, Switzerland
Asea Brown Boveri AG, Zürich, Switzerland
Ascom-Radiocom AG, Solothurn, Switzerland
Crypto AG, Zug, Switzerland
Gretag Ltd., Regensdorf, Switzerland

EUROCRYPT '88 Table of Contents

Lecture Notes in Computer Science

Edited by G. Goos and J. Hartmanis

403

S. Goldwasser (Ed.)

Advances in Cryptology – CRYPTO '88

Proceedings

Springer-Verlag

Berlin Heidelberg New York London Paris Tokyo Hong Kong

Foreword

The papers in this volume were presented at the CRYPTO '88 conference on theory and applications of cryptography, held August 21-25, 1988 in Santa Barbara, California. The conference was sponsored by the International Association for Cryptologic Research (IACR) and hosted by the computer science department at the University of California at Santa Barbara.

The 44 papers presented here comprise: 35 papers selected from 61 extended abstracts submitted in response to the call for papers, 4 invited presentations, and 6 papers selected from a large number of informal rump session presentations.

The papers were chosen by the program committee on the basis of the perceived originality, quality and relevance to the field of cryptography of the extended abstracts submitted. The submissions were not otherwise refereed, and often represent preliminary reports on continuing research.

It is a pleasure to thank many colleagues. Harold Fredricksen single-handedly made CRYPTO '88 a successful reality. Eric Bach, Paul Barret, Tom Berson, Gilles Brassard, Oded Goldreich, Andrew Odlyzko, Charles Rackoff and Ron Rivest did excellent work on the program committee in putting the technical program together, assisted by kind outside reviewers.

Dawn Crowel at MIT did a super job in publicizing the conference and coordinating the activities of the committee, and Deborah Grupp has been most helpful in the production of this volume. Special thanks are due to Joe Kilian whose humor while assisting me to divide the papers into sessions was indispensable.

Finally, I wish to thank the authors who submitted papers for consideration and the attendants of CRYPTO '88 for their continuing support.

June 1989					Shafi Goldwasser
Cambridge, MA

CRYPTO '88

A Conference on the Theory and Application of Cryptography

held at the University of California, Santa Barbara,
August 21-25, 1988
through the cooperation of the Computer Science Department

Sponsored by:

International Association for Cryptologic Research

in cooperation with

The IEEE Computer Society Technical Committee
On Security and Privacy

General Chair
Harold Fredricksen, Naval Postgraduate School

Program Chair
Shafi Goldwasser, Massachusetts Institute of Technology

Program Committee

Eric Bach	University of Wisconsin
Paul Barret	Computer Security Ltd.
Tom Berson	Anagram Laboratories
Gilles Brassard	University of Montreal
Oded Goldreich	Technion Israel Institute of Technology
Andrew Odlyzko	Bell Laboratories
Charles Rackoff	University of Toronto
Ron Rivest	Massachusetts Institute of Technology

CRYPTO '88 Table of Contents

Lecture Notes in Computer Science

Edited by G. Goos and J. Hartmanis

434

J.-J. Quisquater   J. Vandewalle (Eds.)

Advances in Cryptology – EUROCRYPT '89

Workshop on the Theory and Application
of Cryptographic Techniques
Houthalen, Belgium, April 10–13, 1989
Proceedings

Springer-Verlag

Berlin Heidelberg New York London
Paris Tokyo Hong Kong Barcelona

PREFACE

The International Association for Cryptologic Research (IACR) organizes two international conferences every year, one in Europe and one in the United States. EUROCRYPT '89 was the seventh European conference and was held in Houthalen, Belgium on April 10-13, 1989. With close to 300 participants, it was perhaps the largest open conference on cryptography ever held.

The field of cryptography is expanding not only because of the increased vulnerability of computer systems and networks to an increasing range of threats, but also because of the rapid progress in cryptographic methods, that the readers can witness by reading the book.

The present proceedings contain nearly all contributions which were presented including the talks at the rump session. The chapters correspond to the sessions at the conference. It was the first time that a rump session was organized on a Eurocrypt conference. Sixteen impromptu talks were given, and the authors were invited to submit short abstracts of their presentations. Because of the special character of this session, the editors have taken the liberty to shorten some of these.

We are grateful to all authors for the careful preparation of their contributions. It is a pleasure to thank the members of the Program Committee for having made the conference such an interesting and stimulating meeting. In particular, we were very pleased with the interesting rump session organized by J. Gordon and the animated open problem session organized by E. Brickell. We are indebted to the sponsors for their generous donations and to the members of the Organization Committee for the smooth organization of the meeting.

Louvain-la-Neuve, Belgium   J.-J.Q.
Louvain, Belgium   J.V.
July 1990

EUROCRYPT '89 Table of Contents

Lecture Notes in Computer Science

Edited by G. Goos and J. Hartmanis

435

G. Brassard (Ed.)

Advances in Cryptology – CRYPTO '89

Proceedings

Springer-Verlag

New York Berlin Heidelberg London Paris Tokyo Hong Kong

Preface

Pour Alice
Qui est venue au monde
Trois semaines avant l'avalanche

CRYPTO is a conference devoted to all aspects of cryptologic research. It has been held each year on the campus of the University of California at Santa Barbara since 1981, when it was first organized by Alan Gersho. Annual meetings also take place in Europe under the name of EUROCRYPT. Both CRYPTO and EUROCRYPT conferences are now sponsored by the *International Association for Cryptologic Research* (IACR), which was founded in the wake of CRYPTO '82. You are now holding the proceedings of the ninth CRYPTO meeting: CRYPTO '89. Recent previous proceedings of CRYPTO and EUROCRYPT can be cited as [2, 3, 4, 5, 6]. For citations of yet earlier proceedings, please consult the preface of EUROCRYPT '87 [2].

This year's conference took place on August 20–24, 1989. It attracted 263 participants coming from 23 countries, showing a steady increase in size, and requiring a change to a larger lecture room. This growth is better appreciated if one goes back to the preface of CRYPTO '82, which claims that "[it] was the largest conference of its kind [... it] attracted over 100 participants" [1]! Approximately 40% of the attendees were from the industry, 40% from universities, and 20% from governments. The great success of this year's conference was largely due to the enthusiasm and wonderful work done by Kevin McCurley, who was holding the general chair. We all owe him a debt of gratitude for his total commitment to making CRYPTO '89 a memorable event. For a more elaborate report on CRYPTO '89, please read the report that Kevin has written with my collaboration in the *IACR Newsletter* [8]. Details on the new policies that I enforced as program chairperson can be found in [7].

The call for papers resulted in 93 submissions coming from 18 countries. Out of those, 6 were not considered because they arrived after the deadline, 1 was withdrawn, 45 were accepted, and 2 pairs were asked to merge. The accepted papers were selected by the program committee, sometimes on the basis of a rather short abstract. As an experiment for the CRYPTO conference, I enforced a blind refereeing process by which the name of the authors were not revealed to the other members of the program committee. The final papers were not refereed at all, and the authors retain full responsibility for their contents. Several of the papers are preliminary reports of continuing research. It is anticipated that many of these papers will appear in more polished form in various technical journals, including IACR's *Journal of Cryptology*. There will be a special issue of the *Journal of Cryptology* devoted to some of the best papers of the conference this year. These papers will be refereed by the usual process, and Joan Feigenbaum will serve as the special editor for the issue.

VI

In addition to the contributed papers, I scheduled three invited talks: "Keying the German navy's Enigma" by David Kahn, "Digital signatures: The evolution of a fundamental primitive" by Silvio Micali, and "A survey of hardware implementations of RSA" by Ernest F. Brickell. Moreover, in order to encourage a balance between practical and theoretical topics at the conferences, this year's program featured an invited special session on practical aspects of cryptology, which was organized and chaired by Russell L. Brand. Thus, 53 regular papers were presented at the conference. Furthermore, 26 additional papers were submitted on the first day of the conference for the traditional "rump session" of impromptu talks organized as always by Whitfield Diffie. Of those, 17 were accepted for short presentation on Tuesday evening, as selected by Whitfield and me.

These proceedings contain papers for all the contributed and all but one of the invited talks given at the conference. The exception is the invited talk of Silvio Micali. Short papers (I imposed a strict limit of four pages) are also included for 8 of the 17 impromptu talks. Reflecting the structure of the conference, the proceedings are arranged in 13 sections (followed by an author index). Each section corresponds to one session of the conference. The first 12 sections contain the contributed and invited papers in the order in which they were presented. The last section is devoted to the rump session. The sections are organized according to the following themes: opening session, why is cryptography harder than it looks?, pseudo-randomness and sequences, cryptanalysis and implementation, signature and authentication I and II, threshold schemes and key management, key distribution and network security, fast computation, odds and ends, zero-knowledge and oblivious transfer, multiparty computation, and the rump session.

Two papers in this collection are of historical significance. The proceedings open with a short paper by David Kahn on the Enigma. You will also find an antique paper by Ralph Merkle, describing "A certified digital signature", which was accepted a decade ago for publication in the *Communications of the ACM*, but which has never seen the light of day. I trust you will agree that despite its old age, this paper has lost none of its interest. Because I wanted Merkle's paper to appear exactly as it was written ten years ago, I allowed the author one page above the otherwise very strict page limit imposed on all other authors. (Please don't throw bricks at me!)

It is my great pleasure to acknowledge the efforts of those who contributed to making the conference and its proceedings possible. First of all, I wish to thank the program committee, without whom my task would have been hopeless. Most of them read and made detailed comments on at least 29 submissions. Besides myself, the committee consisted of Josh Benaloh (University of Toronto), Russell L. Brand (Special session chairperson, Lawrence Livermore National Laboratory), Claude Crépeau (Massachusetts Institute of Technology), Whitfield Diffie (Bell Northern Research), Joan Feigenbaum (AT&T Bell Laboratories), James L. Massey (ETH Zentrum, Zurich), Jim Omura (Cylink Corporation), Gustavus J. Simmons (Sandia National Laboratories), and Scott Vanstone (University of Waterloo). Moreover many colleagues outside the program committee offered their occasional help. Among them, Manuel Blum, Ernest F. Brickell, Jeff Lagarias, Michael Merritt, Larry Ozarow, Carl Pomerance, Jim Reeds, and Moti Yung.

Of course, the most important contribution was that of the authors (including those whose submissions could not be accepted because of the large number of very high quality submissions to the conference this year). I wish to thank the authors for taking so seriously into account my deadline for submission of the final papers. The timeliness of these proceedings is their doing, together with heavy use of electronic mail. More than 300 messages were exchanged by electronic mail between me and the authors, totalizing over half a megabyte of information. Compared to that, I had to make only about 25 long distance phone calls, and 8 FAX's were exchanged.

I also wish to thank the session chairpersons. In addition to program committee members, sessions were chaired by Bob Blakley, Joan Boyar, Ernest F. Brickell, and Kevin McCurley. James L. Massey was scheduled to chair session 10, but he was unfortunately unable to attend the conference because of an accident on the way to the airport. Bob Blakley was kind enough to chair his session on short notice.

Many other people deserve thanks for the organization of the conference. Chief among them, of course, is Kevin McCurley, the general chairperson. I wish to thank also everyone else who took part in the organization of the meeting, IACR officers and directors, and all attendees. I am also grateful to three students who helped me greatly with my task: André Berthiaume, Philippe Hébrais and Sophie Laplante. Lynn Montz and Suzanne Anthony were instrumental at Springer–Verlag in helping me put the proceedings together.

Last but not least, I wish to express my deepest gratitude to my wife Isabelle and newborn daughter Alice for putting up with me while I was working overtime on the program in the spring and on the proceedings in the fall.

Montréal, December 1989   *Gilles Brassard*

CRYPTO '89

A conference on the Theory and Applications of Cryptology

held at the University of California, Santa Barbara,
through the cooperation of the
Computer Science Department

August 20–24, 1989

sponsored by:

The International Association for Cryptologic Research

in cooperation with

*The IEEE Computer Society Technical Committee
on Security and Privacy*

Organizers

General Chairman: Kevin McCURLEY
(IBM Almaden – Sandia National Laboratories

Program Committee: Josh BENALOH,   University of Toronto
Russell L. BRAND,   Lawrence Livermore Laboratory,
Special Session Chairperson
Gilles BRASSARD,   Université de Montréal,
Program Committee Chairperson
Claude CRÉPEAU,   Massachusetts Institute of Technology
Whitfield DIFFIE,   Bell Northern Research
Joan FEIGENBAUM,   AT&T Bell Laboratories
James L. MASSEY,   ETH Zentrum, Zurich
Jim OMURA,   Cylink Corporation
Gustavus J. SIMMONS,   Sandia National Laboratories
Scott VANSTONE,   University of Waterloo

CRYPTO '89 Table of Contents

108

Lecture Notes in Computer Science

Edited by G. Goos and J. Hartmanis

473

I.B. Damgård (Ed.)

Advances in Cryptology – EUROCRYPT '90

Workshop on the Theory and Application
of Cryptographic Techniques
Aarhus, Denmark, May 21–24, 1990
Proceedings

Springer-Verlag

Berlin Heidelberg New York London
Paris Tokyo Hong Kong Barcelona

Preface

EUROCRYPT is a conference devoted to all aspects of cryptologic research, both theoretical and practical. In the last 7 years, the meeting has taken place once a year at various places in Europe. Both these meetings and the annual Crypto meetings in California are sponsored by The International Association for Cryptologic Research (IACR). Most of the proceedings from these meetings are, like this one, published in Springer-Verlag's *Lecture Notes in Computer Science* series.

EuroCrypt 90 took place on May 21-24 at conference center Scanticon, situated in Århus, Denmark. There were more than 250 participants from all over the world. It is a pleasure to take this opportunity to thank the general chairman Peter Landrock, Århus Congress Bureau, Scanticon, and the organizing committee, who all contributed with hard work and dedication to make a well organized and successful conference.

A total of 85 papers from all over the world were submitted to the conference. This number marks a continuation of the steady growth of interest in the EuroCrypt meetings. Out of the papers submitted, 41 were rejected, 1 was withdrawn, and 2 papers were asked to merge. This resulted in a set of 42 papers presented at the conference. The submissions were in the form of extended abstracts. All program committee members received a full set of submissions, and each submission was refereed independently by at least two members of the program committee (not including the program chairman). The experiment from Crypto 89 with blind refereeing was continued at this conference, and has now become standard policy at IACR conferences. The final papers appearing in these proceedings were not refereed, and the authors retain, of course, full responsibility for the contents. Several of the papers can be expected to appear in various journals in more polished form. There will a special issue of the Journal of Cryptology containing selected papers from the conference.

In addition to the formal contributions, a number of informal talks were given at the traditional rump session. These proceedings include short abstracts of some of these impromptu talks.

Finally, it is a pleasure to acknowledge all those who contributed to putting together the program of EuroCrypt 90 and making these proceedings a reality.

First of all, thanks to the program committee. All of its members put a tremendous amount of hard work into the refereeing, and many of them even took the time to make detailed comment on other papers than the 20 they were asked to read carefully. Also some of my colleagues at Århus University kindly offered their help on various technical questions; among these were Torben Pedersen and Jørgen Brandt.

Of course, no conference could have taken place without the authors' contribution. I would like to thank all those who submitted papers, also those whose submissions could not be accepted because of the large number of high quality submissions we received. Many of the authors have been extremely cooperative in changing the format of their papers to fit into the proceedings. Were it not for this attitude, these proceedings would have been significantly delayed.

Århus, September 1990   Ivan Bjerre Damgård

EuroCrypt 90

A conference on the theory and application of cryptology

Sponsored by The International Association for Cryptologic Research (IACR)

and

CRYPTOMAT$_H$IC AS, DATACO AS, Den Danske Bank AS,

Jutland Telephone Company AS

General Chairman: Peter Landrock (Aarhus University)
Organizing Committee:
Jørgen Brandt (Aarhus University)
Palle Brandt Jensen (Jutland Telephone Company)
Torben Pedersen (Aarhus University)
Århus Congress Bureau

Program Chairman: Ivan Damgård (Aarhus University)
Program Committee:
Ueli Maurer (ETH, Zürich)
Andrew J. Clark (Computer Security Ltd., Brighton)
Claude Crépeau (LRI, Paris)
Thomas Siegenthaler (AWK, Zürich)
Joan Boyar (Aarhus University)
Stig Frode Mjølsnes (ELAB, Trondheim)
Marc Girault (SEPT, Caen)
Walter Fumy (Siemens AG, Erlangen)
Othmar Staffelbach (Gretag, Regensdorf)

EUROCRYPT '90 Table of Contents

A. J. Menezes   S. A. Vanstone (Eds.)

Advances in Cryptology – CRYPTO '90

Proceedings

Lecture Notes in Computer Science 537

Springer-Verlag

Berlin Heidelberg New York
London Paris Tokyo
Hong Kong Barcelona
Budapest

Foreword

Crypto '90 marked the tenth anniversary of the Crypto conferences held at the University of California at Santa Barbara. The conference was held from August 11 to August 15, 1990 and was sponsored by the International Association for Cryptologic Research, in cooperation with the IEEE Computer Society Technical Committee on Security and Privacy and the Department of Computer Science of the University of California at Santa Barbara.

Crypto '90 attracted 227 participants from twenty countries around the world. Roughly 35% of attendees were from academia, 45% from industry and 20% from government. The program was intended to provide a balance between the purely theoretical and the purely practical aspects of cryptography to meet the needs and diversified interests of these various groups.

The overall organization of the conference was superbly handled by the general chairperson Sherry McMahan. All of the outstanding features of Crypto, which we have come to expect over the years, were again present and, in addition to all of this, she did a magnificent job in the preparation of the book of abstracts. This is a crucial part of the program and we owe her a great deal of thanks.

Each year the number and quality of submissions to Crypto has been increasing. This is of course very good for the conference but it does make the task of the program committee more difficult. This year we had 104 papers and abstracts submitted from 18 countries. In anticipation of this larger number, the committee was expanded to twelve members representing seven countries. Having a bigger committee and a wider global representation poses certain problems with communication, but we believe these problems are minute in comparison to the benefits obtained from having each paper scrutinized by more people and by involving a much larger cross-section of the cryptographic community in this process. Each paper was assigned to three committee members who were then responsible for its refereeing. Of the 104 submissions, one was withdrawn, 43 were accepted for presentation and, of these 43, two were merged into one presentation. All papers and abstracts accepted for presentation which contained sufficient detail for the committee to make a reasonably accurate evaluation of the final form of the paper have not been been re-refereed. Rump session contributions and papers accepted for presentation based on abstracts with very little detail have been refereed.

As in other years, Whitfield Diffie kindly agreed to coordinate the Rump Session. We would like to take this opportunity to thank Whit for running this very important aspect of Crypto over the years and for graciously accepting to do it again. In an effort to contain the number of short talks given in this session, a much harder line was adopted this year. Of the 22 abstracts submitted only 12 were accepted for presentation. Of these 12, only 6 were submitted for the proceedings and all of these have gone through a thorough refereeing process.

VIII

For this conference there were three invited speakers and each was given fifty minutes to lecture. It was our goal to have topics of current interest, given by noted authorities in the area and presented in a manner which would make the lectures accessible to a large audience of diversified backgrounds. With this in mind we approached Whitfield Diffie (Bell Northern Research), Adi Shamir (Weizmann Institute) and Gus Simmons (Sandia National Laboratories) and all accepted. We thank them for their outstanding presentations and the enthusiasm which they conveyed for the subject.

We would also like to thank Dr. Tatsuaki Okamoto (NTT Tokyo) for the very valuable assistance he provided to us. Dr. Okamoto was on sabbatical leave from NTT and was spending this time (August 1989 – August 1990) at the University of Waterloo. He kindly volunteered his services and made many very important and significant contributions to our efforts with the program.

Finally, we thank the members of the program committee itself for the very fine job they did. Theirs is a task which takes a great deal of time and effort and which receives a disproportionate amount of gratitude. Without a complete commitment by all members, the task would be impossible. We thank each of them for a very thorough and conscientious effort and also for their very deep dedication in making Crypto '90 successful. Many thanks to Gordon Agnew, Thomas Berson, Johannes Buchmann, Yvo Desmedt, Amos Fiat, Kenji Koyama, Ronald Rivest, Rainer Rueppel, Marijke De Soete, Doug Stinson, and Hugh Williams.

Alfred J. Menezes and Scott A. Vanstone
University of Waterloo
December 1990

CRYPTO '90

A Conference on the Theory and Application of Cryptography

held at the University of California, Santa Barbara,
August 11-15, 1990
through the cooperation of the Computer Science Department

Sponsored by:

International Association for Cryptologic Research

in cooperation with

*The IEEE Computer Society Technical Committee
On Security and Privacy*

General Chair
Sherry McMahan, Cylink

Program Chair
Scott Vanstone, University of Waterloo

Program Committee

Gordon Agnew	University of Waterloo
Thomas Berson	Anagram Laboratories
Johannes Buchmann	Universität des Saarlandes
Yvo Desmedt	University of Wisconsin
Amos Fiat	Tel-Aviv University
Kenji Koyama	NTT Basic Research Lab
Ronald Rivest	Massachusetts Institute of Technology
Rainer Rueppel	Crypto AG
Marijke De Soete	Philips Research Labs
Doug Stinson	University of Nebraska
Hugh Williams	University of Manitoba

CRYPTO '90 Table of Contents

124

D. W. Davies (Ed.)

Advances in Cryptology– EUROCRYPT '91

Workshop on the Theory and Application
of Cryptographic Techniques
Brighton, UK, April 8-11, 1991
Proceedings

Lecture Notes in Computer Science 547

Springer-Verlag
Berlin Heidelberg New York
London Paris Tokyo
Hong Kong Barcelona
Budapest

Preface

A series of open workshops devoted to modern cryptology began in Santa Barbara, California in 1981 and was followed in 1982 by a European counterpart in Burg Feurstein, Germany. The series has been maintained with summer meetings in Santa Barbara and spring meetings somewhere in Europe. At the 1983 meeting in Santa Barbara the International Association for Cryptologic Research was launched and it now sponsors all the meetings of the series.

Following the tradition of the series, papers were invited in the form of extended abstracts and were reviewed by the programme committee, which selected those to be presented. After the meeting, full papers were produced, in some cases with improvements and corrections. These papers form the main part of the present volume. They are placed in the same order that they took at the meeting and under the same headings, for ease of reference by those who attended. The classification under these headings was a little arbitrary, needing to fit the timing of the day's activities, but it makes a workable method of arrangement.

Also following tradition, a "rump session" was held during one evening, under the effective chairmanship of John Gordon. These were short presentations and those present found them to have some real interest, therefore we have taken the unusual step of including short papers contributed by the rump session speakers at the end of this volume, with a necessarily simplified review process.

There was no attempt by the programme committee to guide the programme towards particular themes, though the interests of the committee members may have influeced the shape of the meeting. In our admittedly rough classification the biggest group was about sequences, the term interpreted rather widely. The next biggest group concerned cryptanalysis, which was welcomed because cryptanalysis is the criterion by which algorithms and protocols in cryptography must be judged.

Zero-knowledge interactive protocols figured less this year than at earlier meetings - a consequence of the submissions we received, not of policy.

Smaller groups of papers dealt with S-box criteria, signatures and new ideas in public key cryptography. Then there were many papers placed into sessions labelled "theory" and "applications".

My task as programme chair was made easier by the high quality of papers we received, though we regretted having to reject some of the papers because of time limitations. I would like to thank the programme committee for its hard work of reviewing papers and the organizing committee for ensuring that everything ran smoothly, including the social events. Then, of course, the authors deserve many thanks for favouring Eurocrypt '91 with the publication of their excellent work and for preparing their final papers with (in most cases) admirable despatch.

London, August 1991   Donald W. Davies

EUROCRYPT '91

General Chairman:
Andrew J. Clark
(Logica Aerospace and Defence Ltd.)

Organizing Committee:
Keith Martin
(Royal Holloway and Bedford New College, Univ. of London)
Martin Meikle-Small (Aspen Consultants)
Ben Meisner (RHBNC)
Kathleen Quinn (RHBNC)
Matthew Robshaw (RHBNC)

Program Chairman:
Donald W. Davies (RBHNC)

Program Committee:
Thomas Beth (Univ. of Karlsruhe)
Colin Boyd (Univ. of Manchester)
Norbert Cot (EHEI Université, Paris)
Viveke Fåk (Linköping University)
John Gordon (Cybermation Limited)
Siegfried Herda (GMD, Germany)
Arjen Lenstra (Bellcore, NJ)
Tsutomu Matsumoto (Yokohama National Univ.)
Fred Piper (RHBNC)
Claus Schnorr (Universität Frankfurt)

EUROCRYPT '91 was sponsored by:
International Association for Cryptologic Research (IACR)
in association with:
Logica Aerospace and Defence Limited
ABN Bank
Coopers and Lybrand Deloitte
Northern Telecom
with additional support from:
Computer Security Limited
IBM United Kingdom Limited

EUROCRYPT '91 Table of Contents

132

J. Feigenbaum (Ed.)

Advances in Cryptology – CRYPTO '91

Proceedings

Lecture Notes in Computer Science 576

Springer-Verlag

Berlin Heidelberg New York
London Paris Tokyo
Hong Kong Barcelona
Budapest

Preface

The Crypto '91 conference, sponsored by the International Association for Cryptologic Research (IACR), took place at the University of California in Santa Barbara, August 11 – 15, 1991. The conference was very enjoyable and ran very smoothly, largely because of the efforts of General Chair Burt Kaliski and his colleagues at RSA Data Security, Inc.

There were 115 submissions, two of which were not considered because they arrived after the deadline. Three of the remaining 113 were withdrawn by their authors. Of the 110 submissions considered by the Program Committee, 36 were chosen for presentation at the conference; in two cases, the results presented were combinations of two related submissions. In addition, the Committee chose three invited speakers. All of the contributed talks and two of the invited talks resulted in papers for this volume. Please remember that these are unrefereed papers and that the authors bear full responsibility for their contents. Many of these papers represent work in progress; we expect that the authors will write final papers for refereed journals when their work is complete.

For the third year in a row, submissions were required to be anonymous. This year, we had an explicit rule that each Program Committee member could be an author or coauthor of at most one accepted paper. Program Committee members' submissions were anonymous and went through the same reviewing process as other submissions.

It is my pleasure to acknowledge the efforts of those who contributed to making the conference a success. First of all, I wish to thank the Program Committee, which consisted of Tom Berson (Anagram Laboratories), myself, Ingemar Ingemarsson (University of Linkoping), Ueli Maurer (Princeton University and ETH Zürich), Kevin McCurley (Sandia National Laboratories), Michael Merritt (AT&T Bell Laboratories), Moni Naor (IBM Almaden), Eiji Okamoto (NEC Japan), Josef Pieprzyk (University of New South Wales), Tony Rosati (Newbridge Microsystems), and Moti Yung (IBM Yorktown). Many of us relied on colleagues and friends for help in evaluating the submissions – those who helped include Martín Abadi, Josh Benaloh, Ernie Brickell, Mike Burrows, Don Coppersmith, Uriel Feige, Matt Franklin, Stuart Haber, Mike Luby, Andrew Odlyzko, Alon Orlitsky, and Jim Reeds. As usual, we all thank Whit Diffie for organizing the rump session. I thank Gilles Brassard for agreeing at the last minute to chair the first session of the conference and for providing all of the Latex macros that I used to put together the proceedings. Ruth Shell was extremely helpful in processing all of the submissions, acknowledgements, acceptances, and rejections.

Finally, I thank the authors for sending in their submissions (even the ones that were rejected), the speakers, and all of the participants in this and other IACR conferences. We have established a good tradition, and I hope it continues.

Murray Hill, NJ   Joan Feigenbaum
December, 1991

CRYPTO '91 Table of Contents

138

R. A. Rueppel (Ed.)

Advances in Cryptology – EUROCRYPT '92

Workshop on the Theory and Application
of Cryptographic Techniques
Balatonfüred, Hungary, May 24-28, 1992
Proceedings

Lecture Notes in Computer Science 658

Springer-Verlag
Berlin Heidelberg New York
London Paris Tokyo
Hong Kong Barcelona
Budapest

Preface

A series of open workshops devoted to modern cryptology began in Santa Barbara, California in 1981 and was followed in 1982 by a European counterpart in Burg Feuerstein, Germany. The series has been maintained with summer meetings in Santa Barbara and spring meetings somewhere in Europe. At the 1983 meeting in Santa Barbara the International Association for Cryptologic Research was launched and it now sponsors all the meetings of the series.

Eurocrypt '92 in Hungary was a special meeting in many ways. For the first time, it was held in an Eastern European country. Our charming Hungarian hosts turned the conference into an unforgettable experience for all of us. Also for the first time, the General Chair and the Program Chair were based in different countries. The Program Committee was selected very internationally, which implied that joint meetings were impossible in the course of setting the program. It was encouraging to see how swiftly disputes could be resolved by electronic mail. To ease its burden, the official Program Committee of Eurocrypt '92 obtained help from many renowned researchers and scientists. Here is the final list of all those people (that I know of) who helped during the refereeing phase.

> Brandt, Brickell, Charpin, Crépeau, Csirmaz, Damgård, Denes, Desmedt, Feigenbaum, Fell, Fujioka, Girault, Golic, Helleseth, Itoh, Joux, Kenyon, Koyama, Kurosawa, Landrock, Matsui, Matsumoto, McCurley, Merritt, Miyaguchi, Miyaji, Morain, Morita, Nemetz, Odlyzko, Ohta, Okamoto, Quisquater, Rueppel, Sako, Sakurai, Santha, Seberry, Shamir, Simmons, Staffelbach, Stern, Tanaka, Vajda, Valle, Yang, Yung.

The Rump Session, this time held more in the spirit of a recent results session, was chaired by Laszlo Csirmaz. Some of the presentations, after a simplified review procedure, were selected for publication in these proceedings. They can be found at the end of this volume.

For the first time, a panel discussion was organized, entitled "The Eurocrypt '92 Controversial Issue: Trapdoor Primes and Moduli". The topic was mainly motivated by the public debate on the draft standard on digital signatures proposed by NIST. The panel members produced an interesting report which is included in this volume.

Following the tradition of the series, the authors produced full papers after the meeting, in some cases with revisions. These papers form the main part of the

VI

present volume. They are placed in the same order that they took at the meeting and under the same headings, for ease of reference by those who attended.

My thanks go to the "extended" Program Committee, to the General Chair Tibor Nemetz, to the Organizing Committee, and last but not least to the authors who contributed their recent results. They all have invested their time and effort to make Eurocrypt '92 a success.

Zurich, October 1992   Rainer A. Rueppel

EUROCRYPT '92 Table of Contents

146

Ernest F. Brickell (Ed.)

Advances in Cryptology – CRYPTO '92

12th Annual International Cryptology Conference
Santa Barbara, California, USA
August 16-20, 1992
Proceedings

Lecture Notes in Computer Science 740

Springer-Verlag
Berlin Heidelberg New York
London Paris Tokyo
Hong Kong Barcelona
Budapest

Preface

Crypto'92 took place on August 16-20, 1992. It was the twelfth in the series of annual cryptology conferences held on the beautiful campus of the University of California, Santa Barbara. Once again, it was sponsored by the International Association for Cryptologic Research, in cooperation with the IEEE Computer Society Technical Committee on Security and Privacy. The conference ran smoothly, due to the diligent efforts of the general chair, Spyros Magliveras of the University of Nebraska.

One of the measures of the success of this series of conferences is represented by the ever increasing number of papers submitted. This year, there were 135 submissions to the conference, which represents a new record. Following the practice of recent program committees, the papers received anonymous review. The program committee accepted 38 papers for presentation. In addition, there were two invited presentations, one by Miles Smid on the Digital Signature Standard, and one by Mike Fellows on presenting the concepts of cryptology to elementary-age students. These proceedings contains these 40 papers plus 3 papers that were presented at the Rump Session. I would like to thank all of the authors of the submitted papers and all of the speakers who presented papers.

I would like to express my sincere appreciation to the work of the program committee: Ivan Damgard (Aarhus University, Denmark), Oded Goldreich (Technion, Israel), Burt Kaliski (RSA Data Security, USA), Joe Kilian (NEC, USA), Neal Koblitz (University of Washington, USA), Ueli Maurer (ETH, Switzerland), Chris Mitchell (Royal Holloway, UK), Kazuo Ohta (NTT, Japan), Steven Rudich (Carnegie Mellon, USA), and Yacov Yacobi (Bellcore, USA). I would also like to thank Joan Boyar for agreeing to chair one of the sessions.

Ernest Brickell
Albuquerque, NM
August, 1993

CRYPTO '92 Table of Contents

150

Tor Helleseth (Ed.)

Advances in Cryptology – EUROCRYPT '93

Workshop on the Theory and Application
of Cryptographic Techniques
Lofthus, Norway, May 23-27, 1993
Proceedings

Lecture Notes in Computer Science 765

Springer-Verlag
Berlin Heidelberg New York
London Paris Tokyo
Hong Kong Barcelona
Budapest

Preface

Eurocrypt is a series of open workshops on the theory and application of cryptographic techniques. These meetings have taken place in Europe every year since 1982 and are sponsored by the International Association for Cryptologic Research (IACR).

Eurocrypt'93 was held on May 23-27 at Hotel Ullensvang, beautifully located in the village of Lofthus in the heart of Norway's fjord district. The conference attracted 266 participants from 29 countries. It is a pleasure to thank the local organizers of the conference and the general chair Kåre Presttun. A special acknowledgment to Leif Nilsen whose dedication and tremendous effort was crucial to make the conference a very successful one.

The call for papers resulted in 117 submissions with authors representing 27 different countries. The accepted papers were selected by the program committee after a blind refereeing process where the authors of the papers were unknown to the program committee members. Because of the large number of papers the members of the program committee were encouraged to ask reliable colleagues for assistance in the evaluation of the papers. The program committee had the difficult task selecting only 36 of these papers for presentation at the conference. In addition Professor Ernst Selmer was especially invited to present a talk at the conference.

The rump session this year was chaired by Ingemar Ingemarsson. Some of the presentations were, after a simplified review process, selected for publication in these proceedings and can be found at the end of this volume.

I would like to thank all the people who contributed to the work of putting together the program of Eurocrypt'93. I am indebted to the members of the program committee for their time and conscientious effort in the evaluation and selection of the papers for presentation at the conference. I am also grateful to the 31 additional reviewers who assisted the program committee members in their evaluation. A special thanks to my colleague Øyvind Ytrehus for his valuable assistance in handling the correspondence to the authors and preparing the proceedings. Finally, I would like to thank all the authors for submitting so many good papers and for their cooperation in preparing this volume.

Bergen, October 1993   Tor Helleseth

EUROCRYPT'93

General Chairman:
Kåre Presttun (Alcatel Telecom)

Organizing Committee:
Kenneth Iversen (KITH, Trondheim)
Torleiv Kløve (U. of Bergen)
Leif Nilsen (Alcatel Telecom)
Øystein Rødseth (U. of Bergen)
Øyvind Ytrehus (U. of Bergen)

Programme Chairman:
Tor Helleseth (U. of Bergen)

Programme Committee:
Ivan Damgård (U. of Aarhus)
Alfredo De Santis (U. of Salerno)
Yvo Desmedt (U. of Wisconsin)
Dieter Gollman (U. of London)
Ingemar Ingemarsson (U. of Linköping)
Kaoru Kurosawa (Tokyo Inst. of Techn.)
Jim Massey (ETH Zürich)
Bart Preneel (ESAT/COSIC)
Andrew Odlyzko (AT&T Bell Labs)
Claus Schnorr (U. of Frankfurt)
Jennifer Seberry (U. of Wollongong)

EUROCRYPT '93 Table of Contents

158

Douglas R. Stinson (Ed.)

Advances in Cryptology – CRYPTO '93

13th Annual International Cryptology Conference
Santa Barbara, California, USA
August 22-26, 1993
Proceedings

Lecture Notes in Computer Science 773

Springer-Verlag
Berlin Heidelberg NewYork
London Paris Tokyo
Hong Kong Barcelona
Budapest

PREFACE

The CRYPTO '93 conference was sponsored by the International Association
Cryptologic Research (IACR) and Bell-Northern Research (a subsidiary of
rthern Telecom), in co-operation with the IEEE Computer Society Technical
mmittee. It took place at the University of California, Santa Barbara, from
gust 22–26, 1993. This was the thirteenth annual CRYPTO conference, all of
ich have been held at UCSB. The conference was very enjoyable and ran very
oothly, largely due to the efforts of the General Chair, Paul Van Oorschot.
was a pleasure working with Paul throughout the months leading up to the
ference.

There were 136 submitted papers which were considered by the Program
mmittee. Of these, 38 were selected for presentation at the conference. There
s also one invited talk at the conference, presented by Miles Smid, the title of
ich was "A Status Report On the Federal Government Key Escrow System."

The conference also included the customary Rump Session, which was presided
r by Whit Diffie in his usual inimitable fashion. Thanks again to Whit for
anizing and running the Rump session. This year, the Rump Session included
interesting and lively panel discussion on issues pertaining to key escrowing.
ose taking part were W. Diffie, J. Gilmore, S. Goldwasser, M. Hellman, A.
rzberg, S. Micali, R. Rueppel, G. Simmons and D. Weitzner.

These proceedings contain revised versions of the 38 contributed talks, as
ll as two talks from the Rump Session. Please remember that these papers
: unrefereed, and many of them represent work in progress. Some authors will
ite final versions of their papers for publication in refereed journals at a later
e. Of course, the authors bear full responsibility for the contents of their
pers.

I am very grateful to the members of the Program Committee for their hard
rk and dedication in the difficult task of selecting less than 30% of the sub-
tted papers for presentation at the conference. The members of the program
nmittee were as follows:

> Mihir Bellare (IBM T. J. Watson)
> Eli Biham (Technion, Israel)
> Ernie Brickell (Sandia Laboratories)
> Joan Feigenbaum (AT&T Bell Laboratories)
> Russell Impagliazzo (UCSD)
> Andrew Odlyzko (AT&T Bell Laboratories)
> Tatsuaki Okamoto (NTT, Japan)
> Birgit Pfitzmann (Hildesheim, Germany)
> Rainer Rueppel (R^3, Switzerland)
> Scott Vanstone (Waterloo, Canada)

As has been done since 1989, submissions to CRYPTO '93 were required to
anonymous. As well, we followed recent tradition which dictates that Program

VI

Committee members could be an author or co-author of at most one accepted paper. Papers submitted by members of the Program Committee underwent the normal reviewing process (and, of course, no Program Committee member reviewed his or her own paper).

Thanks to Jimmy Upton for help with the pre-proceedings that were distributed at the conference (incidentally, this is the last year that CRYPTO will have both pre-proceedings and proceedings — starting in 1994, the proceedings will be available at the conference). Thanks also to Gus Simmons and Carol Patterson, who helped out with registration at the conference. And I would also like to convey my gratitude to Deb Heckens and my student, K. Gopalakrishnan, for their assistance.

Finally, I would like to thank everyone who submitted talks for CRYPTO '93. It goes without saying that the success of the conference depends ultimately on the quality of the submissions — CRYPTO has been and remains a leading conference in the discipline due the the high quality of the papers. I am also grateful to the authors for sending me final versions of their papers for publication in these proceedings in a timely fashion.

Douglas Stinson
Program Chair, CRYPTO '93
University of Nebraska
November, 1993

CRYPTO '93 Table of Contents

Alfredo De Santis (Ed.)

Advances in Cryptology – EUROCRYPT '94

Workshop on the Theory and Application
of Cryptographic Techniques
Perugia, Italy, May 9-12, 1994
Proceedings

Lecture Notes in Computer Science 950

Springer

Preface

Eurocrypt is a series of open workshops devoted to all aspects of cryptologic research, both theoretical and practical. The first workshop was held in 1982, and since then the meetings have taken place in various places in Europe. The Eurocrypt meetings and the Crypto meetings in Santa Barbara, California, are sponsored by the International Association for Cryptologic Research (IACR).

Eurocrypt 94 was held on May 9–12, 1994, in Perugia, an Italian city that was a city-state of Etruria in the 7th and 6th centuries BC. It is a pleasure to thank the general chair William Wolfowitcz and the organizing committee, who all contributed to make a well organized and successful conference.

There were 137 submitted papers which were considered by the Program Committee. Of these, 2 were withdrawn and 36 were selected for presentation and publication in the proceedings. Two of the papers appearing in the proceedings are merged papers from two submissions. These proceedings contain revised versions of the 36 contributed talks. Each paper was sent to at least 3 members of the Program Committee for comments. Revisions were not checked on their scientific aspects. Some authors will write final versions of their papers for publication in refereed journals. Of course the authors bear full responsibility for the contents of their papers.

Silvio Micali, MIT, gave a brilliant invited talk on the Clipper Chip and Fair Cryptosystems.

I am very grateful to the 11 members of the Program Committee for their hard work and the difficult task of selecting about 38% of the submitted papers. As usual, submissions to Eurocrypt 94 were required to be anonymous. The more recent tradition that a Program Committee member can be the author of at most one accepted paper has been followed. Papers submitted by members of the Program Committee were sent to all other members. The entire refereeing process was done by electronic mail.

The following referees and external experts helped the Program Committee in reaching their decisions: S. R. Blackburn, Carlo Blundo, S. Boucheron, Gilles Brassard, Odoardo Brugia, Marco Bucci, Mike Burmester, Claude Carlet, Pascale Charpin, Jean-Marc Couveignes, Denes, Giovanni Di Crescenzo, Michele Elia, Piero Filipponi, Toru Fujiwara, Marc Girault, Akira Hayashi, Toshiya Itoh, Hugo Krawczyk, Kaoru Kurosawa, Antoine Joux, James Massey, Mitsuru Matsui, Tsutomu Matsumoto, Natsume Matsuzaki, Renato Menicocci, Chris Mitchell, Atsuko Miyaji, Emilio Montolivo, Francois Morain, David M'raihi,

VI

Sean Murphy, Giuseppe Persiano, Jean-Marc Piveteau, G. M. Poscetti, Jean-Jacques Quisquater, Kouichi Sakurai, Miklos Santha, Nicolas Sendrier, Matteo Sereno, Hiroki Shizuya, Dan Simon, Markus Stadler, Othmar Staffelbach, Doug R. Stinson, S. Trigila, Ugo Vaccaro, Serge Vaudenay, Jeroen van de Graaf, P. R. Wild, William Wolfowicz. The Program Committee appreciates their effort.

The rump session was chaired by Yvo Desmedt. There were 23 presentations, of which 11 appear in the proceedings.

Special thanks to Carlo Blundo and Giovanni Di Crescenzo for their help. Finally, I would like to thank everyone who submitted to Eurocrypt '94.

University of Salerno, Italy   Alfredo De Santis
July 1995   Program Chair, EUROCRYPT '94

EUROCRYPT '94

took place in Perugia, Italy
May 9–12, 1994

Sponsored by the

International Association for Cryptologic Research

General Chair

William Wolfowitcz, Fondazione Ugo Bordoni, Rome, Italy

Program Chair

Alfredo De Santis, Università di Salerno, Italy

Program Committee

Ernie Brickell	Sandia Labs, USA
Claude Crepeau	CNRS, France
Yvo Desmedt	Univ. of Wisconsin, USA
Adina Di Porto	Fondazione Bordoni, Italy
Dieter Gollman	Univ. of London, UK
Louis Guillou	CCETT, France
Ueli Maurer	ETH Zurich, Switzerland
David Naccache	Gemplus, France
Tatsuaki Okamoto	NTT Labs, Japan
Jacques Stern	ENS-DMI, France
Moti Yung	IBM T. J. Watson Research Center, USA

EUROCRYPT '94 Table of Contents

Yvo G. Desmedt (Ed.)

Advances in Cryptology – CRYPTO '94

14th Annual International
Cryptology Conference
Santa Barbara, California, USA
August 21-25, 1994
Proceedings

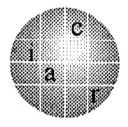

Lecture Notes in Computer Science 839

Springer-Verlag

Berlin Heidelberg New York
London Paris Tokyo
Hong Kong Barcelona
Budapest

PREFACE

The CRYPTO '94 conference is sponsored by the International Association for Cryptologic Research (IACR), in co-operation with the IEEE Computer Society Technical Committee on Security and Privacy. It has taken place at the University of California, Santa Barbara, from August 21–25, 1994. This is the fourteenth annual CRYPTO conference, all of which have been held at UCSB. This is the first time that proceedings are available at the conference. The General Chair, Jimmy R. Upton has been responsible for local organization, registration, etc.

There were 114 submitted papers which were considered by the Program Committee. Of these, 1 was withdrawn and 38 were selected for the proceedings. There are also 3 invited talks. Two of these are on aspects of cryptography in the commercial world. The one on hardware aspects will be presented by David Maher (AT&T), the one on software aspects by Joseph Pato (Hewlett-Packard). There will also be a panel discussion on "Securing an Electronic World: Are We Ready?" The panel members will be: Ross Anderson, Bob Blakley, Matt Blaze, George Davida, Yvo Desmedt (moderator), Whitfield Diffie, Joan Feigenbaum, Blake Greenlee, Martin Hellman, David Maher, Miles Smid. The topic of the panel will be introduced by the invited talk of Whitfield Diffie on "Securing the Information Highway."

These proceedings contain revised versions of the 38 contributed talks. Each paper was sent to at least 3 members of the program committee for comments. Revisions were not checked on their scientific aspects. Some authors will write final versions of their papers for publication in refereed journals. Of course the authors bear full responsibility for the contents of their papers.

I am very grateful to the members of the Program Committee for their hard work and the difficult task of selecting roughly 1 out of 3 of the submitted papers. As has been done since 1989, submissions to CRYPTO '94 were required to be anonymous. The more recent tradition, introduced since 1991, that a Program Committee member can be the author of at most one accepted paper has been followed. Papers submitted by members of the Program Committee were sent to at least 4 referees (and, of course, no Program Committee member reviewed his or her own paper).

The following referees and external experts helped the Program Committee in reaching their decisions: Amos Beimel, Josh Benaloh, Eli Biham, Carlo Blundo, Gilles Brassard, Benny Chor, Philippe Delsarte, Yair Frankel, Atsushi Fujioka, Oded Goldreich, Dan Gordon, Thomas Hardjono, Gene Itkis, Markus Jakobsson, Burt Kaliski, Hugo Krawczyk, Kaoru Kurosawa, Eyal Kushilevitz, Susan Langford, Hendrik Lenstra, Carsten Lund, Kevin McCurley, Yi Mu, Moni Naor, Seffi Naor, Kazuo Ohta, Kevin Phelps, Jean-Jacques Quisquater, Venkatesan Ramarathnam, Jim Reeds, Ron M. Roth, Rei Safavi-Naini, Ryuichi Sakai, Doug Stinson, Jimmy Upton, Paul Van Oorschot, Scott Vanstone and Yuliang Zheng. The Program Committee appreciates their effort.

Thanks to Eli Biham for helping with postscript, Tom Cusick for being willing to provide a backup to read e-mail, Dave Rasmussen for organizing the automatic mailing facility used to distribute information, Marg Feeney and Ann Libert

VI

for secretarial work, Carlo Blundo, Giovanni Di Crescenzo, Ugo Vaccaro and William Wolfowicz for helping out at the last minute. I would also like to thank my hosts of my sabbatical year, Shimon Even, Scott Vanstone and Alfredo De Santis, where most of my work towards the conference took place. Several people have helped the General Chair with sending out the call for papers, registration, registration at the conference, etc.

Finally, I would like to thank everyone who submitted to CRYPTO '94. It goes without saying that the success of the conference depends ultimately on the quality of the submissions — CRYPTO has been and remains a leading conference in the discipline due to the high quality of the papers submitted. I am also grateful to the authors for sending me final versions of their papers for publication in these proceedings in a timely fashion.

Yvo Desmedt
Program Chair, CRYPTO '94
University of Wisconsin – Milwaukee, USA
Salerno, Italy, June, 1994.

CRYPTO '94

will take place at the University of California, Santa Barbara,
August 21–25, 1994

Sponsored by the

International Association for Cryptologic Research

in cooperation with the

*IEEE Computer Society Technical Committee
on Security and Privacy*

General Chair

Jimmy R. Upton, Uptronics Incorporated, USA

Program Chair

Yvo Desmedt, University of Wisconsin – Milwaukee, USA

Program Committee

Tom Berson	Anagram Laboratories, USA
Don Coppersmith	IBM T. J. Watson Research Center, USA
Donald Davies	United Kingdom
Shimon Even	Technion, Israel
Amos Fiat	Tel Aviv University, Israel
Russell Impagliazzo	University of California San Diego, USA
Ingemar Ingemarsson	University of Linköping, Sweden
Mitsuru Matsui	Mitsubishi Electric Corporation, Japan
Alfred Menezes	Auburn University, USA
Andrew Odlyzko	AT&T Bell Laboratories, USA
Jennifer Seberry	University of Wollongong, Australia
Ben Smeets	Lund University, Sweden
Moti Yung	IBM T. J. Watson Research Center, USA

CRYPTO '94 Table of Contents

Louis C. Guillou
Jean-Jacques Quisquater (Eds.)

Advances in Cryptology – EUROCRYPT '95

International Conference on the
Theory and Application of Cryptographic Techniques
Saint-Malo, France, May 21-25, 1995
Proceedings

Lecture Notes in Computer Science 921

 Springer

PREFACE

EUROCRYPT '95. Sponsored by the International Association for Cryptologic Research (IACR), in cooperation with the Centre Commun d'Études de Télévision et Télécommunications (CCETT), a workshop on the theory and applications of cryptographic techniques takes place at the Palais du Grand Large, Saint Malo, France, May 21-25, 1995.

The General Chair of EUROCRYPT '95 is Françoise Scarabin. The Organization Committee was helped by Maryvonne Lahaie and her communication team. Moreover, the CCETT has generously provided the help of a young English lady, Miss Virginia Cooper, for the secretariat of both the Organization and Program Committees. They all did an excellent job in preparing the conference. It is our pleasure to thank them for their essential work.

IACR and EUROCRYPT. According to a very good suggestion expressed during CRYPTO '82, the Association was established at CRYPTO '83. Today, the Association has approximately 600 members and the mailing file managed by its Secretariat consists of more than 2 000 names.

The main goal of the Association is the sponsoring of two annual conferences: CRYPTO, every summer at the University of California, Santa Barbara (UCSB), and EUROCRYPT, every spring in a different European country. Moreover, the Association edits quarterly the Journal of Cryptology (JoC).

After 2 conferences held in 1982 in Burg Feuerstein (Germany) and in 1983 in Udine (Italy), the name EUROCRYPT was used for the very first time in 1984 in Paris (France). Since then, EUROCRYPT has taken place at a variety of venues: in 1985 in Linz (Austria), in 1986 in Linköping (Sweden), in 1987 in Amsterdam (Netherlands), in 1988 in Davos (Switzerland), in 1989 in Houthalen (Belgium), in 1990 in Aarhus (Denmark), in 1991 in Brighton (United Kingdom), in 1992 in Balatonfüred (Hungaria), in 1993 in Lofthus (Norway) and in 1994 in Perugia (Italy). EUROCRYPT '96 is planned to take place in Sarragossa (Spain).

Previous Proceedings. The following 24 proceedings have been published for conferences held at UCSB (CRYPTO) and in Europe (EUROCRYPT).
1. Advances in Cryptology: a Report on CRYPTO 81, ECE Report no. 82-04, Allen Gersho, Ed., ECE Dpt, UCSB, Santa Barbara, CA 93106.
2. Cryptography: Proceedings, Burg Feuerstein, 1982, T. Beth, Ed., LNCS 149, Springer-Verlag, 1983.
3. Advances in Cryptology: Proceedings of Crypto 82, D. Chaum, R. L. Rivest and A. T. Sherman, Eds., Plenum, NY, 1983.
4. Advances in Cryptology: Proceedings of Crypto 83, D. Chaum, Ed., Plenum, NY, 1984.
5. Advances in Cryptology: Proceedings of EUROCRYPT 84, T. Beth, N. Cot and I. Ingermarsson, Eds., LNCS 209, Springer-Verlag, 1985.
6. Advances in Cryptology: Proceedings of CRYPTO 84, R. Blakley and D. Chaum, Eds., LNCS 196, Springer-Verlag, 1985.

VI

7. Advances in Cryptology: Proceedings of EUROCRYPT '85,
   F. Pichler, Ed., LNCS 219, Springer-Verlag, 1986.
8. Advances in Cryptology: CRYPTO '85,
   H. C. Williams, Ed., LNCS 218, Springer-Verlag, 1986.
9. Advances in Cryptology: CRYPTO '86,
   A. M. Odlyzko, Ed., LNCS 263, Springer-Verlag, 1987.
10. Advances in Cryptology: EUROCRYPT '87,
    D. Chaum and W. L. Price, Eds., LNCS 304, Springer-Verlag, 1988.
11. Advances in Cryptology: CRYPTO '87,
    C. Pomerance, Ed., LNCS 293, Springer-Verlag, 1988.
12. Advances in Cryptology: EUROCRYPT '88,
    C. G. Günther, Ed., LNCS 330, Springer-Verlag, 1988.
13. Advances in Cryptology: CRYPTO '88,
    S. Goldwasser, Ed., LNCS 403, Springer-Verlag, 1989.
14. Advances in Cryptology: EUROCRYPT '89,
    J.-J. Quisquater and J. Vandewalle, Eds., LNCS 434, Springer-Verlag, 1990.
15. Advances in Cryptology: CRYPTO '89,
    G. Brassard, Ed., LNCS 435, Springer-Verlag, 1990.
16. Advances in Cryptology: EUROCRYPT '90,
    I. B. Damgard, Ed., LNCS 473, Springer-Verlag, 1991.
17. Advances in Cryptology: CRYPTO '90,
    A. J. Menezes and S. A. Vanstone, Eds., LNCS 537, Springer-Verlag, 1991.
18. Advances in Cryptology: EUROCRYPT '91,
    D. W. Davies, Ed., LNCS 547, Springer-Verlag, 1991.
19. Advances in Cryptology: CRYPTO '91,
    J. Feigenbaum, Ed., LNCS 576, Springer-Verlag, 1992.
20. Advances in Cryptology: EUROCRYPT '92,
    R. A. Rueppel, Ed., LNCS 658, Springer-Verlag, 1993.
21. Advances in Cryptology: CRYPTO '92,
    E. F. Brickell, Ed., LNCS 740, Springer-Verlag, 1993.
22. Advances in Cryptology: EUROCRYPT '93,
    T. Helleseth, Ed., LNCS 765, Springer-Verlag, 1994.
23. Advances in Cryptology: CRYPTO '93,
    D. R. Stinson, Ed., LNCS 773, Springer-Verlag, 1994.
24. Advances in Cryptology: CRYPTO '94,
    Y. G. Desmedt, Ed., LNCS 839, Springer-Verlag, 1994.

No proceedings were published for the conferences held in 1983 in Udine (Italy) and in 1986 in Linköping (Sweden). Moreover at the time of writing this preface, the proceedings of EUROCRYPT '94 held in Perugia (Italy) are still waiting for publication. A careful examination of the list induces the following five remarks.

- The words 'Advances in cryptology' appeared on the first proceedings.
- Since 1984, CRYPTO and EUROCRYPT are written in capitals.
- Since EUROCRYPT '85, the number of the year is preceded by '.
- Since CRYPTO '85, the words 'Proceedings of' have disappeared.
- Among these 24 proceedings, 21 were published by Springer Verlag.

Submissions, Program, Proceedings. CRYPTO '94 and EUROCRYPT '95 are the first two IACR conferences where the proceedings are available at the conference; the subsequent advance of the submission deadlines by two months explains the slight decrease in the number of submissions: 135 at CRYPTO '92, 117 at EUROCRYPT '93, 136 at CRYPTO '93, 137 at EUROCRYPT '94, 114 at CRYPTO '94, 113 at EUROCRYPT '95.

This outcome does not appear to be long term, there being 150 submissions for CRYPTO '95. Equally the Board of Directors of the IACR is currently looking at solutions to address this problem for later conferences.

Thus the Program Committee of EUROCRYPT '95 received 113 submissions among which one was withdrawn by the author and one by the Program Chair for double submission. The editors would like to thank everyone who submitted a paper. The success of a conference depends ultimately upon the quality of the contributions. EUROCRYPT and CRYPTO have been and remain leading conferences in cryptology due to the high quality of the submissions.

Each paper was submitted for evaluation and comments to at least 4 members of the Program Committee. The process was anonymous, as it has been since 1989. The Program Committee has selected 33 papers among the 111 remaining submissions, i.e., slightly less than one third.

The rule, introduced in 1991, whereby a member of the Program Committee can be the author of at most one accepted paper, has been respected. Moreover, a new rule states that the status of Program Chair is not compatible with that of author.

The Program Chair is very grateful to all the members of the Program Committee for their hard work. It was a pleasure working with all of them.

Several experts helped the Program Committee members in reaching their decisions. In the name of the Program Committee, the Program Chair would also like to express here his appreciation for their efforts and their expertises.

The editors thank the authors for providing them in due time with the final versions of their papers. The availability of the proceedings at the conference is a significant progress, appreciated by the editors and also, by each participant.

The Author Index at the end of this book consists of 60 names. We know the date of birth of 30 peoples in this list: 7 are in their forties; 11 in their thirties; 12 in their twenties, four of them being only 24 years old! The youngest one will be 24 on the last day of the conference. The significant percentage of young authors is an encouraging sign of vitality of the IACR conferences.

Rump Session. The rump session is now an established tradition at IACR conferences. It aims at presenting the most recent results and at establishing the constestation of results presented in the other sessions. The publication of the proceedings at the conference seriously reduces the possibility of publishing the rump talks in the book. However, one contestation has been presented in due time and the corresponding rump talk is provided as the last paper of this book. As long as fair play is respected, such a contestation is another proof of the vitality of the IACR conferences. Of course, each author bears the full responsibility for his or her paper.

VIII

Special Session. In the program, a special session is dedicated to the introduction of arithmetic co-processors in the security self-programmable one-chip microcomputers (SPOMs), such as those used in smart cards. Allowing an efficient use of PK and ZK techniques, such arithmetic co-processors will deeply modify the use of smart cards in their various applications.

With the agreement of the Program Committee, the Program Chair set up a Special Committee chaired by Pascal Chour (AQL) and Marc Girault (SEPT). With the help of Guy Monnier (SGS Thomson) and David Arditti (CNET-Paris), the Special Committee has done an admirable job in orienting and focusing the preparation of the three invited talks of the special session and in organizing a corresponding illustrative exhibition.

David Naccache (Gemplus), Michel Ugon (Bull CP8) and Peter Landrock (Cryptomathic) have agreed to draft and to talk respectively on the following three aspects: hardware (architectural principles, trade-offs, performances, provisional calendars of the silicon founders); software (possible security mechanisms for functional aspects, such as digital signature, entity authentication, key management, file management, card issuing); applications (estimated consequences in major applications such as banking, telephone, television, health care, network security, electronic purse, transportation ...). A copy of the three talks is available for each participant as a special pre-publication.

The subject is particularly hot if we consider the major work of Europay International, MasterCard International and Visa International in drafting the so-called EMV specifications. The goal of the three organizations is a general worldwide use of SPOMs in credit cards. The present production of SPOMs for smart cards is about 30 million pieces per year, approximately one half of which are for banking purposes. The needs of the banks which are members of the three international organizations are evaluated around 300 million pieces per year.

Ten years ago, EUROCRYPT '84 held a special session on smart cards; at that time, we were at the very beginning of a general French development with the publication of specifications, in January 1984, by the GIE des Cartes Bancaires, the French interbank association; today, we are on the verge of a general worldwide development with the publication of the EMV specifications.

However the EMV phenomena should not hide all the other emerging applications. Let us quote Gustavus J. Simmons: "Smart cards *will put a sophisticated information-integrity device in the wallet or purse of practically every person in the industrialized world, and will therefore probably be the most extensive application ever made of cryptographic schemes*" (Preface of *Contemporary Cryptology, The Science of Information Integrity*, IEEE Press, 1992).

Louis Claude Guillou, Program Chair

CCETT, Cesson Sévigné, France

Jean-Jacques Quisquater, Co-Editor

March 1995

EUROCRYPT '95

EUROCRYPT '95
Saint-Malo, France
May 21–25, 1995

Sponsored by the

International Association for Cryptologic Research (IACR)

in cooperation with the

Centre Commun d'Études de Télévision et Télécommunications (CCETT)

General Chair

Françoise Scarabin, CCETT, France

Program Chair

Louis C. Guillou, CCETT, France

Program Committee

Mihir Bellare .... IBM T. J. Watson Research Center, USA
Johannes Buchmann .... U. Saarland, Germany
Mike Burmester .... Royal Holloway, U. London, UK
Paul Camion .... INRIA, France
Donald Davies .... Fair Winds, UK
Amos Fiat .... U. Tel Aviv-ARL, Israel
Hideki Imai .... U. Tokyo, Japan
Lars R. Knudsen .... U. Aarhus, Denmark
Ueli Maurer .... ETH, Switzerland
Birgit Pfitzmann .... U. Hildesheim, Germany
Jean-Jacques Quisquater .... UCL-Math RiZK, Belgium
Ronald L. Rivest .... MIT, USA
Jacques Stern .... ENS, France
Douglas Stinson .... U. Nebraska, USA
Moti Yung .... IBM T. J. Watson Research Center, USA
Gideon Yuval .... Microsoft, USA

EUROCRYPT '95 Table of Contents

188

Don Coppersmith (Ed.)

Advances
in Cryptology –
CRYPTO '95

15th Annual International Cryptology Conference
Santa Barbara, California, USA, August 27-31, 1995
Proceedings

Lecture Notes in Computer Science 963

 Springer

PREFACE

The Crypto '95 conference was sponsored by the International Association for Cryptologic Research (IACR), in cooperation with the IEEE Computer Society Technical Committee on Security and Privacy, and the Computer Science Department of the University of California, Santa Barbara. It took place at the University of California, Santa Barbara, from August 27-31, 1995. This was the fifteenth annual Crypto conference; all have been held at UCSB. For the second time, proceedings were available at the conference. The General Chair, Stafford Tavares, was responsible for local organization and registration.

The Program Committee considered 151 papers and selected 36 for presentation. There were also two invited talks. Robert Morris, Sr. gave a talk on "Ways of Losing Information," which included some non-cryptographic means of leaking secrets that are often overlooked by cryptographers. The second talk, "Cryptography - Myths and Realities," was given by Adi Shamir, this year's IACR Distinguished Lecturer. Shamir is the second person to receive this honor, the first having been Gus Simmons at Crypto '94.

These proceedings contain revised versions of the 36 contributed talks. Each paper was sent to at least three members of the program committee for comments. Revisions were not checked on their scientific aspects. Some authors will write final versions of their papers for publication in refereed journals. Of course, the authors bear full responsibility for the contents of their papers.

I am very grateful to the members of the Program Committee for their hard work and the difficult task of selecting one quarter of the submitted papers. Following recent traditions, the submissions were anonymous; and each program committee member could be the author of at most one accepted paper.

We thank the following referees and external experts for their help on various papers: Philippe Béguin, Mihir Bellare, Charles Bennett, Gilles Brassard, Florent Chabaud, Chris Charnes, Yair Frankel, Atsushi Fujioka, Thomas Hardjono, Philippe Hoogvorst, Nobuyuki Imoto, Toshiya Itoh, Sushil Jajodia, Lars Knudsen, Paul Kocher, Mitsuru Matsui, Tsutomu Matsumoto, David M'Raihi, Yi Mu, Rafail Ostrovsky, Eiji Okamoto, Tatsuaki Okamoto, David Pointcheval, Rei Safavi-Naini, Kouichi Sakurai, Jennifer Seberry, Hiroki Shizuya, Dan Simon, Othmar Staffelbach, Jacques Stern, Moti Yung and Xian-Mo Zhang. I apologize for any omissions.

I thank Baruch Schieber and Prabhakar Raghavan for help with software and LaTeX; Barbara White and Peg Cargiulo for secretarial help; and Yvo Desmedt, Jimmy Upton and Peter Landrock for advice on the mechanics.

Finally, thanks go to all who submitted papers for Crypto '95. The success of the conference depends on the quality of its submissions. I am also thankful for all the authors, who cooperated by delivering their final copy to me in a timely fashion for the proceedings.

VI

Don Coppersmith
Program Chair, Crypto '95
IBM Research Division, Yorktown Heights, New York, USA
June, 1995

CRYPTO '95

University of California, Santa Barbara
August 27-31, 1995

Sponsored by the

International Association for Cryptologic Research

in cooperation with the

*IEEE Computer Society Technical Committee
on Security and Privacy*

and the

*Computer Science Department,
University of California, Santa Barbara*

General Chair

Stafford Tavares, Queen's University, Canada

Program Chair

Don Coppersmith, IBM T.J. Watson Research Center, USA

Program Committee

Ross Anderson	Cambridge University, UK
Ernest Brickell	Sandia National Laboratories, USA
Hugo Krawczyk	IBM T.J. Watson Research Center, USA
Susan Langford	Stanford University, USA
Kevin McCurley	Sandia National Laboratories, USA
Willi Meier	HTL Brugg-Windisch, Switzerland
Moni Naor	Weizmann Institute of Science, Israel
Andrew Odlyzko	AT&T Bell Laboratories, USA
Kazuo Ohta	NTT Laboratories, Japan
Josef Pieprzyk	University of Wollongong, Australia
Jean-Jacques Quisquater	UCL-MathRIZK, Belgium
Alan Sherman	Univ. of Maryland Baltimore County, USA
Scott Vanstone	University of Waterloo, Canada
Serge Vaudenay	Ecole Normale Supérieure, France

CRYPTO '95 Table of Contents

Ueli Maurer (Ed.)

Advances in Cryptology – EUROCRYPT '96

International Conference on the Theory
and Application of Cryptographic Techniques
Saragossa, Spain, May 12-16, 1996
Proceedings

Lecture Notes in Computer Science 1070

 Springer

PREFACE

The EUROCRYPT '96 conference was sponsored by the International Association for Cryptologic Research (IACR)[1], in cooperation with the University of Saragossa. It took place at the Palacio de Congresos in Saragossa, Spain, during May 12–16, 1996. This was the fifteenth annual EUROCRYPT conference (this name has been used since the third conference held in 1984), each of which has been held in a different city in Europe. For the second time, proceedings were available at the conference. José Pastor Franco, the General Chair, was responsible for local organization and registration. His contribution to the success of the conference is gratefully acknowledged.

The Program Committee considered 126 submitted papers and selected 34 for presentation. Each paper was sent to all members of the Program Committee and was assigned to at least three of them for careful evaluation. There were also two invited talks. James L. Massey, this year's IACR Distinguished Lecturer, gave a lecture entitled "The difficulty with difficulty". Massey is the third to receive this honor, the first two being Gustavus Simmons and Adi Shamir. Shafi Goldwasser gave an invited talk entitled "Multi party secure protocols: past and present".

These proceedings contain revised versions of the 34 contributed talks. While the papers were carefully selected, they have not been refereed like submissions to a refereed journal. The authors bear full responsibility for the contents of their papers. Some authors may write final versions of their papers for publication in a refereed journal.

I am very grateful to the members of the Program Committee for generously spending much of their time on the difficult task of selecting the papers to be presented at the conference. Following recent tradition, the submissions were anonymous. Each committee member could be an author of at most one accepted paper.

The help of the following referees and external experts in evaluating various papers is gratefully acknowledged: Philippe Béguin, Matt Blaze, Daniel Bleichenbacher, Bert den Boer, Antoon Bosselaers, Jørgen Brandt, Gilles Brassard, Christian Cachin, Jan Camenisch, Ran Canetti, Florent Chabaud, Ronald Cramer, Scott Decatur, Markus Dichtl, Marten van Dijk, Jan-Hendrik Evertse, Joan Feigenbaum, Eiichiro Fujisaki, Rosario Gennaro, Jean Geordiades, Jeroen van de Graaf, Louis Granboulan, Shai Halevi, Erwin Hess, Martin Hirt, Nobuyuki Imoto, David-Olivier Jaquet-Chiffelle, Stasio Jarecki, Mike Just, Gregory Kabatianski, Volker Kessler, Lars Knudsen, Jack Lacy, Françoise Levy-dit-Vehel, Mitsuru Matsui, Willi Meier, J. Merkle, Kazuo Ohta, Torben Pedersen, David Pointcheval, Mike Reiter, Vincent Rijmen, Kazue Sako, Berry Schoenmakers,

---

[1] The main purpose of the IACR is to sponsor two annual conferences: CRYPTO, every summer at the University of California, Santa Barbara (UCSB), and EUROCRYPT, every spring in a different European country. The IACR also publishes the Journal of Cryptology.

VI

Peter Schweitzer, J. P. Seifert, Peter Shor, Markus Stadler, Jacques Stern, Ramarathnam Venkatesan, Stefan Wolf, Aaron Wyner, and Hirosuke Yamamoto. I apologize for possible omissions.

Special thanks go to Martin Hirt for his help with the organization of the committee's work and with the preparation of the proceedings. Martin Burkart provided help with software for automatically handling correspondence with authors. Don Coppersmith, Louis Guillou, Kevin McCurley, and Jean-Jacques Quisquater gave advice for the organization of the committee's work. Louis provided LaTeX files for preparing parts of these proceedings.

Finally, I would like to thank all who have submitted papers to EURO-CRYPT '96 and to the authors of accepted papers for their cooperation.

March 1996   Ueli Maurer

EUROCRYPT '96
Saragossa, Spain
May 12–16, 1996

Sponsored by the

International Association for Cryptologic Research (IACR)

in cooperation with the

University of Saragossa, Spain

General Chairman

Jose Pastor Franco, University of Saragossa, Spain

Program Chairman

Ueli Maurer, ETH Zürich, Switzerland

Program Committee

Stefan Brands .... CWI, The Netherlands
Claude Crépeau .... University of Montréal, Canada
Ivan Damgård .... Aarhus University, Denmark
Josep Domingo .... Universitat Rovira i Virgili, Spain
Walter Fumy .... Siemens, Germany
Jovan Dj. Golić .... QUT, Australia
Arjen K. Lenstra .... Bellcore, USA
David Naccache .... Gemplus, France
Andrew M. Odlyzko .... AT&T Bell Labs., USA
Tatsuaki Okamoto .... NIT Labs., Japan
Jean-Marc Piveteau .... UBILAB, Switzerland
Bart Preneel .... K. U. Leuven, Belgium
Ronald Rivest .... MIT, USA
Claus P. Schnorr .... University of Frankfurt, Germany
Othmar Staffelbach .... Federal Cryptology Section, Switzerland
Serge Vaudenay .... ENS, France

EUROCRYPT '96 Table of Contents

204

Neal Koblitz   (Ed.)

Advances in Cryptology – CRYPTO '96

16th Annual International
Cryptology Conference
Santa Barbara, California, USA
August 18-22, 1996
Proceedings

Lecture Notes in Computer Science 1109

Springer

Preface

Crypto '96, the Sixteenth Annual Crypto Conference, is sponsored by the International Association for Cryptologic Research (IACR), in cooperation with the IEEE Computer Society Technical Committee on Security and Privacy and the Computer Science Department of the University of California at Santa Barbara (UCSB). It takes place at UCSB from August 18 to 22, 1996. The General Chair, Richard Graveman, is responsible for local organization and registration.

The scientific program was organized by the 16-member Program Committee. We considered 115 papers. (An additional 15 submissions had to be summarily rejected because of lateness or major noncompliance with the conditions in the Call for Papers.) Of these, 30 were accepted for presentation. In addition, there will be five invited talks by Ernest Brickell, Andrew Clark, Whitfield Diffie, Ronald Rivest, and Cliff Stoll. A Rump Session will be chaired by Stuart Haber.

These proceedings contain the revised versions of the 30 contributed talks. The submitted version of each paper was examined by at least three committee members and/or outside experts, and their comments were taken into account in the revisions. However, the authors (and not the committee) bear full responsibility for the content of their papers.

A successful Crypto conference requires the combined efforts of many people. In the first place I wish to thank the members of the Program Committee, who devoted a tremendous amount of time and energy to reading the papers and making a difficult selection. They are: Mihir Bellare, Josh Benaloh, Matt Blaze, Johannes Buchmann, Don Coppersmith, Joan Feigenbaum, Andrew Klapper, Lars Knudsen, Peter Landrock, Tsutomu Matsumoto, Chris Mitchell, Paul Van Oorschot, Bart Preneel, Rainer Rueppel, and Jacques Stern. They were assisted by the following outside experts, whom I would also like to thank: Martin Abadi, Birgit Baum, Charles Bennett, Antoon Bosselaers, Gilles Brassard, Florent Chabaud, Giovanni Di Crescenzo, Matthew Franklin, Jovan Golic, Louis Granboulan, Russell Impagliazzo, Markus Jacobsson, Thomas Jakobsen, Jack Lacy, Xuejia Lai, Kevin McCurley, Kaisa Nyberg, David Pointcheval, James Reeds, Mike Reiter, Vincent Rijmen, Dan Simon, Doug Stinson, Serge Vaudenay, Michael Waidner, Michael Wiener, Yakov Yakobi. I apologize for any omissions in this list.

I would next like to thank the authors of all the papers (not just the ones that we were able to accept) for their hard work and cooperation. In particular, I very much appreciated the positive spirit with which they complied with the new requirement of a 1-page statement about the oral presentation, even though this was a further imposition on their time. The authors' 1-page statements turned out to be useful to me and the reviewers in several ways: in determining whom to ask to evaluate the paper, in getting an informal

VI

overview (which the authors might not have found appropriate to include in the formal paper), and sometimes in deciding between acceptance and rejection in a borderline case.

Finally, I want to thank a few other individuals who made the job of Program Chair more tractable and rewarding. It was a pleasure to work with the General Chair, Richard Graveman, who was helpful and cooperative beyond the call of duty. Scott Vanstone was an important source of encouragement in the first period after my appointment as Program Chair, when I was afraid that I would do everything wrong. My wife Ann provided some useful suggestions, as well as the reassuring perspective of a historian of science who knows that any damage caused by my mistakes will be of no importance in the next millennium.

Neal Koblitz
June, 1996

CRYPTO '96

University of California, Santa Barbara
August 18-22, 1996

Sponsored by the

International Association for Cryptologic Research

in cooperation with the

*IEEE Computer Society Technical Committee
on Security and Privacy*

and the

*Computer Science Department,
University of California, Santa Barbara*

General Chair

Richard Graveman, Bellcore, USA

Program Chair

Neal Koblitz, University of Washington, Seattle, USA

Program Committee

Mihir Bellare	Univ. of California, San Diego, USA
Josh Benaloh	Microsoft, USA
Matt Blaze	AT&T Bell Laboratories, USA
Johannes Buchmann	Universität de Saarlandes, Germany
Don Coppersmith	IBM T.J. Watson Research Center, USA
Joan Feigenbaum	AT&T Bell Laboratories, USA
Andrew Klapper	University of Kentucky, USA
Lars Knudsen	Ecole Normale Supérieure, France
Peter Landrock	Aarhus University, Denmark
Tsutomu Matsumoto	Yokohama National University, Japan
Chris Mitchell	University of London, UK
Paul Van Oorschot	Bell-Northern Research, Canada
Bart Preneel	Katholieke Universiteit Leuven, Belgium
Rainer Rueppel	R^3 Security Engineering, Switzerland
Jacques Stern	Ecole Normale Supérieure, France

CRYPTO '96 Table of Contents

Walter Fumy   (Ed.)

Advances in Cryptology — EUROCRYPT '97

International Conference on the Theory and
Application of Cryptographic Techniques
Konstanz, Germany, May 11-15, 1997
Proceedings

Lecture Notes in Computer Science 1233

 Springer

Preface

EUROCRYPT '97, the 15th annual EUROCRYPT conference on the theory and application of cryptographic techniques, was organized and sponsored by the International Association for Cryptologic Research (IACR). The IACR organizes two series of international conferences each year, the EUROCRYPT meeting in Europe and CRYPTO in the United States.

The history of EUROCRYPT started 15 years ago in Germany with the Burg Feuerstein Workshop (see Springer LNCS 149 for the proceedings). It was due to Thomas Beth's initiative and hard work that the 76 participants from 14 countries gathered in Burg Feuerstein for the first open meeting in Europe devoted to modern cryptography. I am proud to have been one of the participants and still fondly remember my first encounters with some of the celebrities in cryptography.

Since those early days the conference has been held in a different location in Europe each year (Udine, Paris, Linz, Linköping, Amsterdam, Davos, Houthalen, Aarhus, Brighton, Balantonfüred, Lofthus, Perugia, Saint-Malo, Saragossa) and it has enjoyed a steady growth. Since the second conference (Udine, 1983) the IACR has been involved, since the Paris meeting in 1984, the name EUROCRYPT has been used. For its 15th anniversary, EUROCRYPT finally returned to Germany.

The scientific program for EUROCRYPT '97 was put together by a 18-member program committee which considered 104 high-quality submissions. These proceedings contain the revised versions of the 34 papers that were accepted for presentation. In addition, there were two invited talks by Ernst Bovelander and by Gerhard Frey.

A successful EUROCRYPT conference requires the combined efforts of many people. First, I would like to thank the members of the program committee, who devoted a tremendous amount of time and energy to reading the papers and making the difficult selection. They are: Michael Burmester, Hans Dobbertin, Marc Girault, Shafi Goldwasser, Alain P. Hiltgen, Don B. Johnson, Pil Joong Lee, Tsutomu Matsumoto, David Naccache, Kaisa Nyberg, Paul Van Oorschot, Torben P. Pedersen, Josef Pieprzyk, Bart Preneel, Rainer Rueppel, Claus Schnorr, and William Wolfowicz.

In addition, I gratefully acknowledge the support to the program committee by the following experts: Albrecht Beutelspacher, Simon R. Blackburn, Carlo Blundo, Antoon Bosselaers, Odoardo Brugia, Marco Bucci, Anne Canteaut, Chris Charnes, Ivan Damgård, Yvo Desmedt, Erik De Win, Markus Dichtl, Michele Elia, Piero Filipponi, Marc Fischlin, Roger Fischlin, Steven Galbraith,

VI

Oded Goldreich, Dieter Gollmann, Shai Halevi, Helena Handschuh, Erwin Hess, Stanislaw Jarecki, Joe Kilian, Lars R. Knudsen, Xuejia Lai, Françoise Levy-dit-Vehel, Keith M. Martin, Willi Meier, Alfred Menezes, Renato Menicocci, Daniele Micciancio, Preda Mihailescu, Thomas Mittelholzer, Sean Murphy, Pascal Paillier, Birgit Pfitzmann, Tal Rabin, David M'Raihi, Vincent Rijmen, Ron Rivest, Rei Safavi-Naini, Jacques Traoré, and Peter Wild. I apologize to those whose names have inadvertently escaped this list.

I also thank Alfred Büllesbach, Roland Müller, Roland Nehl, and Susanne Röhrig for taking the resposibility to organize EUROCRYPT '97, and Christina Strobel for her help with the proceedings.

Finally, I would like to thank the authors of all submissions (including those whose papers could not be accepted because of the large number of high-quality submissions received) for their hard work and cooperation.

March 1997   Walter Fumy

EUROCRYPT '97

May 11-15, 1997, Konstanz, Germany

Sponsored by the

International Association for Cryptologic Research (IACR)

General Chairmen

Roland Nehl, Deutsche Telekom, Germany
Alfred Buellesbach, debis Systemhaus, Germany

Program Chairman

Walter Fumy , Siemens AG, Germany

Program Committee

Michael Burmester .... University of London, U.K.
Hans Dobbertin .... BSI, Germany
Marc Girault .... SEPT, France
Shafi Goldwasser .... MIT, USA
Alain P. Hiltgen .... Crypto AG, Switzerland
Don B. Johnson .... Certicom, USA
Pil Joong Lee .... Postech, Korea
Tsutomu Matsumoto .... Yokohama National University, Japan
David Naccache .... Gemplus, France
Kaisa Nyberg .... Finnish Defence Forces, Finland
Paul Van Oorschot .... Entrust Technologies, Canada
Torben P. Pedersen .... Cryptomathic, Denmark
Josef Pieprzyk .... University of Wollongong, Australia
Bart Preneel .... K.U. Leuven, Belgium
Rainer Rueppel .... R3 Security Engineering, Switzerland
Claus Schnorr .... University of Frankfurt, Germany
William Wolfowicz .... Fondazione Ugo Bordoni, Italy

EUROCRYPT '97 Table of Contents

Burton S. Kaliski Jr. (Ed.)

Advances in Cryptology – CRYPTO '97

17th Annual International
Cryptology Conference
Santa Barbara, California, USA
August 17-21, 1997
Proceedings

Lecture Notes in Computer Science 1294

 Springer

Preface

Crypto '97, the Seventeenth Annual Crypto conference organized by the International Association for Cryptologic Research (IACR) in cooperation with the IEEE Computer Society Technical Committee on Security and Privacy and the Computer Science Department of the University of California, Santa Barbara, represents another step forward in the steady progression of the science of cryptology. There is both a tremendous need for and a great amount of work on securing information with cryptologic technology. As one of the two annual meetings held by the IACR, the Crypto conference provides a focal point for presentation and discussion of research on all aspects of this science.

It is thus a privilege to coordinate the efforts of this community in focusing on its steps forward. Crypto '97 is a conference for its community, and to the researchers who have contributed to it — those whose papers appear in the proceedings, those whose submissions were not accepted, and those who have laid the foundation for the work — the community owes a debt of gratitude.

The process of developing a conference program is a challenging one, and this year's committee made the process both enjoyable and effective. My thanks go to Antoon Bosselaers, Gilles Brassard, Johannes Buchmann, Ivan Damgård, Donald Davies, Alfredo de Santis, Susan Langford, James L. Massey, Moni Naor, David Naccache, Tatsuaki Okamoto, Douglas Stinson, Michael J. Wiener, Rebecca Wright, and Yuliang Zheng for many hours of reviewing submissions and presenting their comments to the committee.

My thanks also to the committee's two advisory members, Neal Koblitz and Hugo Krawcyzk, the program chairs of Crypto '96 and '98. Neal's experience from a year ago and Hugo's perspective on the year ahead have helped to make this year's conference what it is, and should provide continuity to the next one.

Continuing a recent tradition, the review process for Crypto '97 was conducted entirely by e-mail and fax, without a program committee meeting. Each submission was assigned anonymously to three committee members (though many submissions were reviewed by more than three people), and decisions were made through several rounds of e-mail discussions. Of the 160 submissions received, the committee accepted 36, of which 35 appear in final form in these proceedings. Except for the papers themselves, nearly all correspondence with authors was also conducted by e-mail.

VI

Gilles Brassard and Oded Goldreich complete this year's program with their invited lectures on quantum information processing and the theoretical foundations of cryptology. My appreciation to both of them, as well as to Stuart Haber, who chairs the conference's informal rump session (whose papers, due to logistics, cannot be included in these proceedings).

The program committee benefited from the expertise of many colleagues: Carlisle Adams, Carlo Blundo, Dan Boneh, Jørgen Brandt, Ran Canetti, Don Coppersmith, Erik De Win, Giovanni Di Crescenzo, Matthew Franklin, Atsushi Fujioka, Eiichiro Fujisaki, Rosario Gennaro, Helena Handschuh, Michael Jacobson Jr., Markus Jakobsson, Joe Kilian, Lars Knudsen, Tetsutaro Kobayashi, Françoise Levy-dit-Vehel, Keith Martin, Markus Maurer, Andreas Meyer, David M'raïhi, Volker Mueller, Stefan Neis, Kobbi Nissim, Kazuo Ohta, Pascal Paillier, Sachar Paulus, Giuseppe Persiano, Erez Petrank, Benny Pinkas, Bart Preneel, Tal Rabin, Omer Reingold, Mike Reiter, Pankaj Rohatgi, Taiichi Saitoh, Berry Schoenmakers, Martin Strauss, Edlyn Teske, Shigenori Uchiyama, Paul Van Oorschot, Susanne Wetzel, and Hugh Williams. My thanks to each one, as well as to any others whom I have inadvertently omitted.

The successful organization of this year's conference is due to its general chair, Bruce Schneier. The functions of general chair and program chair are for the most part independent, but at those times where collaboration was required, Bruce was very helpful, and I appreciate the opportunity to have worked with him. On behalf of Bruce, I would also like to extend my thanks to Raphael Carter and Karen Cooper for their assistance in the organization of Crypto '97.

My work was also not without assistance, and I would like to thank Ari Juels and Gerri Sireen for their participation in administrative aspects of the program.

In the Proverbs, it is written, "It is the glory of God to conceal a thing; but the honour of kings is to search out a matter." The search for knowledge about cryptology — itself the science of secrets — is an essential part of protecting information in today's increasingly open world. Another step in this search is expressed in these proceedings. May the search of such matters, and the search for knowledge about cryptology, continue for many years to come.

Burt Kaliski

June 16, 1997
Bedford, Massachusetts

VII

CRYPTO '97

August 17–21, 1997, Santa Barbara, California, USA

Sponsored by the

International Association for Cryptologic Research (IACR)

in cooperation with

IEEE Computer Society Technical Committee on Security and Privacy
Computer Science Department, University of California, Santa Barbara

General Chair

Bruce Schneier, Counterpane Systems, USA

Program Chair

Burt Kaliski, RSA Laboratories, USA

Program Committee

Antoon Bosselaers ....Katholieke Universiteit Leuven, Belgium
Gilles Brassard...Université de Montréal, Canada
Johannes Buchmann.....................Techniche Hochschule Darmstadt, Germany
Ivan Damgård...Aarhus University, Denmark
Donald Davies...................Royal Holloway College London, United Kingdom
Alfredo de Santis.. Università di Salerno, Italy
Susan Langford ....Atalla Corporation, USA
James L. Massey ....Swiss Federal Institute of Technology, Switzerland
Moni Naor.. Weizmann Institute, Israel
David Naccache .... Gemplus, France
Tatsuaki Okamoto.. NTT Laboratories, Japan
Douglas Stinson .... University of Nebraska, USA
Michael J. Wiener...Entrust Technologies, Canada
Rebecca Wright... AT&T Labs, USA
Yuliang Zheng.. Monash University, Australia

Advisory Members

Neal Koblitz *(Crypto '96 program chair)* .... University of Washington, USA
Hugo Krawczyk *(Crypto '98 program chair)* IBM T.J. Watson Research Center, USA
....and Technion, Israel

CRYPTO '97 Table of Contents

228

Part II: Indices

Program Committee Listings

CRYPTO '81

- Gersho, Allen (Program Chair)
- Adleman, Leonard
- Diffie, Whitfield
- Hellman, Martin
- Kemmerer, Richard
- Konheim, Alan
- Pickholtz, Raymond
- Schanning, Brian
- Simmons, Gustavus J.
- Weinstein, Stephen

EUROCRYPT '82

- Beth, Thomas (Program Chair)
- Beker, Henry
- Schuchmann, H.-R.
- Sloane, Neil J. A.

CRYPTO '82

- Rivest, Ronald (Program Chair)
- Adleman, Leonard
- Chaum, David
- Denning, Dorothy
- Diffie, Whitfield
- Gersho, Allen
- Gordon, John
- Kent, Stephen
- Sherman, Alan

CRYPTO '83

- Sloane, Neil J. A. (Program Chair)
- Akl, Selim
- Beker, Henry

- Berson, Thomas
- Beth, Thomas
- Chaum, David
- Denning, Dorothy

EUROCRYPT '84

- Ingemarsson, Ingemar (Program Chair)
- Akl, Selim
- Beker, Henry
- Beth, Thomas
- Chaum, David
- Davies, Donald W.
- Denning, Dorothy
- Diffie, Whitfield
- Gordon, John
- Harari, S.
- Lebidois, J.
- Longo, G.
- Massey, James L.
- Mignotte, M.
- Odlyzko, Andrew
- Quisquater, Jean-Jacques
- Rivest, Ronald
- Schnorr, Claus
- Simmons, Gustavus J.

CRYPTO '84

- Blakely, Bob (Program Chair)
- Beker, Henry
- Chaum, David
- Denning, Dorothy
- Diffie, Whitfield
- Rivest, Ronald
- Smid, Miles

EUROCRYPT '85

- Beth, Thomas (Program Chair)
- Beker, Henry
- Denning, Dorothy
- Eier, R.
- Henze, E.
- Herlestam, Tor
- Horak, O.
- Ingemarsson, Ingemar
- Massey, James L.
- Müller-Schloer, Ch.
- Odlyzko, Andrew
- Price, W. L.
- Rivest, Ronald
- Simmons, Gustavus J.

CRYPTO '85

- Williams, Hugh C. (Program Chair)
- Berson, Thomas
- Boyar, Joan
- Davies, Donald W.
- Goldreich, Oded
- Rivest, Ronald

EUROCRYPT '86

- Massey, James L. (Program Chair)
- Glass, Andrew
- Schöbi, Paul
- Staffelbach, Othmar
- Beth, Thomas
- Chaum, David
- Günther, Christof G.
- Nyffleler, Peter
- Siegenthaler, Thomas
- Widman, Kjell Owe
- Cot, Norbert
- Herlestam, Tor

CRYPTO '86

- Coppersmith, Don (Program Chair)
- Berson, Thomas
- Brickell, Ernest
- Goldwasser, Shafi
- Odlyzko, Andrew
- Schnorr, Claus

EUROCRYPT '87

- Price, W. L. (Program Chair)
- Beth, Thomas
- Evertse, J.-H.
- Guillou, Louis C.
- Herlestam, Tor
- Piper, Fred
- Quisquater, Jean-Jacques
- Schnorr, Claus

CRYPTO '87

- Agnew, Gordon (Program Chair)
- Berson, Thomas
- Brickell, Ernest
- Odlyzko, Andrew
- Pomerance, Carl
- Simmons, Gustavus J.

EUROCRYPT '88

- Massey, James L. (Program Chair)
- Blom, Rolf
- Brynielsson, Lennart
- Damgård, Ivan
- Fåk, Viveke
- Helleseth, Tor
- Johannesson, Rolf

CRYPTO '88

- Goldwasser, Shafi (Program Chair)
- Bach, Eric
- Barret, Paul
- Berson, Thomas
- Brassard, Gilles
- Goldreich, Oded
- Odlyzko, Andrew
- Rackoff, Charles
- Rivest, Ronald

EUROCRYPT '89

- Quisquater, Jean-Jacques (Program Chair)
- Camion, Paul
- Desmedt, Yvo
- Guillou, Louis

- Håstad, Johan,
- Huguet, Llorenç
- Price, Wyn
- Rueppel, Rainer
- van Tilburg, Johan

CRYPTO '89

- Brassard, Gilles (Program Chair)
- Benaloh, Josh
- Brand, Russell
- Crépeau, Claude
- Diffie, Whitfield
- Feigenbaum, Joan
- Massey, James L.
- Omura, Jim
- Simmons, Gustavus J.
- Vanstone, Scott

EUROCRYPT '90

- Damgård, Ivan (Program Chair)
- Clark, Andrew J.
- Crépeau, Claude
- Boyar, Joan
- Girault, Marc
- Fumy, Walter
- Mjølsnes, Stig Frode
- Siegenthaler, Thomas
- Staffelbach, Othmar

CRYPTO '90

- Vanstone, Scott (Program Chair)
- Agnew, Gordon
- Berson, Thomas
- Buchmann, Johannes
- Desmedt, Yvo
- Fiat, Amos
- Koyama, Kenji
- Rivest, Ronald
- Rueppel, Rainer
- De Soete, Marijke
- Stinson, Douglas
- Williams, Hugh C.

EUROCRYPT '91

- Davies, Donald W. (Program Chair)
- Beth, Thomas
- Boyd, Colin
- Cot, Norbert
- Fåk, Viveke
- Gordon, John
- Herda, Siegfried
- Lenstra, Arjen K.
- Matsumoto, Tsutomu
- Piper, Fred
- Schnorr, Claus

CRYPTO '91

- Feigenbaum, Joan (Program Chair)
- Ingemarsson, Ingemar
- Maurer, Ueli
- McCurley, Kevin
- Merritt, Michael
- Naor, Moni
- Okamoto, Eiji
- Pieprzyk, Josef
- Rosati, Toni
- Yung, Moti

EUROCRYPT '92

- Rueppel, Rainer (Program Chair)
- Desmedt, Yvo
- Feigenbaum, Joan
- Golic, Jovan Dj.
- Helleseth, Tor
- Landrock, Peter
- McCurley, Kevin
- Okamoto, Tatsuaki
- Seberry, Jennifer
- Staffelbach, Othmar
- Stern, Jacques
- Vajda, Istvan

CRYPTO '92

- Brickell, Ernest (Program Chair)
- Damgård, Ivan
- Goldreich, Oded
- Kaliski, Burt

- Kilian, Joe
- Koblitz, Neal
- Maurer, Ueli
- Mitchell, Chris
- Ohta, Kazuo
- Rudich, Steven
- Yacobi, Yacov

EUROCRYPT '93

- Helleseth, Tor (Program Chair)
- Damgård, Ivan
- De Santis, Alfredo
- Desmedt, Yvo
- Gollmann, Dieter
- Ingemarsson, Ingemar
- Kurosawa, Kaoru
- Massey, James L.
- Preneel, Bart
- Odlyzko, Andrew
- Schnorr, Claus
- Seberry, Jennifer

CRYPTO '93

- Stinson, Douglas (Program Chair)
- Bellare, Mihir
- Biham, Eli
- Brickell, Ernest
- Feigenbaum, Joan
- Imagliazzo, Russell
- Odlyzko, Andrew
- Okamoto, Tatsuaki
- Pfitzmann, Birgit
- Rueppel, Rainer
- Vanstone, Scott

EUROCRYPT '94

- De Santis, Alfredo (Program Chair)
- Brickell, Ernest
- Crépeau, Claude
- Desmedt, Yvo
- Di Porto, Adina
- Gollmann, Dieter
- Guillou, Louis C.
- Maurer, Ueli
- Naccache, David

- Okamoto, Tatsuaki
- Stern, Jacques
- Yung, Moti

CRYPTO '94

- Desmedt, Yvo (Program Chair)
- Berson, Thomas
- Coppersmith, Don
- Davies, Donald W.
- Even, Shimon
- Fiat, Amos
- Impagliazzo, Russell
- Ingemarsson, Ingemar
- Matsui, Mitsuru
- Menezes, Alfred
- Odlyzko, Andrew
- Seberry, Jennifer
- Smeets, Ben
- Yung, Moti

EUROCRYPT '95

- Guillou, Louis C. (Program Chair)
- Bellare, Mihir
- Buchmann, Johannes
- Burmester, Mike
- Camion, Paul
- Davies, Donald W.
- Fiat, Amos
- Imai, Hideki
- Knudsen, Lars
- Maurer, Ueli
- Pfitzmann, Birgit
- Quisquater, Jean-Jacques
- Rivest, Ronald
- Stern, Jacques
- Stinson, Douglas
- Yung, Moti
- Yuval, Gideon

CRYPTO '95

- Coppersmith, Don (Program Chair)
- Anderson, Ross
- Brickell, Ernest
- Krawczyk, Hugo
- Langford, Susan

- McCurley, Kevin
- Meier, Willi
- Naor, Moni
- Odlyzko, Andrew
- Ohta, Kazuo
- Pieprzyk, Josef
- Quisquater, Jean-Jacques
- Sherman, Alan
- Vanstone, Scott
- Vaudenay, Serge

EUROCRYPT '96

- Maurer, Ueli (Program Chair)
- Brands, Stefan
- Crépeau, Claude
- Damgård, Ivan
- Domingo, Josep
- Fumy, Walter
- Golic, Jovan Dj.
- Lenstra, Arjen K.
- Naccache, David
- Odlyzko, Andrew
- Okamoto, Tatsuaki
- Piveteau, Jean-Marc
- Preneel, Bart
- Rivest, Ronald
- Schnorr, Claus
- Staffelbach, Othmar
- Vaudenay, Serge

CRYPTO '96

- Koblitz, Neal (Program Chair)
- Bellare, Mihir
- Benaloh, Josh
- Blaze, Matt
- Buchmann, Johannes
- Coppersmith, Don
- Feigenbaum, Joan
- Klapper, Andrew
- Knudsen, Lars
- Landrock, Peter
- Matsumoto, Tsutomu
- Mitchell, Chris
- Van Oorschot, Paul
- Preneel, Bart

- Rueppel, Rainer
- Stern, Jacques

EUROCRYPT '97

- Fumy, Walter (Program Chair)
- Burmester, Michael
- Dobbertin, Hans
- Girault, Marc
- Goldwasser, Shafi
- Hiltgen, Alain B.
- Johnson, Don B.
- Lee, Pil Joong
- Matsumoto, Tsutomu
- Naccache, David
- Nyberg, Kaisa
- Van Oorschot, Paul
- Pedersen, Torben P.
- Pieprzyk, Josef
- Preneel, Bart
- Rueppel, Rainer
- Schnorr, Claus
- Wolfowicz, William

CRYPTO '97

- Kaliski, Burt (Program Chair)
- Bosselaers, Antoon
- Brassard, Gilles
- Buchmann, Johannes
- Damgård, Ivan
- Davies, Donald W.
- De Santis, Alfredo
- Langford, Susan
- Massey, James L.
- Naor, Moni
- Naccache, David
- Okamoto, Tatsuaki
- Stinson, Douglas
- Wiener, Michael J.
- Wright, Rebecca
- Zheng, Yuliang

Author Index

Abadi, M.

- Abadi, M., Allender, E., Broder, A., Feigenbaum, J. and Hemachandra, L. A., "On generating solved instances of computational problems," *Advances in Cryptology - CRYPTO '88*, p. 297. Springer-Verlag, Berlin, 1989.
- Abadi, M., Burrows, M., Lampson, B. and Plotkin, G., "A calculus for access control in distributed systems," *Advances in Cryptology - CRYPTO '91*, p. 1. Springer-Verlag, Berlin, 1991.

Adams, C. M.

- Adams, C. M. and Meijer, H., "Security-related comments regarding McEliece's public-key cryptosystem," *Advances in Cryptology - CRYPTO '87*, p. 224. Springer-Verlag, Berlin, 1987.
- Adams, C. M. and Tavares, S. E., "Good S-boxes are easy to find," *Advances in Cryptology - CRYPTO '89*, p. 612. Springer-Verlag, Berlin, 1989.

Adleman, L. M.

- Adleman, L. M., "Primality Testing," *Advances in Cryptography*, p. 10. University of California, Santa Barbara, Santa Barbara, California, USA, 1982.
- Adleman, L. M., "Implementing an electronic notary public," *Advances in Cryptology: Proceedings of CRYPTO '82*, p. 259. Plenum Publishing, New York, USA, 1982.
- Adleman, L. M., "On breaking the iterated Merkle-Hellman public-key cryptosystem," *Advances in Cryptology: Proceedings of CRYPTO '82*, p. 303. Plenum Publishing, New York, USA, 1982.
- Estes, D., Adleman, L. M., Kompella, K., McCurley, K. S. and Miller, G. L., "Breaking the Ong-Schnorr-Shamir signature scheme for quadratic number fields," *Advances in Cryptology - CRYPTO '85*, p. 3. Springer-Verlag, Berlin, 1986.
- Adleman, L. M., "An abstract theory of computer viruses (invited talk)," *Advances in Cryptology - CRYPTO '88*, p. 354. Springer-Verlag, Berlin, 1989.
- Kompella, K. and Adleman, L. M., "Fast checkers for cryptography," *Advances in Cryptology - CRYPTO '90*, p. 515. Springer-Verlag, Berlin, 1990.

- Adleman, L. M. and DeMarrais, J., "A subexponential algorithm for discrete logarithms over all finite fields," *Advances in Cryptology - CRYPTO '93*, p. 147. Springer-Verlag, Berlin, 1993.

Agnew, G. B.

- Agnew, G. B., "Secrecy and privacy in the local area network environment," *Advances in Cryptology: Proceedings of EUROCRYPT '84*, p. 349. Springer-Verlag, Berlin, 1984.
- Agnew, G. B., "Modeling of encryption techniques for secrecy and privacy in multi-user networks.," *Advances in Cryptology - EUROCRYPT '85*, p. 221. Springer-Verlag, Berlin, 1985.
- Agnew, G. B., "Another Look at Redundancy in Cryptographic Systems," *Abstracts of Papers: EUROCRYPT '86*, p. 29. Department of Electrical Engineering, University of Linköping, Linkoping, Sweden, 1986.
- Agnew, G. B., "Random sources for cryptographic systems," *Advances in Cryptology - EUROCRYPT '87*, p. 77. Springer-Verlag, Berlin, 1987.
- Agnew, G. B., Mullin, R. C. and Vanstone, S. A., "An interactive data exchange protocol based on discrete exponentiation," *Advances in Cryptology - EUROCRYPT '88*, p. 159. Springer-Verlag, Berlin, 1988.
- Agnew, G. B., Mullin, R. C. and Vanstone, S. A., "Fast exponentiation in $GF(2^n)$," *Advances in Cryptology - EUROCRYPT '88*, p. 251. Springer-Verlag, Berlin, 1988.
- Agnew, G. B., Mullin, R. C. and Vanstone, S. A., "A fast elliptic curve cryptosystem," *Advances in Cryptology - EUROCRYPT '89*, p. 706. Springer-Verlag, Berlin, 1989.
- Agnew, G. B., Mullin, R. C. and Vanstone, S. A., "On the development of a fast elliptic curve cryptosystem," *Advances in Cryptology - EUROCRYPT '92*, p. 482. Springer-Verlag, Berlin, 1992.

Aiello, W.

- Aiello, W. and Venkatesan, R., "Foiling birthday attacks in length-doubling transformations," *Advances in Cryptology - EUROCRYPT '96*, p. 307. Springer-Verlag, Berlin, 1996.

Akl, S. G.

- Meijer, H. and Akl, S. G., "Digital Signature Scheme for Computer Communication Networks," *Advances in Cryptography*, p. 65. University of California, Santa Barbara, Santa Barbara, California, USA, 1982.
- Akl, S. G. and Taylor, P. D., "Cryptographic solution to a multilevel security problem," *Advances in Cryptology: Proceedings of CRYPTO '82*, p. 237. Plenum Publishing, New York, USA, 1982.
- Akl, S. G., "On the security of compressed encodings," *Advances in Cryptology: Proceedings of CRYPTO '83*, p. 209. Plenum Publishing, New York, USA, 1984.

- Akl, S. G. and Meijer, H., "A fast pseudo random permutation generator with applications to cryptology," *Advances in Cryptology: Proceedings of CRYPTO '84*, p. 269. Springer-Verlag, Berlin, 1985.
- Meijer, H. and Akl, S. G., "Two new secret key cryptosystems.," *Advances in Cryptology - EUROCRYPT '85*, p. 96. Springer-Verlag, Berlin, 1985.

Alexi, W.
- Schnorr, C. P. and Alexi, W., "RSA-bits are 0.5 + epsilon secure," *Advances in Cryptology: Proceedings of EUROCRYPT '84*, p. 113. Springer-Verlag, Berlin, 1984.

Allender, E.
- Abadi, M., Allender, E., Broder, A., Feigenbaum, J. and Hemachandra, L. A., "On generating solved instances of computational problems," *Advances in Cryptology - CRYPTO '88*, p. 297. Springer-Verlag, Berlin, 1989.

Amirazizi, H.
- Amirazizi, H. and Hellman, M. E., "Time-Memory-Processor Tradeoffs," *Advances in Cryptography*, p. 7. University of California, Santa Barbara, Santa Barbara, California, USA, 1982.
- Amirazizi, H., Karnin, E. and Reyneri, J. M., "Compact Knapsacks are Polynomially Solvable," *Advances in Cryptography*, p. 17. University of California, Santa Barbara, Santa Barbara, California, USA, 1982.

Anderson, D. P.
- Anderson, D. P. and Venkat Rangan, P., "Highperformance interface architectures for cryptographic hardware," *Advances in Cryptology - EUROCRYPT '87*, p. 301. Springer-Verlag, Berlin, 1987.

Anderson, R.
- Anderson, R. and Needham, R., "Robustness Principles for Public Key Protocols," *Advances in Cryptology - CRYPTO '95*, p. 236. Springer-Verlag, Berlin, 1995.
- Anderson, R. and Roe, M., "The GCHQ Protocol and Its Problems," *Advances in Cryptology - EUROCRYPT '97*, p. 134. Springer-Verlag, Berlin, 1997.

Andreasen, E.
- Orup, H., Svendsen, E. and Andreasen, E., "VICTOR - an efficient RSA hardware implementation," *Advances in Cryptology - EUROCRYPT '90*, p. 245. Springer-Verlag, Berlin, 1990.

Annick, M.
- Quisquater, J. J., Guillou, L. C., Annick, M. and Berson, T. A., "How to explain zero-knowledge protocols to your children," *Advances in Cryptology - CRYPTO '89*, p. 628. Springer-Verlag, Berlin, 1989.

242

Antoine, M.

- Antoine, M., Brakeland, Jean-Franc, Eloy, M. and Poullet, Y., "Legal requirements facing new signature technology (invited)," *Advances in Cryptology - EUROCRYPT '89*, p. 273. Springer-Verlag, Berlin, 1989.

Aoki, K.

- Ohta, K. and Aoki, K., "Linear cryptanalysis of the Fast Data Encipherment Algorithm," *Advances in Cryptology - CRYPTO '94*, p. 12. Springer-Verlag, Berlin, 1994.
- Ohta, K., Moriai, S. and Aoki, K., "Improving the Search Algorithm for the Best Linear Expression," *Advances in Cryptology - CRYPTO '95*, p. 157. Springer-Verlag, Berlin, 1995.

Atici, M.

- Atici, M. and Stinson, D. R., "Universal Hashing and Multiple Authentication," *Advances in Cryptology - CRYPTO '96*, p. 16. Springer-Verlag, Berlin, 1996.

Aumann, Y.

- Aumann, Y. and Feige, U., "One message proof systems with known space verifiers," *Advances in Cryptology - CRYPTO '93*, p. 85. Springer-Verlag, Berlin, 1993.

Avis, G. M.

- Avis, G. M. and Tavares, S. E., "Using data uncertainty to increase the crypto-complexity of simple private key enciphering schemes," *Advances in Cryptology: Proceedings of CRYPTO '82*, p. 139. Plenum Publishing, New York, USA, 1982.

Bach, E.

- Bach, E., "Intractable problems in number theory (invited talk)," *Advances in Cryptology - CRYPTO '88*, p. 77. Springer-Verlag, Berlin, 1989.

Barbaroux, P.

- Barbaroux, P., "Uniform results in polynomial-time security," *Advances in Cryptology - EUROCRYPT '92*, p. 297. Springer-Verlag, Berlin, 1992.

Baric, N.

- Baric, N. and Pfitzmann, B., "Collision-Free Accumulators and Fail-Stop Signature Schemes Without Trees," *Advances in Cryptology - EUROCRYPT '97*, p. 480. Springer-Verlag, Berlin, 1997.

Baritaud, T.

- Baritaud, T., Gilbert, H. and Girault, M., "FFT hashing is not collision-free," *Advances in Cryptology - EUROCRYPT '92*, p. 35. Springer-Verlag, Berlin, 1992.
- Baritaud, T., Campana, M., Chauvaud, P. and Gilbert, H., "On the security of the permuted kernel identification scheme," *Advances in Cryptology - CRYPTO '92*, p. 305. Springer-Verlag, Berlin, 1992.

Barrett, P.

- Barrett, P., "Implementing the Rivest Shamir and Adleman public key encryption algorithm on a standard digital signal processor," *Advances in Cryptology - CRYPTO '86*, p. 311. Springer-Verlag, Berlin, 1986.
- Barrett, P. and Eisele, R., "The smart diskette – A universal user token and personal crypto-engine," *Advances in Cryptology - CRYPTO '89*, p. 74. Springer-Verlag, Berlin, 1989.

Bauer, F. L.

- Bauer, F. L., "Cryptology-methods and maxims," *Cryptography - Proceedings of the Workshop on Cryptography, Burg Feuerstein, Germany*, p. 31. Springer-Verlag, Berlin, 1983.

Bauspiess, F.

- Bauspiess, F. and Knobloch, H.-J., "How to keep authenticity alive in a computer network," *Advances in Cryptology - EUROCRYPT '89*, p. 38. Springer-Verlag, Berlin, 1989.
- Bauspiess, F., Knobloch, H.-J. and Wichmann, P., "Inverting the pseudo exponentiation," *Advances in Cryptology - EUROCRYPT '90*, p. 344. Springer-Verlag, Berlin, 1990.

Bauval, Anne

- Bauval, Anne, "Cryptanalysis of Pseudo-Random Number Sequences Generated by a Linear Recurrence of a Given Order," *Abstracts of Papers: EUROCRYPT '86*, p. 23. Department of Electrical Engineering, University of Linköping, Linkoping, Sweden, 1986.

Baxter, M. S. J.

- Baxter, M. S. J. and Jones, R. W., "The role of encipherment services in distributed systems.," *Advances in Cryptology - EUROCRYPT '85*, p. 214. Springer-Verlag, Berlin, 1985.

244

Beale, M.

- Beale, M., "Properties of De Bruijn Sequences Generated by a Cross-Join Technique," *Abstracts of Papers: EUROCRYPT '86*, p. 45. Department of Electrical Engineering, University of Linköping, Linkoping, Sweden, 1986.
- Buckley, D. D. and Beale, M., "Public Key Encryption of Stream Ciphers," *Abstracts of Papers: EUROCRYPT '86*, p. 53. Department of Electrical Engineering, University of Linköping, Linkoping, Sweden, 1986.
- Kwok, R. T. C. and Beale, M., "Aperiodic linear complexities of de Bruijn sequences," *Advances in Cryptology - CRYPTO '88*, p. 479. Springer-Verlag, Berlin, 1989.

Beauchemin, P.

- Beauchemin, P., Brassard, G., Crépeau, C. and Goutier, C., "Two observations on probabilistic primality testing," *Advances in Cryptology - CRYPTO '86*, p. 443. Springer-Verlag, Berlin, 1986.
- Beauchemin, P. and Brassard, G., "A generalization of Hellman's extension of Shannon's approach to cryptography," *Advances in Cryptology - CRYPTO '87*, p. 461. Springer-Verlag, Berlin, 1987.

Beaver, D.

- Beaver, D., "Multiparty protocols tolerating half faulty processors," *Advances in Cryptology - CRYPTO '89*, p. 560. Springer-Verlag, Berlin, 1989.
- Beaver, D. and Goldwasser, S., "Multiparty computation with faulty majority," *Advances in Cryptology - CRYPTO '89*, p. 589. Springer-Verlag, Berlin, 1989.
- Beaver, D., Feigenbaum, J., Kilian, J. and Rogaway, P., "Security with low communication overhead (Extended abstract)," *Advances in Cryptology - CRYPTO '90*, p. 62. Springer-Verlag, Berlin, 1990.
- Beaver, D., Feigenbaum, J. and Shoup, V., "Hiding instances in zero-knowledge proof systems (Extended abstract)," *Advances in Cryptology - CRYPTO '90*, p. 326. Springer-Verlag, Berlin, 1990.
- Beaver, D., "Foundations of secure interactive computing," *Advances in Cryptology - CRYPTO '91*, p. 377. Springer-Verlag, Berlin, 1991.
- Beaver, D., "Efficient multiparty protocols using circuit randomization," *Advances in Cryptology - CRYPTO '91*, p. 420. Springer-Verlag, Berlin, 1991.
- Beaver, D., "How to break a "secure" oblivious transfer protocol," *Advances in Cryptology - EUROCRYPT '92*, p. 285. Springer-Verlag, Berlin, 1992.
- Beaver, D. and Haber, S., "Cryptographic protocols provably secure against dynamic adversaries," *Advances in Cryptology - EUROCRYPT '92*, p. 307. Springer-Verlag, Berlin, 1992.
- Beaver, D. and So, N., "Global, unpredictable bit generation without broadcast," *Advances in Cryptology - EUROCRYPT '93*, p. 424. Springer-Verlag, Berlin, 1993.

Bellare, M.

- Bellare, M. and Micali, S., "How to sign given any trapdoor function," *Advances in Cryptology - CRYPTO '88*, p. 200. Springer-Verlag, Berlin, 1989.
- Bellare, M. and Goldwasser, S., "New paradigms for digital signatures and message authentication based on non-interactive zero knowledge proofs," *Advances in Cryptology - CRYPTO '89*, p. 194. Springer-Verlag, Berlin, 1989.
- Bellare, M. and Micali, S., "Non-interactive oblivious transfer and applications," *Advances in Cryptology - CRYPTO '89*, p. 547. Springer-Verlag, Berlin, 1989.
- Bellare, M., Cowen, L. and Goldwasser, S., "On the structure of secret key exchange protocols," *Advances in Cryptology - CRYPTO '89*, p. 604. Springer-Verlag, Berlin, 1989.
- Bellare, M. and Goldreich, O., "On defining proofs of knowledge," *Advances in Cryptology - CRYPTO '92*, p. 390. Springer-Verlag, Berlin, 1992.
- Bellare, M. and Yung, M., "Certifying cryptographic tools: The case of trapdoor permutations," *Advances in Cryptology - CRYPTO '92*, p. 442. Springer-Verlag, Berlin, 1992.
- Bellare, M. and Rogaway, P., "Entity authentication and key distribution," *Advances in Cryptology - CRYPTO '93*, p. 232. Springer-Verlag, Berlin, 1993.
- Bellare, M. and Rogaway, P., "Optimal asymmetric encryption," *Advances in Cryptology - EUROCRYPT '94*, p. 92. Springer-Verlag, Berlin, 1995.
- Bellare, M., Goldreich, O. and Goldwasser, S., "Incremental cryptography: the case of hashing and signing," *Advances in Cryptology - CRYPTO '94*, p. 216. Springer-Verlag, Berlin, 1994.
- Bellare, M., Kilian, J. and Rogaway, P., "The security of cipher block chaining," *Advances in Cryptology - CRYPTO '94*, p. 341. Springer-Verlag, Berlin, 1994.
- Bellare, M., Guerin, R. and Rogaway, P., "XOR MACs: New Methods for Message Authentication Using Finite Pseudorandom Functions," *Advances in Cryptology - CRYPTO '95*, p. 15. Springer-Verlag, Berlin, 1995.
- Bellare, M. and Rogaway, P., "The exact security of digital signatures how to sign with RSA and Rabin," *Advances in Cryptology - EUROCRYPT '96*, p. 399. Springer-Verlag, Berlin, 1996.
- Bellare, M., Canetti, R. and Krawczyk, H., "Keying Hash Functions for Message Authentication," *Advances in Cryptology - CRYPTO '96*, p. 1. Springer-Verlag, Berlin, 1996.
- Bellare, M. and Micciancio, D., "A New Paradigm for Collision-Free Hashing: Incrementality at Reduced Cost," *Advances in Cryptology - EUROCRYPT '97*, p. 163. Springer-Verlag, Berlin, 1997.

- Bellare, M., Jakobsson, M. and Yung, M., "Round-Optimal Zero-Knowledge Arguments Based on Any One-Way Function," *Advances in Cryptology - EUROCRYPT '97*, p. 280. Springer-Verlag, Berlin, 1997.
- Bellare, M., Goldwasser, S. and Micciancio, D., ""Pseudo-Random" Number Generation within Cryptographic Algorithms: The DSS Case," *Advances in Cryptology - CRYPTO '97*, p. 277. Springer-Verlag, Berlin, 1997.
- Bellare, M. and Rogaway, P., "Collision-Resistant Hashing: Towards Making UOWHFs Practical," *Advances in Cryptology - CRYPTO '97*, p. 470. Springer-Verlag, Berlin, 1997.

Beller, M. J.

- Beller, M. J. and Yacobi, Y., "Batch Diffie-Hellman key agreement systems and their application to portable communications," *Advances in Cryptology - EUROCRYPT '92*, p. 208. Springer-Verlag, Berlin, 1992.

Ben Aroya, I.

- Ben Aroya, I. and Biham, E., "Differential cryptanalysis of Lucifer," *Advances in Cryptology - CRYPTO '93*, p. 187. Springer-Verlag, Berlin, 1993.

Ben-Or, M.

- Ben-Or, M., Goldreich, O., Goldwasser, S., Hastad, J., Kilian, J., Micali, S. and Rogaway, P., "Everything provable is provable in zero-knowledge," *Advances in Cryptology - CRYPTO '88*, p. 37. Springer-Verlag, Berlin, 1989.
- Ben-Or, M., Goldwasser, S., Kilian, J. and Wigderson, A., "Efficient identification schemes using two prover interactive proofs," *Advances in Cryptology - CRYPTO '89*, p. 498. Springer-Verlag, Berlin, 1989.

Benaloh, J.

- Benaloh, J. and Leichter, J., "Generalized secret sharing and monotone functions," *Advances in Cryptology - CRYPTO '88*, p. 27. Springer-Verlag, Berlin, 1989.
- Benaloh, J. and Mare, M. de, "One-way accumulators: A decentralized alternative to digital signatures," *Advances in Cryptology - EUROCRYPT '93*, p. 274. Springer Verlag, Berlin, 1993.

Bender, A.

- Bender, A. and Castagnoli, G., "On the implementation of elliptic curve cryptosystems," *Advances in Cryptology - CRYPTO '89*, p. 186. Springer-Verlag, Berlin, 1989.

Bengio, S.

- Desmedt, Y., Goutier, C. and Bengio, S., "Special uses and abuses of the Fiat Shamir passport protocol," *Advances in Cryptology - CRYPTO '87*, p. 21. Springer-Verlag, Berlin, 1987.

Bennett, C. H.

- Bennett, C. H., Brassard, G., Breidbart, S. and Wiesner, S., "Quantum cryptography, or unforgeable subway tokens," *Advances in Cryptology: Proceedings of CRYPTO '82*, p. 267. Plenum Publishing, New York, USA, 1982.
- Bennett, C. H. and Brassard, G., "An update on quantum cryptography," *Advances in Cryptology: Proceedings of CRYPTO '84*, p. 475. Springer-Verlag, Berlin, 1985.
- Bennett, C. H., Brassard, G. and Robert, J. M., "How to reduce your enemy's information," *Advances in Cryptology - CRYPTO '85*, p. 468. Springer-Verlag, Berlin, 1986.
- Bennett, C. H., Bessette, F., Brassard, G., Salvail, L. and Smolin, J., "Experimental quantum cryptography," *Advances in Cryptology - EUROCRYPT '90*, p. 253. Springer-Verlag, Berlin, 1990.
- Bennett, C. H., Brassard, G., Crépeau, C. and Skubiszewska, M. H., "Practical quantum oblivious transfer," *Advances in Cryptology - CRYPTO '91*, p. 351. Springer-Verlag, Berlin, 1991.

Berger, R.

- Berger, R., Peralta, R. and Tedrick, T., "A provably secure oblivious transfer protocol," *Advances in Cryptology: Proceedings of EUROCRYPT '84*, p. 379. Springer-Verlag, Berlin, 1984.
- Berger, R., Kannan, S. and Peralta, R., "A framework for the study of cryptographic protocols," *Advances in Cryptology - CRYPTO '85*, p. 87. Springer-Verlag, Berlin, 1986.

Berkovits, S.

- Sachs, J. E. and Berkovits, S., "Probabilistic analysis and performance modelling of the "Swedish" algorithm and modifications," *Advances in Cryptology: Proceedings of CRYPTO '83*, p. 253. Plenum Publishing, New York, USA, 1984.
- Berkovits, S., "How to broadcast a secret," *Advances in Cryptology - EUROCRYPT '91*, p. 535. Springer-Verlag, Berlin, 1991.

Bernasconi, J.

- Bernasconi, J. and Guenther, C. G., "Analysis of a nonlinear feedforward logic for binary sequence generators.," *Advances in Cryptology - EUROCRYPT '85*, p. 161. Springer-Verlag, Berlin, 1985.

Berson, T. A.

- Berson, T. A., "Local Network Cryptosystem Architecture," *Advances in Cryptography*, p. 73. University of California, Santa Barbara, Santa Barbara, California, USA, 1982.
- Berson, T. A., "Local network cryptosystem architecture: access control," *Advances in Cryptology: Proceedings of CRYPTO '82*, p. 251. Plenum Publishing, New York, USA, 1982.
- Berson, T. A., "Long key variants of DES," *Advances in Cryptology: Proceedings of CRYPTO '82*, p. 311. Plenum Publishing, New York, USA, 1982.
- Quisquater, J. J., Guillou, L. C., Annick, M. and Berson, T. A., "How to explain zero-knowledge protocols to your children," *Advances in Cryptology - CRYPTO '89*, p. 628. Springer-Verlag, Berlin, 1989.
- Berson, T. A., "Differential cryptanalysis mod 2^{32} with applications to MD5," *Advances in Cryptology - EUROCRYPT '92*, p. 71. Springer-Verlag, Berlin, 1992.
- Berson, T. A., "Failure of the McEliece Public-Key Cryptosystem Under Message-Resend and Related-Message Attack," *Advances in Cryptology - CRYPTO '97*, p. 213. Springer-Verlag, Berlin, 1997.

Bertilsson, M.

- Bertilsson, M., Brickell, E. F. and Ingemarsson, I., "Cryptanalysis of video encryption based on space-filling curves," *Advances in Cryptology - EUROCRYPT '89*, p. 403. Springer-Verlag, Berlin, 1989.

Bessette, F.

- Bennett, C. H., Bessette, F., Brassard, G., Salvail, L. and Smolin, J., "Experimental quantum cryptography," *Advances in Cryptology - EUROCRYPT '90*, p. 253. Springer-Verlag, Berlin, 1990.

Beth, T.

- Beth, T., "Introduction," *Cryptography - Proceedings of the Workshop on Cryptography, Burg Feuerstein, Germany*, p. 1. Springer-Verlag, Berlin, 1983.
- Beth, T. and Piper, F., "The stop-and-go generator," *Advances in Cryptology: Proceedings of EUROCRYPT '84*, p. 88. Springer-Verlag, Berlin, 1984.
- Beth, T., Cook, B. M. and Gollmann, D., "Architectures for exponentiation in $GF(2^n)$," *Advances in Cryptology - CRYPTO '86*, p. 302. Springer-Verlag, Berlin, 1986.
- Mund, S., Gollmann, D. and Beth, T., "Some remarks on the cross correlation analysis of pseudo random generators," *Advances in Cryptology - EUROCRYPT '87*, p. 25. Springer-Verlag, Berlin, 1987.
- Beth, T., "Efficient zero-knowledged identification scheme for smart cards," *Advances in Cryptology - EUROCRYPT '88*, p. 77. Springer-Verlag, Berlin, 1988.

- Beth, T. and Dai, Z., "On the Complexity of Pseudo-Random Sequences - or: If you Can Describe a Sequence It Can't be Random," *Advances in Cryptology - EUROCRYPT '89*, p. 533. Springer-Verlag, Berlin, 1989.
- Dai, Z., Beth, T. and Gollmann, D., "Lower bounds for the linear complexity of sequences over residue rings," *Advances in Cryptology - EUROCRYPT '90*, p. 189. Springer-Verlag, Berlin, 1990.
- Beth, T. and Desmedt, Y., "Identification tokens – or: Solving the chess grandmaster problem," *Advances in Cryptology - CRYPTO '90*, p. 169. Springer-Verlag, Berlin, 1990.
- Beth, T. and Schaefer, F., "Non supersingular elliptic curves for public key cryptosystems," *Advances in Cryptology - EUROCRYPT '91*, p. 316. Springer-Verlag, Berlin, 1991.
- Beth, T. and Ding, C., "On almost perfect nonlinear permutations," *Advances in Cryptology - EUROCRYPT '93*, p. 65. Springer-Verlag, Berlin, 1993.
- Beth, T., Lazic, D. E. and Mathias, A., "Cryptanalysis of cryptosystems based on remote chaos replication," *Advances in Cryptology - CRYPTO '94*, p. 318. Springer-Verlag, Berlin, 1994.

Beutelspacher, A.

- Beutelspacher, A., "Geometric Structures as Threshold Schemes," *Abstracts of Papers: EUROCRYPT '86*, p. 46. Department of Electrical Engineering, University of Linköping, Linkoping, Sweden, 1986.
- Beutelspacher, A., "Perfect and essentially perfect authentication schemes," *Advances in Cryptology - EUROCRYPT '87*, p. 167. Springer-Verlag, Berlin, 1987.
- Beutelspacher, A., "How to say "no"," *Advances in Cryptology - EUROCRYPT '89*, p. 491. Springer-Verlag, Berlin, 1989.
- Beutelspacher, A. and Rosenbaum, U., "Essentially l-fold secure authentication systems," *Advances in Cryptology - EUROCRYPT '90*, p. 294. Springer-Verlag, Berlin, 1990.

Biehl, I.

- Biehl, I., Buchmann, J. A., Meyer, B., Thiel, C. and Thiel, C., "Tools for proving zero knowledge," *Advances in Cryptology - EUROCRYPT '92*, p. 356. Springer-Verlag, Berlin, 1992.
- Biehl, I., Buchmann, J. A. and Thiel, C., "Cryptographic protocols based on discrete logarithms in real-quadratic orders," *Advances in Cryptology - CRYPTO '94*, p. 56. Springer-Verlag, Berlin, 1994.

Bierbrauer, J.

- Bierbrauer, J., Johansson, T., Kabatianski, G. A. and Smeets, B., "On families of hash functions via geometric codes and concatenation," *Advances in Cryptology - CRYPTO '93*, p. 331. Springer-Verlag, Berlin, 1993.
- Bierbrauer, J., Gopalakrishnan, K. and Stinson, D. R., "Bounds for resilient functions and orthogonal arrays," *Advances in Cryptology - CRYPTO '94*, p. 247. Springer-Verlag, Berlin, 1994.
- Bierbrauer, J., "A2-codes from universal hash classes," *Advances in Cryptology - EUROCRYPT '95*, p. 311. Springer-Verlag, Berlin, 1995.

Bierens, L.

- Cloetens, H., Bierens, L., Vandewalle, J. and Govaerts, R., "Additional Properties in the S-Boxes of the DES," *Abstracts of Papers: EUROCRYPT '86*, p. 20. Department of Electrical Engineering, University of Linköping, Linkoping, Sweden, 1986.

Biham, E.

- Biham, E. and Shamir, A., "Differential cryptanalysis of DES-like cryptosystems (Extended abstract)," *Advances in Cryptology - CRYPTO '90*, p. 2. Springer-Verlag, Berlin, 1990.
- Biham, E. and Shamir, A., "Differential cryptanalysis of Feal and N-Hash," *Advances in Cryptology - EUROCRYPT '91*, p. 1. Springer-Verlag, Berlin, 1991.
- Biham, E., "Cryptanalysis of the chaotic-map cryptosystem suggested at EUROCRYPT'91," *Advances in Cryptology - EUROCRYPT '91*, p. 532. Springer-Verlag, Berlin, 1991.
- Biham, E. and Shamir, A., "Differential cryptanalysis of Snefru, Khafre, REDOC-II, LOKI and Lucifer (Extended abstract)," *Advances in Cryptology - CRYPTO '91*, p. 156. Springer-Verlag, Berlin, 1991.
- Biham, E. and Shamir, A., "Differential cryptanalysis of the full 16-round DES," *Advances in Cryptology - CRYPTO '92*, p. 487. Springer-Verlag, Berlin, 1992.
- Biham, E., "New types of cryptanalytic attacks using related keys," *Advances in Cryptology - EUROCRYPT '93*, p. 398. Springer-Verlag, Berlin, 1993.
- Ben Aroya, I. and Biham, E., "Differential cryptanalysis of Lucifer," *Advances in Cryptology - CRYPTO '93*, p. 187. Springer-Verlag, Berlin, 1993.
- Biham, E., "On Matsui's linear cryptanalysis," *Advances in Cryptology - EUROCRYPT '94*, p. 341. Springer-Verlag, Berlin, 1995.
- Biham, E. and Biryukov, A., "An improvement of Davies' attack on DES," *Advances in Cryptology - EUROCRYPT '94*, p. 461. Springer-Verlag, Berlin, 1995.
- Biham, E. and Shamir, A., "Differential Fault Analysis of Secret Key Cryptosystems," *Advances in Cryptology - CRYPTO '97*, p. 513. Springer-Verlag, Berlin, 1997.

252

Bird, G. J.

- Khoo, D. S. P., Bird, G. J. and Seberry, J., "Encryption Exponent 3 and the Security of RSA," *Abstracts of Papers: EUROCRYPT '86*, p. 55. Department of Electrical Engineering, University of Linköping, Linkoping, Sweden, 1986.

Bird, R.

- Bird, R., Gopal, I., Herzberg, A., Janson, P., Kutten, S., Molva, R. and Yung, M., "Systematic design of two-party authentication protocols," *Advances in Cryptology - CRYPTO '91*, p. 44. Springer-Verlag, Berlin, 1991.

Biryukov, A.

- Biham, E. and Biryukov, A., "An improvement of Davies' attack on DES," *Advances in Cryptology - EUROCRYPT '94*, p. 461. Springer-Verlag, Berlin, 1995.

Blackburn, S. R.

- Blackburn, S. R., Murphy, S. and Stern, J., "Weaknesses of a public-key cryptosystem based on factorizations of finite groups," *Advances in Cryptology - EUROCRYPT '93*, p. 50. Springer-Verlag, Berlin, 1993.
- Blackburn, S. R., Burmester, M. V. D., Desmedt, Y. and Wild, R. P., "Efficient multiplicative sharing schemes," *Advances in Cryptology - EUROCRYPT '96*, p. 107. Springer-Verlag, Berlin, 1996.

Blake, I. F.

- Blake, I. F., Mullin, R. C. and Vanstone, S. A., "Computing logarithms in $GF(2^n)$," *Advances in Cryptology: Proceedings of CRYPTO '84*, p. 73. Springer-Verlag, Berlin, 1985.

Blakley, B.

- Blakley, B., Blakley, G. R., Chan, A. H. and Massey, J. L., "Threshold schemes with disenrollment," *Advances in Cryptology - CRYPTO '92*, p. 540. Springer-Verlag, Berlin, 1992.

Blakley, G. R.

- Blakley, G. R., "Key Management from a Security Viewpoint," *Advances in Cryptography*, p. 82. University of California, Santa Barbara, Santa Barbara, California, USA, 1982.
- Blakley, G. R. and Swanson, L., "Infinite structures in information theory," *Advances in Cryptology: Proceedings of CRYPTO '82*, p. 39. Plenum Publishing, New York, USA, 1982.
- Blakley, G. R. and Meadows, C., "Security of ramp schemes," *Advances in Cryptology: Proceedings of CRYPTO '84*, p. 242. Springer-Verlag, Berlin, 1985.
- Blakley, G. R., "Information theory without the finiteness assumption, I: Cryptosystems as group-theoretic objects," *Advances in Cryptology: Proceedings of CRYPTO '84*, p. 314. Springer-Verlag, Berlin, 1985.
- Blakley, G. R., Meadows, C. and Purdy, G. B., "Fingerprinting long forgiving messages," *Advances in Cryptology - CRYPTO '85*, p. 180. Springer-Verlag, Berlin, 1986.
- Blakley, G. R., "Information theory without the finiteness assumption, II unfolding the DES," *Advances in Cryptology - CRYPTO '85*, p. 282. Springer-Verlag, Berlin, 1986.
- Blakley, G. R. and Dixon, R. D., "Smallest possible message expansion in threshold schemes," *Advances in Cryptology - CRYPTO '86*, p. 266. Springer-Verlag, Berlin, 1986.
- Blakley, G. R. and Rundell, W., "Cryptosystems based on an analog of heat flow," *Advances in Cryptology - CRYPTO '87*, p. 306. Springer-Verlag, Berlin, 1987.
- Blakley, B., Blakley, G. R., Chan, A. H. and Massey, J. L., "Threshold schemes with disenrollment," *Advances in Cryptology - CRYPTO '92*, p. 540. Springer-Verlag, Berlin, 1992.
- Blakley, G. R. and Kabatianski, G. A., "On General Perfect Secret Sharing Schemes," *Advances in Cryptology - CRYPTO '95*, p. 367. Springer-Verlag, Berlin, 1995.

Bleichenbacher, D.

- Bleichenbacher, D. and Maurer, U. M., "Directed acyclic graphs, one-way functions and digital signatures," *Advances in Cryptology - CRYPTO '94*, p. 75. Springer-Verlag, Berlin, 1994.
- Bleichenbacher, D., Bosma, W. and Lenstra, A. K., "Some Remarks on Lucas-Based Cryptosystems," *Advances in Cryptology - CRYPTO '95*, p. 386. Springer-Verlag, Berlin, 1995.
- Bleichenbacher, D., "Generating ElGamal signatures without knowing the secret key," *Advances in Cryptology - EUROCRYPT '96*, p. 10. Springer-Verlag, Berlin, 1996.
- Bleichenbacher, D., "On the Security of the KMOV Public Key Cryptosystem," *Advances in Cryptology - CRYPTO '97*, p. 235. Springer-Verlag, Berlin, 1997.

254

Bleumer, G.

- Bleumer, G., Pfitzmann, B. and Waidner, M., "A remark on signature scheme where forgery can be proved," *Advances in Cryptology - EURO-CRYPT '90*, p. 441. Springer-Verlag, Berlin, 1990.

Blom, R.

- Blom, R., "Non-public key distribution," *Advances in Cryptology: Proceedings of CRYPTO '82*, p. 231. Plenum Publishing, New York, USA, 1982.
- Blom, R., "An optimal class of symmetric key generation systems," *Advances in Cryptology: Proceedings of EUROCRYPT '84*, p. 335. Springer-Verlag, Berlin, 1984.

Blum, A.

- Blum, A., Furst, M., Kearns, M. and Lipton, R. J., "Cryptographic primitives based on hard learning problems," *Advances in Cryptology - CRYPTO '93*, p. 278. Springer-Verlag, Berlin, 1993.

Blum, L.

- Blum, L., Blum, M. and Shub, M., "Comparison of two pseudo-random number generators," *Advances in Cryptology: Proceedings of CRYPTO '82*, p. 61. Plenum Publishing, New York, USA, 1982.

Blum, M.

- Blum, M., "Coin Flipping by Telephone," *Advances in Cryptography*, p. 11. University of California, Santa Barbara, Santa Barbara, California, USA, 1982.
- Blum, L., Blum, M. and Shub, M., "Comparison of two pseudo-random number generators," *Advances in Cryptology: Proceedings of CRYPTO '82*, p. 61. Plenum Publishing, New York, USA, 1982.
- Blum, M., Vazirani, U. V. and Vazirani, V. V., "Reducibility among protocols," *Advances in Cryptology: Proceedings of CRYPTO '83*, p. 137. Plenum Publishing, New York, USA, 1984.
- Blum, M. and Goldwasser, S., "An efficient probabilistic public key encryption scheme which hides all partial information," *Advances in Cryptology: Proceedings of CRYPTO '84*, p. 289. Springer-Verlag, Berlin, 1985.
- Blum, M., Feldman, P. and Micali, S., "Proving security against chosen cyphertext attacks," *Advances in Cryptology - CRYPTO '88*, p. 256. Springer-Verlag, Berlin, 1989.

Blundo, C.

- Blundo, C., De Santis, A., Stinson, D. R. and Vaccaro, U., "Graph decompositions and secret sharing schemes," *Advances in Cryptology - EURO-CRYPT '92*, p. 1. Springer-Verlag, Berlin, 1992.
- Blundo, C., De Santis, A., Gargano, L. and Vaccaro, U., "On the information rate of secret sharing schemes," *Advances in Cryptology - CRYPTO '92*, p. 148. Springer-Verlag, Berlin, 1992.
- Blundo, C., De Santis, A., Herzberg, A., Kutten, S., Vaccaro, U. and Yung, M., "Perfectly-secure key distribution for dynamic conferences," *Advances in Cryptology - CRYPTO '92*, p. 471. Springer-Verlag, Berlin, 1992.
- Blundo, C., Cresti, A., De Santis, A. and Vaccaro, U., "Fully dynamic secret sharing schemes," *Advances in Cryptology - CRYPTO '93*, p. 110. Springer-Verlag, Berlin, 1993.
- Blundo, C., Giorgio Gaggia, A. and Stinson, D. R., "On the dealer's randomness required in secret sharing schemes," *Advances in Cryptology - EUROCRYPT '94*, p. 35. Springer-Verlag, Berlin, 1995.
- Blundo, C. and Cresti, A., "Space requirements for broadcast encryption," *Advances in Cryptology - EUROCRYPT '94*, p. 287. Springer-Verlag, Berlin, 1995.
- Blundo, C., De Santis, A., Di Crescenzo, G., Gaggia, A. Giorgio and Vaccaro, U., "Multi-secret sharing schemes," *Advances in Cryptology - CRYPTO '94*, p. 150. Springer-Verlag, Berlin, 1994.
- Blundo, C., Mattos, L. A. F. and Stinson, D. R., "Trade-offs Between Communication and Storage in Unconditionally Secure Schemes for Broadcast Encryption and Interactive Key Distribution," *Advances in Cryptology - CRYPTO '96*, p. 387. Springer-Verlag, Berlin, 1996.

Boekee, D. E.

- van Tilburg, J. and Boekee, D. E., "Divergence bounds on key equivocation and error probability in cryptanalysis," *Advances in Cryptology - CRYPTO '85*, p. 489. Springer-Verlag, Berlin, 1986.
- Jansen, C. J. A. and Boekee, D. E., "Modes of blockcipher algorithms and their protection against active eavesdropping," *Advances in Cryptology - EUROCRYPT '87*, p. 281. Springer-Verlag, Berlin, 1987.
- Jensen, C. J. A. and Boekee, D. E., "The shortest feedback shift register that can generate a given sequence," *Advances in Cryptology - CRYPTO '89*, p. 90. Springer-Verlag, Berlin, 1989.

Boneh, D.

- Boneh, D. and Lipton, R. J., "Quantum Cryptanalysis of Hidden Linear Functions," *Advances in Cryptology - CRYPTO '95*, p. 424. Springer-Verlag, Berlin, 1995.
- Boneh, D. and Shaw, J., "Collusion-Secure Fingerprinting for Digital Data," *Advances in Cryptology - CRYPTO '95*, p. 452. Springer-Verlag, Berlin, 1995.

- Boneh, D. and Venkatesan, R., "Hardness of Computing the Most Significant Bits of Secret Keys in Diffie-Hellman and Related Schemes," *Advances in Cryptology - CRYPTO '96*, p. 129. Springer-Verlag, Berlin, 1996.
- Boneh, D. and Lipton, R. J., "Algorithms for Black-Box Fields and Their Application to Cryptography," *Advances in Cryptology - CRYPTO '96*, p. 283. Springer-Verlag, Berlin, 1996.
- Boneh, D., DeMillo, R. A. and Lipton, R. J., "On the Importance of Checking Cryptographic Protocols for Faults (Extended Abstract)," *Advances in Cryptology - EUROCRYPT '97*, p. 37. Springer-Verlag, Berlin, 1997.
- Boneh, D. and Franklin, M. K., "Efficient Generation of Shared RSA Keys," *Advances in Cryptology - CRYPTO '97*, p. 425. Springer-Verlag, Berlin, 1997.

Book, R. V.

- Book, R. V. and Otto, F., "The verifiability of two-party protocols.," *Advances in Cryptology - EUROCRYPT '85*, p. 254. Springer-Verlag, Berlin, 1985.

Borst, J.

- Borst, J., Knudsen, L. R. and Rijmen, V., "Two Attacks on Reduced IDEA (Extended Abstract)," *Advances in Cryptology - EUROCRYPT '97*, p. 1. Springer-Verlag, Berlin, 1997.

Bos, J. N. E.

- Bos, J. N. E. and den Boer, B., "Detection of disrupters in the DC protocol," *Advances in Cryptology - EUROCRYPT '89*, p. 320. Springer-Verlag, Berlin, 1989.
- Bos, J. N. E. and Coster, M. J., "Addition chain heuristics," *Advances in Cryptology - CRYPTO '89*, p. 400. Springer-Verlag, Berlin, 1989.
- Bos, J. N. E. and Chaum, D., "Provably unforgeable signatures," *Advances in Cryptology - CRYPTO '92*, p. 1. Springer-Verlag, Berlin, 1992.

Bosma, W.

- Bosma, W. and van der Hulst, M. P., "Faster primality testing (extended abstract)," *Advances in Cryptology - EUROCRYPT '89*, p. 652. Springer-Verlag, Berlin, 1989.
- Bleichenbacher, D., Bosma, W. and Lenstra, A. K., "Some Remarks on Lucas-Based Cryptosystems," *Advances in Cryptology - CRYPTO '95*, p. 386. Springer-Verlag, Berlin, 1995.

Boyd, C.

- Boyd, C., "Some applications of multiple key ciphers," *Advances in Cryptology - EUROCRYPT '88*, p. 455. Springer-Verlag, Berlin, 1988.
- Boyd, C., "A new multiple key cipher and an improved voting scheme," *Advances in Cryptology - EUROCRYPT '89*, p. 617. Springer-Verlag, Berlin, 1989.
- Boyd, C., "Enhancing secrecy by data compression: Theoretical and practical aspects," *Advances in Cryptology - EUROCRYPT '91*, p. 266. Springer-Verlag, Berlin, 1991.
- Boyd, C. and Mao, W., "On a limitation of BAN logic," *Advances in Cryptology - EUROCRYPT '93*, p. 240. Springer-Verlag, Berlin, 1993.

Bradey, R. L.

- Bradey, R. L. and Graham, I. G., "Full encryption in a personal computer system.," *Advances in Cryptology - EUROCRYPT '85*, p. 231. Springer-Verlag, Berlin, 1985.

Brakeland, Jean-Franc

- Antoine, M., Brakeland, Jean-Franc, Eloy, M. and Poullet, Y., "Legal requirements facing new signature technology (invited)," *Advances in Cryptology - EUROCRYPT '89*, p. 273. Springer-Verlag, Berlin, 1989.

Brand, R. L.

- Brand, R. L., "Problems with the normal use of cryptography for providing security on unclassified networks (invited)," *Advances in Cryptology - CRYPTO '89*, p. 30. Springer-Verlag, Berlin, 1989.

Brands, S.

- Brands, S. and Chaum, D., "Distance bounding protocols," *Advances in Cryptology - EUROCRYPT '93*, p. 344. Springer-Verlag, Berlin, 1993.
- Brands, S., "Untraceable off-line cash in wallets with observers," *Advances in Cryptology - CRYPTO '93*, p. 302. Springer-Verlag, Berlin, 1993.
- Brands, S., "Restrictive blinding of secret-key certificates," *Advances in Cryptology - EUROCRYPT '95*, p. 231. Springer-Verlag, Berlin, 1995.
- Brands, S., "Rapid Demonstration of Linear Relations Connected by Boolean Operators," *Advances in Cryptology - EUROCRYPT '97*, p. 318. Springer-Verlag, Berlin, 1997.

Brandt, J.

- Brandt, J., Damgård, I. B. and Landrock, P., "Anonymous and verifiable registration in databases," *Advances in Cryptology - EUROCRYPT '88*, p. 167. Springer-Verlag, Berlin, 1988.
- Brandt, J., Damgård, I. B., Landrock, P. and Pedersen, T. P., "Zero-knowledge authentication scheme with secret key exchange," *Advances in Cryptology - CRYPTO '88*, p. 583. Springer-Verlag, Berlin, 1989.
- Brandt, J. and Damgård, I. B., "On generation of probable primes by incremental search," *Advances in Cryptology - CRYPTO '92*, p. 358. Springer-Verlag, Berlin, 1992.

Branstad, D. K.

- Smid, M. E. and Branstad, D. K., "Response to comments on the NIST proposed Digital Signature Standard," *Advances in Cryptology - CRYPTO '92*, p. 76. Springer-Verlag, Berlin, 1992.

Brassard, G.

- Brassard, G., "An Optimally Secure Relativized Cryptosystem," *Advances in Cryptography*, p. 54. University of California, Santa Barbara, Santa Barbara, California, USA, 1982.
- Brassard, G., "On computationally secure authentication tags requiring short secret shared keys," *Advances in Cryptology: Proceedings of CRYPTO '82*, p. 79. Plenum Publishing, New York, USA, 1982.
- Bennett, C. H., Brassard, G., Breidbart, S. and Wiesner, S., "Quantum cryptography, or unforgeable subway tokens," *Advances in Cryptology: Proceedings of CRYPTO '82*, p. 267. Plenum Publishing, New York, USA, 1982.
- Bennett, C. H. and Brassard, G., "An update on quantum cryptography," *Advances in Cryptology: Proceedings of CRYPTO '84*, p. 475. Springer-Verlag, Berlin, 1985.
- Bennett, C. H., Brassard, G. and Robert, J. M., "How to reduce your enemy's information," *Advances in Cryptology - CRYPTO '85*, p. 468. Springer-Verlag, Berlin, 1986.
- Brassard, G. and Crépeau, C., "Zero-knowledge simulation of Boolean circuits," *Advances in Cryptology - CRYPTO '86*, p. 223. Springer-Verlag, Berlin, 1986.
- Brassard, G., Crépeau, C. and Robert, J. M., "All-or-nothing disclosure of secrets," *Advances in Cryptology - CRYPTO '86*, p. 234. Springer-Verlag, Berlin, 1986.
- Beauchemin, P., Brassard, G., Crépeau, C. and Goutier, C., "Two observations on probabilistic primality testing," *Advances in Cryptology - CRYPTO '86*, p. 443. Springer-Verlag, Berlin, 1986.
- Beauchemin, P. and Brassard, G., "A generalization of Hellman's extension of Shannon's approach to cryptography," *Advances in Cryptology - CRYPTO '87*, p. 461. Springer-Verlag, Berlin, 1987.

- Brassard, G. and Damgård, I. B., ""Practical IP" ¡ MA," *Advances in Cryptology - CRYPTO '88*, p. 580. Springer-Verlag, Berlin, 1989.
- Brassard, G., "How to improve signature schemes," *Advances in Cryptology - EUROCRYPT '89*, p. 16. Springer-Verlag, Berlin, 1989.
- Brassard, G. and Crépeau, C., "Sorting out zero-knowledge," *Advances in Cryptology - EUROCRYPT '89*, p. 181. Springer-Verlag, Berlin, 1989.
- Brassard, G., Crépeau, C. and Yung, M., "Everything in NP can be argued in perfect zero-knowledge in a bounded number of rounds (extended abstract)," *Advances in Cryptology - EUROCRYPT '89*, p. 192. Springer-Verlag, Berlin, 1989.
- Bennett, C. H., Bessette, F., Brassard, G., Salvail, L. and Smolin, J., "Experimental quantum cryptography," *Advances in Cryptology - EURO-CRYPT '90*, p. 253. Springer-Verlag, Berlin, 1990.
- Brassard, G. and Crépeau, C., "Quantum bit commitment and coin tossing protocols," *Advances in Cryptology - CRYPTO '90*, p. 49. Springer-Verlag, Berlin, 1990.
- Brassard, G. and Yung, M., "One-way group actions," *Advances in Cryptology - CRYPTO '90*, p. 94. Springer-Verlag, Berlin, 1990.
- Bennett, C. H., Brassard, G., Crépeau, C. and Skubiszewska, M. H., "Practical quantum oblivious transfer," *Advances in Cryptology - CRYPTO '91*, p. 351. Springer-Verlag, Berlin, 1991.
- Brassard, G. and Salvail, L., "Secret key reconciliation by public discussion," *Advances in Cryptology - EUROCRYPT '93*, p. 410. Springer-Verlag, Berlin, 1993.
- Brassard, G. and Crépeau, C., "Oblivious Transfers and Privacy Amplification," *Advances in Cryptology - EUROCRYPT '97*, p. 334. Springer-Verlag, Berlin, 1997.
- Brassard, G., "Quantum Information Processing: The Good, the Bad and the Ugly," *Advances in Cryptology - CRYPTO '97*, p. 337. Springer-Verlag, Berlin, 1997.

Breidbart, S.

- Bennett, C. H., Brassard, G., Breidbart, S. and Wiesner, S., "Quantum cryptography, or unforgeable subway tokens," *Advances in Cryptology: Proceedings of CRYPTO '82*, p. 267. Plenum Publishing, New York, USA, 1982.

Brickell, E. F.

- Brickell, E. F. and Moore, J. H., "Some remarks on the Herlestam-Johannesson algorithm for computing logarithms over $GF(2^p)$," *Advances in Cryptology: Proceedings of CRYPTO '82*, p. 15. Plenum Publishing, New York, USA, 1982.
- Brickell, E. F., "A fast modular multiplication algorithm with applications to two key cryptography," *Advances in Cryptology: Proceedings of CRYPTO '82*, p. 51. Plenum Publishing, New York, USA, 1982.

- Brickell, E. F., Davis, J. A. and Simmons, G. J., "A preliminary report on the cryptanalysis of Merkle-Hellman knapsack cryptosystems," *Advances in Cryptology: Proceedings of CRYPTO '82*, p. 289. Plenum Publishing, New York, USA, 1982.
- Brickell, E. F., "Solving low density knapsacks," *Advances in Cryptology: Proceedings of CRYPTO '83*, p. 25. Plenum Publishing, New York, USA, 1984.
- Brickell, E. F., Lagarias, J. C. and Odlyzko, A. M., "Evaluation of the Adleman attack on multiply iterated knapsack cryptosystems," *Advances in Cryptology: Proceedings of CRYPTO '83*, p. 39. Plenum Publishing, New York, USA, 1984.
- Brickell, E. F., "Breaking iterated knapsacks," *Advances in Cryptology: Proceedings of CRYPTO '84*, p. 342. Springer-Verlag, Berlin, 1985.
- Brickell, E. F. and DeLaurentis, J. M., "An attack on a signature scheme proposed by Okamoto and Shiraishi," *Advances in Cryptology - CRYPTO '85*, p. 28. Springer-Verlag, Berlin, 1986.
- Brickell, E. F., "Cryptanalysis of the Yagisawa Public Key Cryptosystem," *Abstracts of Papers: EUROCRYPT '86*, p. 21. Department of Electrical Engineering, University of Linköping, Linkoping, Sweden, 1986.
- Brickell, E. F., Moore, J. H. and Purtill, M. R., "Structure in the S-boxes of the DES," *Advances in Cryptology - CRYPTO '86*, p. 3. Springer-Verlag, Berlin, 1986.
- Brickell, E. F. and Yacobi, Y., "On privacy homomorphisms," *Advances in Cryptology - EUROCRYPT '87*, p. 117. Springer-Verlag, Berlin, 1987.
- Brickell, E. F., Chaum, D., Damgård, I. B. and van de Graaf, J., "Gradual and verifiable release of a secret," *Advances in Cryptology - CRYPTO '87*, p. 156. Springer-Verlag, Berlin, 1987.
- Brickell, E. F., Lee, P. J. and Yacobi, Y., "Secure audio teleconference," *Advances in Cryptology - CRYPTO '87*, p. 418. Springer-Verlag, Berlin, 1987.
- Brickell, E. F. and Stinson, D. R., "Authentication codes with multiple arbiters," *Advances in Cryptology - EUROCRYPT '88*, p. 51. Springer-Verlag, Berlin, 1988.
- Lee, P. J. and Brickell, E. F., "An observation on the security of McEliece's public-key cryptosystem," *Advances in Cryptology - EUROCRYPT '88*, p. 275. Springer-Verlag, Berlin, 1988.
- Brickell, E. F. and Stinson, D. R., "The detection of cheaters in threshold schemes," *Advances in Cryptology - CRYPTO '88*, p. 564. Springer-Verlag, Berlin, 1989.
- Bertilsson, M., Brickell, E. F. and Ingemarsson, I., "Cryptanalysis of video encryption based on space-filling curves," *Advances in Cryptology - EUROCRYPT '89*, p. 403. Springer-Verlag, Berlin, 1989.
- Brickell, E. F., "Some ideal secret sharing schemes," *Advances in Cryptology - EUROCRYPT '89*, p. 468. Springer-Verlag, Berlin, 1989.

- Brickell, E. F. and Davenport, D. M., "On the classification of ideal secret sharing schemes (extended abstract)," *Advances in Cryptology - CRYPTO '89*, p. 278. Springer-Verlag, Berlin, 1989.
- Brickell, E. F., "A survey of hardware implementations of RSA (invited)," *Advances in Cryptology - CRYPTO '89*, p. 368. Springer-Verlag, Berlin, 1989.
- Brickell, E. F. and McCurley, K. S., "An interactive identification scheme based on discrete logarithms and factoring (extended abstract)," *Advances in Cryptology - EUROCRYPT '90*, p. 63. Springer-Verlag, Berlin, 1990.
- Brickell, E. F. and Stinson, D. R., "Some improved bounds on the information rate of perfect secret sharing schemes (Extended abstract)," *Advances in Cryptology - CRYPTO '90*, p. 242. Springer-Verlag, Berlin, 1990.
- Brickell, E. F., Gordon, D. M., McCurley, K. S. and Wilson, D. B., "Fast exponentiation with precomputation (Extended abstract)," *Advances in Cryptology - EUROCRYPT '92*, p. 200. Springer-Verlag, Berlin, 1992.

Broder, A.
- Abadi, M., Allender, E., Broder, A., Feigenbaum, J. and Hemachandra, L. A., "On generating solved instances of computational problems," *Advances in Cryptology - CRYPTO '88*, p. 297. Springer-Verlag, Berlin, 1989.

Brookson, C. B.
- Serpell, S. C. and Brookson, C. B., "Encryption and key management for the ECS satellite service," *Advances in Cryptology: Proceedings of EUROCRYPT '84*, p. 426. Springer-Verlag, Berlin, 1984.
- Serpell, S. C., Brookson, C. B. and Clark, B. L., "A prototype encryption system using public key," *Advances in Cryptology: Proceedings of CRYPTO '84*, p. 3. Springer-Verlag, Berlin, 1985.

Broscius, A. G.
- Broscius, A. G. and Smith, J. M., "Exploiting parallelism in hardware implementation of the DES," *Advances in Cryptology - CRYPTO '91*, p. 367. Springer-Verlag, Berlin, 1991.

Brown, L.
- Brown, L. and Seberry, J., "On the design of permutation P in DES type cryptosystems," *Advances in Cryptology - EUROCRYPT '89*, p. 696. Springer-Verlag, Berlin, 1989.

Brugia, O.
- Wolfowicz, W., Brugia, O. and Improta, S., "An encryption and authentication procedure for tele-surveillance systems," *Advances in Cryptology: Proceedings of EUROCRYPT '84*, p. 437. Springer-Verlag, Berlin, 1984.

Brynielsson, L.

- Brynielsson, L., "On the linear complexity of combined shift register sequences.," *Advances in Cryptology - EUROCRYPT '85*, p. 156. Springer-Verlag, Berlin, 1985.
- Brynielsson, L., "The information leakage through a randomly generated function," *Advances in Cryptology - EUROCRYPT '91*, p. 552. Springer-Verlag, Berlin, 1991.

Buchmann, J. A.

- Buchmann, J. A., Duellmann, S. and Williams, H. C., "On the complexity and efficiency of a new key exchange system," *Advances in Cryptology - EUROCRYPT '89*, p. 597. Springer-Verlag, Berlin, 1989.
- Buchmann, J. A. and Williams, H. C., "A key exchange system based on real quadratic fields," *Advances in Cryptology - CRYPTO '89*, p. 335. Springer-Verlag, Berlin, 1989.
- Scheidler, R., Buchmann, J. A. and Williams, H. C., "Implementation of a key exchange protocol using real quadratic fields (extended abstract)," *Advances in Cryptology - EUROCRYPT '90*, p. 98. Springer-Verlag, Berlin, 1990.
- Buchmann, J. A. and Duellmann, S., "On the computation of discrete logarithms in class groups (Extended abstract)," *Advances in Cryptology - CRYPTO '90*, p. 134. Springer-Verlag, Berlin, 1990.
- Biehl, I., Buchmann, J. A., Meyer, B., Thiel, C. and Thiel, C., "Tools for proving zero knowledge," *Advances in Cryptology - EUROCRYPT '92*, p. 356. Springer-Verlag, Berlin, 1992.
- Buchmann, J. A., Loho, J. and Zayer, J., "An implementation of the general number field sieve," *Advances in Cryptology - CRYPTO '93*, p. 159. Springer-Verlag, Berlin, 1993.
- Biehl, I., Buchmann, J. A. and Thiel, C., "Cryptographic protocols based on discrete logarithms in real-quadratic orders," *Advances in Cryptology - CRYPTO '94*, p. 56. Springer-Verlag, Berlin, 1994.
- Buchmann, J. A. and Paulus, S., "A One Way Function Based on Ideal Arithmetic in Number Fields," *Advances in Cryptology - CRYPTO '97*, p. 385. Springer-Verlag, Berlin, 1997.

Buckley, D. D.

- Buckley, D. D. and Beale, M., "Public Key Encryption of Stream Ciphers," *Abstracts of Papers: EUROCRYPT '86*, p. 53. Department of Electrical Engineering, University of Linköping, Linkoping, Sweden, 1986.

Buelens, J.

- Preneel, B., Nuttin, M., Rijmen, V. and Buelens, J., "Cryptanalysis of the CFB mode of the DES with a reduced number of rounds," *Advances in Cryptology - CRYPTO '93*, p. 212. Springer-Verlag, Berlin, 1993.

Burmester, M. V. D.

- Burmester, M. V. D., Desmedt, Y., Piper, F. and Walker, M., "A general zero-knowledge scheme," *Advances in Cryptology - EUROCRYPT '89*, p. 122. Springer-Verlag, Berlin, 1989.
- Burmester, M. V. D. and Desmedt, Y., "All languages in NP have divertible zero-knowledge proofs and arguments under cryptographic assumptions (extended abstract)," *Advances in Cryptology - EUROCRYPT '90*, p. 1. Springer-Verlag, Berlin, 1990.
- Burmester, M. V. D., "A remark on efficiency of identification schemes," *Advances in Cryptology - EUROCRYPT '90*, p. 493. Springer-Verlag, Berlin, 1990.
- Burmester, M. V. D. and Desmedt, Y., "Broadcast interactive proofs," *Advances in Cryptology - EUROCRYPT '91*, p. 81. Springer-Verlag, Berlin, 1991.
- Frankel, Y., Desmedt, Y. and Burmester, M. V. D., "Non-existence of homomorphic general sharing schemes for some key spaces," *Advances in Cryptology - CRYPTO '92*, p. 549. Springer-Verlag, Berlin, 1992.
- Burmester, M. V. D., "Cryptanalysis of the Chang-Wu-Chen key distribution system," *Advances in Cryptology - EUROCRYPT '93*, p. 440. Springer-Verlag, Berlin, 1993.
- Burmester, M. V. D. and Desmedt, Y., "A secure and efficient conference key distribution system," *Advances in Cryptology - EUROCRYPT '94*, p. 275. Springer-Verlag, Berlin, 1995.
- Burmester, M. V. D., "On the risk of opening distributed keys," *Advances in Cryptology - CRYPTO '94*, p. 308. Springer-Verlag, Berlin, 1994.
- Burmester, M. V. D., "Homomorphisms of secret sharing schemes: a tool for verifiable signature sharing," *Advances in Cryptology - EUROCRYPT '96*, p. 96. Springer-Verlag, Berlin, 1996.
- Blackburn, S. R., Burmester, M. V. D., Desmedt, Y. and Wild, R. P., "Efficient multiplicative sharing schemes," *Advances in Cryptology - EUROCRYPT '96*, p. 107. Springer-Verlag, Berlin, 1996.

Burrows, M.

- Abadi, M., Burrows, M., Lampson, B. and Plotkin, G., "A calculus for access control in distributed systems," *Advances in Cryptology - CRYPTO '91*, p. 1. Springer-Verlag, Berlin, 1991.

Cachin, C.

- Cachin, C. and Maurer, U. M., "Linking information reconciliation and privacy amplification," *Advances in Cryptology - EUROCRYPT '94*, p. 266. Springer-Verlag, Berlin, 1995.
- Cachin, C., "Smooth Entropy and Renyi Entropy," *Advances in Cryptology - EUROCRYPT '97*, p. 193. Springer-Verlag, Berlin, 1997.
- Cachin, C. and Maurer, U. M., "Unconditional Security Against Memory-Bounded Adversaries," *Advances in Cryptology - CRYPTO '97*, p. 292. Springer-Verlag, Berlin, 1997.

Cade, J. J.

- Cade, J. J., "A modification of a broken public-key cipher," *Advances in Cryptology - CRYPTO '86*, p. 64. Springer-Verlag, Berlin, 1986.

Cain, M. R.

- Wagner, N. R., Putter, P. S. and Cain, M. R., "Using algorithms as keys in stream ciphers.," *Advances in Cryptology - EUROCRYPT '85*, p. 149. Springer-Verlag, Berlin, 1985.
- Wagner, N. R., Putter, P. S. and Cain, M. R., "Large-scale randomization techniques," *Advances in Cryptology - CRYPTO '86*, p. 393. Springer-Verlag, Berlin, 1986.

Camenisch, J. L.

- Camenisch, J. L., Piveteau, J. M. and Stadler, M. A., "Blind signatures based on the discrete logarithm problem," *Advances in Cryptology - EUROCRYPT '94*, p. 428. Springer-Verlag, Berlin, 1995.
- Stadler, M. A., Piveteau, J. M. and Camenisch, J. L., "Fair blind signatures," *Advances in Cryptology - EUROCRYPT '95*, p. 209. Springer-Verlag, Berlin, 1995.
- Camenisch, J. L., "Efficient and Generalized Group Signatures," *Advances in Cryptology - EUROCRYPT '97*, p. 465. Springer-Verlag, Berlin, 1997.
- Camenisch, J. L. and Stadler, M. A., "Efficient Group Signature Schemes for Large Groups," *Advances in Cryptology - CRYPTO '97*, p. 410. Springer-Verlag, Berlin, 1997.

Camion, P.

- Godlewski, P. and Camion, P., "Manipulations and errors, detection and localization," *Advances in Cryptology - EUROCRYPT '88*, p. 97. Springer-Verlag, Berlin, 1988.
- Camion, P. and Patarin, J., "The knapsack hash function proposed at Crypto'89 can be broken," *Advances in Cryptology - EUROCRYPT '91*, p. 39. Springer-Verlag, Berlin, 1991.
- Camion, P., Carlet, C., Charpin, P. and Sendrier, N., "On correlation-immune functions," *Advances in Cryptology - CRYPTO '91*, p. 86. Springer-Verlag, Berlin, 1991.
- Camion, P. and Canteaut, A., "Construction of t-resilient functions over a finite alphabet," *Advances in Cryptology - EUROCRYPT '96*, p. 283. Springer-Verlag, Berlin, 1996.
- Camion, P. and Canteaut, A., "Generalization of Siegenthaler Inequality and Schnorr-Vaudenay Multipermutations," *Advances in Cryptology - CRYPTO '96*, p. 372. Springer-Verlag, Berlin, 1996.

Campana, M.

- Baritaud, T., Campana, M., Chauvaud, P. and Gilbert, H., "On the security of the permuted kernel identification scheme," *Advances in Cryptology - CRYPTO '92*, p. 305. Springer-Verlag, Berlin, 1992.

Campbell, K. W.

- Campbell, K. W. and Wiener, M. J., "DES is not a group," *Advances in Cryptology - CRYPTO '92*, p. 512. Springer-Verlag, Berlin, 1992.

Canetti, R.

- Canetti, R. and Herzberg, A., "Maintaining security in the presence of transient faults," *Advances in Cryptology - CRYPTO '94*, p. 425. Springer-Verlag, Berlin, 1994.
- Bellare, M., Canetti, R. and Krawczyk, H., "Keying Hash Functions for Message Authentication," *Advances in Cryptology - CRYPTO '96*, p. 1. Springer-Verlag, Berlin, 1996.
- Canetti, R., Dwork, C., Naor, M. and Ostrovsky, R., "Deniable Encryption," *Advances in Cryptology - CRYPTO '97*, p. 90. Springer-Verlag, Berlin, 1997.
- Canetti, R., "Towards Realizing Random Oracles: Hash Functions that Hide All Partial Information," *Advances in Cryptology - CRYPTO '97*, p. 455. Springer-Verlag, Berlin, 1997.

Canteaut, A.

- Camion, P. and Canteaut, A., "Construction of t-resilient functions over a finite alphabet," *Advances in Cryptology - EUROCRYPT '96*, p. 283. Springer-Verlag, Berlin, 1996.
- Camion, P. and Canteaut, A., "Generalization of Siegenthaler Inequality and Schnorr-Vaudenay Multipermutations," *Advances in Cryptology - CRYPTO '96*, p. 372. Springer-Verlag, Berlin, 1996.

Capocelli, R. M.

- Capocelli, R. M., De Santis, A., Gargano, L. and Vaccaro, U., "On the size of shares for secret sharing schemes," *Advances in Cryptology - CRYPTO '91*, p. 101. Springer-Verlag, Berlin, 1991.

Carlet, C.

- Camion, P., Carlet, C., Charpin, P. and Sendrier, N., "On correlation-immune functions," *Advances in Cryptology - CRYPTO '91*, p. 86. Springer-Verlag, Berlin, 1991.
- Carlet, C., "Partially-bent functions," *Advances in Cryptology - CRYPTO '92*, p. 280. Springer-Verlag, Berlin, 1992.
- Carlet, C., "Two new classes of bent functions," *Advances in Cryptology - EUROCRYPT '93*, p. 77. Springer-Verlag, Berlin, 1993.
- Carlet, C., "More Correlation-Immune and Reslient Functions over Galois Fields and Galois Rings," *Advances in Cryptology - EUROCRYPT '97*, p. 422. Springer-Verlag, Berlin, 1997.

Carpentieri, M.

- Carpentieri, M., De Santis, A. and Vaccaro, U., "Size of shares and probability of cheating in threshold schemes," *Advances in Cryptology - EURO-CRYPT '93*, p. 118. Springer-Verlag, Berlin, 1993.

Carter, G.

- Carter, G., "Some conditions on the linear complexity profiles of certain binary sequences," *Advances in Cryptology - EUROCRYPT '89*, p. 691. Springer-Verlag, Berlin, 1989.

Castagnoli, G.

- Bender, A. and Castagnoli, G., "On the implementation of elliptic curve cryptosystems," *Advances in Cryptology - CRYPTO '89*, p. 186. Springer-Verlag, Berlin, 1989.

Chabaud, F.

- Chabaud, F., "On the security of some cryptosystems based on error-correcting codes," *Advances in Cryptology - EUROCRYPT '94*, p. 131. Springer-Verlag, Berlin, 1995.
- Chabaud, F. and Vaudenay, S., "Links between differential and linear cryptanalysis," *Advances in Cryptology - EUROCRYPT '94*, p. 356. Springer-Verlag, Berlin, 1995.

Chambers, W. G.

- Smeets, B. and Chambers, W. G., "Windmill generators: A generalization and an observation of how many there are," *Advances in Cryptology - EUROCRYPT '88*, p. 325. Springer-Verlag, Berlin, 1988.
- Chambers, W. G. and Gollmann, D., "Lock-in effect in cascades of clock-controlled shift-registers," *Advances in Cryptology - EUROCRYPT '88*, p. 331. Springer-Verlag, Berlin, 1988.
- Gollmann, D. and Chambers, W. G., "A cryptanalysis of $Step_{k,m}$-cascades," *Advances in Cryptology - EUROCRYPT '89*, p. 680. Springer-Verlag, Berlin, 1989.
- Chambers, W. G., "On binary sequences from recursions "modulo 2^e" made non-linear by the bit-by-bit "xor" function," *Advances in Cryptology - EUROCRYPT '91*, p. 200. Springer-Verlag, Berlin, 1991.

268

Chan, A. H.

- Chan, A. H. and Games, R. A., "On the linear span of binary sequences obtained from finite geometries," *Advances in Cryptology - CRYPTO '86*, p. 405. Springer-Verlag, Berlin, 1986.
- Chan, A. H., Goresky, M. and Klapper, A., "On the linear complexity of feedback registers (extended abstract)," *Advances in Cryptology - EURO-CRYPT '89*, p. 563. Springer-Verlag, Berlin, 1989.
- Chan, A. H. and Games, R. A., "On the quadratic spans of periodic sequences," *Advances in Cryptology - CRYPTO '89*, p. 82. Springer-Verlag, Berlin, 1989.
- Chan, A. H., Goresky, M. and Klapper, A., "Correlation functions of geometric sequences," *Advances in Cryptology - EUROCRYPT '90*, p. 214. Springer-Verlag, Berlin, 1990.
- Blakley, B., Blakley, G. R., Chan, A. H. and Massey, J. L., "Threshold schemes with disenrollment," *Advances in Cryptology - CRYPTO '92*, p. 540. Springer-Verlag, Berlin, 1992.

Chao, J.

- Tsujii, S. and Chao, J., "A new ID-based key sharing system," *Advances in Cryptology - CRYPTO '91*, p. 288. Springer-Verlag, Berlin, 1991.
- Chao, J., Tanada, K. and Tsujii, S., "Design of elliptic curves with controllable lower boundary of extension degree for reduction attacks," *Advances in Cryptology - CRYPTO '94*, p. 50. Springer-Verlag, Berlin, 1994.

Charnes, C.

- Charnes, C., O'Connor, L., Pieprzyk, J., Safavi-Naini, R. and Zheng, Y., "Comments on Soviet encryption algorithm," *Advances in Cryptology - EUROCRYPT '94*, p. 433. Springer-Verlag, Berlin, 1995.

Charpin, P.

- Camion, P., Carlet, C., Charpin, P. and Sendrier, N., "On correlation-immune functions," *Advances in Cryptology - CRYPTO '91*, p. 86. Springer-Verlag, Berlin, 1991.

Chasse, G.

- Gilbert, H. and Chasse, G., "A statistical attack of the FEAL cryptosystem," *Advances in Cryptology - CRYPTO '90*, p. 22. Springer-Verlag, Berlin, 1990.

Chaum, D.

- Chaum, D., "Verification by Anonymous Monitors (also known as Silo Watching)," *Advances in Cryptography*, p. 138. University of California, Santa Barbara, Santa Barbara, California, USA, 1982.
- Chaum, D., "Blind signatures for untraceable payments," *Advances in Cryptology: Proceedings of CRYPTO '82*, p. 199. Plenum Publishing, New York, USA, 1982.
- Chaum, D., "Blind signature system," *Advances in Cryptology: Proceedings of CRYPTO '83*, p. 153. Plenum Publishing, New York, USA, 1984.
- Chaum, D., "Design concepts for tamper responding systems," *Advances in Cryptology: Proceedings of CRYPTO '83*, p. 387. Plenum Publishing, New York, USA, 1984.
- Chaum, D., "New secret codes can prevent a computerized big brother," *Advances in Cryptology: Proceedings of CRYPTO '84*, p. 432. Springer-Verlag, Berlin, 1985.
- Chaum, D., "How to keep a secret alive: extensible partial key, key safeguarding, and threshold systems," *Advances in Cryptology: Proceedings of CRYPTO '84*, p. 481. Springer-Verlag, Berlin, 1985.
- Chaum, D., "Showing credentials without identification. Signatures transferred between unconditionally unlinkable pseudonyms.," *Advances in Cryptology - EUROCRYPT '85*, p. 241. Springer-Verlag, Berlin, 1985.
- de Jonge, W. and Chaum, D., "Attacks on some RSA signatures," *Advances in Cryptology - CRYPTO '85*, p. 18. Springer-Verlag, Berlin, 1986.
- Chaum, D. and Evertse, J. H., "Cryptanalysis of DES with a reduced number of rounds," *Advances in Cryptology - CRYPTO '85*, p. 192. Springer-Verlag, Berlin, 1986.
- de Jonge, W. and Chaum, D., "Some variations on RSA signatures and their security," *Advances in Cryptology - CRYPTO '86*, p. 49. Springer-Verlag, Berlin, 1986.
- Chaum, D. and Evertse, J. H., "A secure and privacy-protecting protocol for transmitting personal information between organizations," *Advances in Cryptology - CRYPTO '86*, p. 118. Springer-Verlag, Berlin, 1986.
- Chaum, D., "Demonstrating that a public predicate can be satisfied without revealing any information about how," *Advances in Cryptology - CRYPTO '86*, p. 195. Springer-Verlag, Berlin, 1986.
- Chaum, D., Evertse, J. H., van de Graaf, J. and Peralta, R., "Demonstrating possession of a discrete logarithm without revealing it," *Advances in Cryptology - CRYPTO '86*, p. 200. Springer-Verlag, Berlin, 1986.
- Chaum, D., Evertse, J. H. and van de Graaf, J., "An improved protocol for demonstrating possession of discrete logarithms and some generalizations," *Advances in Cryptology - EUROCRYPT '87*, p. 127. Springer-Verlag, Berlin, 1987.
- Chaum, D., "Blinding for unanticipated signatures," *Advances in Cryptology - EUROCRYPT '87*, p. 227. Springer-Verlag, Berlin, 1987.

- Chaum, D., Damgård, I. B. and van de Graaf, J., "Multiparty computations ensuring privacy of each party's input and correctness of the result," *Advances in Cryptology - CRYPTO '87*, p. 87. Springer-Verlag, Berlin, 1987.
- Brickell, E. F., Chaum, D., Damgård, I. B. and van de Graaf, J., "Gradual and verifiable release of a secret," *Advances in Cryptology - CRYPTO '87*, p. 156. Springer-Verlag, Berlin, 1987.
- Chaum, D., Crépeau, C. and Damgård, I. B., "Multiparty unconditionally secure protocols," *Advances in Cryptology - CRYPTO '87*, p. 462. Springer-Verlag, Berlin, 1987.
- Chaum, D., "Elections with unconditionally-secret ballots and disruption equivalent to breaking RSA," *Advances in Cryptology - EUROCRYPT '88*, p. 177. Springer-Verlag, Berlin, 1988.
- Chaum, D., Fiat, A. and Naor, M., "Untraceable electronic cash," *Advances in Cryptology - CRYPTO '88*, p. 319. Springer-Verlag, Berlin, 1989.
- Vandewalle, J., Chaum, D., Fumy, W., Jansen, C. J. A., Landrock, P. and Roelofsen, G., "A European call for cryptographic algorithms: RIPE; Race Integrity Primitives Evaluation," *Advances in Cryptology - EUROCRYPT '89*, p. 267. Springer-Verlag, Berlin, 1989.
- Chaum, D., "Online cash checks," *Advances in Cryptology - EUROCRYPT '89*, p. 288. Springer-Verlag, Berlin, 1989.
- Chaum, D., den Boer, B., van Heyst, E., Mjoelsnes, S. F. and Steenbeek, A., "Efficient offline electronic checks (extended abstract)," *Advances in Cryptology - EUROCRYPT '89*, p. 294. Springer-Verlag, Berlin, 1989.
- Chaum, D. and van Antwerpen, H., "Undeniable signatures," *Advances in Cryptology - CRYPTO '89*, p. 212. Springer-Verlag, Berlin, 1989.
- Chaum, D., "The spymasters double-agent problem: Multiparty computations secure unconditionally from minorities and cryptograhically from majorities," *Advances in Cryptology - CRYPTO '89*, p. 591. Springer-Verlag, Berlin, 1989.
- Chaum, D., "Zero-knowledge undeniable signatures (extended abstract)," *Advances in Cryptology - EUROCRYPT '90*, p. 458. Springer-Verlag, Berlin, 1990.
- Boyar, J., Chaum, D., Damgård, I. B. and Pedersen, T. P., "Convertible undeniable signatures," *Advances in Cryptology - CRYPTO '90*, p. 189. Springer-Verlag, Berlin, 1990.
- Chaum, D. and Roijakkers, Sandra, "Unconditionally Secure Digital Signatures," *Advances in Cryptology - CRYPTO '90*, p. 206. Springer-Verlag, Berlin, 1990.
- Okamoto, T., Chaum, D. and Ohta, K., "Direct zero knowledge proofs of computational power in five rounds," *Advances in Cryptology - EUROCRYPT '91*, p. 96. Springer-Verlag, Berlin, 1991.
- Chaum, D. and Heyst, E. van, "Group signatures," *Advances in Cryptology - EUROCRYPT '91*, p. 257. Springer-Verlag, Berlin, 1991.

- Preneel, B., Chaum, D., Fumy, W., Jansen, C. J. A., Landrock, P. and Roelofsen, G., "Race Integrity Primitives Evaluation," *Advances in Cryptology - EUROCRYPT '91*, p. 547. Springer-Verlag, Berlin, 1991.
- Chaum, D., "Some Weaknesses of "Weaknesses of Undeniable Signatures"," *Advances in Cryptology - EUROCRYPT '91*, p. 554. Springer-Verlag, Berlin, 1991.
- Chaum, D., van Heijst, E. and Pfitzmann, B., "Cryptographically strong undeniable signatures, unconditionally secure for the signer," *Advances in Cryptology - CRYPTO '91*, p. 470. Springer-Verlag, Berlin, 1991.
- Chaum, D. and Pedersen, T. P., "Transferred cash grows in size," *Advances in Cryptology - EUROCRYPT '92*, p. 390. Springer-Verlag, Berlin, 1992.
- Bos, J. N. E. and Chaum, D., "Provably unforgeable signatures," *Advances in Cryptology - CRYPTO '92*, p. 1. Springer-Verlag, Berlin, 1992.
- Chaum, D. and Pedersen, T. P., "Wallet databases with observers," *Advances in Cryptology - CRYPTO '92*, p. 89. Springer-Verlag, Berlin, 1992.
- Brands, S. and Chaum, D., "Distance bounding protocols," *Advances in Cryptology - EUROCRYPT '93*, p. 344. Springer-Verlag, Berlin, 1993.
- Chaum, D., "Designated confirmer signatures," *Advances in Cryptology - EUROCRYPT '94*, p. 86. Springer-Verlag, Berlin, 1995.

Chauvaud, P.

- Baritaud, T., Campana, M., Chauvaud, P. and Gilbert, H., "On the security of the permuted kernel identification scheme," *Advances in Cryptology - CRYPTO '92*, p. 305. Springer-Verlag, Berlin, 1992.
- Patarin, J. and Chauvaud, P., "Improved algorithms for the permuted kernel problem," *Advances in Cryptology - CRYPTO '93*, p. 391. Springer-Verlag, Berlin, 1993.
- Gilbert, H. and Chauvaud, P., "A chosen plaintext attack of the 16-round cryptosystem," *Advances in Cryptology - CRYPTO '94*, p. 359. Springer-Verlag, Berlin, 1994.

Chee, Y. Meng

- Chee, Y. Meng, Joux, A. and Stern, J., "The cryptanalysis of a new public-key cryptosystem based on modular knapsacks," *Advances in Cryptology - CRYPTO '91*, p. 204. Springer-Verlag, Berlin, 1991.

Chen, D.

- Chen, D. and Dai, Z., "On feedforward transforms and p-fold periodic p-arrays.," *Advances in Cryptology - EUROCRYPT '85*, p. 130. Springer-Verlag, Berlin, 1985.

Chen, L.

- Chen, L. and Damgård, I. B., "Security bounds for parallel versions of identification protocols," *Advances in Cryptology - EUROCRYPT '92*, p. 461. Springer-Verlag, Berlin, 1992.
- Chen, L., Damgård, I. B. and Pedersen, T. P., "Parallel divertibility of proofs of knowledge," *Advances in Cryptology - EUROCRYPT '94*, p. 140. Springer-Verlag, Berlin, 1995.
- Chen, L. and Pedersen, T. P., "New group signature schemes," *Advances in Cryptology - EUROCRYPT '94*, p. 171. Springer-Verlag, Berlin, 1995.
- Chen, L. and Pedersen, T. P., "On the efficiency of group signatures providing information-theoretic anonymity," *Advances in Cryptology - EUROCRYPT '95*, p. 39. Springer-Verlag, Berlin, 1995.

Chen, Su-shing

- Chen, Su-shing, "On rotation group and encryption of analog signals," *Advances in Cryptology: Proceedings of CRYPTO '84*, p. 95. Springer-Verlag, Berlin, 1985.

Chepyzhov, V.

- Chepyzhov, V. and Smeets, B., "On a fast correlation attack on certain stream ciphers," *Advances in Cryptology - EUROCRYPT '91*, p. 176. Springer-Verlag, Berlin, 1991.

Chick, G. C.

- Chick, G. C. and Tavares, S. E., "Flexible access control with master keys," *Advances in Cryptology - CRYPTO '89*, p. 316. Springer-Verlag, Berlin, 1989.

Chor, B.

- Chor, B. and Rivest, R. L., "A knapsack type public key cryptosystem based on arithmetic in finite fields," *Advances in Cryptology: Proceedings of CRYPTO '84*, p. 54. Springer-Verlag, Berlin, 1985.
- Chor, B. and Goldreich, O., "RSA/Rabin least significant bits are $1/2 + 1/poly(logN)$ secure," *Advances in Cryptology: Proceedings of CRYPTO '84*, p. 303. Springer-Verlag, Berlin, 1985.
- Chor, B., Goldreich, O. and Goldwasser, S., "The bit security of modular squaring given partial factorization of the modulos," *Advances in Cryptology - CRYPTO '85*, p. 448. Springer-Verlag, Berlin, 1986.
- Chor, B. and Kushilevitz, E., "Secret sharing over infinite domains (extended abstract)," *Advances in Cryptology - CRYPTO '89*, p. 299. Springer-Verlag, Berlin, 1989.
- Beimel, A. and Chor, B., "Universally ideal secret sharing schemes (preliminary version)," *Advances in Cryptology - CRYPTO '92*, p. 183. Springer-Verlag, Berlin, 1992.
- Beimel, A. and Chor, B., "Interaction in key distribution schemes," *Advances in Cryptology - CRYPTO '93*, p. 444. Springer-Verlag, Berlin, 1993.

- Chor, B., Fiat, A. and Naor, M., "Tracing traitors," *Advances in Cryptology - CRYPTO '94*, p. 257. Springer-Verlag, Berlin, 1994.
- Beimel, A. and Chor, B., "Secret Sharing with Public Reconstruction," *Advances in Cryptology - CRYPTO '95*, p. 353. Springer-Verlag, Berlin, 1995.

Chow, G.

- Lee, L. and Chow, G., "Results on Sampling-based Scrambling for Secure Speech Communication," *Advances in Cryptography*, p. 115. University of California, Santa Barbara, Santa Barbara, California, USA, 1982.

Chuang, Chih-Chwen

- Chuang, Chih-Chwen and Dunham, J. George, "Matrix extensions of the RSA algorithm," *Advances in Cryptology - CRYPTO '90*, p. 140. Springer-Verlag, Berlin, 1990.

Clark, A. J.

- Clark, A. J., "Physical protection of cryptographic devices," *Advances in Cryptology - EUROCRYPT '87*, p. 83. Springer-Verlag, Berlin, 1987.

Clark, B. L.

- Serpell, S. C., Brookson, C. B. and Clark, B. L., "A prototype encryption system using public key," *Advances in Cryptology: Proceedings of CRYPTO '84*, p. 3. Springer-Verlag, Berlin, 1985.

Cleve, R.

- Cleve, R., "Controlled gradual disclosure schemes for random bits and their applications," *Advances in Cryptology - CRYPTO '89*, p. 573. Springer-Verlag, Berlin, 1989.
- Cleve, R., "Complexity theoretic issues concerning block ciphers related to D.E.S.," *Advances in Cryptology - CRYPTO '90*, p. 530. Springer-Verlag, Berlin, 1990.

Cloetens, H.

- Cloetens, H., Bierens, L., Vandewalle, J. and Govaerts, R., "Additional Properties in the S-Boxes of the DES," *Abstracts of Papers: EUROCRYPT '86*, p. 20. Department of Electrical Engineering, University of Linköping, Linkoping, Sweden, 1986.

Cnudde, H.

- Cnudde, H., "Cryptel—the practical protection of an existing electronic mail system," *Advances in Cryptology - EUROCRYPT '89*, p. 237. Springer-Verlag, Berlin, 1989.

Cohen Benaloh, J.

- Cohen Benaloh, J., "Cryptographic capsules: a disjunctive primitive for interactive protocols," *Advances in Cryptology - CRYPTO '86*, p. 213. Springer-Verlag, Berlin, 1986.
- Cohen Benaloh, J., "Secret sharing homomorphisms: keeping shares of a secret secret," *Advances in Cryptology - CRYPTO '86*, p. 251. Springer-Verlag, Berlin, 1986.

Cohen, G. D.

- Godlewski, P. and Cohen, G. D., "Authorized writing for "write-once" memories.," *Advances in Cryptology - EUROCRYPT '85*, p. 111. Springer-Verlag, Berlin, 1985.
- Godlewski, P. and Cohen, G. D., "Some cryptographic aspects of wom-codes," *Advances in Cryptology - CRYPTO '85*, p. 458. Springer-Verlag, Berlin, 1986.

Cole, G. M.

- Beker, H. J. and Cole, G. M., "Message authentication and dynamic passwords," *Advances in Cryptology - EUROCRYPT '87*, p. 171. Springer-Verlag, Berlin, 1987.

Cook, B. M.

- Beth, T., Cook, B. M. and Gollmann, D., "Architectures for exponentiation in $GF(2^n)$," *Advances in Cryptology - CRYPTO '86*, p. 302. Springer-Verlag, Berlin, 1986.

Coppersmith, D.

- Coppersmith, D., "Another birthday attack," *Advances in Cryptology - CRYPTO '85*, p. 14. Springer-Verlag, Berlin, 1986.
- Coppersmith, D., "Cheating at mental poker," *Advances in Cryptology - CRYPTO '85*, p. 104. Springer-Verlag, Berlin, 1986.
- Coppersmith, D., "The real reason for Rivest's phenomenon," *Advances in Cryptology - CRYPTO '85*, p. 535. Springer-Verlag, Berlin, 1986.
- Coppersmith, D., Krawczyk, H. and Mansour, Y., "The shrinking generator," *Advances in Cryptology - CRYPTO '93*, p. 22. Springer-Verlag, Berlin, 1993.
- Coppersmith, D., Stern, J. and Vaudenay, S., "Attacks on the birational permutation signature schemes," *Advances in Cryptology - CRYPTO '93*, p. 435. Springer-Verlag, Berlin, 1993.
- Coppersmith, D., "Attack on the cryptographic scheme NIKS-TAS," *Advances in Cryptology - CRYPTO '94*, p. 294. Springer-Verlag, Berlin, 1994.
- Coppersmith, D., Franklin, M. K., Patarin, J. and Reiter, M. K., "Low-exponent RSA with related messages," *Advances in Cryptology - EUROCRYPT '96*, p. 1. Springer-Verlag, Berlin, 1996.

- Coppersmith, D., "Finding a small root of a univariate modular equation," *Advances in Cryptology - EUROCRYPT '96*, p. 155. Springer-Verlag, Berlin, 1996.
- Coppersmith, D., "Finding a small root of a bivariate integer equation; factoring with high bits known," *Advances in Cryptology - EUROCRYPT '96*, p. 178. Springer-Verlag, Berlin, 1996.
- Coppersmith, D. and Shamir, A., "Lattice Attacks on NTRU," *Advances in Cryptology - EUROCRYPT '97*, p. 52. Springer-Verlag, Berlin, 1997.

Coster, M. J.

- Bos, J. N. E. and Coster, M. J., "Addition chain heuristics," *Advances in Cryptology - CRYPTO '89*, p. 400. Springer-Verlag, Berlin, 1989.
- Coster, M. J., LaMacchia, B. A., Odlyzko, A. M. and Schnorr, C. P., "An improved low-density subset sum algorithm," *Advances in Cryptology - EUROCRYPT '91*, p. 54. Springer-Verlag, Berlin, 1991.

Coulthart, K. B.

- Fairfield, R. C., Mortenson, R. L. and Coulthart, K. B., "An LSI random number generator (RNG)," *Advances in Cryptology: Proceedings of CRYPTO '84*, p. 203. Springer-Verlag, Berlin, 1985.

Cowen, L.

- Bellare, M., Cowen, L. and Goldwasser, S., "On the structure of secret key exchange protocols," *Advances in Cryptology - CRYPTO '89*, p. 604. Springer-Verlag, Berlin, 1989.

Crépeau, C.

- Crépeau, C., "A secure poker protocol that minimizes the effect of player coalitions," *Advances in Cryptology - CRYPTO '85*, p. 73. Springer-Verlag, Berlin, 1986.
- Brassard, G. and Crépeau, C., "Zero-knowledge simulation of Boolean circuits," *Advances in Cryptology - CRYPTO '86*, p. 223. Springer-Verlag, Berlin, 1986.
- Brassard, G., Crépeau, C. and Robert, J. M., "All-or-nothing disclosure of secrets," *Advances in Cryptology - CRYPTO '86*, p. 234. Springer-Verlag, Berlin, 1986.
- Crépeau, C., "A zero-knowledge poker protocol that achieves confidentiality of the players' strategy or How to achieve an electronic poker face," *Advances in Cryptology - CRYPTO '86*, p. 239. Springer-Verlag, Berlin, 1986.
- Beauchemin, P., Brassard, G., Crépeau, C. and Goutier, C., "Two observations on probabilistic primality testing," *Advances in Cryptology - CRYPTO '86*, p. 443. Springer-Verlag, Berlin, 1986.
- Crépeau, C., "Equivalence between two flavours of oblivious transfers (cryptography)," *Advances in Cryptology - CRYPTO '87*, p. 350. Springer-Verlag, Berlin, 1987.

- Chaum, D., Crépeau, C. and Damgård, I. B., "Multiparty unconditionally secure protocols," *Advances in Cryptology - CRYPTO '87*, p. 462. Springer-Verlag, Berlin, 1987.
- Crépeau, C. and Kilian, J., "Weakening security assumptions and oblivious transfer," *Advances in Cryptology - CRYPTO '88*, p. 2. Springer-Verlag, Berlin, 1989.
- Crépeau, C., "Verifiable disclose for secrets and applications (abstract)," *Advances in Cryptology - EUROCRYPT '89*, p. 150. Springer-Verlag, Berlin, 1989.
- Brassard, G. and Crépeau, C., "Sorting out zero-knowledge," *Advances in Cryptology - EUROCRYPT '89*, p. 181. Springer-Verlag, Berlin, 1989.
- Brassard, G., Crépeau, C. and Yung, M., "Everything in NP can be argued in perfect zero-knowledge in a bounded number of rounds (extended abstract)," *Advances in Cryptology - EUROCRYPT '89*, p. 192. Springer-Verlag, Berlin, 1989.
- Brassard, G. and Crépeau, C., "Quantum bit commitment and coin tossing protocols," *Advances in Cryptology - CRYPTO '90*, p. 49. Springer-Verlag, Berlin, 1990.
- Crépeau, C. and Santha, M., "On the reversibility of oblivious transfer," *Advances in Cryptology - EUROCRYPT '91*, p. 106. Springer-Verlag, Berlin, 1991.
- Bennett, C. H., Brassard, G., Crépeau, C. and Skubiszewska, M. H., "Practical quantum oblivious transfer," *Advances in Cryptology - CRYPTO '91*, p. 351. Springer-Verlag, Berlin, 1991.
- Crépeau, C. and Kilian, J., "Discreet solitary games," *Advances in Cryptology - CRYPTO '93*, p. 319. Springer-Verlag, Berlin, 1993.
- Crépeau, C. and Salvail, L., "Quantum oblivious mutual identification," *Advances in Cryptology - EUROCRYPT '95*, p. 133. Springer-Verlag, Berlin, 1995.
- Crépeau, C., Graaf, J. van de and Tapp, A., "Committed Oblivious Transfer and Private Multi-Party Computation," *Advances in Cryptology - CRYPTO '95*, p. 110. Springer-Verlag, Berlin, 1995.
- Crépeau, C., "Efficient Cryptographic Protocols Based on Noisy Channels," *Advances in Cryptology - EUROCRYPT '97*, p. 306. Springer-Verlag, Berlin, 1997.
- Brassard, G. and Crépeau, C., "Oblivious Transfers and Privacy Amplification," *Advances in Cryptology - EUROCRYPT '97*, p. 334. Springer-Verlag, Berlin, 1997.

Cramer, R.
- Cramer, R. and Pedersen, T. P., "Improved privacy in wallets with observers," *Advances in Cryptology - EUROCRYPT '93*, p. 329. Springer-Verlag, Berlin, 1993.

- Cramer, R., Damgård, I. B. and Schoenmakers, B., "Proofs of partial knowledge and simplified design of witness hiding protocols," *Advances in Cryptology - CRYPTO '94*, p. 174. Springer-Verlag, Berlin, 1994.
- Cramer, R. and Damgård, I. B., "Secure Signature Schemes based on Interactive Protocols," *Advances in Cryptology - CRYPTO '95*, p. 297. Springer-Verlag, Berlin, 1995.
- Cramer, R., Franklin, M. K., Schoenmakers, B. and Yung, M., "Multi-authority secret-ballot elections with linear work," *Advances in Cryptology - EUROCRYPT '96*, p. 72. Springer-Verlag, Berlin, 1996.
- Cramer, R. and Damgård, I. B., "New Generation of Secure and Practical RSA-Based Signatures," *Advances in Cryptology - CRYPTO '96*, p. 173. Springer-Verlag, Berlin, 1996.
- Cramer, R. and Damgård, I. B., "Fast and Secure Immunization Against Adaptive Man-in-the-Middle Impersonation," *Advances in Cryptology - EUROCRYPT '97*, p. 75. Springer-Verlag, Berlin, 1997.
- Cramer, R., Gennaro, R. and Schoenmakers, B., "A Secure and Optimally Efficient Multi-Authority Election Scheme," *Advances in Cryptology - EUROCRYPT '97*, p. 103. Springer-Verlag, Berlin, 1997.

Cresti, A.

- Blundo, C., Cresti, A., De Santis, A. and Vaccaro, U., "Fully dynamic secret sharing schemes," *Advances in Cryptology - CRYPTO '93*, p. 110. Springer-Verlag, Berlin, 1993.
- Blundo, C. and Cresti, A., "Space requirements for broadcast encryption," *Advances in Cryptology - EUROCRYPT '94*, p. 287. Springer-Verlag, Berlin, 1995.
- Beguin, P. and Cresti, A., "General short computational secret sharing schemes," *Advances in Cryptology - EUROCRYPT '95*, p. 194. Springer-Verlag, Berlin, 1995.

Csirmaz, L.

- Csirmaz, L., "The size of a share must be large," *Advances in Cryptology - EUROCRYPT '94*, p. 13. Springer-Verlag, Berlin, 1995.

Cusick, T. W.

- Cusick, T. W. and Wood, M. C., "The REDOC II cryptosystem," *Advances in Cryptology - CRYPTO '90*, p. 545. Springer-Verlag, Berlin, 1990.
- Cusick, T. W., "Boolean functions satisfying a higher order strict avalanche criterion," *Advances in Cryptology - EUROCRYPT '93*, p. 102. Springer-Verlag, Berlin, 1993.

D'Amiano, S.

- D'Amiano, S. and Di Crescenzo, G., "Methodology for digital money based on general cryptographic tools," *Advances in Cryptology - EUROCRYPT '94*, p. 156. Springer-Verlag, Berlin, 1995.
- D'Amiano, S. and Di Crescenzo, G., "Anonymous NIZK proofs of knowledge with preprocessing," *Advances in Cryptology - EUROCRYPT '95*, p. 413. Springer-Verlag, Berlin, 1995.

Daemen, J.

- Daemen, J., Govaerts, R. and Vandewalle, J., "Resynchronization weaknesses in synchronous stream ciphers," *Advances in Cryptology - EUROCRYPT '93*, p. 159. Springer-Verlag, Berlin, 1993.
- Daemen, J., Govaerts, R. and Vandewalle, J., "Weak keys for IDEA," *Advances in Cryptology - CRYPTO '93*, p. 224. Springer-Verlag, Berlin, 1993.

Dai, Z.

- Chen, D. and Dai, Z., "On feedforward transforms and p-fold periodic p-arrays.," *Advances in Cryptology - EUROCRYPT '85*, p. 130. Springer-Verlag, Berlin, 1985.
- Zeng, K., Yang, J.-H. and Dai, Z., "Patterns of entropy drop of the key in an S-box of the DES," *Advances in Cryptology - CRYPTO '87*, p. 438. Springer-Verlag, Berlin, 1987.
- Beth, T. and Dai, Z., "On the Complexity of Pseudo-Random Sequences - or: If you Can Describe a Sequence It Can't be Random," *Advances in Cryptology - EUROCRYPT '89*, p. 533. Springer-Verlag, Berlin, 1989.
- Dai, Z. and Zeng, K., "Feedforward functions defined by de Brujin sequences," *Advances in Cryptology - EUROCRYPT '89*, p. 544. Springer-Verlag, Berlin, 1989.
- Dai, Z., Beth, T. and Gollmann, D., "Lower bounds for the linear complexity of sequences over residue rings," *Advances in Cryptology - EUROCRYPT '90*, p. 189. Springer-Verlag, Berlin, 1990.
- Dai, Z. and Yang, J.-H., "Linear complexity of periodically repeated random sequences," *Advances in Cryptology - EUROCRYPT '91*, p. 168. Springer-Verlag, Berlin, 1991.

Damgård, I. B.

- Damgård, I. B., "Collision free hash functions and public key signature schemes," *Advances in Cryptology - EUROCRYPT '87*, p. 203. Springer-Verlag, Berlin, 1987.
- Chaum, D., Damgård, I. B. and van de Graaf, J., "Multiparty computations ensuring privacy of each party's input and correctness of the result," *Advances in Cryptology - CRYPTO '87*, p. 87. Springer-Verlag, Berlin, 1987.
- Brickell, E. F., Chaum, D., Damgård, I. B. and van de Graaf, J., "Gradual and verifiable release of a secret," *Advances in Cryptology - CRYPTO '87*, p. 156. Springer-Verlag, Berlin, 1987.
- Chaum, D., Crépeau, C. and Damgård, I. B., "Multiparty unconditionally secure protocols," *Advances in Cryptology - CRYPTO '87*, p. 462. Springer-Verlag, Berlin, 1987.
- Brandt, J., Damgård, I. B. and Landrock, P., "Anonymous and verifiable registration in databases," *Advances in Cryptology - EUROCRYPT '88*, p. 167. Springer-Verlag, Berlin, 1988.
- Damgård, I. B., "On the randomness of Legendre and Jacobi sequences," *Advances in Cryptology - CRYPTO '88*, p. 163. Springer-Verlag, Berlin, 1989.
- Damgård, I. B., "Payment systems and credential mechanisms with provable security against abuse by individuals," *Advances in Cryptology - CRYPTO '88*, p. 328. Springer-Verlag, Berlin, 1989.
- Brassard, G. and Damgård, I. B., ""Practical IP" ¡ MA," *Advances in Cryptology - CRYPTO '88*, p. 580. Springer-Verlag, Berlin, 1989.
- Brandt, J., Damgård, I. B., Landrock, P. and Pedersen, T. P., "Zero-knowledge authentication scheme with secret key exchange," *Advances in Cryptology - CRYPTO '88*, p. 583. Springer-Verlag, Berlin, 1989.
- Damgård, I. B., "On the existence of bit commitment schemes and zero-knowledge proofs," *Advances in Cryptology - CRYPTO '89*, p. 17. Springer-Verlag, Berlin, 1989.
- Damgård, I. B., "A design principle for hash functions," *Advances in Cryptology - CRYPTO '89*, p. 416. Springer-Verlag, Berlin, 1989.
- Boyar, J., Chaum, D., Damgård, I. B. and Pedersen, T. P., "Convertible undeniable signatures," *Advances in Cryptology - CRYPTO '90*, p. 189. Springer-Verlag, Berlin, 1990.
- Damgård, I. B., "Towards practical public key systems secure against chosen ciphertext attacks," *Advances in Cryptology - CRYPTO '91*, p. 445. Springer-Verlag, Berlin, 1991.
- Damgård, I. B., "Non-interactive circuit based proofs and non-interactive perfect zero-knowledge with preprocessing," *Advances in Cryptology - EUROCRYPT '92*, p. 341. Springer-Verlag, Berlin, 1992.

280

- Chen, L. and Damgård, I. B., "Security bounds for parallel versions of identification protocols," *Advances in Cryptology - EUROCRYPT '92*, p. 461. Springer-Verlag, Berlin, 1992.
- Brandt, J. and Damgård, I. B., "On generation of probable primes by incremental search," *Advances in Cryptology - CRYPTO '92*, p. 358. Springer-Verlag, Berlin, 1992.
- Damgård, I. B., "Practical and provably secure release of a secret and exchange of signatures," *Advances in Cryptology - EUROCRYPT '93*, p. 200. Springer-Verlag, Berlin, 1993.
- Damgård, I. B. and Knudsen, L. R., "The breaking of the AR hash function," *Advances in Cryptology - EUROCRYPT '93*, p. 286. Springer-Verlag, Berlin, 1993.
- Damgård, I. B., "Interactive hashing can simplify zero-knowledge protocol design without computational assumptions," *Advances in Cryptology - CRYPTO '93*, p. 100. Springer-Verlag, Berlin, 1993.
- Damgård, I. B., Pedersen, T. P. and Pfitzmann, B., "On the existence of statistically hiding bit commitment schemes and fail-stop signatures," *Advances in Cryptology - CRYPTO '93*, p. 250. Springer-Verlag, Berlin, 1993.
- Chen, L., Damgård, I. B. and Pedersen, T. P., "Parallel divertibility of proofs of knowledge," *Advances in Cryptology - EUROCRYPT '94*, p. 140. Springer-Verlag, Berlin, 1995.
- Cramer, R., Damgård, I. B. and Schoenmakers, B., "Proofs of partial knowledge and simplified design of witness hiding protocols," *Advances in Cryptology - CRYPTO '94*, p. 174. Springer-Verlag, Berlin, 1994.
- Cramer, R. and Damgård, I. B., "Secure Signature Schemes based on Interactive Protocols," *Advances in Cryptology - CRYPTO '95*, p. 297. Springer-Verlag, Berlin, 1995.
- Damgård, I. B., Goldreich, O., Okamoto, T. and Wigderson, A., "Honest Verifier vs Dishonest Verifier in Public Coin Zero-Knowledge Proofs," *Advances in Cryptology - CRYPTO '95*, p. 325. Springer-Verlag, Berlin, 1995.
- Damgård, I. B. and Pedersen, T. P., "New convertible undeniable signature schemes," *Advances in Cryptology - EUROCRYPT '96*, p. 372. Springer-Verlag, Berlin, 1996.
- Cramer, R. and Damgård, I. B., "New Generation of Secure and Practical RSA-Based Signatures," *Advances in Cryptology - CRYPTO '96*, p. 173. Springer-Verlag, Berlin, 1996.
- Cramer, R. and Damgård, I. B., "Fast and Secure Immunization Against Adaptive Man-in-the-Middle Impersonation," *Advances in Cryptology - EUROCRYPT '97*, p. 75. Springer-Verlag, Berlin, 1997.

Damm, F.

- Damm, F., Heider, F. P. and Wambach, G., "MIMD-factorisation on hypercubes," *Advances in Cryptology - EUROCRYPT '94*, p. 400. Springer-Verlag, Berlin, 1995.

Dancs, F. B.

- Davida, G. I. and Dancs, F. B., "A cryptoengine," *Advances in Cryptology - CRYPTO '87*, p. 257. Springer-Verlag, Berlin, 1987.

Davenport, D. M.

- Brickell, E. F. and Davenport, D. M., "On the classification of ideal secret sharing schemes (extended abstract)," *Advances in Cryptology - CRYPTO '89*, p. 278. Springer-Verlag, Berlin, 1989.

Davida, G. I.

- Davida, G. I. and Yeh, Y. S., "Multilevel Cryptosecure Relational Database," *Abstracts of Papers: EUROCRYPT '86*, p. 50. Department of Electrical Engineering, University of Linköping, Linkoping, Sweden, 1986.
- Davida, G. I. and Walter, G. G., "A public key analog cryptosystem," *Advances in Cryptology - EUROCRYPT '87*, p. 143. Springer-Verlag, Berlin, 1987.
- Davida, G. I. and Matt, B. J., "Arbitration in tamper proof systems. If DES approximately=RSA then what's the difference between true signature and arbitrated signature schemes?," *Advances in Cryptology - CRYPTO '87*, p. 216. Springer-Verlag, Berlin, 1987.
- Davida, G. I. and Dancs, F. B., "A cryptoengine," *Advances in Cryptology - CRYPTO '87*, p. 257. Springer-Verlag, Berlin, 1987.
- Davida, G. I. and Desmedt, Y., "Passports and Visas versus IDs," *Advances in Cryptology - EUROCRYPT '88*, p. 183. Springer-Verlag, Berlin, 1988.
- Davida, G. I., Desmedt, Y. and Peralta, R., "A key distribution system based on any one-way function (extended abstract)," *Advances in Cryptology - EUROCRYPT '89*, p. 75. Springer-Verlag, Berlin, 1989.
- Davida, G. I., Desmedt, Y. and Peralta, R., "On the importance of memory resources in the security of key exchange protocols (extended abstract)," *Advances in Cryptology - EUROCRYPT '90*, p. 11. Springer-Verlag, Berlin, 1990.

Davies, D. W.

- Davies, D. W., "Some Regular Properties of the DES," *Advances in Cryptography*, p. 41. University of California, Santa Barbara, Santa Barbara, California, USA, 1982.
- Davies, D. W. and Parkin, G. I. P., "The average cycle size of the key-stream in output feedback encipherment," *Cryptography - Proceedings of the Workshop on Cryptography, Burg Feuerstein, Germany*, p. 263. Springer-Verlag, Berlin, 1983.
- Davies, D. W., "Some regular properties of the 'Data Encryption Standard' algorithm (Presented at CRYPTO 81)," *Advances in Cryptology: Proceedings of CRYPTO '82*, p. 89. Plenum Publishing, New York, USA, 1982.
- Davies, D. W. and Parkin, G. I. P., "The average cycle size of the key stream in output feedback encipherment (Abstract)," *Advances in Cryptology: Proceedings of CRYPTO '82*, p. 97. Plenum Publishing, New York, USA, 1982.
- Davies, D. W., "Use of the "signature token" to create a negotiable document," *Advances in Cryptology: Proceedings of CRYPTO '83*, p. 377. Plenum Publishing, New York, USA, 1984.
- Davies, D. W., "A message authenticator algorithm suitable for a mainframe computer," *Advances in Cryptology: Proceedings of CRYPTO '84*, p. 393. Springer-Verlag, Berlin, 1985.
- Davies, D. W. and Price, W. L., "Engineering secure information systems.," *Advances in Cryptology - EUROCRYPT '85*, p. 191. Springer-Verlag, Berlin, 1985.

Davio, M.

- Davio, M., Goethals, J. M. and Quisquater, J. J., "Authentication procedures," *Cryptography - Proceedings of the Workshop on Cryptography, Burg Feuerstein, Germany*, p. 283. Springer-Verlag, Berlin, 1983.
- Davio, M., Desmedt, Y., Fosseprez, M., Govaerts, R., Hulsbosch, J., Neutjens, P., Piret, P., Quisquater, J. J., Vandewalle, J. and Wouters, P., "Analytical characteristics of the DES," *Advances in Cryptology: Proceedings of CRYPTO '83*, p. 171. Plenum Publishing, New York, USA, 1984.
- Davio, M., Desmedt, Y. and Quisquater, J. J., "Propagation characteristics of the DES," *Advances in Cryptology: Proceedings of EUROCRYPT '84*, p. 62. Springer-Verlag, Berlin, 1984.
- Davio, M., Desmedt, Y., Goubert, J., Hoornaert, F. and Quisquater, J. J., "Efficient hardware and software implementations for the DES," *Advances in Cryptology: Proceedings of CRYPTO '84*, p. 144. Springer-Verlag, Berlin, 1985.
- Desmedt, Y., Quisquater, J. J. and Davio, M., "Dependence of output on input in DES: small avalanche characteristics," *Advances in Cryptology: Proceedings of CRYPTO '84*, p. 359. Springer-Verlag, Berlin, 1985.

- Quisquater, J. J., Desmedt, Y. and Davio, M., "The importance of "good" key scheduling schemes (how to make a secure DES scheme with < 48 bits keys?)," *Advances in Cryptology - CRYPTO '85*, p. 537. Springer-Verlag, Berlin, 1986.

Davis, D.

- Davis, D., Ihaka, R. and Fenstermacher, P., "Cryptographic randomness from air turbulence in disk drives," *Advances in Cryptology - CRYPTO '94*, p. 114. Springer-Verlag, Berlin, 1994.

Davis, J. A.

- Brickell, E. F., Davis, J. A. and Simmons, G. J., "A preliminary report on the cryptanalysis of Merkle-Hellman knapsack cryptosystems," *Advances in Cryptology: Proceedings of CRYPTO '82*, p. 289. Plenum Publishing, New York, USA, 1982.
- Davis, J. A. and Holdridge, D. B., "Factorization using the Quadratic Sieve algorithm," *Advances in Cryptology: Proceedings of CRYPTO '83*, p. 103. Plenum Publishing, New York, USA, 1984.
- Davis, J. A., Holdridge, D. B. and Simmons, G. J., "Status report on factoring (at the Sandia National Labs)," *Advances in Cryptology: Proceedings of EUROCRYPT '84*, p. 183. Springer-Verlag, Berlin, 1984.
- Davis, J. A. and Holdridge, D. B., "An update on factorization at Sandia National Laboratories," *Advances in Cryptology: Proceedings of CRYPTO '84*, p. 114. Springer-Verlag, Berlin, 1985.
- Davis, J. A. and Holdridge, D. B., "Factorization of large integers on a massively parallel computer," *Advances in Cryptology - EUROCRYPT '88*, p. 235. Springer-Verlag, Berlin, 1988.

Dawson, E.

- Goldburg, B., Dawson, E. and Sridharan, S., "The Automated Cryptanalysis of Analog Speech Scramblers," *Advances in Cryptology - EUROCRYPT '91*, p. 422. Springer-Verlag, Berlin, 1991.

Dawson, M. H.

- Dawson, M. H. and Tavares, S. E., "An expanded set of S-box design criteria based on information theory and its relation to differential-like attacks," *Advances in Cryptology - EUROCRYPT '91*, p. 352. Springer-Verlag, Berlin, 1991.

De Becker, W.

- Vandewalle, J., Govaerts, R., De Becker, W., Decroos, M. and Speybrouck, G., "Implementation study of public key cryptography protection in an existing electronic mail and document handling system.," *Advances in Cryptology - EUROCRYPT '85*, p. 43. Springer-Verlag, Berlin, 1985.

de Jonge, W.

- de Jonge, W. and Chaum, D., "Attacks on some RSA signatures," *Advances in Cryptology - CRYPTO '85*, p. 18. Springer-Verlag, Berlin, 1986.
- de Jonge, W. and Chaum, D., "Some variations on RSA signatures and their security," *Advances in Cryptology - CRYPTO '86*, p. 49. Springer-Verlag, Berlin, 1986.

De Man, H.

- Verbauwhede, I., Hoornaert, F., Vandewalle, J. and De Man, H., "Security considerations in the design and implementation of a new DES chip," *Advances in Cryptology - EUROCRYPT '87*, p. 287. Springer-Verlag, Berlin, 1987.

De Santis, A.

- De Santis, A., Micali, S. and Persiano, G., "Noninteractive zero-knowledge proof systems," *Advances in Cryptology - CRYPTO '87*, p. 52. Springer-Verlag, Berlin, 1987.
- De Santis, A., Micali, S. and Persiano, G., "Non-interactive zero-knowledge with preprocessing," *Advances in Cryptology - CRYPTO '88*, p. 269. Springer-Verlag, Berlin, 1989.
- De Santis, A. and Persiano, G., "Public-randomness in public-key cryptography (extended abstract)," *Advances in Cryptology - EUROCRYPT '90*, p. 46. Springer-Verlag, Berlin, 1990.
- De Santis, A. and Yung, M., "On the design of provably-secure cryptographic hash functions," *Advances in Cryptology - EUROCRYPT '90*, p. 412. Springer-Verlag, Berlin, 1990.
- De Santis, A. and Yung, M., "Cryptographic applications of the non-interactive metaproof and many-prover systems (Preliminary version)," *Advances in Cryptology - CRYPTO '90*, p. 366. Springer-Verlag, Berlin, 1990.
- Capocelli, R. M., De Santis, A., Gargano, L. and Vaccaro, U., "On the size of shares for secret sharing schemes," *Advances in Cryptology - CRYPTO '91*, p. 101. Springer-Verlag, Berlin, 1991.
- Blundo, C., De Santis, A., Stinson, D. R. and Vaccaro, U., "Graph decompositions and secret sharing schemes," *Advances in Cryptology - EUROCRYPT '92*, p. 1. Springer-Verlag, Berlin, 1992.
- Blundo, C., De Santis, A., Gargano, L. and Vaccaro, U., "On the information rate of secret sharing schemes," *Advances in Cryptology - CRYPTO '92*, p. 148. Springer-Verlag, Berlin, 1992.
- Blundo, C., De Santis, A., Herzberg, A., Kutten, S., Vaccaro, U. and Yung, M., "Perfectly-secure key distribution for dynamic conferences," *Advances in Cryptology - CRYPTO '92*, p. 471. Springer-Verlag, Berlin, 1992.
- Carpentieri, M., De Santis, A. and Vaccaro, U., "Size of shares and probability of cheating in threshold schemes," *Advances in Cryptology - EUROCRYPT '93*, p. 118. Springer-Verlag, Berlin, 1993.

- De Santis, A., Di Crescenzo, G. and Persiano, G., "Secret sharing and perfect zero-knowledge," *Advances in Cryptology - CRYPTO '93*, p. 73. Springer-Verlag, Berlin, 1993.
- Blundo, C., Cresti, A., De Santis, A. and Vaccaro, U., "Fully dynamic secret sharing schemes," *Advances in Cryptology - CRYPTO '93*, p. 110. Springer-Verlag, Berlin, 1993.
- Blundo, C., De Santis, A., Di Crescenzo, G., Gaggia, A. Giorgio and Vaccaro, U., "Multi-secret sharing schemes," *Advances in Cryptology - CRYPTO '94*, p. 150. Springer-Verlag, Berlin, 1994.

De Soete, M.

- De Soete, M., "Some constructions for authentication-secrecy codes," *Advances in Cryptology - EUROCRYPT '88*, p. 57. Springer-Verlag, Berlin, 1988.
- De Soete, M. and Vedder, K., "Some new classes of geometric threshold schemes," *Advances in Cryptology - EUROCRYPT '88*, p. 389. Springer-Verlag, Berlin, 1988.
- De Soete, M., "Bounds and Constructions for Authentication-Secrecy Codes with Splitting," *Advances in Cryptology - CRYPTO '88*, p. 311. Springer-Verlag, Berlin, 1989.
- De Soete, M., Vedder, K. and Walker, M., "Cartesian authentication schemes," *Advances in Cryptology - EUROCRYPT '89*, p. 476. Springer-Verlag, Berlin, 1989.
- De Soete, M., Quisquater, J. J. and Vedder, K., "A signature with shared verification scheme," *Advances in Cryptology - CRYPTO '89*, p. 253. Springer-Verlag, Berlin, 1989.

De Waleffe, D.

- De Waleffe, D. and Quisquater, J. J., "CORSAIR: A smart card for public key cryptosystems," *Advances in Cryptology - CRYPTO '90*, p. 502. Springer-Verlag, Berlin, 1990.

Decroos, M.

- Vandewalle, J., Govaerts, R., De Becker, W., Decroos, M. and Speybrouck, G., "Implementation study of public key cryptography protection in an existing electronic mail and document handling system.," *Advances in Cryptology - EUROCRYPT '85*, p. 43. Springer-Verlag, Berlin, 1985.
- Hoornaert, F., Decroos, M., Vandewalle, J. and Govaerts, R., "Fast RSA-hardware: dream or reality," *Advances in Cryptology - EUROCRYPT '88*, p. 257. Springer-Verlag, Berlin, 1988.

DeLaurentis, J. M.

- Brickell, E. F. and DeLaurentis, J. M., "An attack on a signature scheme proposed by Okamoto and Shiraishi," *Advances in Cryptology - CRYPTO '85*, p. 28. Springer-Verlag, Berlin, 1986.
- DeLaurentis, J. M., "Components and cycles of a random function," *Advances in Cryptology - CRYPTO '87*, p. 231. Springer-Verlag, Berlin, 1987.

Delescaille, J. P.

- Quisquater, J. J. and Delescaille, J. P., "Other cycling tests for DES," *Advances in Cryptology - CRYPTO '87*, p. 255. Springer-Verlag, Berlin, 1987.
- Quisquater, J. J. and Delescaille, J. P., "How easy is collision search? Application to DES," *Advances in Cryptology - EUROCRYPT '89*, p. 429. Springer-Verlag, Berlin, 1989.
- Quisquater, J. J. and Delescaille, J. P., "How easy is collision search. New results and applications to DES," *Advances in Cryptology - CRYPTO '89*, p. 408. Springer-Verlag, Berlin, 1989.

Delos, O.

- Delos, O. and Quisquater, J. J., "An identity-based signature scheme with bounded life-span," *Advances in Cryptology - CRYPTO '94*, p. 83. Springer-Verlag, Berlin, 1994.

Delsarte, P.

- Desmedt, Y., Delsarte, P., Odlyzko, A. M. and Piret, P., "Fast cryptanalysis of the Matsumoto-Imai public key scheme," *Advances in Cryptology: Proceedings of EUROCRYPT '84*, p. 142. Springer-Verlag, Berlin, 1984.

DeMarrais, J.

- Adleman, L. M. and DeMarrais, J., "A subexponential algorithm for discrete logarithms over all finite fields," *Advances in Cryptology - CRYPTO '93*, p. 147. Springer-Verlag, Berlin, 1993.

DeMillo, R. A.

- Boneh, D., DeMillo, R. A. and Lipton, R. J., "On the Importance of Checking Cryptographic Protocols for Faults (Extended Abstract)," *Advances in Cryptology - EUROCRYPT '97*, p. 37. Springer-Verlag, Berlin, 1997.

Demytko, N.

- Demytko, N., "A new elliptic curve based analogue of RSA," *Advances in Cryptology - EUROCRYPT '93*, p. 40. Springer-Verlag, Berlin, 1993.

den Boer, B.

- den Boer, B., "Cryptanalysis of F.E.A.L.," *Advances in Cryptology - EUROCRYPT '88*, p. 293. Springer-Verlag, Berlin, 1988.
- den Boer, B., "Diffie-Hellman is as strong as discrete log for certain primes," *Advances in Cryptology - CRYPTO '88*, p. 530. Springer-Verlag, Berlin, 1989.
- den Boer, B., "More efficient match-making and satisfiability," *Advances in Cryptology - EUROCRYPT '89*, p. 208. Springer-Verlag, Berlin, 1989.
- Chaum, D., den Boer, B., van Heyst, E., Mjoelsnes, S. F. and Steenbeek, A., "Efficient offline electronic checks (extended abstract)," *Advances in Cryptology - EUROCRYPT '89*, p. 294. Springer-Verlag, Berlin, 1989.
- Bos, J. N. E. and den Boer, B., "Detection of disrupters in the DC protocol," *Advances in Cryptology - EUROCRYPT '89*, p. 320. Springer-Verlag, Berlin, 1989.
- den Boer, B., "Oblivious transfer protecting secrecy," *Advances in Cryptology - EUROCRYPT '90*, p. 31. Springer-Verlag, Berlin, 1990.
- den Boer, B. and Bosselaers, A., "An attack on the last two rounds of MD4," *Advances in Cryptology - CRYPTO '91*, p. 194. Springer-Verlag, Berlin, 1991.
- den Boer, B. and Bosselaers, A., "Collisions for the compression function of MD-5," *Advances in Cryptology - EUROCRYPT '93*, p. 293. Springer-Verlag, Berlin, 1993.

Denayer, T.

- Vandemeulebroecke, A., Vanzieleghem, E., Jespers, P. G. A. and Denayer, T., "A single chip 1024 bits RSA processor," *Advances in Cryptology - EUROCRYPT '89*, p. 219. Springer-Verlag, Berlin, 1989.

Denning, D. E.

- Denning, D. E., "Field encryption and authentication.," *Advances in Cryptology: Proceedings of CRYPTO '83*, p. 231. Plenum Publishing, New York, USA, 1984.

Denny, T.

- Denny, T., Dodson, B., Lenstra, A. K. and Manasse, M. S., "On the factorization of RSA-120," *Advances in Cryptology - CRYPTO '93*, p. 166. Springer-Verlag, Berlin, 1993.

Dertouzos, M. L.

- Diffie, W., Klein, M., Dertouzos, M. L., Gleason, A. and Smith, D., "Panel Discussion: National Security and Commercial Security: Division of Responsibility," *Advances in Cryptography*, p. 154. University of California, Santa Barbara, Santa Barbara, California, USA, 1982.

Desmedt, Y.

- Davio, M., Desmedt, Y., Fosseprez, M., Govaerts, R., Hulsbosch, J., Neutjens, P., Piret, P., Quisquater, J. J., Vandewalle, J. and Wouters, P., "Analytical characteristics of the DES," *Advances in Cryptology: Proceedings of CRYPTO '83*, p. 171. Plenum Publishing, New York, USA, 1984.
- Davio, M., Desmedt, Y. and Quisquater, J. J., "Propagation characteristics of the DES," *Advances in Cryptology: Proceedings of EUROCRYPT '84*, p. 62. Springer-Verlag, Berlin, 1984.
- Desmedt, Y., Delsarte, P., Odlyzko, A. M. and Piret, P., "Fast cryptanalysis of the Matsumoto-Imai public key scheme," *Advances in Cryptology: Proceedings of EUROCRYPT '84*, p. 142. Springer-Verlag, Berlin, 1984.
- Davio, M., Desmedt, Y., Goubert, J., Hoornaert, F. and Quisquater, J. J., "Efficient hardware and software implementations for the DES," *Advances in Cryptology: Proceedings of CRYPTO '84*, p. 144. Springer-Verlag, Berlin, 1985.
- Hoornaert, F., Goubert, J. and Desmedt, Y., "Efficient hardware implementation of the DES," *Advances in Cryptology: Proceedings of CRYPTO '84*, p. 147. Springer-Verlag, Berlin, 1985.
- Desmedt, Y., Quisquater, J. J. and Davio, M., "Dependence of output on input in DES: small avalanche characteristics," *Advances in Cryptology: Proceedings of CRYPTO '84*, p. 359. Springer-Verlag, Berlin, 1985.
- Desmedt, Y., "Unconditionally secure authentication schemes and practical and theoretical consequences," *Advances in Cryptology - CRYPTO '85*, p. 42. Springer-Verlag, Berlin, 1986.
- Desmedt, Y. and Odlyzko, A. M., "A chosen text attack on the RSA cryptosystem and some discrete logarithm schemes," *Advances in Cryptology - CRYPTO '85*, p. 516. Springer-Verlag, Berlin, 1986.
- Quisquater, J. J., Desmedt, Y. and Davio, M., "The importance of "good" key scheduling schemes (how to make a secure DES scheme with < 48 bits keys?)," *Advances in Cryptology - CRYPTO '85*, p. 537. Springer-Verlag, Berlin, 1986.
- Desmedt, Y., Hoornaert, F. and Quisquater, J. J., "Several Exhaustive Key Search Machines and DES," *Abstracts of Papers: EUROCRYPT '86*, p. 17. Department of Electrical Engineering, University of Linköping, Linkoping, Sweden, 1986.
- Desmedt, Y. and Quisquater, J. J., "Public-key systems based on the difficulty of tampering (Is there a difference between DES and RSA?)," *Advances in Cryptology - CRYPTO '86*, p. 111. Springer-Verlag, Berlin, 1986.
- Desmedt, Y., "Is there an ultimate use of cryptography?," *Advances in Cryptology - CRYPTO '86*, p. 459. Springer-Verlag, Berlin, 1986.
- Desmedt, Y., Goutier, C. and Bengio, S., "Special uses and abuses of the Fiat Shamir passport protocol," *Advances in Cryptology - CRYPTO '87*, p. 21. Springer-Verlag, Berlin, 1987.

- Desmedt, Y., "Society and group oriented cryptography: a new concept," *Advances in Cryptology - CRYPTO '87*, p. 120. Springer-Verlag, Berlin, 1987.
- Desmedt, Y., "Subliminal-free authentication and signature," *Advances in Cryptology - EUROCRYPT '88*, p. 23. Springer-Verlag, Berlin, 1988.
- Davida, G. I. and Desmedt, Y., "Passports and Visas versus IDs," *Advances in Cryptology - EUROCRYPT '88*, p. 183. Springer-Verlag, Berlin, 1988.
- Desmedt, Y., "Abuses in cryptography and how to fight them," *Advances in Cryptology - CRYPTO '88*, p. 375. Springer-Verlag, Berlin, 1989.
- Davida, G. I., Desmedt, Y. and Peralta, R., "A key distribution system based on any one-way function (extended abstract)," *Advances in Cryptology - EUROCRYPT '89*, p. 75. Springer-Verlag, Berlin, 1989.
- Burmester, M. V. D., Desmedt, Y., Piper, F. and Walker, M., "A general zero-knowledge scheme," *Advances in Cryptology - EUROCRYPT '89*, p. 122. Springer-Verlag, Berlin, 1989.
- Desmedt, Y., "Making conditionally secure cryptosystems unconditionally abuse-free in a general context," *Advances in Cryptology - CRYPTO '89*, p. 6. Springer-Verlag, Berlin, 1989.
- Desmedt, Y. and Frankel, Y., "Threshold cryptosystems," *Advances in Cryptology - CRYPTO '89*, p. 307. Springer-Verlag, Berlin, 1989.
- Burmester, M. V. D. and Desmedt, Y., "All languages in NP have divertible zero-knowledge proofs and arguments under cryptographic assumptions (extended abstract)," *Advances in Cryptology - EUROCRYPT '90*, p. 1. Springer-Verlag, Berlin, 1990.
- Davida, G. I., Desmedt, Y. and Peralta, R., "On the importance of memory resources in the security of key exchange protocols (extended abstract)," *Advances in Cryptology - EUROCRYPT '90*, p. 11. Springer-Verlag, Berlin, 1990.
- Beth, T. and Desmedt, Y., "Identification tokens – or: Solving the chess grandmaster problem," *Advances in Cryptology - CRYPTO '90*, p. 169. Springer-Verlag, Berlin, 1990.
- Desmedt, Y. and Yung, M., "Arbitrated unconditionally secure authentication can be unconditionally protected against arbiter's attacks (Extended abstract)," *Advances in Cryptology - CRYPTO '90*, p. 177. Springer-Verlag, Berlin, 1990.
- Burmester, M. V. D. and Desmedt, Y., "Broadcast interactive proofs," *Advances in Cryptology - EUROCRYPT '91*, p. 81. Springer-Verlag, Berlin, 1991.
- Desmedt, Y. and Yung, M., "Weaknesses of undeniable signature schemes," *Advances in Cryptology - EUROCRYPT '91*, p. 205. Springer-Verlag, Berlin, 1991.
- Desmedt, Y. and Frankel, Y., "Shared generation of authenticators and signatures," *Advances in Cryptology - CRYPTO '91*, p. 457. Springer-Verlag, Berlin, 1991.

- Frankel, Y. and Desmedt, Y., "Classification of ideal homomorphic threshold schemes over finite Abelian groups (Extended abstract)," *Advances in Cryptology - EUROCRYPT '92*, p. 25. Springer-Verlag, Berlin, 1992.
- Desmedt, Y., Landrock, P., Lenstra, A. K., McCurley, K. S., Odlyzko, A. M., Rueppel, R. A. and Smid, M. E., "The Eurocrypt '92 Controversial Issue: Trapdoor Primes and Moduli," *Advances in Cryptology - EUROCRYPT '92*, p. 194. Springer-Verlag, Berlin, 1992.
- Frankel, Y., Desmedt, Y. and Burmester, M. V. D., "Non-existence of homomorphic general sharing schemes for some key spaces," *Advances in Cryptology - CRYPTO '92*, p. 549. Springer-Verlag, Berlin, 1992.
- Burmester, M. V. D. and Desmedt, Y., "A secure and efficient conference key distribution system," *Advances in Cryptology - EUROCRYPT '94*, p. 275. Springer-Verlag, Berlin, 1995.
- Desmedt, Y., "Securing traceability of ciphertexts - Towards a secure software key escrow system," *Advances in Cryptology - EUROCRYPT '95*, p. 147. Springer-Verlag, Berlin, 1995.
- Blackburn, S. R., Burmester, M. V. D., Desmedt, Y. and Wild, R. P., "Efficient multiplicative sharing schemes," *Advances in Cryptology - EUROCRYPT '96*, p. 107. Springer-Verlag, Berlin, 1996.

Di Crescenzo, G.

- De Santis, A., Di Crescenzo, G. and Persiano, G., "Secret sharing and perfect zero-knowledge," *Advances in Cryptology - CRYPTO '93*, p. 73. Springer-Verlag, Berlin, 1993.
- D'Amiano, S. and Di Crescenzo, G., "Methodology for digital money based on general cryptographic tools," *Advances in Cryptology - EUROCRYPT '94*, p. 156. Springer-Verlag, Berlin, 1995.
- Blundo, C., De Santis, A., Di Crescenzo, G., Gaggia, A. Giorgio and Vaccaro, U., "Multi-secret sharing schemes," *Advances in Cryptology - CRYPTO '94*, p. 150. Springer-Verlag, Berlin, 1994.
- Di Crescenzo, G., "Recycling random bits in composed perfect zero-knowledge," *Advances in Cryptology - EUROCRYPT '95*, p. 367. Springer-Verlag, Berlin, 1995.
- D'Amiano, S. and Di Crescenzo, G., "Anonymous NIZK proofs of knowledge with preprocessing," *Advances in Cryptology - EUROCRYPT '95*, p. 413. Springer-Verlag, Berlin, 1995.
- Di Crescenzo, G., Okamoto, T. and Yung, M., "Keeping the SZK-Verifier Honest Unconditionally," *Advances in Cryptology - CRYPTO '97*, p. 31. Springer-Verlag, Berlin, 1997.

Di Porto, A.

- Di Porto, A. and Filipponi, P., "A probabilistic primality test based on the properties of certain generalized Lucas numbers," *Advances in Cryptology - EUROCRYPT '88*, p. 211. Springer-Verlag, Berlin, 1988.

Dial, G.

- Dial, G. and Pessoa, F., "Sharma-Mittal Entropy and Shannon's Random Cipher Result," *Abstracts of Papers: EUROCRYPT '86*, p. 28. Department of Electrical Engineering, University of Linköping, Linkoping, Sweden, 1986.

Dietel, A.

- Sauerbrey, J. and Dietel, A., "Resource requirements for the application of addition chains in modulo exponentiation," *Advances in Cryptology - EUROCRYPT '92*, p. 174. Springer-Verlag, Berlin, 1992.

Diffie, W.

- Diffie, W., Klein, M., Dertouzos, M. L., Gleason, A. and Smith, D., "Panel Discussion: National Security and Commercial Security: Division of Responsibility," *Advances in Cryptography*, p. 154. University of California, Santa Barbara, Santa Barbara, California, USA, 1982.
- Diffie, W., "Security for the DoD transmission control protocol," *Advances in Cryptology - CRYPTO '85*, p. 108. Springer-Verlag, Berlin, 1986.
- Fell, H. and Diffie, W., "Analysis of a public key approach based on polynomial substitution," *Advances in Cryptology - CRYPTO '85*, p. 340. Springer-Verlag, Berlin, 1986.
- Steer, D. G., Strawczynski, L., Diffie, W. and Wiener, M. J., "A secure audio teleconference system," *Advances in Cryptology - CRYPTO '88*, p. 520. Springer-Verlag, Berlin, 1989.
- Diffie, W., "The adolescence of public-key cryptography (invited)," *Advances in Cryptology - EUROCRYPT '89*, p. 2. Springer-Verlag, Berlin, 1989.

Dijk, M. van

- Dijk, M. van, "A linear construction of perfect secret sharing schemes," *Advances in Cryptology - EUROCRYPT '94*, p. 23. Springer-Verlag, Berlin, 1995.

Ding, C.

- Ding, C., "Proof of Massey's conjectured algorithm," *Advances in Cryptology - EUROCRYPT '88*, p. 345. Springer-Verlag, Berlin, 1988.
- Beth, T. and Ding, C., "On almost perfect nonlinear permutations," *Advances in Cryptology - EUROCRYPT '93*, p. 65. Springer-Verlag, Berlin, 1993.

Dixon, B.

- Dixon, B. and Lenstra, A. K., "Massively parallel elliptic curve factoring," *Advances in Cryptology - EUROCRYPT '92*, p. 183. Springer-Verlag, Berlin, 1992.
- Dixon, B. and Lenstra, A. K., "Factoring integers using SIMD sieves," *Advances in Cryptology - EUROCRYPT '93*, p. 28. Springer-Verlag, Berlin, 1993.

Dixon, R. D.

- Blakley, G. R. and Dixon, R. D., "Smallest possible message expansion in threshold schemes," *Advances in Cryptology - CRYPTO '86*, p. 266. Springer-Verlag, Berlin, 1986.

Dlay, S. S.

- Gorgui-Naguib, R. N. and Dlay, S. S., "Properties of the Euler totient function modulo 24 and some of its cryptographic implications," *Advances in Cryptology - EUROCRYPT '88*, p. 267. Springer-Verlag, Berlin, 1988.

Dodson, B.

- Denny, T., Dodson, B., Lenstra, A. K. and Manasse, M. S., "On the factorization of RSA-120," *Advances in Cryptology - CRYPTO '93*, p. 166. Springer-Verlag, Berlin, 1993.
- Dodson, B. and Lenstra, A. K., "NFS with Four Large Primes: An Explosive Experiment," *Advances in Cryptology - CRYPTO '95*, p. 372. Springer-Verlag, Berlin, 1995.

Dolev, D.

- Dolev, D. and Wigderson, A., "On the security of multi-party protocols in distributed systems," *Advances in Cryptology: Proceedings of CRYPTO '82*, p. 167. Plenum Publishing, New York, USA, 1982.
- Dolev, D., Even, S. and Karp, R. M., "On the security of ping-pong protocols (Extended abstract)," *Advances in Cryptology: Proceedings of CRYPTO '82*, p. 177. Plenum Publishing, New York, USA, 1982.

Dolev, S.

- Dolev, S. and Ostrovsky, R., "Efficient Anonymous Multicast and Reception," *Advances in Cryptology - CRYPTO '97*, p. 395. Springer-Verlag, Berlin, 1997.

Domingo-Ferrer, J.

- Domingo-Ferrer, J. and Huguet i Rotger, L., "Full secure key exchange and authentication with no previously shared secrets," *Advances in Cryptology - EUROCRYPT '89*, p. 665. Springer-Verlag, Berlin, 1989.
- Domingo-Ferrer, J., "Software run-time protection: A cryptographic issue," *Advances in Cryptology - EUROCRYPT '90*, p. 474. Springer-Verlag, Berlin, 1990.
- Domingo-Ferrer, J., "Un transferable rights in a client-independent server environment," *Advances in Cryptology - EUROCRYPT '93*, p. 260. Springer-Verlag, Berlin, 1993.

Droste, S.

- Droste, S., "New Results on Visual Cryptography," *Advances in Cryptology - CRYPTO '96*, p. 401. Springer-Verlag, Berlin, 1996.

Duellmann, S.

- Buchmann, J. A., Duellmann, S. and Williams, H. C., "On the complexity and efficiency of a new key exchange system," *Advances in Cryptology - EUROCRYPT '89*, p. 597. Springer-Verlag, Berlin, 1989.
- Buchmann, J. A. and Duellmann, S., "On the computation of discrete logarithms in class groups (Extended abstract)," *Advances in Cryptology - CRYPTO '90*, p. 134. Springer-Verlag, Berlin, 1990.

Duhoux, Y.

- Duhoux, Y., "Deciphering bronze age scripts of Crete. The case of Linear A (invited)," *Advances in Cryptology - EUROCRYPT '89*, p. 649. Springer-Verlag, Berlin, 1989.

Dunham, J. George

- Chuang, Chih-Chwen and Dunham, J. George, "Matrix extensions of the RSA algorithm," *Advances in Cryptology - CRYPTO '90*, p. 140. Springer-Verlag, Berlin, 1990.

Dusse, S. R.

- Dusse, S. R. and Kaliski, B. S., "A cryptographic library for the Motorola DSP 56000," *Advances in Cryptology - EUROCRYPT '90*, p. 230. Springer-Verlag, Berlin, 1990.

Dwork, C.

- Dwork, C. and Stockmeyer, L., "Zero-knowledge with finite state verifiers (invited talk)," *Advances in Cryptology - CRYPTO '88*, p. 71. Springer-Verlag, Berlin, 1989.
- Dwork, C., "On verification in secret sharing," *Advances in Cryptology - CRYPTO '91*, p. 114. Springer-Verlag, Berlin, 1991.
- Dwork, C. and Naor, M., "Pricing via processing or combatting junk mail," *Advances in Cryptology - CRYPTO '92*, p. 139. Springer-Verlag, Berlin, 1992.
- Dwork, C., Feige, U., Kilian, J., Naor, M. and Safra, M., "Low communication 2-prover zero-knowledge proofs for NP," *Advances in Cryptology - CRYPTO '92*, p. 215. Springer-Verlag, Berlin, 1992.
- Dwork, C. and Naor, M., "An efficient existentially unforgeable signature scheme and its applications," *Advances in Cryptology - CRYPTO '94*, p. 234. Springer-Verlag, Berlin, 1994.
- Canetti, R., Dwork, C., Naor, M. and Ostrovsky, R., "Deniable Encryption," *Advances in Cryptology - CRYPTO '97*, p. 90. Springer-Verlag, Berlin, 1997.

Eberle, H.

- Eberle, H., "A high-speed DES implementation for network applications," *Advances in Cryptology - CRYPTO '92*, p. 521. Springer-Verlag, Berlin, 1992.

Ecker, A.

- Ecker, A., "Finite semigroups and the RSA-cryptosystem," *Cryptography - Proceedings of the Workshop on Cryptography, Burg Feuerstein, Germany,* p. 353. Springer-Verlag, Berlin, 1983.
- Ecker, A., "Time-division multiplexing scramblers: selecting permutations and testing the systems," *Advances in Cryptology: Proceedings of EURO-CRYPT '84,* p. 399. Springer-Verlag, Berlin, 1984.
- Ecker, A., "Tactical Configurations and Threshold Schemes," *Abstracts of Papers: EUROCRYPT '86,* p. 47. Department of Electrical Engineering, University of Linköping, Linkoping, Sweden, 1986.

Eichinger, B. O.

- Kowatsch, M., Eichinger, B. O. and Seifert, F. J., "Message protection by spread spectrum modulation in a packet voice radio link.," *Advances in Cryptology - EUROCRYPT '85,* p. 273. Springer-Verlag, Berlin, 1985.

Eier, R.

- Eier, R. and Lagger, H., "Trapdoors in knapsack cryptosystems," *Cryptography - Proceedings of the Workshop on Cryptography, Burg Feuerstein, Germany,* p. 316. Springer-Verlag, Berlin, 1983.

Eisele, R.

- Barrett, P. and Eisele, R., "The smart diskette – A universal user token and personal crypto-engine," *Advances in Cryptology - CRYPTO '89,* p. 74. Springer-Verlag, Berlin, 1989.

Eisfeld, J.

- Schwenk, J. and Eisfeld, J., "Public key encryption and signature schemes based on polynominals over Z_n," *Advances in Cryptology - EUROCRYPT '96,* p. 60. Springer-Verlag, Berlin, 1996.

ElGamal, T.

- ElGamal, T., "A subexponential time algorithm for computing discrete logarithms over $GF(p^2)$," *Advances in Cryptology: Proceedings of CRYPTO '83,* p. 275. Plenum Publishing, New York, USA, 1984.
- ElGamal, T., "A public key cryptosystem and a signature scheme based on discrete logarithms," *Advances in Cryptology: Proceedings of CRYPTO '84,* p. 10. Springer-Verlag, Berlin, 1985.
- ElGamal, T., "On computing logarithms over finite fields," *Advances in Cryptology - CRYPTO '85,* p. 396. Springer-Verlag, Berlin, 1986.

Eloy, M.

- Antoine, M., Brakeland, Jean-Franc, Eloy, M. and Poullet, Y., "Legal requirements facing new signature technology (invited)," *Advances in Cryptology - EUROCRYPT '89,* p. 273. Springer-Verlag, Berlin, 1989.

Eng, T.

- Eng, T. and Okamoto, T., "Single-term divisible electronic coins," *Advances in Cryptology - EUROCRYPT '94*, p. 306. Springer-Verlag, Berlin, 1995.

Estes, D.

- Estes, D., Adleman, L. M., Kompella, K., McCurley, K. S. and Miller, G. L., "Breaking the Ong-Schnorr-Shamir signature scheme for quadratic number fields," *Advances in Cryptology - CRYPTO '85*, p. 3. Springer-Verlag, Berlin, 1986.

Even, S.

- Even, S., "Protocol for Signing Contracts," *Advances in Cryptography*, p. 148. University of California, Santa Barbara, Santa Barbara, California, USA, 1982.
- Dolev, D., Even, S. and Karp, R. M., "On the security of ping-pong protocols (Extended abstract)," *Advances in Cryptology: Proceedings of CRYPTO '82*, p. 177. Plenum Publishing, New York, USA, 1982.
- Even, S., Goldreich, O. and Lempel, A., "A randomized protocol for signing contracts (Extended abstract)," *Advances in Cryptology: Proceedings of CRYPTO '82*, p. 205. Plenum Publishing, New York, USA, 1982.
- Even, S. and Goldreich, O., "On the security of multi-party ping-pong protocols (Abstract)," *Advances in Cryptology: Proceedings of CRYPTO '82*, p. 315. Plenum Publishing, New York, USA, 1982.
- Even, S. and Goldreich, O., "On the power of cascade ciphers," *Advances in Cryptology: Proceedings of CRYPTO '83*, p. 43. Plenum Publishing, New York, USA, 1984.
- Even, S. and Goldreich, O., "Electronic wallet," *Advances in Cryptology: Proceedings of CRYPTO '83*, p. 383. Plenum Publishing, New York, USA, 1984.
- Even, S., Goldreich, O. and Shamir, A., "On the security of ping-pong protocols when implemented using the RSA," *Advances in Cryptology - CRYPTO '85*, p. 58. Springer-Verlag, Berlin, 1986.
- Even, S., Goldreich, O. and Micali, S., "On-line/off-line digital signatures," *Advances in Cryptology - CRYPTO '89*, p. 263. Springer-Verlag, Berlin, 1989.
- Even, S., "Systolic modular multiplication," *Advances in Cryptology - CRYPTO '90*, p. 619. Springer-Verlag, Berlin, 1990.

Evertse, J. H.

- Chaum, D. and Evertse, J. H., "Cryptanalysis of DES with a reduced number of rounds," *Advances in Cryptology - CRYPTO '85*, p. 192. Springer-Verlag, Berlin, 1986.
- Chaum, D. and Evertse, J. H., "A secure and privacy-protecting protocol for transmitting personal information between organizations," *Advances in Cryptology - CRYPTO '86*, p. 118. Springer-Verlag, Berlin, 1986.
- Chaum, D., Evertse, J. H., van de Graaf, J. and Peralta, R., "Demonstrating possession of a discrete logarithm without revealing it," *Advances in Cryptology - CRYPTO '86*, p. 200. Springer-Verlag, Berlin, 1986.
- Chaum, D., Evertse, J. H. and van de Graaf, J., "An improved protocol for demonstrating possession of discrete logarithms and some generalizations," *Advances in Cryptology - EUROCRYPT '87*, p. 127. Springer-Verlag, Berlin, 1987.
- Evertse, J. H., "Linear structures in block ciphers," *Advances in Cryptology - EUROCRYPT '87*, p. 249. Springer-Verlag, Berlin, 1987.
- Evertse, J. H. and van Heyst, E., "Which new RSA signatures can be computed from some given RSA signatures? (extended abstract)," *Advances in Cryptology - EUROCRYPT '90*, p. 83. Springer-Verlag, Berlin, 1990.
- Evertse, J. H. and Heyst, E. van, "Which new RSA signatures can be computed from RSA signatures, obtained in a specific interactive protocol?," *Advances in Cryptology - EUROCRYPT '92*, p. 378. Springer-Verlag, Berlin, 1992.

Fairfield, R. C.

- Fairfield, R. C., Matusevich, A and Plany, J, "An LSI digital encryption processor (DEP)," *Advances in Cryptology: Proceedings of CRYPTO '84*, p. 115. Springer-Verlag, Berlin, 1985.
- Fairfield, R. C., Mortenson, R. L. and Coulthart, K. B., "An LSI random number generator (RNG)," *Advances in Cryptology: Proceedings of CRYPTO '84*, p. 203. Springer-Verlag, Berlin, 1985.

Fam, B. W.

- Fam, B. W., "Improving the security of exponential key exchange," *Advances in Cryptology: Proceedings of CRYPTO '83*, p. 359. Plenum Publishing, New York, USA, 1984.

Feige, U.

- Feige, U., Shamir, A. and Tennenholtz, M., "The noisy oracle problem," *Advances in Cryptology - CRYPTO '88*, p. 284. Springer-Verlag, Berlin, 1989.
- Feige, U. and Shamir, A., "Zero knowledge proofs of knowledge in two rounds," *Advances in Cryptology - CRYPTO '89*, p. 526. Springer-Verlag, Berlin, 1989.
- Dwork, C., Feige, U., Kilian, J., Naor, M. and Safra, M., "Low communication 2-prover zero-knowledge proofs for NP," *Advances in Cryptology - CRYPTO '92*, p. 215. Springer-Verlag, Berlin, 1992.
- Aumann, Y. and Feige, U., "One message proof systems with known space verifiers," *Advances in Cryptology - CRYPTO '93*, p. 85. Springer-Verlag, Berlin, 1993.

Feigenbaum, J.

- Feigenbaum, J., "Encrypting problem instances: Or ... can you take advantage of someone without having to trust him?," *Advances in Cryptology - CRYPTO '85*, p. 477. Springer-Verlag, Berlin, 1986.
- Abadi, M., Allender, E., Broder, A., Feigenbaum, J. and Hemachandra, L. A., "On generating solved instances of computational problems," *Advances in Cryptology - CRYPTO '88*, p. 297. Springer-Verlag, Berlin, 1989.
- Beaver, D., Feigenbaum, J., Kilian, J. and Rogaway, P., "Security with low communication overhead (Extended abstract)," *Advances in Cryptology - CRYPTO '90*, p. 62. Springer-Verlag, Berlin, 1990.
- Beaver, D., Feigenbaum, J. and Shoup, V., "Hiding instances in zero-knowledge proof systems (Extended abstract)," *Advances in Cryptology - CRYPTO '90*, p. 326. Springer-Verlag, Berlin, 1990.

Feldman, F. A.

- Feldman, F. A., "Fast spectral tests for measuring nonrandomness and the DES," *Advances in Cryptology - CRYPTO '87*, p. 243. Springer-Verlag, Berlin, 1987.

Feldman, P.

- Blum, M., Feldman, P. and Micali, S., "Proving security against chosen cyphertext attacks," *Advances in Cryptology - CRYPTO '88*, p. 256. Springer-Verlag, Berlin, 1989.

Feldmeier, D. C.

- Feldmeier, D. C. and Karn, P. R., "UNIX password security—ten years later (invited)," *Advances in Cryptology - CRYPTO '89*, p. 44. Springer-Verlag, Berlin, 1989.

Fell, H.

- Fell, H. and Diffie, W., "Analysis of a public key approach based on polynomial substitution," *Advances in Cryptology - CRYPTO '85*, p. 340. Springer-Verlag, Berlin, 1986.

Fellows, M.

- Fellows, M. and Koblitz, N., "Kid Krypto," *Advances in Cryptology - CRYPTO '92*, p. 371. Springer-Verlag, Berlin, 1992.

Fenstermacher, P.

- Davis, D., Ihaka, R. and Fenstermacher, P., "Cryptographic randomness from air turbulence in disk drives," *Advances in Cryptology - CRYPTO '94*, p. 114. Springer-Verlag, Berlin, 1994.

Ferguson, N.

- Ferguson, N., "Single term off-line coins," *Advances in Cryptology - EUROCRYPT '93*, p. 318. Springer-Verlag, Berlin, 1993.
- Ferguson, N., "Extensions of single-term coins," *Advances in Cryptology - CRYPTO '93*, p. 292. Springer-Verlag, Berlin, 1993.

Fiat, A.

- Fiat, A. and Shamir, A., "How to prove yourself: practical solutions to identification and signature problems," *Advances in Cryptology - CRYPTO '86*, p. 186. Springer-Verlag, Berlin, 1986.
- Chaum, D., Fiat, A. and Naor, M., "Untraceable electronic cash," *Advances in Cryptology - CRYPTO '88*, p. 319. Springer-Verlag, Berlin, 1989.
- Fiat, A., "Batch RSA," *Advances in Cryptology - CRYPTO '89*, p. 175. Springer-Verlag, Berlin, 1989.
- Fiat, A. and Naor, M., "Broadcast encryption," *Advances in Cryptology - CRYPTO '93*, p. 480. Springer-Verlag, Berlin, 1993.
- Chor, B., Fiat, A. and Naor, M., "Tracing traitors," *Advances in Cryptology - CRYPTO '94*, p. 257. Springer-Verlag, Berlin, 1994.

Filipponi, P.

- Di Porto, A. and Filipponi, P., "A probabilistic primality test based on the properties of certain generalized Lucas numbers," *Advances in Cryptology - EUROCRYPT '88*, p. 211. Springer-Verlag, Berlin, 1988.

Findlay, P. A.

- Findlay, P. A. and Johnson, B. A., "Modular exponentiation using recursive sums of residues," *Advances in Cryptology - CRYPTO '89*, p. 371. Springer-Verlag, Berlin, 1989.

Fischer, J. B.

- Fischer, J. B. and Stern, J., "An efficient pseudo-random generator provably as secure as syndrome decoding," *Advances in Cryptology - EUROCRYPT '96*, p. 245. Springer-Verlag, Berlin, 1996.

Fischer, M. J.

- Fischer, M. J. and Wright, R. N., "Multiparty secret key exchange using a random deal of cards," *Advances in Cryptology - CRYPTO '91*, p. 141. Springer-Verlag, Berlin, 1991.

Fischlin, M.

- Fischlin, M., "Incremental Cryptography and Memory Checkers," *Advances in Cryptology - EUROCRYPT '97*, p. 393. Springer-Verlag, Berlin, 1997.

Fischlin, R.

- Fischlin, R. and Schnorr, C. P., "Stronger Security Proofs for RSA and Rabin Bits," *Advances in Cryptology - EUROCRYPT '97*, p. 267. Springer-Verlag, Berlin, 1997.

Flajolet, P.

- Flajolet, P. and Odlyzko, A. M., "Random mapping statistics (invited)," *Advances in Cryptology - EUROCRYPT '89*, p. 329. Springer-Verlag, Berlin, 1989.

Forre, R.

- Siegenthaler, T., Kleiner, A. W. and Forre, R., "Generation of binary sequences with controllable complexity and ideal r-tuple distribution," *Advances in Cryptology - EUROCRYPT '87*, p. 15. Springer-Verlag, Berlin, 1987.
- Forre, R., "The strict avalanche criterion: spectral properties of boolean functions and an extended definition," *Advances in Cryptology - CRYPTO '88*, p. 450. Springer-Verlag, Berlin, 1989.
- Forre, R., "A fast correlation attack on nonlinearly feed-forward filtered shift-register sequences," *Advances in Cryptology - EUROCRYPT '89*, p. 586. Springer-Verlag, Berlin, 1989.

Fortune, S.

- Fortune, S. and Merritt, M., "Poker protocols," *Advances in Cryptology: Proceedings of CRYPTO '84*, p. 454. Springer-Verlag, Berlin, 1985.

Fosseprez, M.

- Davio, M., Desmedt, Y., Fosseprez, M., Govaerts, R., Hulsbosch, J., Neutjens, P., Piret, P., Quisquater, J. J., Vandewalle, J. and Wouters, P., "Analytical characteristics of the DES," *Advances in Cryptology: Proceedings of CRYPTO '83*, p. 171. Plenum Publishing, New York, USA, 1984.

Frank, O.

- Frank, O. and Weidenman, P., "Controlling Individual Information in Statistics by Coding," *Abstracts of Papers: EUROCRYPT '86*, p. 49. Department of Electrical Engineering, University of Linköping, Linkoping, Sweden, 1986.

Frankel, Y.

- Frankel, Y., "A practical protocol for large group oriented networks," *Advances in Cryptology - EUROCRYPT '89*, p. 56. Springer-Verlag, Berlin, 1989.
- Desmedt, Y. and Frankel, Y., "Threshold cryptosystems," *Advances in Cryptology - CRYPTO '89*, p. 307. Springer-Verlag, Berlin, 1989.
- Desmedt, Y. and Frankel, Y., "Shared generation of authenticators and signatures," *Advances in Cryptology - CRYPTO '91*, p. 457. Springer-Verlag, Berlin, 1991.
- Frankel, Y. and Desmedt, Y., "Classification of ideal homomorphic threshold schemes over finite Abelian groups (Extended abstract)," *Advances in Cryptology - EUROCRYPT '92*, p. 25. Springer-Verlag, Berlin, 1992.
- Frankel, Y., Desmedt, Y. and Burmester, M. V. D., "Non-existence of homomorphic general sharing schemes for some key spaces," *Advances in Cryptology - CRYPTO '92*, p. 549. Springer-Verlag, Berlin, 1992.
- Frankel, Y. and Yung, M., "Escrow Encryption Systems Visited: Attacks, Analysis and Designs," *Advances in Cryptology - CRYPTO '95*, p. 222. Springer-Verlag, Berlin, 1995.
- Frankel, Y. and Yung, M., "Cryptanalysis of the Immunized LL Public Key Systems," *Advances in Cryptology - CRYPTO '95*, p. 287. Springer-Verlag, Berlin, 1995.
- Frankel, Y., Gemmell, P., MacKenzie, P. D. and Yung, M., "Proactive RSA," *Advances in Cryptology - CRYPTO '97*, p. 440. Springer-Verlag, Berlin, 1997.

Franklin, M. K.

- Franklin, M. K. and Haber, S., "Joint encryption and message-efficient secure computation," *Advances in Cryptology - CRYPTO '93*, p. 266. Springer-Verlag, Berlin, 1993.
- Franklin, M. K. and Yung, M., "The blinding of weak signatures," *Advances in Cryptology - EUROCRYPT '94*, p. 67. Springer-Verlag, Berlin, 1995.
- Franklin, M. K. and Reiter, M. K., "Verifiable signature sharing," *Advances in Cryptology - EUROCRYPT '95*, p. 50. Springer-Verlag, Berlin, 1995.
- Coppersmith, D., Franklin, M. K., Patarin, J. and Reiter, M. K., "Low-exponent RSA with related messages," *Advances in Cryptology - EUROCRYPT '96*, p. 1. Springer-Verlag, Berlin, 1996.
- Cramer, R., Franklin, M. K., Schoenmakers, B. and Yung, M., "Multi-authority secret-ballot elections with linear work," *Advances in Cryptology - EUROCRYPT '96*, p. 72. Springer-Verlag, Berlin, 1996.
- Boneh, D. and Franklin, M. K., "Efficient Generation of Shared RSA Keys," *Advances in Cryptology - CRYPTO '97*, p. 425. Springer-Verlag, Berlin, 1997.

Friedl, K.

- Boyar, J., Friedl, K. and Lund, C., "Practical zero-knowledge proofs: Giving hints and using deficiencies," *Advances in Cryptology - EUROCRYPT '89*, p. 155. Springer-Verlag, Berlin, 1989.

Fujioka, A.

- Shinozaki, S., Itoh, T., Fujioka, A. and Tsujii, S., "Provably secure key-updating schemes in identity-based systems," *Advances in Cryptology - EUROCRYPT '90*, p. 16. Springer-Verlag, Berlin, 1990.
- Fujioka, A., Okamoto, T. and Ohta, K., "Interactive bi-proof systems and undeniable signature schemes," *Advances in Cryptology - EUROCRYPT '91*, p. 243. Springer-Verlag, Berlin, 1991.
- Fujioka, A., Okamoto, T. and Miyaguchi, S., "ESIGN: An efficient digital signature implementation for smart cards," *Advances in Cryptology - EUROCRYPT '91*, p. 446. Springer-Verlag, Berlin, 1991.
- Ohta, K., Okamoto, T. and Fujioka, A., "Secure bit commitment function against divertibility," *Advances in Cryptology - EUROCRYPT '92*, p. 324. Springer-Verlag, Berlin, 1992.
- Okamoto, T., Fujioka, A. and Fujisaki, E., "An efficient digital signature scheme based on an elliptic curve over the ring Z_n," *Advances in Cryptology - CRYPTO '92*, p. 54. Springer-Verlag, Berlin, 1992.

Fujisaki, E.

- Okamoto, T., Fujioka, A. and Fujisaki, E., "An efficient digital signature scheme based on an elliptic curve over the ring Z_n," *Advances in Cryptology - CRYPTO '92*, p. 54. Springer-Verlag, Berlin, 1992.
- Fujisaki, E. and Okamoto, T., "Statistical Zero Knowledge Protocols to Prove Modular Polynomial Relations," *Advances in Cryptology - CRYPTO '97*, p. 16. Springer-Verlag, Berlin, 1997.

Fumy, W.

- Fumy, W., "On the F function of FEAL (cryptography)," *Advances in Cryptology - CRYPTO '87*, p. 434. Springer-Verlag, Berlin, 1987.
- Vandewalle, J., Chaum, D., Fumy, W., Jansen, C. J. A., Landrock, P. and Roelofsen, G., "A European call for cryptographic algorithms: RIPE; Race Integrity Primitives Evaluation," *Advances in Cryptology - EUROCRYPT '89*, p. 267. Springer-Verlag, Berlin, 1989.
- Fumy, W. and Munzert, M., "A modular approach to key distribution," *Advances in Cryptology - CRYPTO '90*, p. 274. Springer-Verlag, Berlin, 1990.
- Preneel, B., Chaum, D., Fumy, W., Jansen, C. J. A., Landrock, P. and Roelofsen, G., "Race Integrity Primitives Evaluation," *Advances in Cryptology - EUROCRYPT '91*, p. 547. Springer-Verlag, Berlin, 1991.

Furst, M.

- Blum, A., Furst, M., Kearns, M. and Lipton, R. J., "Cryptographic primitives based on hard learning problems," *Advances in Cryptology - CRYPTO '93*, p. 278. Springer-Verlag, Berlin, 1993.

Gabidulin, E. M.

- Gabidulin, E. M., Paramonov, A. V. and Tretjakov, O. V., "Ideals over a non-commutative ring and their application in cryptology," *Advances in Cryptology - EUROCRYPT '91*, p. 482. Springer-Verlag, Berlin, 1991.

Gaggia, A. Giorgio

- Blundo, C., De Santis, A., Di Crescenzo, G., Gaggia, A. Giorgio and Vaccaro, U., "Multi-secret sharing schemes," *Advances in Cryptology - CRYPTO '94*, p. 150. Springer-Verlag, Berlin, 1994.

Galil, Z.

- Galil, Z., Haber, S. and Yung, M., "Symmetric public-key encryption," *Advances in Cryptology - CRYPTO '85*, p. 128. Springer-Verlag, Berlin, 1986.
- Galil, Z., Haber, S. and Yung, M., "Cryptographic computation: secure fault tolerant protocols and the publickey model," *Advances in Cryptology - CRYPTO '87*, p. 135. Springer-Verlag, Berlin, 1987.
- Galil, Z., Haber, S. and Yung, M., "A secure public-key authentication scheme," *Advances in Cryptology - EUROCRYPT '89*, p. 3. Springer-Verlag, Berlin, 1989.

Gallo, V. A.

- Sherwood, J. R. and Gallo, V. A., "The application of smart cards for RSA digital signatures in a network comprising both interactive and store-and-forward facilities," *Advances in Cryptology - CRYPTO '88*, p. 484. Springer-Verlag, Berlin, 1989.

Games, R. A.

- Chan, A. H. and Games, R. A., "On the linear span of binary sequences obtained from finite geometries," *Advances in Cryptology - CRYPTO '86*, p. 405. Springer-Verlag, Berlin, 1986.
- Chan, A. H. and Games, R. A., "On the quadratic spans of periodic sequences," *Advances in Cryptology - CRYPTO '89*, p. 82. Springer-Verlag, Berlin, 1989.
- Games, R. A. and Rushanan, J. J., "Blind synchronization of m-sequences with even span," *Advances in Cryptology - EUROCRYPT '93*, p. 168. Springer-Verlag, Berlin, 1993.

Gargano, L.
- Capocelli, R. M., De Santis, A., Gargano, L. and Vaccaro, U., "On the size of shares for secret sharing schemes," *Advances in Cryptology - CRYPTO '91*, p. 101. Springer-Verlag, Berlin, 1991.
- Blundo, C., De Santis, A., Gargano, L. and Vaccaro, U., "On the information rate of secret sharing schemes," *Advances in Cryptology - CRYPTO '92*, p. 148. Springer-Verlag, Berlin, 1992.

Gasser, M.
- Gasser, M., "Limitations on the Use of Encryption to Enforce Mandatory Security," *Advances in Cryptography*, p. 130. University of California, Santa Barbara, Santa Barbara, California, USA, 1982.

Gehrmann, C.
- Gehrmann, C., "Cryptanalysis of the Gemmell and Naor multiround authentication protocol," *Advances in Cryptology - CRYPTO '94*, p. 121. Springer-Verlag, Berlin, 1994.

Gehrmann, C.
- Gehrmann, C., "Secure multiround authentication protocols," *Advances in Cryptology - EUROCRYPT '95*, p. 158. Springer-Verlag, Berlin, 1995.

Gemmell, P.
- Gemmell, P. and Naor, M., "Codes for interactive authentication," *Advances in Cryptology - CRYPTO '93*, p. 355. Springer-Verlag, Berlin, 1993.
- Frankel, Y., Gemmell, P., MacKenzie, P. D. and Yung, M., "Proactive RSA," *Advances in Cryptology - CRYPTO '97*, p. 440. Springer-Verlag, Berlin, 1997.

Gennaro, R.
- Gennaro, R. and Micali, S., "Verifiable secret sharing as secure computation," *Advances in Cryptology - EUROCRYPT '95*, p. 168. Springer-Verlag, Berlin, 1995.
- Gennaro, R., Jarecki, S., Krawczyk, H. and Rabin, T., "Robust threshold DSS signatures," *Advances in Cryptology - EUROCRYPT '96*, p. 354. Springer-Verlag, Berlin, 1996.
- Gennaro, R., Jarecki, S., Krawczyk, H. and Rabin, T., "Robust and Efficient Sharing of RSA Functions," *Advances in Cryptology - CRYPTO '96*, p. 157. Springer-Verlag, Berlin, 1996.
- Cramer, R., Gennaro, R. and Schoenmakers, B., "A Secure and Optimally Efficient Multi-Authority Election Scheme," *Advances in Cryptology - EUROCRYPT '97*, p. 103. Springer-Verlag, Berlin, 1997.
- Gennaro, R., Krawczyk, H. and Rabin, T., "RSA-Based Undeniable Signatures," *Advances in Cryptology - CRYPTO '97*, p. 132. Springer-Verlag, Berlin, 1997.
- Gennaro, R. and Rohatgi, P., "How to Sign Digital Streams," *Advances in Cryptology - CRYPTO '97*, p. 180. Springer-Verlag, Berlin, 1997.

Gibson, J. K.

- Gibson, J. K., "Equivalent Goppa codes and trapdoors to McEliece's public key cryptosystem," *Advances in Cryptology - EUROCRYPT '91*, p. 517. Springer-Verlag, Berlin, 1991.
- Gibson, J. K., "The security of the Gabidulin public key cryptosystem," *Advances in Cryptology - EUROCRYPT '96*, p. 212. Springer-Verlag, Berlin, 1996.

Gilbert, H.

- Gilbert, H. and Chasse, G., "A statistical attack of the FEAL cryptosystem," *Advances in Cryptology - CRYPTO '90*, p. 22. Springer-Verlag, Berlin, 1990.
- Tardy-Corfdir, A. and Gilbert, H., "A known plaintext attack of FEAL and FEAL-6," *Advances in Cryptology - CRYPTO '91*, p. 172. Springer-Verlag, Berlin, 1991.
- Baritaud, T., Gilbert, H. and Girault, M., "FFT hashing is not collision-free," *Advances in Cryptology - EUROCRYPT '92*, p. 35. Springer-Verlag, Berlin, 1992.
- Baritaud, T., Campana, M., Chauvaud, P. and Gilbert, H., "On the security of the permuted kernel identification scheme," *Advances in Cryptology - CRYPTO '92*, p. 305. Springer-Verlag, Berlin, 1992.
- Gilbert, H. and Chauvaud, P., "A chosen plaintext attack of the 16-round cryptosystem," *Advances in Cryptology - CRYPTO '94*, p. 359. Springer-Verlag, Berlin, 1994.

Giorgio Gaggia, A.

- Blundo, C., Giorgio Gaggia, A. and Stinson, D. R., "On the dealer's randomness required in secret sharing schemes," *Advances in Cryptology - EUROCRYPT '94*, p. 35. Springer-Verlag, Berlin, 1995.

Girardot, Y.

- Girardot, Y., "Bull CP8 smart card uses in cryptology," *Advances in Cryptology: Proceedings of EUROCRYPT '84*, p. 464. Springer-Verlag, Berlin, 1984.

Godlewski, P.

- Godlewski, P. and Cohen, G. D., "Authorized writing for "write-once" memories.," *Advances in Cryptology - EUROCRYPT '85*, p. 111. Springer-Verlag, Berlin, 1985.
- Godlewski, P. and Cohen, G. D., "Some cryptographic aspects of wom-codes," *Advances in Cryptology - CRYPTO '85*, p. 458. Springer-Verlag, Berlin, 1986.
- Godlewski, P. and Camion, P., "Manipulations and errors, detection and localization," *Advances in Cryptology - EUROCRYPT '88*, p. 97. Springer-Verlag, Berlin, 1988.
- Godlewski, P. and Mitchell, C., "Key minimal authentication systems for unconditional secrecy," *Advances in Cryptology - EUROCRYPT '89*, p. 497. Springer-Verlag, Berlin, 1989.

Goethals, J. M.

- Davio, M., Goethals, J. M. and Quisquater, J. J., "Authentication procedures," *Cryptography - Proceedings of the Workshop on Cryptography, Burg Feuerstein, Germany*, p. 283. Springer-Verlag, Berlin, 1983.

Goettfert, R.

- Goettfert, R. and Niederreiter, H., "On the linear complexity of products of shift-register sequences," *Advances in Cryptology - EUROCRYPT '93*, p. 151. Springer-Verlag, Berlin, 1993.
- Goettfert, R. and Niederreiter, H., "A general lower bound for the linear complexity of the product of shift-register sequences," *Advances in Cryptology - EUROCRYPT '94*, p. 223. Springer-Verlag, Berlin, 1995.

Goh, S. C.

- Park, S. J., Lee, S. J. and Goh, S. C., "On the Security of the Gollmann Cascades," *Advances in Cryptology - CRYPTO '95*, p. 148. Springer-Verlag, Berlin, 1995.

Goldburg, B.

- Goldburg, B., Dawson, E. and Sridharan, S., "The Automated Cryptanalysis of Analog Speech Scramblers," *Advances in Cryptology - EUROCRYPT '91*, p. 422. Springer-Verlag, Berlin, 1991.

Goldmann, M.

- Goldmann, M. and Naslund, M., "The Complexity of Computing Hard Core Predicates," *Advances in Cryptology - CRYPTO '97*, p. 1. Springer-Verlag, Berlin, 1997.

Goldreich, O.

- Even, S., Goldreich, O. and Lempel, A., "A randomized protocol for signing contracts (Extended abstract)," *Advances in Cryptology: Proceedings of CRYPTO '82*, p. 205. Plenum Publishing, New York, USA, 1982.
- Even, S. and Goldreich, O., "On the security of multi-party ping-pong protocols (Abstract)," *Advances in Cryptology: Proceedings of CRYPTO '82*, p. 315. Plenum Publishing, New York, USA, 1982.
- Even, S. and Goldreich, O., "On the power of cascade ciphers," *Advances in Cryptology: Proceedings of CRYPTO '83*, p. 43. Plenum Publishing, New York, USA, 1984.
- Goldreich, O., "A simple protocol for signing contracts," *Advances in Cryptology: Proceedings of CRYPTO '83*, p. 133. Plenum Publishing, New York, USA, 1984.
- Even, S. and Goldreich, O., "Electronic wallet," *Advances in Cryptology: Proceedings of CRYPTO '83*, p. 383. Plenum Publishing, New York, USA, 1984.
- Goldreich, O., "On the number of close-and-equal pairs of bits in a string," *Advances in Cryptology: Proceedings of EUROCRYPT '84*, p. 127. Springer-Verlag, Berlin, 1984.
- Goldreich, O., "On concurrent identification protocols," *Advances in Cryptology: Proceedings of EUROCRYPT '84*, p. 387. Springer-Verlag, Berlin, 1984.
- Goldreich, O., Goldwasser, S. and Micali, S., "On the cryptographic applications of random functions," *Advances in Cryptology: Proceedings of CRYPTO '84*, p. 276. Springer-Verlag, Berlin, 1985.
- Chor, B. and Goldreich, O., "RSA/Rabin least significant bits are $1/2 + 1/poly(logN)$ secure," *Advances in Cryptology: Proceedings of CRYPTO '84*, p. 303. Springer-Verlag, Berlin, 1985.
- Even, S., Goldreich, O. and Shamir, A., "On the security of ping-pong protocols when implemented using the RSA," *Advances in Cryptology - CRYPTO '85*, p. 58. Springer-Verlag, Berlin, 1986.
- Chor, B., Goldreich, O. and Goldwasser, S., "The bit security of modular squaring given partial factorization of the modulos," *Advances in Cryptology - CRYPTO '85*, p. 448. Springer-Verlag, Berlin, 1986.
- Goldreich, O., "Two remarks concerning the Goldwasser-Micali-Rivest signature scheme," *Advances in Cryptology - CRYPTO '86*, p. 104. Springer-Verlag, Berlin, 1986.
- Goldreich, O., Micali, S. and Wigderson, A., "How to prove all NP-statements in zero-knowledge, and a methodology of cryptographic protocol design," *Advances in Cryptology - CRYPTO '86*, p. 171. Springer-Verlag, Berlin, 1986.
- Goldreich, O., "Towards a theory of software protection," *Advances in Cryptology - CRYPTO '86*, p. 426. Springer-Verlag, Berlin, 1986.

- Goldreich, O. and Vainish, R., "How to solve any protocol probleman efficiency improvement," *Advances in Cryptology - CRYPTO '87*, p. 73. Springer-Verlag, Berlin, 1987.
- Ben-Or, M., Goldreich, O., Goldwasser, S., Hastad, J., Kilian, J., Micali, S. and Rogaway, P., "Everything provable is provable in zero-knowledge," *Advances in Cryptology - CRYPTO '88*, p. 37. Springer-Verlag, Berlin, 1989.
- Goldreich, O. and Kushilevitz, E., "A perfect zero-knowledge proof for a problem equivalent to discrete logarithm," *Advances in Cryptology - CRYPTO '88*, p. 57. Springer-Verlag, Berlin, 1989.
- Goldreich, O., Krawczyk, H. and Luby, M., "On the existence of pseudorandom generators," *Advances in Cryptology - CRYPTO '88*, p. 146. Springer-Verlag, Berlin, 1989.
- Goldreich, O. and Krawczyk, H., "Sparse pseudorandom distributions (extended abstract)," *Advances in Cryptology - CRYPTO '89*, p. 113. Springer-Verlag, Berlin, 1989.
- Even, S., Goldreich, O. and Micali, S., "On-line/off-line digital signatures," *Advances in Cryptology - CRYPTO '89*, p. 263. Springer-Verlag, Berlin, 1989.
- Bellare, M. and Goldreich, O., "On defining proofs of knowledge," *Advances in Cryptology - CRYPTO '92*, p. 390. Springer-Verlag, Berlin, 1992.
- Bellare, M., Goldreich, O. and Goldwasser, S., "Incremental cryptography: the case of hashing and signing," *Advances in Cryptology - CRYPTO '94*, p. 216. Springer-Verlag, Berlin, 1994.
- Damgård, I. B., Goldreich, O., Okamoto, T. and Wigderson, A., "Honest Verifier vs Dishonest Verifier in Public Coin Zero-Knowledge Proofs," *Advances in Cryptology - CRYPTO '95*, p. 325. Springer-Verlag, Berlin, 1995.
- Goldreich, O., "On the Foundations of Modern Cryptography," *Advances in Cryptology - CRYPTO '97*, p. 46. Springer-Verlag, Berlin, 1997.
- Goldreich, O., Goldwasser, S. and Halevi, S., "Eliminating Decryption Errors in the Ajtai-Dwork Cryptosystem," *Advances in Cryptology - CRYPTO '97*, p. 105. Springer-Verlag, Berlin, 1997.
- Goldreich, O., Goldwasser, S. and Halevi, S., "Public-Key Cryptosystems from Lattice Reduction Problems," *Advances in Cryptology - CRYPTO '97*, p. 112. Springer-Verlag, Berlin, 1997.

Goldwasser, S.

- Goldwasser, S., Micali, S. and Yao, A., "On signatures and authentication," *Advances in Cryptology: Proceedings of CRYPTO '82*, p. 211. Plenum Publishing, New York, USA, 1982.
- Goldreich, O., Goldwasser, S. and Micali, S., "On the cryptographic applications of random functions," *Advances in Cryptology: Proceedings of CRYPTO '84*, p. 276. Springer-Verlag, Berlin, 1985.

- Blum, M. and Goldwasser, S., "An efficient probabilistic public key encryption scheme which hides all partial information," *Advances in Cryptology: Proceedings of CRYPTO '84*, p. 289. Springer-Verlag, Berlin, 1985.
- Chor, B., Goldreich, O. and Goldwasser, S., "The bit security of modular squaring given partial factorization of the modulos," *Advances in Cryptology - CRYPTO '85*, p. 448. Springer-Verlag, Berlin, 1986.
- Ben-Or, M., Goldreich, O., Goldwasser, S., Hastad, J., Kilian, J., Micali, S. and Rogaway, P., "Everything provable is provable in zero-knowledge," *Advances in Cryptology - CRYPTO '88*, p. 37. Springer-Verlag, Berlin, 1989.
- Bellare, M. and Goldwasser, S., "New paradigms for digital signatures and message authentication based on non-interactive zero knowledge proofs," *Advances in Cryptology - CRYPTO '89*, p. 194. Springer-Verlag, Berlin, 1989.
- Ben-Or, M., Goldwasser, S., Kilian, J. and Wigderson, A., "Efficient identification schemes using two prover interactive proofs," *Advances in Cryptology - CRYPTO '89*, p. 498. Springer-Verlag, Berlin, 1989.
- Beaver, D. and Goldwasser, S., "Multiparty computation with faulty majority," *Advances in Cryptology - CRYPTO '89*, p. 589. Springer-Verlag, Berlin, 1989.
- Bellare, M., Cowen, L. and Goldwasser, S., "On the structure of secret key exchange protocols," *Advances in Cryptology - CRYPTO '89*, p. 604. Springer-Verlag, Berlin, 1989.
- Goldwasser, S. and Levin, L., "Fair computation of general functions in presence of immoral majority," *Advances in Cryptology - CRYPTO '90*, p. 77. Springer-Verlag, Berlin, 1990.
- Goldwasser, S. and Ostrovsky, R., "Invariant signatures and non-interactive zero-knowledge proofs are equivalent," *Advances in Cryptology - CRYPTO '92*, p. 228. Springer-Verlag, Berlin, 1992.
- Bellare, M., Goldreich, O. and Goldwasser, S., "Incremental cryptography: the case of hashing and signing," *Advances in Cryptology - CRYPTO '94*, p. 216. Springer-Verlag, Berlin, 1994.
- Goldreich, O., Goldwasser, S. and Halevi, S., "Eliminating Decryption Errors in the Ajtai-Dwork Cryptosystem," *Advances in Cryptology - CRYPTO '97*, p. 105. Springer-Verlag, Berlin, 1997.
- Goldreich, O., Goldwasser, S. and Halevi, S., "Public-Key Cryptosystems from Lattice Reduction Problems," *Advances in Cryptology - CRYPTO '97*, p. 112. Springer-Verlag, Berlin, 1997.
- Bellare, M., Goldwasser, S. and Micciancio, D., ""Pseudo-Random" Number Generation within Cryptographic Algorithms: The DSS Case," *Advances in Cryptology - CRYPTO '97*, p. 277. Springer-Verlag, Berlin, 1997.

Golic, J. D.

- Golic, J. D. and Mihaljevic, M. J., "A noisy clock-controlled shift register cryptanalysis concept based on sequence comparison approach," *Advances in Cryptology - EUROCRYPT '90*, p. 487. Springer-Verlag, Berlin, 1990.
- Golic, J. D., "The number of output sequences of a binary sequence generator," *Advances in Cryptology - EUROCRYPT '91*, p. 160. Springer-Verlag, Berlin, 1991.
- Mihaljevic, M. J. and Golic, J. D., "A comparison of cryptoanalytic principles based on iterative error-correction," *Advances in Cryptology - EUROCRYPT '91*, p. 527. Springer-Verlag, Berlin, 1991.
- Golic, J. D., "Correlation via linear sequential circuit approximation of combiners with memory," *Advances in Cryptology - EUROCRYPT '92*, p. 113. Springer-Verlag, Berlin, 1992.
- Mihaljevic, M. J. and Golic, J. D., "Convergence of a Bayesian iterative error-correction procedure on a noisy shift register sequence," *Advances in Cryptology - EUROCRYPT '92*, p. 124. Springer-Verlag, Berlin, 1992.
- Golic, J. D. and Petrovic, S. V., "A generalized correlation attack with a probabilistic constrained edit distance," *Advances in Cryptology - EUROCRYPT '92*, p. 472. Springer-Verlag, Berlin, 1992.
- Golic, J. D. and O'Connor, L., "Embedding and probabilistic correlation attacks on clock-controlled shift registers," *Advances in Cryptology - EUROCRYPT '94*, p. 230. Springer-Verlag, Berlin, 1995.
- Golic, J. D., "Towards fast correlation attacks on irregularly clocked shift registers," *Advances in Cryptology - EUROCRYPT '95*, p. 248. Springer-Verlag, Berlin, 1995.
- Golic, J. D., "Fast low order approximation of cryptographic functions," *Advances in Cryptology - EUROCRYPT '96*, p. 268. Springer-Verlag, Berlin, 1996.
- Golic, J. D., "Linear Statistical Weakness of Alleged RC4 Keystream Generator," *Advances in Cryptology - EUROCRYPT '97*, p. 226. Springer-Verlag, Berlin, 1997.
- Golic, J. D., "Cryptanalysis of Alleged A5 Stream Cipher," *Advances in Cryptology - EUROCRYPT '97*, p. 239. Springer-Verlag, Berlin, 1997.
- Golic, J. D. and Menicocci, R., "Edit Distance Correlation Attack on the Alternating Step Generator," *Advances in Cryptology - CRYPTO '97*, p. 499. Springer-Verlag, Berlin, 1997.

Gollmann, D.

- Gollmann, D., "Pseudo random properties of cascade connections of clock controlled shift registers," *Advances in Cryptology: Proceedings of EUROCRYPT '84*, p. 93. Springer-Verlag, Berlin, 1984.
- Gollmann, D., "Linear Complexity of Sequences with Period p^n," *Abstracts of Papers: EUROCRYPT '86*, p. 33. Department of Electrical Engineering, University of Linköping, Linkoping, Sweden, 1986.

Gordon, J. A.

- Gordon, J. A., "Towards a Design Procedure for Cryptosecure Substitution Boxes," *Advances in Cryptography*, p. 53. University of California, Santa Barbara, Santa Barbara, California, USA, 1982.
- Gordon, J. A. and Retkin, H., "Are big S-boxes best?," *Cryptography - Proceedings of the Workshop on Cryptography, Burg Feuerstein, Germany*, p. 257. Springer-Verlag, Berlin, 1983.
- Gordon, J. A., "Strong primes are easy to find," *Advances in Cryptology: Proceedings of EUROCRYPT '84*, p. 216. Springer-Verlag, Berlin, 1984.

Goresky, M.

- Chan, A. H., Goresky, M. and Klapper, A., "On the linear complexity of feedback registers (extended abstract)," *Advances in Cryptology - EUROCRYPT '89*, p. 563. Springer-Verlag, Berlin, 1989.
- Chan, A. H., Goresky, M. and Klapper, A., "Correlation functions of geometric sequences," *Advances in Cryptology - EUROCRYPT '90*, p. 214. Springer-Verlag, Berlin, 1990.
- Goresky, M. and Klapper, A., "Feedback registers based on ramified extensions of the 2-adic numbers," *Advances in Cryptology - EUROCRYPT '94*, p. 215. Springer-Verlag, Berlin, 1995.
- Klapper, A. and Goresky, M., "Large periods nearly de Bruijn FCSR sequences," *Advances in Cryptology - EUROCRYPT '95*, p. 263. Springer-Verlag, Berlin, 1995.
- Klapper, A. and Goresky, M., "Cryptanalysis Based on 2-Adic Rational Approximation," *Advances in Cryptology - CRYPTO '95*, p. 262. Springer-Verlag, Berlin, 1995.

Gorgui-Naguib, R. N.

- Gorgui-Naguib, R. N. and Dlay, S. S., "Properties of the Euler totient function modulo 24 and some of its cryptographic implications," *Advances in Cryptology - EUROCRYPT '88*, p. 267. Springer-Verlag, Berlin, 1988.

Gosler, J. R.

- Gosler, J. R., "Software protection: myth or reality?," *Advances in Cryptology - CRYPTO '85*, p. 140. Springer-Verlag, Berlin, 1986.

Goubert, J.

- Davio, M., Desmedt, Y., Goubert, J., Hoornaert, F. and Quisquater, J. J., "Efficient hardware and software implementations for the DES," *Advances in Cryptology: Proceedings of CRYPTO '84*, p. 144. Springer-Verlag, Berlin, 1985.
- Hoornaert, F., Goubert, J. and Desmedt, Y., "Efficient hardware implementation of the DES," *Advances in Cryptology: Proceedings of CRYPTO '84*, p. 147. Springer-Verlag, Berlin, 1985.

Goutay, J.

- Goutay, J., "Smart card applications in security and data protection," *Advances in Cryptology: Proceedings of EUROCRYPT '84*, p. 459. Springer-Verlag, Berlin, 1984.

Goutier, C.

- Beauchemin, P., Brassard, G., Crépeau, C. and Goutier, C., "Two observations on probabilistic primality testing," *Advances in Cryptology - CRYPTO '86*, p. 443. Springer-Verlag, Berlin, 1986.
- Desmedt, Y., Goutier, C. and Bengio, S., "Special uses and abuses of the Fiat Shamir passport protocol," *Advances in Cryptology - CRYPTO '87*, p. 21. Springer-Verlag, Berlin, 1987.

Govaerts, R.

- Davio, M., Desmedt, Y., Fosseprez, M., Govaerts, R., Hulsbosch, J., Neutjens, P., Piret, P., Quisquater, J. J., Vandewalle, J. and Wouters, P., "Analytical characteristics of the DES," *Advances in Cryptology: Proceedings of CRYPTO '83*, p. 171. Plenum Publishing, New York, USA, 1984.
- Vandewalle, J., Govaerts, R., De Becker, W., Decroos, M. and Speybrouck, G., "Implementation study of public key cryptography protection in an existing electronic mail and document handling system.," *Advances in Cryptology - EUROCRYPT '85*, p. 43. Springer-Verlag, Berlin, 1985.
- Cloetens, H., Bierens, L., Vandewalle, J. and Govaerts, R., "Additional Properties in the S-Boxes of the DES," *Abstracts of Papers: EUROCRYPT '86*, p. 20. Department of Electrical Engineering, University of Linköping, Linkoping, Sweden, 1986.
- Jorissen, F., Vandewalle, J. and Govaerts, R., "Extension of Brickell's algorithm for breaking high density knapsacks," *Advances in Cryptology - EUROCRYPT '87*, p. 109. Springer-Verlag, Berlin, 1987.
- Hoornaert, F., Decroos, M., Vandewalle, J. and Govaerts, R., "Fast RSA-hardware: dream or reality," *Advances in Cryptology - EUROCRYPT '88*, p. 257. Springer-Verlag, Berlin, 1988.
- Preneel, B., Bosselaers, A., Govaerts, R. and Vandewalle, J., "A chosen text attack on the modified cryptographic checksum algorithm of Cohen and Huang," *Advances in Cryptology - CRYPTO '89*, p. 154. Springer-Verlag, Berlin, 1989.
- Preneel, B., Van Leekwijck, W., Van Linden, L., Govaerts, R. and Vandewalle, J., "Propagation characteristics of Boolean functions," *Advances in Cryptology - EUROCRYPT '90*, p. 161. Springer-Verlag, Berlin, 1990.
- Preneel, B., Govaerts, R. and Vandewalle, J., "Boolean functions satisfying higher order propagation criteria," *Advances in Cryptology - EUROCRYPT '91*, p. 141. Springer-Verlag, Berlin, 1991.
- Daemen, J., Govaerts, R. and Vandewalle, J., "Resynchronization weaknesses in synchronous stream ciphers," *Advances in Cryptology - EUROCRYPT '93*, p. 159. Springer-Verlag, Berlin, 1993.

- Bosselaers, A., Govaerts, R. and Vandewalle, J., "Comparison of three modular reduction functions," *Advances in Cryptology - CRYPTO '93*, p. 175. Springer-Verlag, Berlin, 1993.
- Daemen, J., Govaerts, R. and Vandewalle, J., "Weak keys for IDEA," *Advances in Cryptology - CRYPTO '93*, p. 224. Springer-Verlag, Berlin, 1993.
- Preneel, B., Govaerts, R. and Vandewalle, J., "Hashfunctions based on block ciphers: a synthetic approach," *Advances in Cryptology - CRYPTO '93*, p. 368. Springer-Verlag, Berlin, 1993.
- Bosselaers, A., Govaerts, R. and Vandewalle, J., "Fast Hashing on the Pentium," *Advances in Cryptology - CRYPTO '96*, p. 298. Springer-Verlag, Berlin, 1996.
- Bosselaers, A., Govaerts, R. and Vandewalle, J., "SHA: A Design for Parallel Architectures?," *Advances in Cryptology - EUROCRYPT '97*, p. 348. Springer-Verlag, Berlin, 1997.

Graaf, J. van de
- Crépeau, C., Graaf, J. van de and Tapp, A., "Committed Oblivious Transfer and Private Multi-Party Computation," *Advances in Cryptology - CRYPTO '95*, p. 110. Springer-Verlag, Berlin, 1995.

Graham, I. G.
- Bradey, R. L. and Graham, I. G., "Full encryption in a personal computer system.," *Advances in Cryptology - EUROCRYPT '85*, p. 231. Springer-Verlag, Berlin, 1985.

Granboulan, L.
- Joux, A. and Granboulan, L., "A practical attack against knapsack based hash functions," *Advances in Cryptology - EUROCRYPT '94*, p. 58. Springer-Verlag, Berlin, 1995.

Groscot, H.
- Groscot, H., "Estimation of some encryption functions implemented into smart cards," *Advances in Cryptology: Proceedings of EUROCRYPT '84*, p. 470. Springer-Verlag, Berlin, 1984.

Guajardo, J.
- Guajardo, J. and Paar, C., "Efficient Algorithms for Elliptic Curve Cryptosystems," *Advances in Cryptology - CRYPTO '97*, p. 342. Springer-Verlag, Berlin, 1997.

Guenther, C. G.

- Bernasconi, J. and Guenther, C. G., "Analysis of a nonlinear feedforward logic for binary sequence generators.," *Advances in Cryptology - EURO-CRYPT '85*, p. 161. Springer-Verlag, Berlin, 1985.
- Guenther, C. G., "On Some Properties of the Sum of Two Pseudorandom Sequences," *Abstracts of Papers: EUROCRYPT '86*, p. 40. Department of Electrical Engineering, University of Linköping, Linkoping, Sweden, 1986.
- Guenther, C. G., "Alternating step generators controlled by de Bruijn sequences," *Advances in Cryptology - EUROCRYPT '87*, p. 5. Springer-Verlag, Berlin, 1987.
- Guenther, C. G., "A universal algorithm for homophonic coding," *Advances in Cryptology - EUROCRYPT '88*, p. 405. Springer-Verlag, Berlin, 1988.
- Guenther, C. G., "An identity-based key-exchange protocol," *Advances in Cryptology - EUROCRYPT '89*, p. 29. Springer-Verlag, Berlin, 1989.
- Guenther, C. G., "Parallel generation of recurring sequences," *Advances in Cryptology - EUROCRYPT '89*, p. 503. Springer-Verlag, Berlin, 1989.

Guerin, R.

- Bellare, M., Guerin, R. and Rogaway, P., "XOR MACs: New Methods for Message Authentication Using Finite Pseudorandom Functions," *Advances in Cryptology - CRYPTO '95*, p. 15. Springer-Verlag, Berlin, 1995.

Guillou, L. C.

- Guillou, L. C., "Smart cards and conditional access," *Advances in Cryptology: Proceedings of EUROCRYPT '84*, p. 480. Springer-Verlag, Berlin, 1984.
- Guillou, L. C. and Ugon, M., "Smart card, a highly reliable and portable security device," *Advances in Cryptology - CRYPTO '86*, p. 464. Springer-Verlag, Berlin, 1986.
- Guillou, L. C. and Quisquater, J. J., "Efficient digital publickey signatures with shadow," *Advances in Cryptology - CRYPTO '87*, p. 223. Springer-Verlag, Berlin, 1987.
- Guillou, L. C. and Quisquater, J. J., "A practical zero-knowledge protocol fitted to security microprocessor minimizing both transmission and memory," *Advances in Cryptology - EUROCRYPT '88*, p. 123. Springer-Verlag, Berlin, 1988.
- Guillou, L. C. and Quisquater, J. J., "A "paradoxical" identity-based signature scheme resulting from zero-knowledge," *Advances in Cryptology - CRYPTO '88*, p. 216. Springer-Verlag, Berlin, 1989.
- Quisquater, J. J., Guillou, L. C., Annick, M. and Berson, T. A., "How to explain zero-knowledge protocols to your children," *Advances in Cryptology - CRYPTO '89*, p. 628. Springer-Verlag, Berlin, 1989.
- Guillou, L. C., Quisquater, J. J., Walker, M., Landrock, P. and Shaer, C., "Precautions taken against various potential attacks in ISO/IEC DIS 9796," *Advances in Cryptology - EUROCRYPT '90*, p. 465. Springer-Verlag, Berlin, 1990.

Gyoerfi, L.

- Gyoerfi, L. and Kerekes, I., "Analysis of multiple access channel using multiple level FSK," *Cryptography - Proceedings of the Workshop on Cryptography, Burg Feuerstein, Germany*, p. 165. Springer-Verlag, Berlin, 1983.

Gyoery, R.

- Gyoery, R. and Seberry, J., "Electronic funds transfer point of sale in Australia," *Advances in Cryptology - CRYPTO '86*, p. 347. Springer-Verlag, Berlin, 1986.

Haber, S.

- Galil, Z., Haber, S. and Yung, M., "Symmetric public-key encryption," *Advances in Cryptology - CRYPTO '85*, p. 128. Springer-Verlag, Berlin, 1986.
- Galil, Z., Haber, S. and Yung, M., "Cryptographic computation: secure fault tolerant protocols and the publickey model," *Advances in Cryptology - CRYPTO '87*, p. 135. Springer-Verlag, Berlin, 1987.
- Galil, Z., Haber, S. and Yung, M., "A secure public-key authentication scheme," *Advances in Cryptology - EUROCRYPT '89*, p. 3. Springer-Verlag, Berlin, 1989.
- Haber, S. and Stornetta, W. Scott, "How to time-stamp a digital document," *Advances in Cryptology - CRYPTO '90*, p. 437. Springer-Verlag, Berlin, 1990.
- Beaver, D. and Haber, S., "Cryptographic protocols provably secure against dynamic adversaries," *Advances in Cryptology - EUROCRYPT '92*, p. 307. Springer-Verlag, Berlin, 1992.
- Franklin, M. K. and Haber, S., "Joint encryption and message-efficient secure computation," *Advances in Cryptology - CRYPTO '93*, p. 266. Springer-Verlag, Berlin, 1993.

Habutsu, T.

- Habutsu, T., Nishio, Y., Sasase, Iwao and Mori, S., "A secret key cryptosystem by iterating a chaotic map," *Advances in Cryptology - EUROCRYPT '91*, p. 127. Springer-Verlag, Berlin, 1991.

Haemers, W.

- Haemers, W., "Access control at the Netherlands postal and telecommunications services," *Advances in Cryptology - CRYPTO '85*, p. 543. Springer-Verlag, Berlin, 1986.

Halevi, S.

- Halevi, S., "Efficient Commitment Schemes with Bounded Sender and Unbounded Receiver," *Advances in Cryptology - CRYPTO '95*, p. 84. Springer-Verlag, Berlin, 1995.
- Halevi, S. and Micali, S., "Practical and Provably-Secure Commitment Schemes from Collision-Free Hashing," *Advances in Cryptology - CRYPTO '96*, p. 201. Springer-Verlag, Berlin, 1996.
- Goldreich, O., Goldwasser, S. and Halevi, S., "Eliminating Decryption Errors in the Ajtai-Dwork Cryptosystem," *Advances in Cryptology - CRYPTO '97*, p. 105. Springer-Verlag, Berlin, 1997.
- Goldreich, O., Goldwasser, S. and Halevi, S., "Public-Key Cryptosystems from Lattice Reduction Problems," *Advances in Cryptology - CRYPTO '97*, p. 112. Springer-Verlag, Berlin, 1997.

Harari, S.

- Harari, S., "Non-linear, non-commutative functions for data integrity," *Advances in Cryptology: Proceedings of EUROCRYPT '84*, p. 25. Springer-Verlag, Berlin, 1984.

Harn, L.

- Laih, C. S., Harn, L., Lee, J. Y. and Hwang, T., "Dynamic threshold scheme based on the definition of cross-product in an N-dimensional linear space," *Advances in Cryptology - CRYPTO '89*, p. 286. Springer-Verlag, Berlin, 1989.
- Harn, L. and Lin, Hung-Yu, "An l-span generalized secret sharing scheme," *Advances in Cryptology - CRYPTO '92*, p. 558. Springer-Verlag, Berlin, 1992.

Harper, G.

- Harper, G., Menezes, A. and Vanstone, S. A., "Public-key cryptosystems with very small key lengths," *Advances in Cryptology - EUROCRYPT '92*, p. 163. Springer-Verlag, Berlin, 1992.

Harpes, C.

- Harpes, C., Kramer, G. G. and Massey, J. L., "A generalization of linear cryptanalysis and the applicability of Matsui's piling-up lemma," *Advances in Cryptology - EUROCRYPT '95*, p. 24. Springer-Verlag, Berlin, 1995.

Hastad, J.

- Hastad, J., "On using RSA with low exponent in a public key network," *Advances in Cryptology - CRYPTO '85*, p. 403. Springer-Verlag, Berlin, 1986.
- Ben-Or, M., Goldreich, O., Goldwasser, S., Hastad, J., Kilian, J., Micali, S. and Rogaway, P., "Everything provable is provable in zero-knowledge," *Advances in Cryptology - CRYPTO '88*, p. 37. Springer-Verlag, Berlin, 1989.

Heider, F. P.

- Heider, F. P., Kraus, D. and Welschenbach, M., "Some Preliminary Remarks on the Decimal, Shift an Add-Algorithm (DSA)," *Abstracts of Papers: EUROCRYPT '86*, p. 3. Department of Electrical Engineering, University of Linköping, Linkoping, Sweden, 1986.
- Damm, F., Heider, F. P. and Wambach, G., "MIMD-factorisation on hypercubes," *Advances in Cryptology - EUROCRYPT '94*, p. 400. Springer-Verlag, Berlin, 1995.

Heiman, R.

- Heiman, R., "A note on discrete logarithms with special structure," *Advances in Cryptology - EUROCRYPT '92*, p. 454. Springer-Verlag, Berlin, 1992.

Heiman, Rafi

- Heiman, Rafi, "Secure Audio Teleconferencing: A Practical Solution," *Advances in Cryptology - EUROCRYPT '92*, p. 437. Springer-Verlag, Berlin, 1992.

Heimann, J.

- Nelson, R. and Heimann, J., "SDNS architecture and end-to-end encryption," *Advances in Cryptology - CRYPTO '89*, p. 356. Springer-Verlag, Berlin, 1989.

Helleseth, T.

- Helleseth, T. and Johansson, T., "Universal Hash Functions from Exponential Sums over Finite Fields and Galois Rings," *Advances in Cryptology - CRYPTO '96*, p. 31. Springer-Verlag, Berlin, 1996.

Hellman, M. E.

- Hellman, M. E., Karnin, E. and Reyneri, J. M., "On the Necessity or Exhaustive Search for System-Invariant Cryptanalysis," *Advances in Cryptography*, p. 2. University of California, Santa Barbara, Santa Barbara, California, USA, 1982.
- Amirazizi, H. and Hellman, M. E., "Time-Memory-Processor Tradeoffs," *Advances in Cryptography*, p. 7. University of California, Santa Barbara, Santa Barbara, California, USA, 1982.
- Hellman, M. E. and Reyneri, J. M., "Fast computation of discrete logarithms in GF(q)," *Advances in Cryptology: Proceedings of CRYPTO '82*, p. 3. Plenum Publishing, New York, USA, 1982.
- Hellman, M. E. and Reyneri, J. M., "Drainage and the DES," *Advances in Cryptology: Proceedings of CRYPTO '82*, p. 129. Plenum Publishing, New York, USA, 1982.
- Langford, S. K. and Hellman, M. E., "Differential-linear cryptanalysis," *Advances in Cryptology - CRYPTO '94*, p. 17. Springer-Verlag, Berlin, 1994.

Hemachandra, L. A.

- Abadi, M., Allender, E., Broder, A., Feigenbaum, J. and Hemachandra, L. A., "On generating solved instances of computational problems," *Advances in Cryptology - CRYPTO '88*, p. 297. Springer-Verlag, Berlin, 1989.

Henry, P. S.

- Henry, P. S. and Nash, R. D., "High-Speed Hardware Implementation of the Knapsack Cipher," *Advances in Cryptography*, p. 16. University of California, Santa Barbara, Santa Barbara, California, USA, 1982.

Henze, E.

- Henze, E., "A Solution of the General Equation for Public Key Distribution Systems," *Advances in Cryptography*, p. 140. University of California, Santa Barbara, Santa Barbara, California, USA, 1982.

Herbison, B. J.

- Herbison, B. J., "Developing Ethernet Enhanced-Security System," *Advances in Cryptology - CRYPTO '88*, p. 507. Springer-Verlag, Berlin, 1989.

Herlestam, T.

- Herlestam, T., "Discussion of Adleman's Subexponential Algorithm for Computing Discrete Logarithms," *Advances in Cryptography*, p. 142. University of California, Santa Barbara, Santa Barbara, California, USA, 1982.
- Herlestam, T., "On using prime polynomials in crypto generators," *Cryptography - Proceedings of the Workshop on Cryptography, Burg Feuerstein, Germany*, p. 207. Springer-Verlag, Berlin, 1983.
- Herlestam, T., "On functions of linear shift register sequences.," *Advances in Cryptology - EUROCRYPT '85*, p. 119. Springer-Verlag, Berlin, 1985.
- Herlestam, T., "On Linear Shift Registers with Permuted Feedback," *Abstracts of Papers: EUROCRYPT '86*, p. 38. Department of Electrical Engineering, University of Linköping, Linkoping, Sweden, 1986.

Herlihy, M. P.

- Herlihy, M. P. and Tygar, J. D., "How to make replicated data secure," *Advances in Cryptology - CRYPTO '87*, p. 379. Springer-Verlag, Berlin, 1987.

320

Herzberg, A.

- Herzberg, A. and Pinter, S., "Public protection of software," *Advances in Cryptology - CRYPTO '85*, p. 158. Springer-Verlag, Berlin, 1986.
- Bird, R., Gopal, I., Herzberg, A., Janson, P., Kutten, S., Molva, R. and Yung, M., "Systematic design of two-party authentication protocols," *Advances in Cryptology - CRYPTO '91*, p. 44. Springer-Verlag, Berlin, 1991.
- Herzberg, A. and Luby, M., "Public randomness in cryptography," *Advances in Cryptology - CRYPTO '92*, p. 421. Springer-Verlag, Berlin, 1992.
- Blundo, C., De Santis, A., Herzberg, A., Kutten, S., Vaccaro, U. and Yung, M., "Perfectly-secure key distribution for dynamic conferences," *Advances in Cryptology - CRYPTO '92*, p. 471. Springer-Verlag, Berlin, 1992.
- Canetti, R. and Herzberg, A., "Maintaining security in the presence of transient faults," *Advances in Cryptology - CRYPTO '94*, p. 425. Springer-Verlag, Berlin, 1994.
- Herzberg, A., Jarecki, S., Krawczyk, H. and Yung, M., "Proactive Secret Sharing Or: How to Cope With Perpetual Leakage," *Advances in Cryptology - CRYPTO '95*, p. 339. Springer-Verlag, Berlin, 1995.

Hess, P.

- Hess, P. and Wirl, K., "A voice scrambling system for testing and demonstration," *Cryptography - Proceedings of the Workshop on Cryptography, Burg Feuerstein, Germany*, p. 147. Springer-Verlag, Berlin, 1983.

Heyst, E. van

- Chaum, D. and Heyst, E. van, "Group signatures," *Advances in Cryptology - EUROCRYPT '91*, p. 257. Springer-Verlag, Berlin, 1991.
- Heyst, E. van and Pedersen, T. P., "How to make efficient fail-stop signatures," *Advances in Cryptology - EUROCRYPT '92*, p. 366. Springer-Verlag, Berlin, 1992.
- Evertse, J. H. and Heyst, E. van, "Which new RSA signatures can be computed from RSA signatures, obtained in a specific interactive protocol?," *Advances in Cryptology - EUROCRYPT '92*, p. 378. Springer-Verlag, Berlin, 1992.

Hirano, K.

- Kawamura, S. and Hirano, K., "A fast modular arithmetic algorithm using a residue table," *Advances in Cryptology - EUROCRYPT '88*, p. 245. Springer-Verlag, Berlin, 1988.

Hirschfeld, R.

- Hirschfeld, R., "Making electronic refunds safer," *Advances in Cryptology - CRYPTO '92*, p. 106. Springer-Verlag, Berlin, 1992.

Hoerner, H. H.

- Schnorr, C. P. and Hoerner, H. H., "Attacking the Chor-Rivest cryptosystem by improved lattice reduction," *Advances in Cryptology - EUROCRYPT '95*, p. 1. Springer-Verlag, Berlin, 1995.

Hohl, W.

- Hohl, W., Lai, X., Meier, T. and Waldvogel, C., "Security of iterated hash functions based on block ciphers," *Advances in Cryptology - CRYPTO '93*, p. 379. Springer-Verlag, Berlin, 1993.

Holdridge, D. B.

- Davis, J. A. and Holdridge, D. B., "Factorization using the Quadratic Sieve algorithm," *Advances in Cryptology: Proceedings of CRYPTO '83*, p. 103. Plenum Publishing, New York, USA, 1984.
- Davis, J. A., Holdridge, D. B. and Simmons, G. J., "Status report on factoring (at the Sandia National Labs)," *Advances in Cryptology: Proceedings of EUROCRYPT '84*, p. 183. Springer-Verlag, Berlin, 1984.
- Davis, J. A. and Holdridge, D. B., "An update on factorization at Sandia National Laboratories," *Advances in Cryptology: Proceedings of CRYPTO '84*, p. 114. Springer-Verlag, Berlin, 1985.
- Davis, J. A. and Holdridge, D. B., "Factorization of large integers on a massively parallel computer," *Advances in Cryptology - EUROCRYPT '88*, p. 235. Springer-Verlag, Berlin, 1988.

Hong, S. M.

- Hong, S. M., Oh, S. Y. and Yoon, H., "New modular multiplication algorithms for fast modular exponentiation," *Advances in Cryptology - EUROCRYPT '96*, p. 166. Springer-Verlag, Berlin, 1996.

Hoornaert, F.

- Davio, M., Desmedt, Y., Goubert, J., Hoornaert, F. and Quisquater, J. J., "Efficient hardware and software implementations for the DES," *Advances in Cryptology: Proceedings of CRYPTO '84*, p. 144. Springer-Verlag, Berlin, 1985.
- Hoornaert, F., Goubert, J. and Desmedt, Y., "Efficient hardware implementation of the DES," *Advances in Cryptology: Proceedings of CRYPTO '84*, p. 147. Springer-Verlag, Berlin, 1985.
- Desmedt, Y., Hoornaert, F. and Quisquater, J. J., "Several Exhaustive Key Search Machines and DES," *Abstracts of Papers: EUROCRYPT '86*, p. 17. Department of Electrical Engineering, University of Linköping, Linkoping, Sweden, 1986.
- Verbauwhede, I., Hoornaert, F., Vandewalle, J. and De Man, H., "Security considerations in the design and implementation of a new DES chip," *Advances in Cryptology - EUROCRYPT '87*, p. 287. Springer-Verlag, Berlin, 1987.
- Hoornaert, F., Decroos, M., Vandewalle, J. and Govaerts, R., "Fast RSA-hardware: dream or reality," *Advances in Cryptology - EUROCRYPT '88*, p. 257. Springer-Verlag, Berlin, 1988.

Horak, O. J.

- Horak, O. J., "The contribution of E.B. Fleissner and A. Figl for today's cryptography.," *Advances in Cryptology - EUROCRYPT '85*, p. 3. Springer-Verlag, Berlin, 1985.

Horbach, L.

- Horbach, L., "Privacy and data protection in medicine," *Cryptography - Proceedings of the Workshop on Cryptography, Burg Feuerstein, Germany*, p. 228. Springer-Verlag, Berlin, 1983.

Hornauer, G.

- Hornauer, G., Stephan, W. and Wernsdorf, R., "Markov ciphers and alternating groups," *Advances in Cryptology - EUROCRYPT '93*, p. 453. Springer-Verlag, Berlin, 1993.

Horster, P.

- Horster, P. and Knobloch, H.-J., "Discrete logarithm based protocols," *Advances in Cryptology - EUROCRYPT '91*, p. 399. Springer-Verlag, Berlin, 1991.

Horvath, T.

- Horvath, T., Magliveras, S. S. and van Trung, T., "A parallel permutation multiplier for a PGM crypto-chip," *Advances in Cryptology - CRYPTO '94*, p. 108. Springer-Verlag, Berlin, 1994.

Hoshi, M.

- Itoh, T., Hoshi, M. and Tsujii, S., "A low communication competitive interactive proof system for promised quadratic residuosity," *Advances in Cryptology - CRYPTO '93*, p. 61. Springer-Verlag, Berlin, 1993.

Hruby, J.

- Hruby, J., "Q-deformed quantum cryptography," *Advances in Cryptology - EUROCRYPT '94*, p. 468. Springer-Verlag, Berlin, 1995.

Huang, M.

- Huang, M. and Teng, S. H., "A universal problem in secure and verifiable distributed computation," *Advances in Cryptology - CRYPTO '88*, p. 336. Springer-Verlag, Berlin, 1989.
- Zeng, K. and Huang, M., "On the linear syndrome method in cryptoanalysis," *Advances in Cryptology - CRYPTO '88*, p. 469. Springer-Verlag, Berlin, 1989.

Huber, K.

- Huber, K., "Some considerations concerning the selection of RSA moduli," *Advances in Cryptology - EUROCRYPT '91*, p. 294. Springer-Verlag, Berlin, 1991.

Hughes, R. J.

- Hughes, R. J., Luther, G. G., Morgan, G. L., Peterson, C. G. and Simmons, C., "Quantum Cryptography over Underground Optical Fibers," *Advances in Cryptology - CRYPTO '96*, p. 329. Springer-Verlag, Berlin, 1996.

Huguet i Rotger, L.

- Domingo-Ferrer, J. and Huguet i Rotger, L., "Full secure key exchange and authentication with no previously shared secrets," *Advances in Cryptology - EUROCRYPT '89*, p. 665. Springer-Verlag, Berlin, 1989.

Hulsbosch, J.

- Davio, M., Desmedt, Y., Fosseprez, M., Govaerts, R., Hulsbosch, J., Neutjens, P., Piret, P., Quisquater, J. J., Vandewalle, J. and Wouters, P., "Analytical characteristics of the DES," *Advances in Cryptology: Proceedings of CRYPTO '83*, p. 171. Plenum Publishing, New York, USA, 1984.

Hwang, T.

- Hwang, T. and Rao, T. R. N., "Secret error-correcting codes (SECC)," *Advances in Cryptology - CRYPTO '88*, p. 540. Springer-Verlag, Berlin, 1989.
- Hwang, T. and Rao, T. R. N., "Private-key algebraic-code cryptosystems with high information rates," *Advances in Cryptology - EUROCRYPT '89*, p. 657. Springer-Verlag, Berlin, 1989.
- Laih, C. S., Harn, L., Lee, J. Y. and Hwang, T., "Dynamic threshold scheme based on the definition of cross-product in an N-dimensional linear space," *Advances in Cryptology - CRYPTO '89*, p. 286. Springer-Verlag, Berlin, 1989.
- Hwang, T., "Cryptosystem for group oriented cryptography," *Advances in Cryptology - EUROCRYPT '90*, p. 352. Springer-Verlag, Berlin, 1990.
- Li, C. M., Hwang, T. and Lee, N. Y., "Remark on the threshold RSA signature scheme," *Advances in Cryptology - CRYPTO '93*, p. 413. Springer-Verlag, Berlin, 1993.
- Li, C. M., Hwang, T. and Lee, N. Y., "Threshold-multisignature schemes where suspected forgery implies traceability of adversarial shareholders," *Advances in Cryptology - EUROCRYPT '94*, p. 194. Springer-Verlag, Berlin, 1995.
- Wang, C. H., Hwang, T. and Tsai, J. J., "On the Matsumoto and Imai's human identification scheme," *Advances in Cryptology - EUROCRYPT '95*, p. 382. Springer-Verlag, Berlin, 1995.

Ihaka, R.

- Davis, D., Ihaka, R. and Fenstermacher, P., "Cryptographic randomness from air turbulence in disk drives," *Advances in Cryptology - CRYPTO '94*, p. 114. Springer-Verlag, Berlin, 1994.

Imai, H.

- Matsumoto, T. and Imai, H., "On the key predistribution system: a practical solution to the key distribution problem," *Advances in Cryptology - CRYPTO '87*, p. 185. Springer-Verlag, Berlin, 1987.
- Matsumoto, T. and Imai, H., "Public quadratic polynomial-tuples for efficient signature-verification and message-encryption," *Advances in Cryptology - EUROCRYPT '88*, p. 419. Springer-Verlag, Berlin, 1988.
- Matsumoto, T., Kato, K. and Imai, H., "Speeding up secret computations with insecure auxiliary devices," *Advances in Cryptology - CRYPTO '88*, p. 497. Springer-Verlag, Berlin, 1989.
- Zheng, Y., Matsumoto, T. and Imai, H., "Impossibility and optimally results on constructing pseudorandom permutations (extended abstract)," *Advances in Cryptology - EUROCRYPT '89*, p. 412. Springer-Verlag, Berlin, 1989.
- Zheng, Y., Matsumoto, T. and Imai, H., "On the construction of block ciphers provably secure and not relying on any unproved hypotheses (extended abstract)," *Advances in Cryptology - CRYPTO '89*, p. 461. Springer-Verlag, Berlin, 1989.
- Zheng, Y., Matsumoto, T. and Imai, H., "Structural properties of one-way hash functions," *Advances in Cryptology - CRYPTO '90*, p. 285. Springer-Verlag, Berlin, 1990.
- Kim, K., Matsumoto, T. and Imai, H., "A recursive construction method of S-boxes satisfying strict avalanche criterion," *Advances in Cryptology - CRYPTO '90*, p. 564. Springer-Verlag, Berlin, 1990.
- Matsumoto, T. and Imai, H., "Human identification through insecure channel," *Advances in Cryptology - EUROCRYPT '91*, p. 409. Springer-Verlag, Berlin, 1991.
- Iwamura, K., Matsumoto, T. and Imai, H., "High-speed implementation methods for RSA scheme," *Advances in Cryptology - EUROCRYPT '92*, p. 221. Springer-Verlag, Berlin, 1992.
- Iwamura, K., Matsumoto, T. and Imai, H., "Systolic-arrays for modular exponentiation using Montgomery method," *Advances in Cryptology - EUROCRYPT '92*, p. 477. Springer-Verlag, Berlin, 1992.

Impagliazzo, R.

- Impagliazzo, R. and Yung, M., "Direct minimum knowledge computations," *Advances in Cryptology - CRYPTO '87*, p. 40. Springer-Verlag, Berlin, 1987.
- Impagliazzo, R. and Rudich, S., "Limits on the provable consequences of one-way permutations (invited talk)," *Advances in Cryptology - CRYPTO '88*, p. 8. Springer-Verlag, Berlin, 1989.
- Jakobsson, M., Sako, K. and Impagliazzo, R., "Designated verifier proofs and their applications," *Advances in Cryptology - EUROCRYPT '96*, p. 143. Springer-Verlag, Berlin, 1996.

Improta, S.

- Wolfowicz, W., Brugia, O. and Improta, S., "An encryption and authentication procedure for tele-surveillance systems," *Advances in Cryptology: Proceedings of EUROCRYPT '84*, p. 437. Springer-Verlag, Berlin, 1984.

Ingemarsson, I.

- Ingemarsson, I., "Some Comments on the Knapsack Problem," *Advances in Cryptography*, p. 20. University of California, Santa Barbara, Santa Barbara, California, USA, 1982.
- Ingemarsson, I., "A new algorithm for the solution of the knapsack problem," *Cryptography - Proceedings of the Workshop on Cryptography, Burg Feuerstein, Germany*, p. 309. Springer-Verlag, Berlin, 1983.
- Bertilsson, M., Brickell, E. F. and Ingemarsson, I., "Cryptanalysis of video encryption based on space-filling curves," *Advances in Cryptology - EUROCRYPT '89*, p. 403. Springer-Verlag, Berlin, 1989.
- Ingemarsson, I. and Simmons, G. J., "A protocol to set up shared secret schemes without the assistance of mutually trusted party," *Advances in Cryptology - EUROCRYPT '90*, p. 266. Springer-Verlag, Berlin, 1990.

Isselhorst, H.

- Isselhorst, H., "The use of fractions in public-key cryptosystems," *Advances in Cryptology - EUROCRYPT '89*, p. 47. Springer-Verlag, Berlin, 1989.

Itoh, K.

- Park, C., Itoh, K. and Kurosawa, K., "Efficient anonymous channel and all/nothing election scheme," *Advances in Cryptology - EUROCRYPT '93*, p. 248. Springer-Verlag, Berlin, 1993.

Itoh, T.

- Shinozaki, S., Itoh, T., Fujioka, A. and Tsujii, S., "Provably secure key-updating schemes in identity-based systems," *Advances in Cryptology - EUROCRYPT '90*, p. 16. Springer-Verlag, Berlin, 1990.
- Sakurai, K. and Itoh, T., "On the discrepancy between serial and parallel of zero-knowledge protocols," *Advances in Cryptology - CRYPTO '92*, p. 246. Springer-Verlag, Berlin, 1992.
- Itoh, T., Hoshi, M. and Tsujii, S., "A low communication competitive interactive proof system for promised quadratic residuosity," *Advances in Cryptology - CRYPTO '93*, p. 61. Springer-Verlag, Berlin, 1993.
- Itoh, T., Ohta, Y. and Shizuya, H., "Language dependent secure bit commitment," *Advances in Cryptology - CRYPTO '94*, p. 188. Springer-Verlag, Berlin, 1994.

Iversen, K. R.

- Iversen, K. R., "A cryptographic scheme for computerized general elections," *Advances in Cryptology - CRYPTO '91*, p. 405. Springer-Verlag, Berlin, 1991.

Iwamura, K.

- Iwamura, K., Matsumoto, T. and Imai, H., "High-speed implementation methods for RSA scheme," *Advances in Cryptology - EUROCRYPT '92*, p. 221. Springer-Verlag, Berlin, 1992.
- Iwamura, K., Matsumoto, T. and Imai, H., "Systolic-arrays for modular exponentiation using Montgomery method," *Advances in Cryptology - EUROCRYPT '92*, p. 477. Springer-Verlag, Berlin, 1992.

Iwata, M.

- Miyaguchi, S., Ohta, K. and Iwata, M., "Confirmation that some hash functions are not collision free," *Advances in Cryptology - EUROCRYPT '90*, p. 326. Springer-Verlag, Berlin, 1990.

Jaburek, W. J.

- Jaburek, W. J. and Vienna, G., "A generalization of ElGamal's public key cryptosystem," *Advances in Cryptology - EUROCRYPT '89*, p. 23. Springer-Verlag, Berlin, 1989.

Jackson, W. A.

- Jackson, W. A., Martin, K. M. and O'Keefe, C. M., "Multisecret threshold schemes," *Advances in Cryptology - CRYPTO '93*, p. 126. Springer-Verlag, Berlin, 1993.
- Jackson, W. A., Martin, K. M. and O'Keefe, C. M., "Efficient secret sharing without a mutually trusted authority," *Advances in Cryptology - EUROCRYPT '95*, p. 183. Springer-Verlag, Berlin, 1995.

Jakobsson, M.

- Jakobsson, M., "Blackmailing using undeniable signatures," *Advances in Cryptology - EUROCRYPT '94*, p. 425. Springer-Verlag, Berlin, 1995.
- Jakobsson, M., "Ripping coins for a fair exchange," *Advances in Cryptology - EUROCRYPT '95*, p. 220. Springer-Verlag, Berlin, 1995.
- Jakobsson, M., Sako, K. and Impagliazzo, R., "Designated verifier proofs and their applications," *Advances in Cryptology - EUROCRYPT '96*, p. 143. Springer-Verlag, Berlin, 1996.
- Jakobsson, M. and Yung, M., "Proving Without Knowing: On Oblivious, Agnostic and Blindfolded Provers," *Advances in Cryptology - CRYPTO '96*, p. 186. Springer-Verlag, Berlin, 1996.
- Bellare, M., Jakobsson, M. and Yung, M., "Round-Optimal Zero-Knowledge Arguments Based on Any One-Way Function," *Advances in Cryptology - EUROCRYPT '97*, p. 280. Springer-Verlag, Berlin, 1997.
- Jakobsson, M. and Yung, M., "Distributed "Magic Ink" Signatures," *Advances in Cryptology - EUROCRYPT '97*, p. 450. Springer-Verlag, Berlin, 1997.

James, N. S.

- James, N. S., Lidl, R. and Niederreiter, H., "A Cryptanalytic Attack on the CADE Cryptosystem," *Abstracts of Papers: EUROCRYPT '86*, p. 27. Department of Electrical Engineering, University of Linköping, Linkoping, Sweden, 1986.
- James, N. S., Lidl, R. and Niederreiter, H., "Breaking the Cade cipher," *Advances in Cryptology - CRYPTO '86*, p. 60. Springer-Verlag, Berlin, 1986.

Janardan, R.

- Janardan, R. and Lakshmanan, K. B., "A public-key cryptosystem based on the matrix cover NP-complete problem," *Advances in Cryptology: Proceedings of CRYPTO '82*, p. 21. Plenum Publishing, New York, USA, 1982.

Jansen, C. J. A.

- Jansen, C. J. A., "Protection Against Active Eavesdropping," *Abstracts of Papers: EUROCRYPT '86*, p. 4. Department of Electrical Engineering, University of Linköping, Linkoping, Sweden, 1986.
- Jansen, C. J. A. and Boekee, D. E., "Modes of blockcipher algorithms and their protection against active eavesdropping," *Advances in Cryptology - EUROCRYPT '87*, p. 281. Springer-Verlag, Berlin, 1987.
- Vandewalle, J., Chaum, D., Fumy, W., Jansen, C. J. A., Landrock, P. and Roelofsen, G., "A European call for cryptographic algorithms: RIPE; Race Integrity Primitives Evaluation," *Advances in Cryptology - EUROCRYPT '89*, p. 267. Springer-Verlag, Berlin, 1989.
- Jansen, C. J. A., "On the construction of run permuted sequences," *Advances in Cryptology - EUROCRYPT '90*, p. 196. Springer-Verlag, Berlin, 1990.
- Jansen, C. J. A., "The maximum order complexity of sequence ensembles," *Advances in Cryptology - EUROCRYPT '91*, p. 153. Springer-Verlag, Berlin, 1991.
- Preneel, B., Chaum, D., Fumy, W., Jansen, C. J. A., Landrock, P. and Roelofsen, G., "Race Integrity Primitives Evaluation," *Advances in Cryptology - EUROCRYPT '91*, p. 547. Springer-Verlag, Berlin, 1991.

Janson, P.

- Bird, R., Gopal, I., Herzberg, A., Janson, P., Kutten, S., Molva, R. and Yung, M., "Systematic design of two-party authentication protocols," *Advances in Cryptology - CRYPTO '91*, p. 44. Springer-Verlag, Berlin, 1991.

328

Jarecki, S.

- Herzberg, A., Jarecki, S., Krawczyk, H. and Yung, M., "Proactive Secret Sharing Or: How to Cope With Perpetual Leakage," *Advances in Cryptology - CRYPTO '95*, p. 339. Springer-Verlag, Berlin, 1995.
- Gennaro, R., Jarecki, S., Krawczyk, H. and Rabin, T., "Robust threshold DSS signatures," *Advances in Cryptology - EUROCRYPT '96*, p. 354. Springer-Verlag, Berlin, 1996.
- Gennaro, R., Jarecki, S., Krawczyk, H. and Rabin, T., "Robust and Efficient Sharing of RSA Functions," *Advances in Cryptology - CRYPTO '96*, p. 157. Springer-Verlag, Berlin, 1996.

Jendal, H. N.

- Jendal, H. N., Kuhn, Y. J. B. and Massey, J. L., "An information-theoretic treatment of homophonic substitution," *Advances in Cryptology - EUROCRYPT '89*, p. 382. Springer-Verlag, Berlin, 1989.

Jennings, S. M.

- Jennings, S. M., "Multiplexed sequences: some properties of the minimum polynomial," *Cryptography - Proceedings of the Workshop on Cryptography, Burg Feuerstein, Germany*, p. 189. Springer-Verlag, Berlin, 1983.

Jensen, C. J. A.

- Jensen, C. J. A. and Boekee, D. E., "The shortest feedback shift register that can generate a given sequence," *Advances in Cryptology - CRYPTO '89*, p. 90. Springer-Verlag, Berlin, 1989.

Jespers, P. G. A.

- Vandemeulebroecke, A., Vanzieleghem, E., Jespers, P. G. A. and Denayer, T., "A single chip 1024 bits RSA processor," *Advances in Cryptology - EUROCRYPT '89*, p. 219. Springer-Verlag, Berlin, 1989.

Jingmin, H.

- Jingmin, H. and Kaicheng, L., "A new probabilistic encryption scheme," *Advances in Cryptology - EUROCRYPT '88*, p. 415. Springer-Verlag, Berlin, 1988.

Johansson, T.

- Johansson, T., Kabatianski, G. A. and Smeets, B., "On the relation between A-codes and codes correcting independent errors," *Advances in Cryptology - EUROCRYPT '93*, p. 1. Springer-Verlag, Berlin, 1993.
- Bierbrauer, J., Johansson, T., Kabatianski, G. A. and Smeets, B., "On families of hash functions via geometric codes and concatenation," *Advances in Cryptology - CRYPTO '93*, p. 331. Springer-Verlag, Berlin, 1993.
- Johansson, T., "On the construction of perfect authentication codes that permit arbitration," *Advances in Cryptology - CRYPTO '93*, p. 343. Springer-Verlag, Berlin, 1993.
- Johansson, T. and Smeets, B., "On A2-codes including arbiter's attacks," *Advances in Cryptology - EUROCRYPT '94*, p. 456. Springer-Verlag, Berlin, 1995.
- Helleseth, T. and Johansson, T., "Universal Hash Functions from Exponential Sums over Finite Fields and Galois Rings," *Advances in Cryptology - CRYPTO '96*, p. 31. Springer-Verlag, Berlin, 1996.
- Johansson, T., "Bucket Hashing with a Small Key Size," *Advances in Cryptology - EUROCRYPT '97*, p. 149. Springer-Verlag, Berlin, 1997.
- Kurosawa, K., Johansson, T. and Stinson, D. R., "Almost k-wise Independent Sample Spaces and Their Cryptologic Applications," *Advances in Cryptology - EUROCRYPT '97*, p. 409. Springer-Verlag, Berlin, 1997.

Johnson, B. A.

- Findlay, P. A. and Johnson, B. A., "Modular exponentiation using recursive sums of residues," *Advances in Cryptology - CRYPTO '89*, p. 371. Springer-Verlag, Berlin, 1989.

Jones, R. W.

- Jones, R. W., "User functions for the generation and distribution of encipherment keys," *Advances in Cryptology: Proceedings of EUROCRYPT '84*, p. 317. Springer-Verlag, Berlin, 1984.
- Baxter, M. S. J. and Jones, R. W., "The role of encipherment services in distributed systems.," *Advances in Cryptology - EUROCRYPT '85*, p. 214. Springer-Verlag, Berlin, 1985.

Jordan, J. P.

- Jordan, J. P., "Variant of a Public Key Cryptosystem based Goppa codes," *Advances in Cryptography*, p. 25. University of California, Santa Barbara, Santa Barbara, California, USA, 1982.

Jorissen, F.

- Jorissen, F., Vandewalle, J. and Govaerts, R., "Extension of Brickell's algorithm for breaking high density knapsacks," *Advances in Cryptology - EUROCRYPT '87*, p. 109. Springer-Verlag, Berlin, 1987.

Joux, A.

- Chee, Y. Meng, Joux, A. and Stern, J., "The cryptanalysis of a new public-key cryptosystem based on modular knapsacks," *Advances in Cryptology - CRYPTO '91*, p. 204. Springer-Verlag, Berlin, 1991.
- Joux, A. and Granboulan, L., "A practical attack against knapsack based hash functions," *Advances in Cryptology - EUROCRYPT '94*, p. 58. Springer-Verlag, Berlin, 1995.

Juels, A.

- Juels, A., Luby, M. and Ostrovsky, R., "Security of Blind Digital Signatures," *Advances in Cryptology - CRYPTO '97*, p. 150. Springer-Verlag, Berlin, 1997.

Jueneman, R. R.

- Jueneman, R. R., "Analysis of certain aspects of output feedback mode," *Advances in Cryptology: Proceedings of CRYPTO '82*, p. 99. Plenum Publishing, New York, USA, 1982.
- Jueneman, R. R., "A high speed manipulation detection code," *Advances in Cryptology - CRYPTO '86*, p. 327. Springer-Verlag, Berlin, 1986.

Juergensen, H.

- Juergensen, H. and Matthews, D. E., "Some results on the information theoretic analysis of cryptosystems," *Advances in Cryptology: Proceedings of CRYPTO '83*, p. 303. Plenum Publishing, New York, USA, 1984.

Kabatianski, G. A.

- Johansson, T., Kabatianski, G. A. and Smeets, B., "On the relation between A-codes and codes correcting independent errors," *Advances in Cryptology - EUROCRYPT '93*, p. 1. Springer-Verlag, Berlin, 1993.
- Bierbrauer, J., Johansson, T., Kabatianski, G. A. and Smeets, B., "On families of hash functions via geometric codes and concatenation," *Advances in Cryptology - CRYPTO '93*, p. 331. Springer-Verlag, Berlin, 1993.
- Blakley, G. R. and Kabatianski, G. A., "On General Perfect Secret Sharing Schemes," *Advances in Cryptology - CRYPTO '95*, p. 367. Springer-Verlag, Berlin, 1995.

Kahn, D.

- Kahn, D., "Keying the German Navy's Enigma (invited)," *Advances in Cryptology - CRYPTO '89*, p. 2. Springer-Verlag, Berlin, 1989.

Kaicheng, L.

- Jingmin, H. and Kaicheng, L., "A new probabilistic encryption scheme," *Advances in Cryptology - EUROCRYPT '88*, p. 415. Springer-Verlag, Berlin, 1988.

Karnin, E.

- Hellman, M. E., Karnin, E. and Reyneri, J. M., "On the Necessity or Exhaustive Search for System-Invariant Cryptanalysis," *Advances in Cryptography*, p. 2. University of California, Santa Barbara, Santa Barbara, California, USA, 1982.
- Amirazizi, H., Karnin, E. and Reyneri, J. M., "Compact Knapsacks are Polynomially Solvable," *Advances in Cryptography*, p. 17. University of California, Santa Barbara, Santa Barbara, California, USA, 1982.

Karp, R. M.

- Dolev, D., Even, S. and Karp, R. M., "On the security of ping-pong protocols (Extended abstract)," *Advances in Cryptology: Proceedings of CRYPTO '82*, p. 177. Plenum Publishing, New York, USA, 1982.

Katayama, Y.

- Kurosawa, K., Katayama, Y., Ogata, W. and Tsujii, S., "General public key residue cryptosystems and mental poker protocols," *Advances in Cryptology - EUROCRYPT '90*, p. 374. Springer-Verlag, Berlin, 1990.

Kato, K.

- Matsumoto, T., Kato, K. and Imai, H., "Speeding up secret computations with insecure auxiliary devices," *Advances in Cryptology - CRYPTO '88*, p. 497. Springer-Verlag, Berlin, 1989.

Kawamura, S.

- Kawamura, S. and Hirano, K., "A fast modular arithmetic algorithm using a residue table," *Advances in Cryptology - EUROCRYPT '88*, p. 245. Springer-Verlag, Berlin, 1988.

Kearns, M.

- Blum, A., Furst, M., Kearns, M. and Lipton, R. J., "Cryptographic primitives based on hard learning problems," *Advances in Cryptology - CRYPTO '93*, p. 278. Springer-Verlag, Berlin, 1993.

Kelsey, J.

- Kelsey, J., Schneier, B. and Wagner, D., "Key-Schedule Cryptanalysis of IDEA, G-DES, GOST, SAFER, and Triple-DES," *Advances in Cryptology - CRYPTO '96*, p. 237. Springer-Verlag, Berlin, 1996.
- Wagner, D., Schneier, B. and Kelsey, J., "Cryptanalysis of the Cellular Message Encryption Algorithm," *Advances in Cryptology - CRYPTO '97*, p. 526. Springer-Verlag, Berlin, 1997.

- Kilian, J., "Interactive proofs with provable security against honest verifiers," *Advances in Cryptology - CRYPTO '90*, p. 378. Springer-Verlag, Berlin, 1990.
- Kilian, J. and Rubinfeld, R., "Interactive proofs with space bounded provers," *Advances in Cryptology - CRYPTO '91*, p. 225. Springer-Verlag, Berlin, 1991.
- Dwork, C., Feige, U., Kilian, J., Naor, M. and Safra, M., "Low communication 2-prover zero-knowledge proofs for NP," *Advances in Cryptology - CRYPTO '92*, p. 215. Springer-Verlag, Berlin, 1992.
- Crépeau, C. and Kilian, J., "Discreet solitary games," *Advances in Cryptology - CRYPTO '93*, p. 319. Springer-Verlag, Berlin, 1993.
- Bellare, M., Kilian, J. and Rogaway, P., "The security of cipher block chaining," *Advances in Cryptology - CRYPTO '94*, p. 341. Springer-Verlag, Berlin, 1994.
- Sako, K. and Kilian, J., "Secure voting using partially compatible homomorphisms," *Advances in Cryptology - CRYPTO '94*, p. 411. Springer-Verlag, Berlin, 1994.
- Sako, K. and Kilian, J., "Receipt-free mix-type voting scheme A practical solution to the implementation of a voting booth," *Advances in Cryptology - EUROCRYPT '95*, p. 393. Springer-Verlag, Berlin, 1995.
- Kilian, J. and Leighton, T., "Fair Crypto systems, Revisited," *Advances in Cryptology - CRYPTO '95*, p. 208. Springer-Verlag, Berlin, 1995.
- Kilian, J., "Improved Efficient Arguments," *Advances in Cryptology - CRYPTO '95*, p. 311. Springer-Verlag, Berlin, 1995.
- Kilian, J. and Rogaway, P., "How to Protect DES Against Exhaustive Key Search," *Advances in Cryptology - CRYPTO '96*, p. 252. Springer-Verlag, Berlin, 1996.

Kim, K.
- Kim, K., Matsumoto, T. and Imai, H., "A recursive construction method of S-boxes satisfying strict avalanche criterion," *Advances in Cryptology - CRYPTO '90*, p. 564. Springer-Verlag, Berlin, 1990.

Klapper, A.
- Chan, A. H., Goresky, M. and Klapper, A., "On the linear complexity of feedback registers (extended abstract)," *Advances in Cryptology - EUROCRYPT '89*, p. 563. Springer-Verlag, Berlin, 1989.
- Chan, A. H., Goresky, M. and Klapper, A., "Correlation functions of geometric sequences," *Advances in Cryptology - EUROCRYPT '90*, p. 214. Springer-Verlag, Berlin, 1990.
- Goresky, M. and Klapper, A., "Feedback registers based on ramified extensions of the 2-adic numbers," *Advances in Cryptology - EUROCRYPT '94*, p. 215. Springer-Verlag, Berlin, 1995.

- Klapper, A. and Goresky, M., "Large periods nearly de Bruijn FCSR sequences," *Advances in Cryptology - EUROCRYPT '95*, p. 263. Springer-Verlag, Berlin, 1995.
- Klapper, A. and Goresky, M., "Cryptanalysis Based on 2-Adic Rational Approximation," *Advances in Cryptology - CRYPTO '95*, p. 262. Springer-Verlag, Berlin, 1995.
- Klapper, A., "On the existence of secure feedback registers," *Advances in Cryptology - EUROCRYPT '96*, p. 256. Springer-Verlag, Berlin, 1996.

Klein, M.

- Diffie, W., Klein, M., Dertouzos, M. L., Gleason, A. and Smith, D., "Panel Discussion: National Security and Commercial Security: Division of Responsibility," *Advances in Cryptography*, p. 154. University of California, Santa Barbara, Santa Barbara, California, USA, 1982.

Kleiner, A. W.

- Siegenthaler, T., Kleiner, A. W. and Forre, R., "Generation of binary sequences with controllable complexity and ideal r-tuple distribution," *Advances in Cryptology - EUROCRYPT '87*, p. 15. Springer-Verlag, Berlin, 1987.

Knapskog, S. J.

- Knapskog, S. J., "Privacy protected payments–realization of a protocol that guarantees payer anonymity," *Advances in Cryptology - EUROCRYPT '88*, p. 107. Springer-Verlag, Berlin, 1988.

Knobloch, H.-J.

- Knobloch, H.-J., "A smart card implementation of the Fiat-Shamir identification scheme," *Advances in Cryptology - EUROCRYPT '88*, p. 87. Springer-Verlag, Berlin, 1988.
- Bauspiess, F. and Knobloch, H.-J., "How to keep authenticity alive in a computer network," *Advances in Cryptology - EUROCRYPT '89*, p. 38. Springer-Verlag, Berlin, 1989.
- Bauspiess, F., Knobloch, H.-J. and Wichmann, P., "Inverting the pseudo exponentiation," *Advances in Cryptology - EUROCRYPT '90*, p. 344. Springer-Verlag, Berlin, 1990.
- Horster, P. and Knobloch, H.-J., "Discrete logarithm based protocols," *Advances in Cryptology - EUROCRYPT '91*, p. 399. Springer-Verlag, Berlin, 1991.

Knudsen, L. R.

- Knudsen, L. R., "Iterative characteristics of DES and s^2-DES," *Advances in Cryptology - CRYPTO '92*, p. 497. Springer-Verlag, Berlin, 1992.
- Nyberg, K. and Knudsen, L. R., "Provable security against differential cryptanalysis," *Advances in Cryptology - CRYPTO '92*, p. 566. Springer-Verlag, Berlin, 1992.
- Damgård, I. B. and Knudsen, L. R., "The breaking of the AR hash function," *Advances in Cryptology - EUROCRYPT '93*, p. 286. Springer-Verlag, Berlin, 1993.
- Knudsen, L. R. and Lai, X., "New attacks on all double block length hash functions of hash rate 1, including the parallel-DM," *Advances in Cryptology - EUROCRYPT '94*, p. 410. Springer-Verlag, Berlin, 1995.
- Knudsen, L. R., "New potentially "weak" keys for DES and LOKI," *Advances in Cryptology - EUROCRYPT '94*, p. 419. Springer-Verlag, Berlin, 1995.
- Knudsen, L. R., "A Key-schedule Weakness in SAFER K-64," *Advances in Cryptology - CRYPTO '95*, p. 274. Springer-Verlag, Berlin, 1995.
- Knudsen, L. R. and Robshaw, M. J. B., "Non-linear approximations in linear cryptanalysis," *Advances in Cryptology - EUROCRYPT '96*, p. 224. Springer-Verlag, Berlin, 1996.
- Knudsen, L. R. and Pedersen, T. P., "On the difficulty of software key escrow," *Advances in Cryptology - EUROCRYPT '96*, p. 237. Springer-Verlag, Berlin, 1996.
- Knudsen, L. R. and Meier, W., "Improved Differential Attacks on RC5," *Advances in Cryptology - CRYPTO '96*, p. 216. Springer-Verlag, Berlin, 1996.
- Borst, J., Knudsen, L. R. and Rijmen, V., "Two Attacks on Reduced IDEA (Extended Abstract)," *Advances in Cryptology - EUROCRYPT '97*, p. 1. Springer-Verlag, Berlin, 1997.
- Knudsen, L. R. and Preneel, B., "Fast and Secure Hashing Based on Codes," *Advances in Cryptology - CRYPTO '97*, p. 485. Springer-Verlag, Berlin, 1997.

Koblitz, N.

- Koblitz, N., "A family of Jacobians suitable for discrete log cryptosystems," *Advances in Cryptology - CRYPTO '88*, p. 94. Springer-Verlag, Berlin, 1989.
- Koblitz, N., "Constructing elliptic curve cryptosystems in characteristic 2," *Advances in Cryptology - CRYPTO '90*, p. 156. Springer-Verlag, Berlin, 1990.
- Koblitz, N., "CM-curves with good cryptographic properties," *Advances in Cryptology - CRYPTO '91*, p. 279. Springer-Verlag, Berlin, 1991.
- Fellows, M. and Koblitz, N., "Kid Krypto," *Advances in Cryptology - CRYPTO '92*, p. 371. Springer-Verlag, Berlin, 1992.

Kochanski, M.

- Kochanski, M., "Developing an RSA chip," *Advances in Cryptology - CRYPTO '85*, p. 350. Springer-Verlag, Berlin, 1986.

Kocher, P. C.

- Kocher, P. C., "Timing Attacks on Implementations of Diffie-Hellman, RSA, DSS, and Other Systems," *Advances in Cryptology - CRYPTO '96*, p. 104. Springer-Verlag, Berlin, 1996.

Kohl, J. T.

- Kohl, J. T., "The use of encryption in Kerberos for network authentication (invited)," *Advances in Cryptology - CRYPTO '89*, p. 35. Springer-Verlag, Berlin, 1989.

Kompella, K.

- Estes, D., Adleman, L. M., Kompella, K., McCurley, K. S. and Miller, G. L., "Breaking the Ong-Schnorr-Shamir signature scheme for quadratic number fields," *Advances in Cryptology - CRYPTO '85*, p. 3. Springer-Verlag, Berlin, 1986.
- Kompella, K. and Adleman, L. M., "Fast checkers for cryptography," *Advances in Cryptology - CRYPTO '90*, p. 515. Springer-Verlag, Berlin, 1990.

Konheim, A. G.

- Konheim, A. G., "One-way Sequence for Transaction Verification," *Advances in Cryptography*, p. 38. University of California, Santa Barbara, Santa Barbara, California, USA, 1982.
- Konheim, A. G., "Cryptoanalysis of a Kryha machine," *Cryptography - Proceedings of the Workshop on Cryptography, Burg Feuerstein, Germany*, p. 49. Springer-Verlag, Berlin, 1983.
- Konheim, A. G., "Cryptanalysis of ADFGVX encipherment systems," *Advances in Cryptology: Proceedings of CRYPTO '84*, p. 339. Springer-Verlag, Berlin, 1985.

Korzhik, Valery I.

- Korzhik, Valery I. and Turkin, Andrey I., "Cryptanalysis of McEliece's Public-Key Cryptosystem," *Advances in Cryptology - EUROCRYPT '91*, p. 68. Springer-Verlag, Berlin, 1991.

Kothari, S. C.

- Kothari, S. C., "Generalized linear threshold scheme," *Advances in Cryptology: Proceedings of CRYPTO '84*, p. 231. Springer-Verlag, Berlin, 1985.

Kowalchuk, J.

- Scnanning, B. P. and Kowalchuk, J., "MEMO: A Hybrid Approach to Encrypted Electronic Mail," *Advances in Cryptography*, p. 64. University of California, Santa Barbara, Santa Barbara, California, USA, 1982.

Kowatsch, M.

- Kowatsch, M., Eichinger, B. O. and Seifert, F. J., "Message protection by spread spectrum modulation in a packet voice radio link.," *Advances in Cryptology - EUROCRYPT '85*, p. 273. Springer-Verlag, Berlin, 1985.

Koyama, K.

- Koyama, K. and Ohta, K., "Identity based conference key distribution systems," *Advances in Cryptology - CRYPTO '87*, p. 175. Springer-Verlag, Berlin, 1987.
- Koyama, K. and Ohta, K., "Security of improved identity-based conference key distribution systems," *Advances in Cryptology - EUROCRYPT '88*, p. 11. Springer-Verlag, Berlin, 1988.
- Ohta, K., Okamoto, T. and Koyama, K., "Membership authentication for hierarchical multigroups using the extended Fiat-Shamir scheme," *Advances in Cryptology - EUROCRYPT '90*, p. 446. Springer-Verlag, Berlin, 1990.
- Koyama, K. and Terada, R., "Nonlinear parity circuits and their cryptographic applications," *Advances in Cryptology - CRYPTO '90*, p. 582. Springer-Verlag, Berlin, 1990.
- Koyama, K., Maurer, U. M., Okamoto, T. and Vanstone, S. A., "New public-key schemes based on elliptic curves over the ring Z_n," *Advances in Cryptology - CRYPTO '91*, p. 252. Springer-Verlag, Berlin, 1991.
- Koyama, K., "Secure conference key distribution schemes for conspiracy attack," *Advances in Cryptology - EUROCRYPT '92*, p. 449. Springer-Verlag, Berlin, 1992.
- Koyama, K. and Tsuruoka, Y., "Speeding up elliptic cryptosystems by using a signed binary window method," *Advances in Cryptology - CRYPTO '92*, p. 345. Springer-Verlag, Berlin, 1992.
- Koyama, K., "Fast RSA-type schemes based on singular cubic curves $y^2 + axy = x^3$ (mod n)," *Advances in Cryptology - EUROCRYPT '95*, p. 329. Springer-Verlag, Berlin, 1995.

Kramer, G. G.

- Harpes, C., Kramer, G. G. and Massey, J. L., "A generalization of linear cryptanalysis and the applicability of Matsui's piling-up lemma," *Advances in Cryptology - EUROCRYPT '95*, p. 24. Springer-Verlag, Berlin, 1995.

Kraus, D.

- Heider, F. P., Kraus, D. and Welschenbach, M., "Some Preliminary Remarks on the Decimal, Shift an Add-Algorithm (DSA)," *Abstracts of Papers: EUROCRYPT '86*, p. 3. Department of Electrical Engineering, University of Linköping, Linkoping, Sweden, 1986.

Krawczyk, H.

- Goldreich, O., Krawczyk, H. and Luby, M., "On the existence of pseudorandom generators," *Advances in Cryptology - CRYPTO '88*, p. 146. Springer-Verlag, Berlin, 1989.
- Goldreich, O. and Krawczyk, H., "Sparse pseudorandom distributions (extended abstract)," *Advances in Cryptology - CRYPTO '89*, p. 113. Springer-Verlag, Berlin, 1989.
- Krawczyk, H., "How to predict congruential generators," *Advances in Cryptology - CRYPTO '89*, p. 138. Springer-Verlag, Berlin, 1989.
- Coppersmith, D., Krawczyk, H. and Mansour, Y., "The shrinking generator," *Advances in Cryptology - CRYPTO '93*, p. 22. Springer-Verlag, Berlin, 1993.
- Krawczyk, H., "Secret sharing made short," *Advances in Cryptology - CRYPTO '93*, p. 136. Springer-Verlag, Berlin, 1993.
- Krawczyk, H., "LFSR-based hashing and authentication," *Advances in Cryptology - CRYPTO '94*, p. 129. Springer-Verlag, Berlin, 1994.
- Krawczyk, H., "New hash functions for message authentication," *Advances in Cryptology - EUROCRYPT '95*, p. 301. Springer-Verlag, Berlin, 1995.
- Herzberg, A., Jarecki, S., Krawczyk, H. and Yung, M., "Proactive Secret Sharing Or: How to Cope With Perpetual Leakage," *Advances in Cryptology - CRYPTO '95*, p. 339. Springer-Verlag, Berlin, 1995.
- Gennaro, R., Jarecki, S., Krawczyk, H. and Rabin, T., "Robust threshold DSS signatures," *Advances in Cryptology - EUROCRYPT '96*, p. 354. Springer-Verlag, Berlin, 1996.
- Bellare, M., Canetti, R. and Krawczyk, H., "Keying Hash Functions for Message Authentication," *Advances in Cryptology - CRYPTO '96*, p. 1. Springer-Verlag, Berlin, 1996.
- Gennaro, R., Jarecki, S., Krawczyk, H. and Rabin, T., "Robust and Efficient Sharing of RSA Functions," *Advances in Cryptology - CRYPTO '96*, p. 157. Springer-Verlag, Berlin, 1996.
- Gennaro, R., Krawczyk, H. and Rabin, T., "RSA-Based Undeniable Signatures," *Advances in Cryptology - CRYPTO '97*, p. 132. Springer-Verlag, Berlin, 1997.

Krivachy, T.

- Krivachy, T., "The chipcard–an identification card with cryptographic protection.," *Advances in Cryptology - EUROCRYPT '85*, p. 200. Springer-Verlag, Berlin, 1985.

Kuhn, Y. J. B.

- Jendal, H. N., Kuhn, Y. J. B. and Massey, J. L., "An information-theoretic treatment of homophonic substitution," *Advances in Cryptology - EUROCRYPT '89*, p. 382. Springer-Verlag, Berlin, 1989.

Kurosawa, K.

- Kurosawa, K., Katayama, Y., Ogata, W. and Tsujii, S., "General public key residue cryptosystems and mental poker protocols," *Advances in Cryptology - EUROCRYPT '90*, p. 374. Springer-Verlag, Berlin, 1990.
- Kurosawa, K. and Tsujii, S., "Multi-language zero knowledge interactive proof systems," *Advances in Cryptology - CRYPTO '90*, p. 339. Springer-Verlag, Berlin, 1990.
- Kurosawa, K., Okada, K., Sakano, K., Ogata, W. and Tsujii, S., "Non-perfect secret sharing schemes and matroids," *Advances in Cryptology - EUROCRYPT '93*, p. 126. Springer-Verlag, Berlin, 1993.
- Park, C., Itoh, K. and Kurosawa, K., "Efficient anonymous channel and all/nothing election scheme," *Advances in Cryptology - EUROCRYPT '93*, p. 248. Springer-Verlag, Berlin, 1993.
- Park, C., Kurosawa, K., Okamoto, T. and Tsujii, S., "On key distribution and authentication in mobile radio networks," *Advances in Cryptology - EUROCRYPT '93*, p. 461. Springer-Verlag, Berlin, 1993.
- Kurosawa, K., "New bound on authentication code with arbitration," *Advances in Cryptology - CRYPTO '94*, p. 140. Springer-Verlag, Berlin, 1994.
- Kurosawa, K. and Obana, S., "Combinatorial bounds for authentication codes with arbitration," *Advances in Cryptology - EUROCRYPT '95*, p. 289. Springer-Verlag, Berlin, 1995.
- Kurosawa, K., Obana, S. and Ogata, W., "t-Cheater Identifiable (k, n) Threshold Secret Sharing Schemes," *Advances in Cryptology - CRYPTO '95*, p. 410. Springer-Verlag, Berlin, 1995.
- Ogata, W. and Kurosawa, K., "Optimum secret sharing scheme secure against cheating," *Advances in Cryptology - EUROCRYPT '96*, p. 200. Springer-Verlag, Berlin, 1996.
- Kurosawa, K., Johansson, T. and Stinson, D. R., "Almost k-wise Independent Sample Spaces and Their Cryptologic Applications," *Advances in Cryptology - EUROCRYPT '97*, p. 409. Springer-Verlag, Berlin, 1997.
- Kurosawa, K. and Satoh, T., "Design of SAC/PC(1) of Order k Boolean Functions and Three Other Cryptographic Criteria," *Advances in Cryptology - EUROCRYPT '97*, p. 434. Springer-Verlag, Berlin, 1997.

Kurtz, S. A.

- Kurtz, S. A., Mahaney, S. R. and Royer, J. S., "On the power of 1-way functions," *Advances in Cryptology - CRYPTO '88*, p. 578. Springer-Verlag, Berlin, 1989.

Kushilevitz, E.

- Goldreich, O. and Kushilevitz, E., "A perfect zero-knowledge proof for a problem equivalent to discrete logarithm," *Advances in Cryptology - CRYPTO '88*, p. 57. Springer-Verlag, Berlin, 1989.
- Chor, B. and Kushilevitz, E., "Secret sharing over infinite domains (extended abstract)," *Advances in Cryptology - CRYPTO '89*, p. 299. Springer-Verlag, Berlin, 1989.
- Kushilevitz, E. and Rosen, A., "A randomness-rounds tradeoff in private computation," *Advances in Cryptology - CRYPTO '94*, p. 397. Springer-Verlag, Berlin, 1994.

Kutten, S.

- Bird, R., Gopal, I., Herzberg, A., Janson, P., Kutten, S., Molva, R. and Yung, M., "Systematic design of two-party authentication protocols," *Advances in Cryptology - CRYPTO '91*, p. 44. Springer-Verlag, Berlin, 1991.
- Blundo, C., De Santis, A., Herzberg, A., Kutten, S., Vaccaro, U. and Yung, M., "Perfectly-secure key distribution for dynamic conferences," *Advances in Cryptology - CRYPTO '92*, p. 471. Springer-Verlag, Berlin, 1992.

Kwok, R. T. C.

- Kwok, R. T. C. and Beale, M., "Aperiodic linear complexities of de Bruijn sequences," *Advances in Cryptology - CRYPTO '88*, p. 479. Springer-Verlag, Berlin, 1989.

Lagarias, J. C.

- Lagarias, J. C., "Knapsack public key cryptosystems and Diophantine approximation," *Advances in Cryptology: Proceedings of CRYPTO '83*, p. 3. Plenum Publishing, New York, USA, 1984.
- Brickell, E. F., Lagarias, J. C. and Odlyzko, A. M., "Evaluation of the Adleman attack on multiply iterated knapsack cryptosystems," *Advances in Cryptology: Proceedings of CRYPTO '83*, p. 39. Plenum Publishing, New York, USA, 1984.

Lagger, H.

- Eier, R. and Lagger, H., "Trapdoors in knapsack cryptosystems," *Cryptography - Proceedings of the Workshop on Cryptography, Burg Feuerstein, Germany*, p. 316. Springer-Verlag, Berlin, 1983.

Lai, X.

- Lai, X. and Massey, J. L., "A proposal for a new block encryption standard," *Advances in Cryptology - EUROCRYPT '90*, p. 389. Springer-Verlag, Berlin, 1990.
- Lai, X. and Massey, J. L., "Markov ciphers and differential cryptanalysis," *Advances in Cryptology - EUROCRYPT '91*, p. 17. Springer-Verlag, Berlin, 1991.
- Lai, X. and Massey, J. L., "Hash functions based on block ciphers," *Advances in Cryptology - EUROCRYPT '92*, p. 55. Springer-Verlag, Berlin, 1992.
- Hohl, W., Lai, X., Meier, T. and Waldvogel, C., "Security of iterated hash functions based on block ciphers," *Advances in Cryptology - CRYPTO '93*, p. 379. Springer-Verlag, Berlin, 1993.
- Knudsen, L. R. and Lai, X., "New attacks on all double block length hash functions of hash rate 1, including the parallel-DM," *Advances in Cryptology - EUROCRYPT '94*, p. 410. Springer-Verlag, Berlin, 1995.

Laih, C. S.

- Laih, C. S., Harn, L., Lee, J. Y. and Hwang, T., "Dynamic threshold scheme based on the definition of cross-product in an N-dimensional linear space," *Advances in Cryptology - CRYPTO '89*, p. 286. Springer-Verlag, Berlin, 1989.

Lakshmanan, K. B.

- Janardan, R. and Lakshmanan, K. B., "A public-key cryptosystem based on the matrix cover NP-complete problem," *Advances in Cryptology: Proceedings of CRYPTO '82*, p. 21. Plenum Publishing, New York, USA, 1982.

LaMacchia, B. A.

- LaMacchia, B. A. and Odlyzko, A. M., "Solving large sparse linear systems over finite fields," *Advances in Cryptology - CRYPTO '90*, p. 109. Springer-Verlag, Berlin, 1990.
- LaMacchia, B. A. and Odlyzko, A. M., "Computation of discrete logarithms in prime fields (Extended abstract)," *Advances in Cryptology - CRYPTO '90*, p. 616. Springer-Verlag, Berlin, 1990.
- Coster, M. J., LaMacchia, B. A., Odlyzko, A. M. and Schnorr, C. P., "An improved low-density subset sum algorithm," *Advances in Cryptology - EUROCRYPT '91*, p. 54. Springer-Verlag, Berlin, 1991.

Lampson, B.

- Abadi, M., Burrows, M., Lampson, B. and Plotkin, G., "A calculus for access control in distributed systems," *Advances in Cryptology - CRYPTO '91*, p. 1. Springer-Verlag, Berlin, 1991.

Landrock, P.

- Brandt, J., Damgård, I. B. and Landrock, P., "Anonymous and verifiable registration in databases," *Advances in Cryptology - EUROCRYPT '88*, p. 167. Springer-Verlag, Berlin, 1988.
- Brandt, J., Damgård, I. B., Landrock, P. and Pedersen, T. P., "Zero-knowledge authentication scheme with secret key exchange," *Advances in Cryptology - CRYPTO '88*, p. 583. Springer-Verlag, Berlin, 1989.
- Vandewalle, J., Chaum, D., Fumy, W., Jansen, C. J. A., Landrock, P. and Roelofsen, G., "A European call for cryptographic algorithms: RIPE; Race Integrity Primitives Evaluation," *Advances in Cryptology - EUROCRYPT '89*, p. 267. Springer-Verlag, Berlin, 1989.
- Guillou, L. C., Quisquater, J. J., Walker, M., Landrock, P. and Shaer, C., "Precautions taken against various potential attacks in ISO/IEC DIS 9796," *Advances in Cryptology - EUROCRYPT '90*, p. 465. Springer-Verlag, Berlin, 1990.
- Preneel, B., Chaum, D., Fumy, W., Jansen, C. J. A., Landrock, P. and Roelofsen, G., "Race Integrity Primitives Evaluation," *Advances in Cryptology - EUROCRYPT '91*, p. 547. Springer-Verlag, Berlin, 1991.
- Desmedt, Y., Landrock, P., Lenstra, A. K., McCurley, K. S., Odlyzko, A. M., Rueppel, R. A. and Smid, M. E., "The Eurocrypt '92 Controversial Issue: Trapdoor Primes and Moduli," *Advances in Cryptology - EURO-CRYPT '92*, p. 194. Springer-Verlag, Berlin, 1992.

Lang, A. L.

- Lang, A. L. and Vasek, J. T., "Evaluating Relative Security or Commercial ComSec Devices," *Advances in Cryptography*, p. 124. University of California, Santa Barbara, Santa Barbara, California, USA, 1982.

Langford, S. K.

- Langford, S. K. and Hellman, M. E., "Differential-linear cryptanalysis," *Advances in Cryptology - CRYPTO '94*, p. 17. Springer-Verlag, Berlin, 1994.
- Langford, S. K., "Threshold DSS Signatures without a Trusted Party," *Advances in Cryptology - CRYPTO '95*, p. 397. Springer-Verlag, Berlin, 1995.
- Langford, S. K., "Weaknesses in Some Threshold Cryptosystems," *Advances in Cryptology - CRYPTO '96*, p. 74. Springer-Verlag, Berlin, 1996.

Lapidot, D.

- Lapidot, D. and Shamir, A., "Publicly verifiable non-interactive zero-knowledge proofs," *Advances in Cryptology - CRYPTO '90*, p. 353. Springer-Verlag, Berlin, 1990.
- Lapidot, D. and Shamir, A., "A one-round, two-prover, zero-knowledge protocol for NP," *Advances in Cryptology - CRYPTO '91*, p. 213. Springer-Verlag, Berlin, 1991.

Lau, Y. A.

- Lau, Y. A. and McPherson, T., "Implementation of a Hybrid RSA/DES Key Management System," *Advances in Cryptography*, p. 83. University of California, Santa Barbara, Santa Barbara, California, USA, 1982.

Lazic, D. E.

- Beth, T., Lazic, D. E. and Mathias, A., "Cryptanalysis of cryptosystems based on remote chaos replication," *Advances in Cryptology - CRYPTO '94*, p. 318. Springer-Verlag, Berlin, 1994.

Lee, J. Y.

- Laih, C. S., Harn, L., Lee, J. Y. and Hwang, T., "Dynamic threshold scheme based on the definition of cross-product in an N-dimensional linear space," *Advances in Cryptology - CRYPTO '89*, p. 286. Springer-Verlag, Berlin, 1989.

Lee, L.

- Lee, L. and Chow, G., "Results on Sampling-based Scrambling for Secure Speech Communication," *Advances in Cryptography*, p. 115. University of California, Santa Barbara, Santa Barbara, California, USA, 1982.

Lee, N. Y.

- Li, C. M., Hwang, T. and Lee, N. Y., "Remark on the threshold RSA signature scheme," *Advances in Cryptology - CRYPTO '93*, p. 413. Springer-Verlag, Berlin, 1993.
- Li, C. M., Hwang, T. and Lee, N. Y., "Threshold-multisignature schemes where suspected forgery implies traceability of adversarial shareholders," *Advances in Cryptology - EUROCRYPT '94*, p. 194. Springer-Verlag, Berlin, 1995.

Lee, P. J.

- Brickell, E. F., Lee, P. J. and Yacobi, Y., "Secure audio teleconference," *Advances in Cryptology - CRYPTO '87*, p. 418. Springer-Verlag, Berlin, 1987.
- Lee, P. J. and Brickell, E. F., "An observation on the security of McEliece's public-key cryptosystem," *Advances in Cryptology - EUROCRYPT '88*, p. 275. Springer-Verlag, Berlin, 1988.
- Lim, C. H. and Lee, P. J., "Another method for attaining security against adaptively chosen ciphertext attacks," *Advances in Cryptology - CRYPTO '93*, p. 420. Springer-Verlag, Berlin, 1993.
- Lim, C. H. and Lee, P. J., "More flexible exponentiation with precomputation," *Advances in Cryptology - CRYPTO '94*, p. 95. Springer-Verlag, Berlin, 1994.
- Lim, C. H. and Lee, P. J., "Server (prover/signer)-aided verification of identity proofs and signatures," *Advances in Cryptology - EUROCRYPT '95*, p. 64. Springer-Verlag, Berlin, 1995.
- Lim, C. H. and Lee, P. J., "Security and Performance of Server-Aided RSA Computation Protocols," *Advances in Cryptology - CRYPTO '95*, p. 70. Springer-Verlag, Berlin, 1995.
- Lim, C. H. and Lee, P. J., "A Key Recovery Attack on Discrete Log-Based Schemes Using a Prime Order Subgroup," *Advances in Cryptology - CRYPTO '97*, p. 249. Springer-Verlag, Berlin, 1997.

Lee, S. J.

- Park, S. J., Lee, S. J. and Goh, S. C., "On the Security of the Gollmann Cascades," *Advances in Cryptology - CRYPTO '95*, p. 148. Springer-Verlag, Berlin, 1995.

Leichter, J.

- Benaloh, J. and Leichter, J., "Generalized secret sharing and monotone functions," *Advances in Cryptology - CRYPTO '88*, p. 27. Springer-Verlag, Berlin, 1989.

Leighton, A. C.

- Leighton, A. C. and Matyas, S. M., "The history of book ciphers," *Advances in Cryptology: Proceedings of CRYPTO '84*, p. 101. Springer-Verlag, Berlin, 1985.

Leighton, T.

- Leighton, T. and Micali, S., "Secret-key agreement without public-key cryptography," *Advances in Cryptology - CRYPTO '93*, p. 456. Springer-Verlag, Berlin, 1993.
- Kilian, J. and Leighton, T., "Fair Crypto systems, Revisited," *Advances in Cryptology - CRYPTO '95*, p. 208. Springer-Verlag, Berlin, 1995.

Lempel, A.

- Even, S., Goldreich, O. and Lempel, A., "A randomized protocol for signing contracts (Extended abstract)," *Advances in Cryptology: Proceedings of CRYPTO '82*, p. 205. Plenum Publishing, New York, USA, 1982.

Lenstra, A. K.

- Lenstra, A. K. and Manasse, M. S., "Factoring by electronic mail," *Advances in Cryptology - EUROCRYPT '89*, p. 355. Springer-Verlag, Berlin, 1989.
- Lenstra, A. K. and Manasse, M. S., "Factoring with two large primes (extended abstract)," *Advances in Cryptology - EUROCRYPT '90*, p. 72. Springer-Verlag, Berlin, 1990.
- Dixon, B. and Lenstra, A. K., "Massively parallel elliptic curve factoring," *Advances in Cryptology - EUROCRYPT '92*, p. 183. Springer-Verlag, Berlin, 1992.
- Desmedt, Y., Landrock, P., Lenstra, A. K., McCurley, K. S., Odlyzko, A. M., Rueppel, R. A. and Smid, M. E., "The Eurocrypt '92 Controversial Issue: Trapdoor Primes and Moduli," *Advances in Cryptology - EUROCRYPT '92*, p. 194. Springer-Verlag, Berlin, 1992.
- Dixon, B. and Lenstra, A. K., "Factoring integers using SIMD sieves," *Advances in Cryptology - EUROCRYPT '93*, p. 28. Springer-Verlag, Berlin, 1993.
- Denny, T., Dodson, B., Lenstra, A. K. and Manasse, M. S., "On the factorization of RSA-120," *Advances in Cryptology - CRYPTO '93*, p. 166. Springer-Verlag, Berlin, 1993.
- Lenstra, A. K., Winkler, P. and Yacobi, Y., "A Key Escrow System with Warrant Bounds," *Advances in Cryptology - CRYPTO '95*, p. 197. Springer-Verlag, Berlin, 1995.
- Dodson, B. and Lenstra, A. K., "NFS with Four Large Primes: An Explosive Experiment," *Advances in Cryptology - CRYPTO '95*, p. 372. Springer-Verlag, Berlin, 1995.
- Bleichenbacher, D., Bosma, W. and Lenstra, A. K., "Some Remarks on Lucas-Based Cryptosystems," *Advances in Cryptology - CRYPTO '95*, p. 386. Springer-Verlag, Berlin, 1995.

Lercier, R.

- Lercier, R. and Morain, F., "Counting the number of points on elliptic curves over finite fields: strategies and performances," *Advances in Cryptology - EUROCRYPT '95*, p. 79. Springer-Verlag, Berlin, 1995.
- Lercier, R., "Finding Good Random Elliptic Curves for Cryptosystems Defined Over F_2^n," *Advances in Cryptology - EUROCRYPT '97*, p. 379. Springer-Verlag, Berlin, 1997.

Leung, A. K.

- Leung, A. K. and Tavares, S. E., "Sequence complexity as a test for cryptographic systems," *Advances in Cryptology: Proceedings of CRYPTO '84*, p. 468. Springer-Verlag, Berlin, 1985.

Levin, L.

- Goldwasser, S. and Levin, L., "Fair computation of general functions in presence of immoral majority," *Advances in Cryptology - CRYPTO '90*, p. 77. Springer-Verlag, Berlin, 1990.

Li, C. M.

- Li, C. M., Hwang, T. and Lee, N. Y., "Remark on the threshold RSA signature scheme," *Advances in Cryptology - CRYPTO '93*, p. 413. Springer-Verlag, Berlin, 1993.
- Li, C. M., Hwang, T. and Lee, N. Y., "Threshold-multisignature schemes where suspected forgery implies traceability of adversarial shareholders," *Advances in Cryptology - EUROCRYPT '94*, p. 194. Springer-Verlag, Berlin, 1995.

Lidl, R.

- Lidl, R. and Mueller, W. B., "Permutation polynomials in RSA cryptosystems," *Advances in Cryptology: Proceedings of CRYPTO '83*, p. 293. Plenum Publishing, New York, USA, 1984.
- Lidl, R., "On cryptosystems based on polynomials and finite fields," *Advances in Cryptology: Proceedings of EUROCRYPT '84*, p. 10. Springer-Verlag, Berlin, 1984.
- James, N. S., Lidl, R. and Niederreiter, H., "A Cryptanalytic Attack on the CADE Cryptosystem," *Abstracts of Papers: EUROCRYPT '86*, p. 27. Department of Electrical Engineering, University of Linköping, Linkoping, Sweden, 1986.
- James, N. S., Lidl, R. and Niederreiter, H., "Breaking the Cade cipher," *Advances in Cryptology - CRYPTO '86*, p. 60. Springer-Verlag, Berlin, 1986.

348

Lim, C. H.

- Lim, C. H. and Lee, P. J., "Another method for attaining security against adaptively chosen ciphertext attacks," *Advances in Cryptology - CRYPTO '93*, p. 420. Springer-Verlag, Berlin, 1993.
- Lim, C. H. and Lee, P. J., "More flexible exponentiation with precomputation," *Advances in Cryptology - CRYPTO '94*, p. 95. Springer-Verlag, Berlin, 1994.
- Lim, C. H. and Lee, P. J., "Server (prover/signer)-aided verification of identity proofs and signatures," *Advances in Cryptology - EUROCRYPT '95*, p. 64. Springer-Verlag, Berlin, 1995.
- Lim, C. H. and Lee, P. J., "Security and Performance of Server-Aided RSA Computation Protocols," *Advances in Cryptology - CRYPTO '95*, p. 70. Springer-Verlag, Berlin, 1995.
- Lim, C. H. and Lee, P. J., "A Key Recovery Attack on Discrete Log-Based Schemes Using a Prime Order Subgroup," *Advances in Cryptology - CRYPTO '97*, p. 249. Springer-Verlag, Berlin, 1997.

Lin, D.

- Lin, D. and Liu, M., "Linear recurring m-arrays," *Advances in Cryptology - EUROCRYPT '88*, p. 351. Springer-Verlag, Berlin, 1988.

Lin, Hung-Yu

- Harn, L. and Lin, Hung-Yu, "An l-span generalized secret sharing scheme," *Advances in Cryptology - CRYPTO '92*, p. 558. Springer-Verlag, Berlin, 1992.

Lipton, R. J.

- Blum, A., Furst, M., Kearns, M. and Lipton, R. J., "Cryptographic primitives based on hard learning problems," *Advances in Cryptology - CRYPTO '93*, p. 278. Springer-Verlag, Berlin, 1993.
- Boneh, D. and Lipton, R. J., "Quantum Cryptanalysis of Hidden Linear Functions," *Advances in Cryptology - CRYPTO '95*, p. 424. Springer-Verlag, Berlin, 1995.
- Boneh, D. and Lipton, R. J., "Algorithms for Black-Box Fields and Their Application to Cryptography," *Advances in Cryptology - CRYPTO '96*, p. 283. Springer-Verlag, Berlin, 1996.
- Boneh, D., DeMillo, R. A. and Lipton, R. J., "On the Importance of Checking Cryptographic Protocols for Faults (Extended Abstract)," *Advances in Cryptology - EUROCRYPT '97*, p. 37. Springer-Verlag, Berlin, 1997.

Liu, M.

- Liu, M. and Wan, Z., "Generalized multiplexed sequences.," *Advances in Cryptology - EUROCRYPT '85*, p. 135. Springer-Verlag, Berlin, 1985.
- Lin, D. and Liu, M., "Linear recurring m-arrays," *Advances in Cryptology - EUROCRYPT '88*, p. 351. Springer-Verlag, Berlin, 1988.

Lloyd, S.

- Lloyd, S., "Counting functions satisfying a higher order strict avalanche criterion," *Advances in Cryptology - EUROCRYPT '89*, p. 63. Springer-Verlag, Berlin, 1989.
- Lloyd, S., "Properties of binary functions," *Advances in Cryptology - EUROCRYPT '90*, p. 124. Springer-Verlag, Berlin, 1990.

Loho, J.

- Buchmann, J. A., Loho, J. and Zayer, J., "An implementation of the general number field sieve," *Advances in Cryptology - CRYPTO '93*, p. 159. Springer-Verlag, Berlin, 1993.

Longpre, L.

- Longpre, L., "The use of public-key cryptography for signing checks," *Advances in Cryptology: Proceedings of CRYPTO '82*, p. 187. Plenum Publishing, New York, USA, 1982.

Luby, M.

- Luby, M. and Rackoff, C., "How to construct pseudo-random permutations from pseudo-random functions," *Advances in Cryptology - CRYPTO '85*, p. 447. Springer-Verlag, Berlin, 1986.
- Luby, M. and Rackoff, C., "A study of password security," *Advances in Cryptology - CRYPTO '87*, p. 392. Springer-Verlag, Berlin, 1987.
- Goldreich, O., Krawczyk, H. and Luby, M., "On the existence of pseudorandom generators," *Advances in Cryptology - CRYPTO '88*, p. 146. Springer-Verlag, Berlin, 1989.
- Luby, M., "Psuedo-random generators from one-way functions," *Advances in Cryptology - CRYPTO '91*, p. 300. Springer-Verlag, Berlin, 1991.
- Herzberg, A. and Luby, M., "Public randomness in cryptography," *Advances in Cryptology - CRYPTO '92*, p. 421. Springer-Verlag, Berlin, 1992.
- Juels, A., Luby, M. and Ostrovsky, R., "Security of Blind Digital Signatures," *Advances in Cryptology - CRYPTO '97*, p. 150. Springer-Verlag, Berlin, 1997.

Lucks, M.

- Lucks, M., "A constraint satisfaction algorithm for the automated decryption of simple substitution ciphers," *Advances in Cryptology - CRYPTO '88*, p. 132. Springer-Verlag, Berlin, 1989.

Lund, C.

- Boyar, J., Friedl, K. and Lund, C., "Practical zero-knowledge proofs: Giving hints and using deficiencies," *Advances in Cryptology - EUROCRYPT '89*, p. 155. Springer-Verlag, Berlin, 1989.

Luther, G. G.

- Hughes, R. J., Luther, G. G., Morgan, G. L., Peterson, C. G. and Simmons, C., "Quantum Cryptography over Underground Optical Fibers," *Advances in Cryptology - CRYPTO '96*, p. 329. Springer-Verlag, Berlin, 1996.

Lynch, N.

- Millo, R. de, Lynch, N. and Merritt, M., "The Design and Analysis of Cryptographic Protocols," *Advances in Cryptography*, p. 71. University of California, Santa Barbara, Santa Barbara, California, USA, 1982.

M'raihi, D.

- Naccache, D., M'raihi, D., Vaudenay, S. and Raphaeli, D., "Can D. S. A. be improved? Complexity trade-offs with the digital signature standard," *Advances in Cryptology - EUROCRYPT '94*, p. 77. Springer-Verlag, Berlin, 1995.
- Naccache, D., M'raihi, D., Wolfowicz, W. and Porto, A. di, "Are crypto-accelerators really inevitable? 20 bit zero-knowledge in less than a second on simple 8-bit microcontrollers," *Advances in Cryptology - EUROCRYPT '95*, p. 404. Springer-Verlag, Berlin, 1995.

MacKenzie, P. D.

- Frankel, Y., Gemmell, P., MacKenzie, P. D. and Yung, M., "Proactive RSA," *Advances in Cryptology - CRYPTO '97*, p. 440. Springer-Verlag, Berlin, 1997.

Magliveras, S. S.

- Magliveras, S. S. and Memon, N. D., "Properties of cryptosystem PGM," *Advances in Cryptology - CRYPTO '89*, p. 447. Springer-Verlag, Berlin, 1989.
- Horvath, T., Magliveras, S. S. and van Trung, T., "A parallel permutation multiplier for a PGM crypto-chip," *Advances in Cryptology - CRYPTO '94*, p. 108. Springer-Verlag, Berlin, 1994.

Magyarik, M. R.

- Wagner, N. R. and Magyarik, M. R., "A public key cryptosystem based on the word problem," *Advances in Cryptology: Proceedings of CRYPTO '84*, p. 19. Springer-Verlag, Berlin, 1985.

Mahaney, S. R.

- Kurtz, S. A., Mahaney, S. R. and Royer, J. S., "On the power of 1-way functions," *Advances in Cryptology - CRYPTO '88*, p. 578. Springer-Verlag, Berlin, 1989.

Manasse, M. S.

- Lenstra, A. K. and Manasse, M. S., "Factoring by electronic mail," *Advances in Cryptology - EUROCRYPT '89*, p. 355. Springer-Verlag, Berlin, 1989.
- Lenstra, A. K. and Manasse, M. S., "Factoring with two large primes (extended abstract)," *Advances in Cryptology - EUROCRYPT '90*, p. 72. Springer-Verlag, Berlin, 1990.
- Denny, T., Dodson, B., Lenstra, A. K. and Manasse, M. S., "On the factorization of RSA-120," *Advances in Cryptology - CRYPTO '93*, p. 166. Springer-Verlag, Berlin, 1993.

Manferdelli, J. L.

- Reeds, J. A. and Manferdelli, J. L., "DES has no per round linear factors," *Advances in Cryptology: Proceedings of CRYPTO '84*, p. 377. Springer-Verlag, Berlin, 1985.

Mansour, Y.

- Coppersmith, D., Krawczyk, H. and Mansour, Y., "The shrinking generator," *Advances in Cryptology - CRYPTO '93*, p. 22. Springer-Verlag, Berlin, 1993.

Mao, W.

- Boyd, C. and Mao, W., "On a limitation of BAN logic," *Advances in Cryptology - EUROCRYPT '93*, p. 240. Springer-Verlag, Berlin, 1993.

Mare, M. de

- Benaloh, J. and Mare, M. de, "One-way accumulators: A decentralized alternative to digital signatures," *Advances in Cryptology - EUROCRYPT '93*, p. 274. Springer-Verlag, Berlin, 1993.

Martin, K. M.

- Jackson, W. A., Martin, K. M. and O'Keefe, C. M., "Multisecret threshold schemes," *Advances in Cryptology - CRYPTO '93*, p. 126. Springer-Verlag, Berlin, 1993.
- Jackson, W. A., Martin, K. M. and O'Keefe, C. M., "Efficient secret sharing without a mutually trusted authority," *Advances in Cryptology - EUROCRYPT '95*, p. 183. Springer-Verlag, Berlin, 1995.

Massey, J. L.

- Schoebi, P. and Massey, J. L., "Fast authentication in a trapdoor - knapsack public key cryptosystem," *Cryptography - Proceedings of the Workshop on Cryptography, Burg Feuerstein, Germany*, p. 289. Springer-Verlag, Berlin, 1983.
- Massey, J. L. and Rueppel, R. A., "Linear ciphers and random sequence generators with multiple clocks," *Advances in Cryptology: Proceedings of EUROCRYPT '84*, p. 74. Springer-Verlag, Berlin, 1984.
- Wang, M. and Massey, J. L., "The Characterization of All Binary Sequences with Perfect Linear Complexity Profiles," *Abstracts of Papers: EUROCRYPT '86*, p. 35. Department of Electrical Engineering, University of Linköping, Linkoping, Sweden, 1986.
- Massey, J. L., "In Memoriam Tore Herlestam (1929-1986)," *Advances in Cryptology - EUROCRYPT '87*, p. 3. Springer-Verlag, Berlin, 1987.
- Massey, J. L., Maurer, U. M. and Wang, M., "Nonexpanding, key-minimal, robustly-perfect, linear and bilinear ciphers," *Advances in Cryptology - EUROCRYPT '87*, p. 237. Springer-Verlag, Berlin, 1987.
- Jendal, H. N., Kuhn, Y. J. B. and Massey, J. L., "An information-theoretic treatment of homophonic substitution," *Advances in Cryptology - EUROCRYPT '89*, p. 382. Springer-Verlag, Berlin, 1989.
- Maurer, U. M. and Massey, J. L., "Perfect local randomness in pseudo-random sequences," *Advances in Cryptology - CRYPTO '89*, p. 100. Springer-Verlag, Berlin, 1989.
- Lai, X. and Massey, J. L., "A proposal for a new block encryption standard," *Advances in Cryptology - EUROCRYPT '90*, p. 389. Springer-Verlag, Berlin, 1990.
- Lai, X. and Massey, J. L., "Markov ciphers and differential cryptanalysis," *Advances in Cryptology - EUROCRYPT '91*, p. 17. Springer-Verlag, Berlin, 1991.
- Lai, X. and Massey, J. L., "Hash functions based on block ciphers," *Advances in Cryptology - EUROCRYPT '92*, p. 55. Springer-Verlag, Berlin, 1992.
- Blakley, B., Blakley, G. R., Chan, A. H. and Massey, J. L., "Threshold schemes with disenrollment," *Advances in Cryptology - CRYPTO '92*, p. 540. Springer-Verlag, Berlin, 1992.
- Massey, J. L. and Serconek, S., "A Fourier transform approach to the linear complexity of nonlinearly filtered sequences," *Advances in Cryptology - CRYPTO '94*, p. 332. Springer-Verlag, Berlin, 1994.
- Harpes, C., Kramer, G. G. and Massey, J. L., "A generalization of linear cryptanalysis and the applicability of Matsui's piling-up lemma," *Advances in Cryptology - EUROCRYPT '95*, p. 24. Springer-Verlag, Berlin, 1995.
- Massey, J. L. and Serconek, S., "Linear Complexity of Periodic Sequences: A General Theory," *Advances in Cryptology - CRYPTO '96*, p. 358. Springer-Verlag, Berlin, 1996.

Mathias, A.

- Beth, T., Lazic, D. E. and Mathias, A., "Cryptanalysis of cryptosystems based on remote chaos replication," *Advances in Cryptology - CRYPTO '94*, p. 318. Springer-Verlag, Berlin, 1994.

Matias, Y.

- Matias, Y. and Shamir, A., "A video scrambling technique based on space filling curves," *Advances in Cryptology - CRYPTO '87*, p. 398. Springer-Verlag, Berlin, 1987.

Matsui, M.

- Matsui, M. and Yamagishi, A., "A new method for known plaintext attack of FEAL cipher," *Advances in Cryptology - EUROCRYPT '92*, p. 81. Springer-Verlag, Berlin, 1992.
- Matsui, M., "Linear cryptanalysis method for DES cipher," *Advances in Cryptology - EUROCRYPT '93*, p. 386. Springer-Verlag, Berlin, 1993.
- Ohta, K. and Matsui, M., "Differential attack on message authentication codes," *Advances in Cryptology - CRYPTO '93*, p. 200. Springer-Verlag, Berlin, 1993.
- Matsui, M., "On correlation between the order of S-boxes and the strength of DES," *Advances in Cryptology - EUROCRYPT '94*, p. 366. Springer-Verlag, Berlin, 1995.
- Matsui, M., "The first experimental crypt analysis of the Data Encryption Standard," *Advances in Cryptology - CRYPTO '94*, p. 1. Springer-Verlag, Berlin, 1994.

Matsumoto, T.

- Matsumoto, T. and Imai, H., "On the key predistribution system: a practical solution to the key distribution problem," *Advances in Cryptology - CRYPTO '87*, p. 185. Springer-Verlag, Berlin, 1987.
- Matsumoto, T. and Imai, H., "Public quadratic polynomial-tuples for efficient signature-verification and message-encryption," *Advances in Cryptology - EUROCRYPT '88*, p. 419. Springer-Verlag, Berlin, 1988.
- Matsumoto, T., Kato, K. and Imai, H., "Speeding up secret computations with insecure auxiliary devices," *Advances in Cryptology - CRYPTO '88*, p. 497. Springer-Verlag, Berlin, 1989.
- Zheng, Y., Matsumoto, T. and Imai, H., "Impossibility and optimally results on constructing pseudorandom permutations (extended abstract)," *Advances in Cryptology - EUROCRYPT '89*, p. 412. Springer-Verlag, Berlin, 1989.
- Zheng, Y., Matsumoto, T. and Imai, H., "On the construction of block ciphers provably secure and not relying on any unproved hypotheses (extended abstract)," *Advances in Cryptology - CRYPTO '89*, p. 461. Springer-Verlag, Berlin, 1989.

- Zheng, Y., Matsumoto, T. and Imai, H., "Structural properties of one-way hash functions," *Advances in Cryptology - CRYPTO '90*, p. 285. Springer-Verlag, Berlin, 1990.
- Kim, K., Matsumoto, T. and Imai, H., "A recursive construction method of S-boxes satisfying strict avalanche criterion," *Advances in Cryptology - CRYPTO '90*, p. 564. Springer-Verlag, Berlin, 1990.
- Matsumoto, T. and Imai, H., "Human identification through insecure channel," *Advances in Cryptology - EUROCRYPT '91*, p. 409. Springer-Verlag, Berlin, 1991.
- Iwamura, K., Matsumoto, T. and Imai, H., "High-speed implementation methods for RSA scheme," *Advances in Cryptology - EUROCRYPT '92*, p. 221. Springer-Verlag, Berlin, 1992.
- Iwamura, K., Matsumoto, T. and Imai, H., "Systolic-arrays for modular exponentiation using Montgomery method," *Advances in Cryptology - EUROCRYPT '92*, p. 477. Springer-Verlag, Berlin, 1992.

Matsuzaki, N.
- Tatebayashi, M., Matsuzaki, N. and Newman, D. B. Jr., "Key distribution protocol for digital mobile communication systems," *Advances in Cryptology - CRYPTO '89*, p. 324. Springer-Verlag, Berlin, 1989.

Matt, B. J.
- Davida, G. I. and Matt, B. J., "Arbitration in tamper proof systems. If DES approximately=RSA then what's the difference between true signature and arbitrated signature schemes?," *Advances in Cryptology - CRYPTO '87*, p. 216. Springer-Verlag, Berlin, 1987.

Matthews, D. E.
- Juergensen, H. and Matthews, D. E., "Some results on the information theoretic analysis of cryptosystems," *Advances in Cryptology: Proceedings of CRYPTO '83*, p. 303. Plenum Publishing, New York, USA, 1984.

Mattos, L. A. F.
- Blundo, C., Mattos, L. A. F. and Stinson, D. R., "Trade-offs Between Communication and Storage in Unconditionally Secure Schemes for Broadcast Encryption and Interactive Key Distribution," *Advances in Cryptology - CRYPTO '96*, p. 387. Springer-Verlag, Berlin, 1996.

Matusevich, A
- Fairfield, R. C., Matusevich, A and Plany, J, "An LSI digital encryption processor (DEP)," *Advances in Cryptology: Proceedings of CRYPTO '84*, p. 115. Springer-Verlag, Berlin, 1985.

Matyas, S. M.

- Leighton, A. C. and Matyas, S. M., "The history of book ciphers," *Advances in Cryptology: Proceedings of CRYPTO '84*, p. 101. Springer-Verlag, Berlin, 1985.
- Matyas, S. M., "Public-key registration," *Advances in Cryptology - CRYPTO '86*, p. 451. Springer-Verlag, Berlin, 1986.

Maurer, U. M.

- Massey, J. L., Maurer, U. M. and Wang, M., "Nonexpanding, key-minimal, robustly-perfect, linear and bilinear ciphers," *Advances in Cryptology - EUROCRYPT '87*, p. 237. Springer-Verlag, Berlin, 1987.
- Maurer, U. M., "Fast generation of secure RSA-moduli with almost maximal diversity," *Advances in Cryptology - EUROCRYPT '89*, p. 636. Springer-Verlag, Berlin, 1989.
- Maurer, U. M. and Massey, J. L., "Perfect local randomness in pseudo-random sequences," *Advances in Cryptology - CRYPTO '89*, p. 100. Springer-Verlag, Berlin, 1989.
- Maurer, U. M., "A provably-secure strongly-randomized cipher," *Advances in Cryptology - EUROCRYPT '90*, p. 361. Springer-Verlag, Berlin, 1990.
- Maurer, U. M., "A universal statistical test for random bit generators," *Advances in Cryptology - CRYPTO '90*, p. 409. Springer-Verlag, Berlin, 1990.
- Maurer, U. M., "New approaches to the design of self-synchronizing stream ciphers," *Advances in Cryptology - EUROCRYPT '91*, p. 458. Springer-Verlag, Berlin, 1991.
- Maurer, U. M. and Yacobi, Y., "Non-interative public-key cryptography," *Advances in Cryptology - EUROCRYPT '91*, p. 498. Springer-Verlag, Berlin, 1991.
- Koyama, K., Maurer, U. M., Okamoto, T. and Vanstone, S. A., "New public-key schemes based on elliptic curves over the ring Z_n," *Advances in Cryptology - CRYPTO '91*, p. 252. Springer-Verlag, Berlin, 1991.
- Maurer, U. M., "A simplified and generalized treatment of Luby-Rackoff pseudorandom permutation generators," *Advances in Cryptology - EUROCRYPT '92*, p. 239. Springer-Verlag, Berlin, 1992.
- Maurer, U. M., "Factoring with an oracle," *Advances in Cryptology - EUROCRYPT '92*, p. 429. Springer-Verlag, Berlin, 1992.
- Maurer, U. M. and Yacobi, Y., "A remark on a non-interactive public-key distribution system," *Advances in Cryptology - EUROCRYPT '92*, p. 458. Springer-Verlag, Berlin, 1992.
- Maurer, U. M., "Protocols for secret key agreement by public discussion based on common information," *Advances in Cryptology - CRYPTO '92*, p. 461. Springer-Verlag, Berlin, 1992.
- Cachin, C. and Maurer, U. M., "Linking information reconciliation and privacy amplification," *Advances in Cryptology - EUROCRYPT '94*, p. 266. Springer-Verlag, Berlin, 1995.

- Bleichenbacher, D. and Maurer, U. M., "Directed acyclic graphs, one-way functions and digital signatures," *Advances in Cryptology - CRYPTO '94*, p. 75. Springer-Verlag, Berlin, 1994.
- Maurer, U. M., "Towards the equivalence of breaking the Diffie-Hellman protocol and computing discrete logarithms," *Advances in Cryptology - CRYPTO '94*, p. 271. Springer-Verlag, Berlin, 1994.
- Maurer, U. M. and Wolf, S., "Diffie-Hellman Oracles," *Advances in Cryptology - CRYPTO '96*, p. 268. Springer-Verlag, Berlin, 1996.
- Maurer, U. M., "Information-Theoretically Secure Secret-Key Agreement by NOT Authenticated Public Discussion," *Advances in Cryptology - EUROCRYPT '97*, p. 209. Springer-Verlag, Berlin, 1997.
- Cachin, C. and Maurer, U. M., "Unconditional Security Against Memory-Bounded Adversaries," *Advances in Cryptology - CRYPTO '97*, p. 292. Springer-Verlag, Berlin, 1997.
- Maurer, U. M. and Wolf, S., "Privacy Amplification Secure Against Active Adversaries," *Advances in Cryptology - CRYPTO '97*, p. 307. Springer-Verlag, Berlin, 1997.

Mayers, D.
- Mayers, D., "On the Security of the Quantum Oblivious Transfer and Key Distribution Protocols," *Advances in Cryptology - CRYPTO '95*, p. 124. Springer-Verlag, Berlin, 1995.
- Mayers, D., "Quantum Key Distribution and String Oblivious Transfer in Noisy Channels," *Advances in Cryptology - CRYPTO '96*, p. 343. Springer-Verlag, Berlin, 1996.

McAuley, A. J.
- Goodman, R. F. and McAuley, A. J., "A new trapdoor knapsack public-key cryptosystem," *Advances in Cryptology: Proceedings of EUROCRYPT '84*, p. 150. Springer-Verlag, Berlin, 1984.

McCurley, K. S.
- Estes, D., Adleman, L. M., Kompella, K., McCurley, K. S. and Miller, G. L., "Breaking the Ong-Schnorr-Shamir signature scheme for quadratic number fields," *Advances in Cryptology - CRYPTO '85*, p. 3. Springer-Verlag, Berlin, 1986.
- Brickell, E. F. and McCurley, K. S., "An interactive identification scheme based on discrete logarithms and factoring (extended abstract)," *Advances in Cryptology - EUROCRYPT '90*, p. 63. Springer-Verlag, Berlin, 1990.
- Desmedt, Y., Landrock, P., Lenstra, A. K., McCurley, K. S., Odlyzko, A. M., Rueppel, R. A. and Smid, M. E., "The Eurocrypt '92 Controversial Issue: Trapdoor Primes and Moduli," *Advances in Cryptology - EUROCRYPT '92*, p. 194. Springer-Verlag, Berlin, 1992.
- Brickell, E. F., Gordon, D. M., McCurley, K. S. and Wilson, D. B., "Fast exponentiation with precomputation (Extended abstract)," *Advances in Cryptology - EUROCRYPT '92*, p. 200. Springer-Verlag, Berlin, 1992.

- Gordon, D. M. and McCurley, K. S., "Massively parallel computation of discrete logarithms," *Advances in Cryptology - CRYPTO '92*, p. 312. Springer-Verlag, Berlin, 1992.

McInnes, J. L.

- McInnes, J. L. and Pinkas, B., "On the impossibility of private key cryptography with weakly random keys," *Advances in Cryptology - CRYPTO '90*, p. 421. Springer-Verlag, Berlin, 1990.

McPherson, T.

- Lau, Y. A. and McPherson, T., "Implementation of a Hybrid RSA/DES Key Management System," *Advances in Cryptography*, p. 83. University of California, Santa Barbara, Santa Barbara, California, USA, 1982.

Meadows, C.

- Blakley, G. R. and Meadows, C., "Security of ramp schemes," *Advances in Cryptology: Proceedings of CRYPTO '84*, p. 242. Springer-Verlag, Berlin, 1985.
- Blakley, G. R., Meadows, C. and Purdy, G. B., "Fingerprinting long forgiving messages," *Advances in Cryptology - CRYPTO '85*, p. 180. Springer-Verlag, Berlin, 1986.
- Syverson, P. and Meadows, C., "Formal requirements for key distribution protocols," *Advances in Cryptology - EUROCRYPT '94*, p. 320. Springer-Verlag, Berlin, 1995.

Meier, T.

- Hohl, W., Lai, X., Meier, T. and Waldvogel, C., "Security of iterated hash functions based on block ciphers," *Advances in Cryptology - CRYPTO '93*, p. 379. Springer-Verlag, Berlin, 1993.

Meier, W.

- Meier, W. and Staffelbach, O., "Fast correlation attacks on stream ciphers," *Advances in Cryptology - EUROCRYPT '88*, p. 301. Springer-Verlag, Berlin, 1988.
- Meier, W. and Staffelbach, O., "Nonlinearity criteria for cryptographic functions," *Advances in Cryptology - EUROCRYPT '89*, p. 549. Springer-Verlag, Berlin, 1989.
- Meier, W. and Staffelbach, O., "Correlation properties of combiners with memory in stream ciphers (extended abstract)," *Advances in Cryptology - EUROCRYPT '90*, p. 204. Springer-Verlag, Berlin, 1990.
- Staffelbach, O. and Meier, W., "Cryptographic significance of the carry for ciphers based on integer addition," *Advances in Cryptology - CRYPTO '90*, p. 601. Springer-Verlag, Berlin, 1990.
- Meier, W. and Staffelbach, O., "Analysis of pseudo random sequences generated by cellular automata," *Advances in Cryptology - EUROCRYPT '91*, p. 186. Springer-Verlag, Berlin, 1991.
- Meier, W. and Staffelbach, O., "Efficient multiplication on certain non-supersingular elliptic curves," *Advances in Cryptology - CRYPTO '92*, p. 333. Springer-Verlag, Berlin, 1992.
- Meier, W., "On the security of the IDEA block cipher," *Advances in Cryptology - EUROCRYPT '93*, p. 371. Springer-Verlag, Berlin, 1993.
- Meier, W. and Staffelbach, O., "The self-shrinking generator," *Advances in Cryptology - EUROCRYPT '94*, p. 205. Springer-Verlag, Berlin, 1995.
- Knudsen, L. R. and Meier, W., "Improved Differential Attacks on RC5," *Advances in Cryptology - CRYPTO '96*, p. 216. Springer-Verlag, Berlin, 1996.

Meijer, H.

- Meijer, H. and Akl, S. G., "Digital Signature Scheme for Computer Communication Networks," *Advances in Cryptography*, p. 65. University of California, Santa Barbara, Santa Barbara, California, USA, 1982.
- Akl, S. G. and Meijer, H., "A fast pseudo random permutation generator with applications to cryptology," *Advances in Cryptology: Proceedings of CRYPTO '84*, p. 269. Springer-Verlag, Berlin, 1985.
- Meijer, H. and Akl, S. G., "Two new secret key cryptosystems.," *Advances in Cryptology - EUROCRYPT '85*, p. 96. Springer-Verlag, Berlin, 1985.
- Adams, C. M. and Meijer, H., "Security-related comments regarding McEliece's public-key cryptosystem," *Advances in Cryptology - CRYPTO '87*, p. 224. Springer-Verlag, Berlin, 1987.

Meister, G.

- Meister, G., "On an implementation of the Mohan-Adiga algorithm," *Advances in Cryptology - EUROCRYPT '90*, p. 496. Springer-Verlag, Berlin, 1990.

Memon, N. D.

- Magliveras, S. S. and Memon, N. D., "Properties of cryptosystem PGM," *Advances in Cryptology - CRYPTO '89*, p. 447. Springer-Verlag, Berlin, 1989.

Menezes, A.

- Harper, G., Menezes, A. and Vanstone, S. A., "Public-key cryptosystems with very small key lengths," *Advances in Cryptology - EUROCRYPT '92*, p. 163. Springer-Verlag, Berlin, 1992.

Menicocci, R.

- Menicocci, R., "A systematic attack on clock controlled cascades," *Advances in Cryptology - EUROCRYPT '94*, p. 450. Springer-Verlag, Berlin, 1995.
- Golic, J. D. and Menicocci, R., "Edit Distance Correlation Attack on the Alternating Step Generator," *Advances in Cryptology - CRYPTO '97*, p. 499. Springer-Verlag, Berlin, 1997.

Merkle, R. C.

- Merkle, R. C., "A digital signature based on a conventional encryption function," *Advances in Cryptology - CRYPTO '87*, p. 369. Springer-Verlag, Berlin, 1987.
- Merkle, R. C., "A certified digital signature," *Advances in Cryptology - CRYPTO '89*, p. 218. Springer-Verlag, Berlin, 1989.
- Merkle, R. C., "One way hash functions and DES," *Advances in Cryptology - CRYPTO '89*, p. 428. Springer-Verlag, Berlin, 1989.
- Merkle, R. C., "Fast software encryption functions," *Advances in Cryptology - CRYPTO '90*, p. 476. Springer-Verlag, Berlin, 1990.

Merritt, M.

- Millo, R. de, Lynch, N. and Merritt, M., "The Design and Analysis of Cryptographic Protocols," *Advances in Cryptography*, p. 71. University of California, Santa Barbara, Santa Barbara, California, USA, 1982.
- Merritt, M., "Key reconstruction (Abstract)," *Advances in Cryptology: Proceedings of CRYPTO '82*, p. 321. Plenum Publishing, New York, USA, 1982.
- Fortune, S. and Merritt, M., "Poker protocols," *Advances in Cryptology: Proceedings of CRYPTO '84*, p. 454. Springer-Verlag, Berlin, 1985.

Meyer, B.

- Biehl, I., Buchmann, J. A., Meyer, B., Thiel, C. and Thiel, C., "Tools for proving zero knowledge," *Advances in Cryptology - EUROCRYPT '92*, p. 356. Springer-Verlag, Berlin, 1992.
- Meyer, B. and Mueller, V., "A public key cryptosystem based on elliptic curves over Z/nZ equivalent to factoring," *Advances in Cryptology - EUROCRYPT '96*, p. 49. Springer-Verlag, Berlin, 1996.

2360

Micali, S.

- Goldwasser, S., Micali, S. and Yao, A., "On signatures and authentication," *Advances in Cryptology: Proceedings of CRYPTO '82*, p. 211. Plenum Publishing, New York, USA, 1982.
- Goldreich, O., Goldwasser, S. and Micali, S., "On the cryptographic applications of random functions," *Advances in Cryptology: Proceedings of CRYPTO '84*, p. 276. Springer-Verlag, Berlin, 1985.
- Goldreich, O., Micali, S. and Wigderson, A., "How to prove all NP-statements in zero-knowledge, and a methodology of cryptographic protocol design," *Advances in Cryptology - CRYPTO '86*, p. 171. Springer-Verlag, Berlin, 1986.
- Micali, S., Rackoff, C. and Sloan, B., "The notion of security for probabilistic cryptosystems," *Advances in Cryptology - CRYPTO '86*, p. 381. Springer-Verlag, Berlin, 1986.
- De Santis, A., Micali, S. and Persiano, G., "Noninteractive zero-knowledge proof systems," *Advances in Cryptology - CRYPTO '87*, p. 52. Springer-Verlag, Berlin, 1987.
- Ben-Or, M., Goldreich, O., Goldwasser, S., Hastad, J., Kilian, J., Micali, S. and Rogaway, P., "Everything provable is provable in zero-knowledge," *Advances in Cryptology - CRYPTO '88*, p. 37. Springer-Verlag, Berlin, 1989.
- Micali, S. and Schnorr, C. P., "Efficient, perfect random number generators," *Advances in Cryptology - CRYPTO '88*, p. 173. Springer-Verlag, Berlin, 1989.
- Bellare, M. and Micali, S., "How to sign given any trapdoor function," *Advances in Cryptology - CRYPTO '88*, p. 200. Springer-Verlag, Berlin, 1989.
- Micali, S. and Shamir, A., "An improvement of the Fiat-Shamir identification and signature scheme," *Advances in Cryptology - CRYPTO '88*, p. 244. Springer-Verlag, Berlin, 1989.
- Blum, M., Feldman, P. and Micali, S., "Proving security against chosen cyphertext attacks," *Advances in Cryptology - CRYPTO '88*, p. 256. Springer-Verlag, Berlin, 1989.
- De Santis, A., Micali, S. and Persiano, G., "Non-interactive zero-knowledge with preprocessing," *Advances in Cryptology - CRYPTO '88*, p. 269. Springer-Verlag, Berlin, 1989.
- Even, S., Goldreich, O. and Micali, S., "On-line/off-line digital signatures," *Advances in Cryptology - CRYPTO '89*, p. 263. Springer-Verlag, Berlin, 1989.
- Kilian, J., Micali, S. and Ostrovsky, R., "Minimum resource zero-knowledge proofs (extended abstracts)," *Advances in Cryptology - CRYPTO '89*, p. 545. Springer-Verlag, Berlin, 1989.

- Bellare, M. and Micali, S., "Non-interactive oblivious transfer and applications," *Advances in Cryptology - CRYPTO '89*, p. 547. Springer-Verlag, Berlin, 1989.
- Micali, S. and Rabin, T., "Collective coin tossing without assumptions nor broadcasting," *Advances in Cryptology - CRYPTO '90*, p. 253. Springer-Verlag, Berlin, 1990.
- Micali, S. and Rogaway, P., "Secure computation," *Advances in Cryptology - CRYPTO '91*, p. 392. Springer-Verlag, Berlin, 1991.
- Micali, S., "Fair public-key cryptosystems," *Advances in Cryptology - CRYPTO '92*, p. 113. Springer-Verlag, Berlin, 1992.
- Leighton, T. and Micali, S., "Secret-key agreement without public-key cryptography," *Advances in Cryptology - CRYPTO '93*, p. 456. Springer-Verlag, Berlin, 1993.
- Gennaro, R. and Micali, S., "Verifiable secret sharing as secure computation," *Advances in Cryptology - EUROCRYPT '95*, p. 168. Springer-Verlag, Berlin, 1995.
- Micali, S. and Sidney, R., "A Simple Method for Generating and Sharing Pseudo-Random Functions, with Applications to Clipper-like Key Escrow Systems," *Advances in Cryptology - CRYPTO '95*, p. 185. Springer-Verlag, Berlin, 1995.
- Halevi, S. and Micali, S., "Practical and Provably-Secure Commitment Schemes from Collision-Free Hashing," *Advances in Cryptology - CRYPTO '96*, p. 201. Springer-Verlag, Berlin, 1996.

Micciancio, D.

- Bellare, M. and Micciancio, D., "A New Paradigm for Collision-Free Hashing: Incrementality at Reduced Cost," *Advances in Cryptology - EUROCRYPT '97*, p. 163. Springer-Verlag, Berlin, 1997.
- Bellare, M., Goldwasser, S. and Micciancio, D., ""Pseudo-Random" Number Generation within Cryptographic Algorithms: The DSS Case," *Advances in Cryptology - CRYPTO '97*, p. 277. Springer-Verlag, Berlin, 1997.

Mignotte, M.

- Mignotte, M., "How to share a secret?," *Cryptography - Proceedings of the Workshop on Cryptography, Burg Feuerstein, Germany*, p. 371. Springer-Verlag, Berlin, 1983.

Mihailescu, P.

- Mihailescu, P., "Fast generation of provable primes using search in arithmetic progressions," *Advances in Cryptology - CRYPTO '94*, p. 282. Springer-Verlag, Berlin, 1994.

Mihaljevic, M. J.

- Golic, J. D. and Mihaljevic, M. J., "A noisy clock-controlled shift register cryptanalysis concept based on sequence comparison approach," *Advances in Cryptology - EUROCRYPT '90*, p. 487. Springer-Verlag, Berlin, 1990.
- Mihaljevic, M. J. and Golic, J. D., "A comparison of cryptoanalytic principles based on iterative error-correction," *Advances in Cryptology - EUROCRYPT '91*, p. 527. Springer-Verlag, Berlin, 1991.
- Mihaljevic, M. J. and Golic, J. D., "Convergence of a Bayesian iterative error-correction procedure on a noisy shift register sequence," *Advances in Cryptology - EUROCRYPT '92*, p. 124. Springer-Verlag, Berlin, 1992.

Miller, G. L.

- Estes, D., Adleman, L. M., Kompella, K., McCurley, K. S. and Miller, G. L., "Breaking the Ong-Schnorr-Shamir signature scheme for quadratic number fields," *Advances in Cryptology - CRYPTO '85*, p. 3. Springer-Verlag, Berlin, 1986.

Miller, V. S.

- Miller, V. S., "Use of elliptic curves in cryptography," *Advances in Cryptology - CRYPTO '85*, p. 417. Springer-Verlag, Berlin, 1986.

Millo, R. de

- Millo, R. de, Lynch, N. and Merritt, M., "The Design and Analysis of Cryptographic Protocols," *Advances in Cryptography*, p. 71. University of California, Santa Barbara, Santa Barbara, California, USA, 1982.

Misarsky, J.-F.

- Girault, M. and Misarsky, J.-F., "Selective Forgery of RSA Signatures Using Redundancy," *Advances in Cryptology - EUROCRYPT '97*, p. 495. Springer-Verlag, Berlin, 1997.
- Misarsky, J.-F., "A Multiplicative Attack Using LLL Algorithm on RSA Signatures with Redundancy," *Advances in Cryptology - CRYPTO '97*, p. 221. Springer-Verlag, Berlin, 1997.

Mitchell, C.

- Godlewski, P. and Mitchell, C., "Key minimal authentication systems for unconditional secrecy," *Advances in Cryptology - EUROCRYPT '89*, p. 497. Springer-Verlag, Berlin, 1989.

Miyaguchi, S.

- Shimizu, A. and Miyaguchi, S., "Fast data encipherment algorithm FEAL," *Advances in Cryptology - EUROCRYPT '87*, p. 267. Springer-Verlag, Berlin, 1987.
- Miyaguchi, S., "The FEAL–8 cryptosystem and a call for attack," *Advances in Cryptology - CRYPTO '89*, p. 624. Springer-Verlag, Berlin, 1989.
- Miyaguchi, S., Ohta, K. and Iwata, M., "Confirmation that some hash functions are not collision free," *Advances in Cryptology - EUROCRYPT '90*, p. 326. Springer-Verlag, Berlin, 1990.
- Miyaguchi, S., "The FEAL Cipher Family," *Advances in Cryptology - CRYPTO '90*, p. 627. Springer-Verlag, Berlin, 1990.
- Fujioka, A., Okamoto, T. and Miyaguchi, S., "ESIGN: An efficient digital signature implementation for smart cards," *Advances in Cryptology - EUROCRYPT '91*, p. 446. Springer-Verlag, Berlin, 1991.
- Morita, H., Ohta, K. and Miyaguchi, S., "A switching closure test to analyze cryptosystems (Extended abstract)," *Advances in Cryptology - CRYPTO '91*, p. 183. Springer-Verlag, Berlin, 1991.

Mjoelsnes, S. F.

- Mjoelsnes, S. F., "A simple technique for diffusing cryptoperiods," *Advances in Cryptology - EUROCRYPT '89*, p. 110. Springer-Verlag, Berlin, 1989.
- Chaum, D., den Boer, B., van Heyst, E., Mjoelsnes, S. F. and Steenbeek, A., "Efficient offline electronic checks (extended abstract)," *Advances in Cryptology - EUROCRYPT '89*, p. 294. Springer-Verlag, Berlin, 1989.

Molva, R.

- Bird, R., Gopal, I., Herzberg, A., Janson, P., Kutten, S., Molva, R. and Yung, M., "Systematic design of two-party authentication protocols," *Advances in Cryptology - CRYPTO '91*, p. 44. Springer-Verlag, Berlin, 1991.

Montgomery, P. L.

- Montgomery, P. L., "A block Lanczos algorithm for finding dependencies over GF(2)," *Advances in Cryptology - EUROCRYPT '95*, p. 106. Springer-Verlag, Berlin, 1995.

Moore, J. H.

- Brickell, E. F. and Moore, J. H., "Some remarks on the Herlestam-Johannesson algorithm for computing logarithms over $GF(2^p)$," *Advances in Cryptology: Proceedings of CRYPTO '82*, p. 15. Plenum Publishing, New York, USA, 1982.
- Moore, J. H. and Simmons, G. J., "Cycle Structure of the Weak and Semi-Weak DES Keys," *Abstracts of Papers: EUROCRYPT '86*, p. 16. Department of Electrical Engineering, University of Linköping, Linkoping, Sweden, 1986.
- Brickell, E. F., Moore, J. H. and Purtill, M. R., "Structure in the S-boxes of the DES," *Advances in Cryptology - CRYPTO '86*, p. 3. Springer-Verlag, Berlin, 1986.
- Moore, J. H. and Simmons, G. J., "Cycle structure of the DES with weak and semi-weak keys," *Advances in Cryptology - CRYPTO '86*, p. 9. Springer-Verlag, Berlin, 1986.
- Moore, J. H., "Strong practical protocols," *Advances in Cryptology - CRYPTO '87*, p. 167. Springer-Verlag, Berlin, 1987.

Moore, T. E.

- Moore, T. E. and Tavares, S. E., "A layered approach to the design of private key cryptosystems," *Advances in Cryptology - CRYPTO '85*, p. 227. Springer-Verlag, Berlin, 1986.

Morain, F.

- Morain, F., "Atkin's test: News from the front," *Advances in Cryptology - EUROCRYPT '89*, p. 626. Springer-Verlag, Berlin, 1989.
- Morain, F., "Distributed primality proving and the primality of $(2^{3539} + 1)/3$," *Advances in Cryptology - EUROCRYPT '90*, p. 110. Springer-Verlag, Berlin, 1990.
- Morain, F., "Building cyclic elliptic curves modulo large primes," *Advances in Cryptology - EUROCRYPT '91*, p. 328. Springer-Verlag, Berlin, 1991.
- Lercier, R. and Morain, F., "Counting the number of points on elliptic curves over finite fields: strategies and performances," *Advances in Cryptology - EUROCRYPT '95*, p. 79. Springer-Verlag, Berlin, 1995.

Morgan, G. L.

- Hughes, R. J., Luther, G. G., Morgan, G. L., Peterson, C. G. and Simmons, C., "Quantum Cryptography over Underground Optical Fibers," *Advances in Cryptology - CRYPTO '96*, p. 329. Springer-Verlag, Berlin, 1996.

Mori, S.

- Habutsu, T., Nishio, Y., Sasase, Iwao and Mori, S., "A secret key cryptosystem by iterating a chaotic map," *Advances in Cryptology - EUROCRYPT '91*, p. 127. Springer-Verlag, Berlin, 1991.

Moriai, S.

- Ohta, K., Moriai, S. and Aoki, K., "Improving the Search Algorithm for the Best Linear Expression," *Advances in Cryptology - CRYPTO '95*, p. 157. Springer-Verlag, Berlin, 1995.

Morita, H.

- Morita, H., "A fast modular-multiplication algorithm based on a higher radix," *Advances in Cryptology - CRYPTO '89*, p. 387. Springer-Verlag, Berlin, 1989.
- Morita, H., Ohta, K. and Miyaguchi, S., "A switching closure test to analyze cryptosystems (Extended abstract)," *Advances in Cryptology - CRYPTO '91*, p. 183. Springer-Verlag, Berlin, 1991.

Morrison, D. R.

- Morrison, D. R., "Subtractive Encryptors - Alternatives to the DES," *Advances in Cryptography*, p. 42. University of California, Santa Barbara, Santa Barbara, California, USA, 1982.

Mortenson, R. L.

- Fairfield, R. C., Mortenson, R. L. and Coulthart, K. B., "An LSI random number generator (RNG)," *Advances in Cryptology: Proceedings of CRYPTO '84*, p. 203. Springer-Verlag, Berlin, 1985.

Mueller, V.

- Meyer, B. and Mueller, V., "A public key cryptosystem based on elliptic curves over Z/nZ equivalent to factoring," *Advances in Cryptology - EUROCRYPT '96*, p. 49. Springer-Verlag, Berlin, 1996.

Mueller, W. B.

- Lidl, R. and Mueller, W. B., "Permutation polynomials in RSA cryptosystems," *Advances in Cryptology: Proceedings of CRYPTO '83*, p. 293. Plenum Publishing, New York, USA, 1984.
- Mueller, W. B. and Noebauer, R., "Cryptanalysis of the Dickson-scheme.," *Advances in Cryptology - EUROCRYPT '85*, p. 50. Springer-Verlag, Berlin, 1985.
- Mueller, W. B. and Noebauer, R., "On Commutative Semigroups of Polynomials and their Application in Cryptography," *Abstracts of Papers: EUROCRYPT '86*, p. 51. Department of Electrical Engineering, University of Linköping, Linkoping, Sweden, 1986.
- Mueller, W. B. and Oswald, A., "Dickson pseudoprimes and primality testing," *Advances in Cryptology - EUROCRYPT '91*, p. 512. Springer-Verlag, Berlin, 1991.

Mueller-Schloer, C.

- Mueller-Schloer, C. and Wagner, N. R., "Cryptographic protection of personal data cards," *Advances in Cryptology: Proceedings of CRYPTO '82*, p. 219. Plenum Publishing, New York, USA, 1982.

Mullin, R. C.

- Blake, I. F., Mullin, R. C. and Vanstone, S. A., "Computing logarithms in GF(2^n)," *Advances in Cryptology: Proceedings of CRYPTO '84*, p. 73. Springer-Verlag, Berlin, 1985.
- Agnew, G. B., Mullin, R. C. and Vanstone, S. A., "An interactive data exchange protocol based on discrete exponentiation," *Advances in Cryptology - EUROCRYPT '88*, p. 159. Springer-Verlag, Berlin, 1988.
- Agnew, G. B., Mullin, R. C. and Vanstone, S. A., "Fast exponentiation in GF(2^n)," *Advances in Cryptology - EUROCRYPT '88*, p. 251. Springer-Verlag, Berlin, 1988.
- Agnew, G. B., Mullin, R. C. and Vanstone, S. A., "A fast elliptic curve cryptosystem," *Advances in Cryptology - EUROCRYPT '89*, p. 706. Springer-Verlag, Berlin, 1989.
- Agnew, G. B., Mullin, R. C. and Vanstone, S. A., "On the development of a fast elliptic curve cryptosystem," *Advances in Cryptology - EUROCRYPT '92*, p. 482. Springer-Verlag, Berlin, 1992.

Mund, S.

- Mund, S., Gollmann, D. and Beth, T., "Some remarks on the cross correlation analysis of pseudo random generators," *Advances in Cryptology - EUROCRYPT '87*, p. 25. Springer-Verlag, Berlin, 1987.
- Mund, S., "Ziv-Lempel complexity for periodic sequences and its cryptographic application," *Advances in Cryptology - EUROCRYPT '91*, p. 114. Springer-Verlag, Berlin, 1991.

Munzert, M.

- Fumy, W. and Munzert, M., "A modular approach to key distribution," *Advances in Cryptology - CRYPTO '90*, p. 274. Springer-Verlag, Berlin, 1990.

Murphy, S.

- Blackburn, S. R., Murphy, S. and Stern, J., "Weaknesses of a public-key cryptosystem based on factorizations of finite groups," *Advances in Cryptology - EUROCRYPT '93*, p. 50. Springer-Verlag, Berlin, 1993.

Naccache, D.

- Naccache, D., "A Montgomery-suitable Fiat-Shamir-like authentication scheme," *Advances in Cryptology - EUROCRYPT '92*, p. 488. Springer-Verlag, Berlin, 1992.
- Naccache, D., "Can O.S.S. be Repaired? - Proposal for a new practical signature scheme," *Advances in Cryptology - EUROCRYPT '93*, p. 233. Springer-Verlag, Berlin, 1993.
- Naccache, D., M'raihi, D., Vaudenay, S. and Raphaeli, D., "Can D. S. A. be improved? Complexity trade-offs with the digital signature standard," *Advances in Cryptology - EUROCRYPT '94*, p. 77. Springer-Verlag, Berlin, 1995.
- Naccache, D., M'raihi, D., Wolfowicz, W. and Porto, A. di, "Are crypto-accelerators really inevitable? 20 bit zero-knowledge in less than a second on simple 8-bit microcontrollers," *Advances in Cryptology - EUROCRYPT '95*, p. 404. Springer-Verlag, Berlin, 1995.
- Naccache, D. and Stern, J., "A New Public-Key Cryptosystem," *Advances in Cryptology - EUROCRYPT '97*, p. 27. Springer-Verlag, Berlin, 1997.

Naeslund, M.

- Naeslund, M., "Universal hash functions & hard core bits," *Advances in Cryptology - EUROCRYPT '95*, p. 356. Springer-Verlag, Berlin, 1995.

Nakamura, K.

- Okamoto, E. and Nakamura, K., "Lifetimes of keys in cryptographic key management systems," *Advances in Cryptology - CRYPTO '85*, p. 246. Springer-Verlag, Berlin, 1986.

Nam, K. H.

- Rao, T. R. N. and Nam, K. H., "Private-key algebraic-coded cryptosystems," *Advances in Cryptology - CRYPTO '86*, p. 35. Springer-Verlag, Berlin, 1986.

Naor, M.

- Chaum, D., Fiat, A. and Naor, M., "Untraceable electronic cash," *Advances in Cryptology - CRYPTO '88*, p. 319. Springer-Verlag, Berlin, 1989.
- Naor, M., "Bit commitment using pseudo-randomness (extended abstract)," *Advances in Cryptology - CRYPTO '89*, p. 128. Springer-Verlag, Berlin, 1989.
- Dwork, C. and Naor, M., "Pricing via processing or combatting junk mail," *Advances in Cryptology - CRYPTO '92*, p. 139. Springer-Verlag, Berlin, 1992.
- Naor, M., Ostrovsky, R., Venkatesan, R. and Yung, M., "Perfect zero-knowledge arguments for NP can be based on general complexity assumptions," *Advances in Cryptology - CRYPTO '92*, p. 196. Springer-Verlag, Berlin, 1992.
- Dwork, C., Feige, U., Kilian, J., Naor, M. and Safra, M., "Low communication 2-prover zero-knowledge proofs for NP," *Advances in Cryptology - CRYPTO '92*, p. 215. Springer-Verlag, Berlin, 1992.
- Gemmell, P. and Naor, M., "Codes for interactive authentication," *Advances in Cryptology - CRYPTO '93*, p. 355. Springer-Verlag, Berlin, 1993.
- Fiat, A. and Naor, M., "Broadcast encryption," *Advances in Cryptology - CRYPTO '93*, p. 480. Springer-Verlag, Berlin, 1993.
- Naor, M. and Shamir, A., "Visual cryptography," *Advances in Cryptology - EUROCRYPT '94*, p. 1. Springer-Verlag, Berlin, 1995.
- Dwork, C. and Naor, M., "An efficient existentially unforgeable signature scheme and its applications," *Advances in Cryptology - CRYPTO '94*, p. 234. Springer-Verlag, Berlin, 1994.
- Chor, B., Fiat, A. and Naor, M., "Tracing traitors," *Advances in Cryptology - CRYPTO '94*, p. 257. Springer-Verlag, Berlin, 1994.
- Canetti, R., Dwork, C., Naor, M. and Ostrovsky, R., "Deniable Encryption," *Advances in Cryptology - CRYPTO '97*, p. 90. Springer-Verlag, Berlin, 1997.
- Naor, M. and Pinkas, B., "Visual Authentication and Identification," *Advances in Cryptology - CRYPTO '97*, p. 322. Springer-Verlag, Berlin, 1997.

Nash, R. D.

- Henry, P. S. and Nash, R. D., "High-Speed Hardware Implementation of the Knapsack Cipher," *Advances in Cryptography*, p. 16. University of California, Santa Barbara, Santa Barbara, California, USA, 1982.

Naslund, M.

- Naslund, M., "All Bits in $ax + b$ mod p are Hard," *Advances in Cryptology - CRYPTO '96*, p. 114. Springer-Verlag, Berlin, 1996.
- Goldmann, M. and Naslund, M., "The Complexity of Computing Hard Core Predicates," *Advances in Cryptology - CRYPTO '97*, p. 1. Springer-Verlag, Berlin, 1997.

Needham, R.

- Anderson, R. and Needham, R., "Robustness Principles for Public Key Protocols," *Advances in Cryptology - CRYPTO '95*, p. 236. Springer-Verlag, Berlin, 1995.

Nelson, R.

- Nelson, R. and Heimann, J., "SDNS architecture and end-to-end encryption," *Advances in Cryptology - CRYPTO '89*, p. 356. Springer-Verlag, Berlin, 1989.

Neutjens, P.

- Davio, M., Desmedt, Y., Fosseprez, M., Govaerts, R., Hulsbosch, J., Neutjens, P., Piret, P., Quisquater, J. J., Vandewalle, J. and Wouters, P., "Analytical characteristics of the DES," *Advances in Cryptology: Proceedings of CRYPTO '83*, p. 171. Plenum Publishing, New York, USA, 1984.

Newman, D. B. Jr.

- Tatebayashi, M., Matsuzaki, N. and Newman, D. B. Jr., "Key distribution protocol for digital mobile communication systems," *Advances in Cryptology - CRYPTO '89*, p. 324. Springer-Verlag, Berlin, 1989.

Nguyen, P.

- Nguyen, P. and Stern, J., "Merkle-Hellman Revisited: A Cryptanalysis of the Qu-Vanstone Cryptosystem Based on Group Factorizations," *Advances in Cryptology - CRYPTO '97*, p. 198. Springer-Verlag, Berlin, 1997.

Nicolai, C.

- Nicolai, C., "Nondeterministic cryptography," *Advances in Cryptology: Proceedings of CRYPTO '82*, p. 323. Plenum Publishing, New York, USA, 1982.

Niederreiter, H.

- Niederreiter, H., "A public-key cryptosystem based on shift register sequences.," *Advances in Cryptology - EUROCRYPT '85*, p. 35. Springer-Verlag, Berlin, 1985.
- James, N. S., Lidl, R. and Niederreiter, H., "A Cryptanalytic Attack on the CADE Cryptosystem," *Abstracts of Papers: EUROCRYPT '86*, p. 27. Department of Electrical Engineering, University of Linköping, Linkoping, Sweden, 1986.
- James, N. S., Lidl, R. and Niederreiter, H., "Breaking the Cade cipher," *Advances in Cryptology - CRYPTO '86*, p. 60. Springer-Verlag, Berlin, 1986.
- Niederreiter, H., "Sequences with almost perfect linear complexity profile," *Advances in Cryptology - EUROCRYPT '87*, p. 37. Springer-Verlag, Berlin, 1987.
- Niederreiter, H., "The probabilistic theory of linear complexity," *Advances in Cryptology - EUROCRYPT '88*, p. 191. Springer-Verlag, Berlin, 1988.
- Niederreiter, H., "Keystream sequences with a good linear complexity profile for every starting point," *Advances in Cryptology - EUROCRYPT '89*, p. 523. Springer-Verlag, Berlin, 1989.
- Niederreiter, H., "The linear complexity profile and the jump complexity of keystream sequences," *Advances in Cryptology - EUROCRYPT '90*, p. 174. Springer-Verlag, Berlin, 1990.
- Niederreiter, H. and Schnorr, C. P., "Local randomness in candidate one-way functions," *Advances in Cryptology - EUROCRYPT '92*, p. 408. Springer-Verlag, Berlin, 1992.
- Goettfert, R. and Niederreiter, H., "On the linear complexity of products of shift-register sequences," *Advances in Cryptology - EUROCRYPT '93*, p. 151. Springer-Verlag, Berlin, 1993.
- Goettfert, R. and Niederreiter, H., "A general lower bound for the linear complexity of the product of shift-register sequences," *Advances in Cryptology - EUROCRYPT '94*, p. 223. Springer-Verlag, Berlin, 1995.

Niemi, V.

- Niemi, V., "A new trapdoor in knapsacks," *Advances in Cryptology - EUROCRYPT '90*, p. 405. Springer-Verlag, Berlin, 1990.

Nishio, Y.

- Habutsu, T., Nishio, Y., Sasase, Iwao and Mori, S., "A secret key cryptosystem by iterating a chaotic map," *Advances in Cryptology - EUROCRYPT '91*, p. 127. Springer-Verlag, Berlin, 1991.

Noebauer, R.

- Mueller, W. B. and Noebauer, R., "Cryptanalysis of the Dickson-scheme.," *Advances in Cryptology - EUROCRYPT '85*, p. 50. Springer-Verlag, Berlin, 1985.
- Mueller, W. B. and Noebauer, R., "On Commutative Semigroups of Polynomials and their Application in Cryptography," *Abstracts of Papers: EUROCRYPT '86*, p. 51. Department of Electrical Engineering, University of Linköping, Linkoping, Sweden, 1986.

Nuttin, M.

- Preneel, B., Nuttin, M., Rijmen, V. and Buelens, J., "Cryptanalysis of the CFB mode of the DES with a reduced number of rounds," *Advances in Cryptology - CRYPTO '93*, p. 212. Springer-Verlag, Berlin, 1993.

Nyberg, K.

- Nyberg, K., "Constructions of bent functions and difference sets," *Advances in Cryptology - EUROCRYPT '90*, p. 151. Springer-Verlag, Berlin, 1990.
- Nyberg, K., "Perfect nonlinear S-boxes," *Advances in Cryptology - EUROCRYPT '91*, p. 378. Springer-Verlag, Berlin, 1991.
- Nyberg, K., "On the construction of highly nonlinear permutations," *Advances in Cryptology - EUROCRYPT '92*, p. 92. Springer-Verlag, Berlin, 1992.
- Nyberg, K. and Knudsen, L. R., "Provable security against differential cryptanalysis," *Advances in Cryptology - CRYPTO '92*, p. 566. Springer-Verlag, Berlin, 1992.
- Nyberg, K., "Differentially uniform mappings for cryptography," *Advances in Cryptology - EUROCRYPT '93*, p. 55. Springer-Verlag, Berlin, 1993.
- Nyberg, K. and Rueppel, R. A., "Message recovery for signature schemes based on the discrete logarithm problem," *Advances in Cryptology - EUROCRYPT '94*, p. 182. Springer-Verlag, Berlin, 1995.
- Nyberg, K., "Linear approximation of block ciphers," *Advances in Cryptology - EUROCRYPT '94*, p. 439. Springer-Verlag, Berlin, 1995.

Nye, J. M.

- Nye, J. M., "Current Market: Products, Costs, Trends," *Advances in Cryptography*, p. 110. University of California, Santa Barbara, Santa Barbara, California, USA, 1982.
- Nye, J. M., "The Import/Export Dilemma," *Advances in Cryptography*, p. 135. University of California, Santa Barbara, Santa Barbara, California, USA, 1982.

O'Connor, L.

- O'Connor, L., "Enumerating nondegenerate permutations," *Advances in Cryptology - EUROCRYPT '91*, p. 368. Springer-Verlag, Berlin, 1991.
- O'Connor, L. and Snider, T., "Suffix trees and string complexity," *Advances in Cryptology - EUROCRYPT '92*, p. 138. Springer-Verlag, Berlin, 1992.
- O'Connor, L., "On the distribution of characteristics in bijective mappings," *Advances in Cryptology - EUROCRYPT '93*, p. 360. Springer-Verlag, Berlin, 1993.
- O'Connor, L., "On the distribution of characteristics in composite permutations," *Advances in Cryptology - CRYPTO '93*, p. 403. Springer-Verlag, Berlin, 1993.
- Golic, J. D. and O'Connor, L., "Embedding and probabilistic correlation attacks on clock-controlled shift registers," *Advances in Cryptology - EUROCRYPT '94*, p. 230. Springer-Verlag, Berlin, 1995.
- Charnes, C., O'Connor, L., Pieprzyk, J., Safavi-Naini, R. and Zheng, Y., "Comments on Soviet encryption algorithm," *Advances in Cryptology - EUROCRYPT '94*, p. 433. Springer-Verlag, Berlin, 1995.
- O'Connor, L., "Convergence in differential distributions," *Advances in Cryptology - EUROCRYPT '95*, p. 13. Springer-Verlag, Berlin, 1995.

O'Keefe, C. M.

- Jackson, W. A., Martin, K. M. and O'Keefe, C. M., "Multisecret threshold schemes," *Advances in Cryptology - CRYPTO '93*, p. 126. Springer-Verlag, Berlin, 1993.
- Jackson, W. A., Martin, K. M. and O'Keefe, C. M., "Efficient secret sharing without a mutually trusted authority," *Advances in Cryptology - EUROCRYPT '95*, p. 183. Springer-Verlag, Berlin, 1995.

O'Malley, S.

- Schroeppel, R., Orman, H., O'Malley, S. and Spatscheck, O., "Fast Key Exchange with Elliptic Curve Systems," *Advances in Cryptology - CRYPTO '95*, p. 43. Springer-Verlag, Berlin, 1995.

Obana, S.

- Kurosawa, K. and Obana, S., "Combinatorial bounds for authentication codes with arbitration," *Advances in Cryptology - EUROCRYPT '95*, p. 289. Springer-Verlag, Berlin, 1995.
- Kurosawa, K., Obana, S. and Ogata, W., "t-Cheater Identifiable (k, n) Threshold Secret Sharing Schemes," *Advances in Cryptology - CRYPTO '95*, p. 410. Springer-Verlag, Berlin, 1995.

Oberman, M. R.

- Oberman, M. R., "Communication security in remote controlled computer systems," *Cryptography - Proceedings of the Workshop on Cryptography, Burg Feuerstein, Germany*, p. 219. Springer-Verlag, Berlin, 1983.

Odlyzko, A. M.

- Brickell, E. F., Lagarias, J. C. and Odlyzko, A. M., "Evaluation of the Adleman attack on multiply iterated knapsack cryptosystems," *Advances in Cryptology: Proceedings of CRYPTO '83*, p. 39. Plenum Publishing, New York, USA, 1984.
- Desmedt, Y., Delsarte, P., Odlyzko, A. M. and Piret, P., "Fast cryptanalysis of the Matsumoto-Imai public key scheme," *Advances in Cryptology: Proceedings of EUROCRYPT '84*, p. 142. Springer-Verlag, Berlin, 1984.
- Odlyzko, A. M., "Discrete logarithms in finite fields and their cryptographic significance," *Advances in Cryptology: Proceedings of EUROCRYPT '84*, p. 224. Springer-Verlag, Berlin, 1984.
- Desmedt, Y. and Odlyzko, A. M., "A chosen text attack on the RSA cryptosystem and some discrete logarithm schemes," *Advances in Cryptology - CRYPTO '85*, p. 516. Springer-Verlag, Berlin, 1986.
- Flajolet, P. and Odlyzko, A. M., "Random mapping statistics (invited)," *Advances in Cryptology - EUROCRYPT '89*, p. 329. Springer-Verlag, Berlin, 1989.
- LaMacchia, B. A. and Odlyzko, A. M., "Solving large sparse linear systems over finite fields," *Advances in Cryptology - CRYPTO '90*, p. 109. Springer-Verlag, Berlin, 1990.
- LaMacchia, B. A. and Odlyzko, A. M., "Computation of discrete logarithms in prime fields (Extended abstract)," *Advances in Cryptology - CRYPTO '90*, p. 616. Springer-Verlag, Berlin, 1990.
- Coster, M. J., LaMacchia, B. A., Odlyzko, A. M. and Schnorr, C. P., "An improved low-density subset sum algorithm," *Advances in Cryptology - EUROCRYPT '91*, p. 54. Springer-Verlag, Berlin, 1991.
- Desmedt, Y., Landrock, P., Lenstra, A. K., McCurley, K. S., Odlyzko, A. M., Rueppel, R. A. and Smid, M. E., "The Eurocrypt '92 Controversial Issue: Trapdoor Primes and Moduli," *Advances in Cryptology - EUROCRYPT '92*, p. 194. Springer-Verlag, Berlin, 1992.

Ogata, W.

- Kurosawa, K., Katayama, Y., Ogata, W. and Tsujii, S., "General public key residue cryptosystems and mental poker protocols," *Advances in Cryptology - EUROCRYPT '90*, p. 374. Springer-Verlag, Berlin, 1990.
- Kurosawa, K., Okada, K., Sakano, K., Ogata, W. and Tsujii, S., "Nonperfect secret sharing schemes and matroids," *Advances in Cryptology - EUROCRYPT '93*, p. 126. Springer-Verlag, Berlin, 1993.
- Kurosawa, K., Obana, S. and Ogata, W., "t-Cheater Identifiable (k, n) Threshold Secret Sharing Schemes," *Advances in Cryptology - CRYPTO '95*, p. 410. Springer-Verlag, Berlin, 1995.
- Ogata, W. and Kurosawa, K., "Optimum secret sharing scheme secure against cheating," *Advances in Cryptology - EUROCRYPT '96*, p. 200. Springer-Verlag, Berlin, 1996.

Oh, S. Y.

- Hong, S. M., Oh, S. Y. and Yoon, H., "New modular multiplication algorithms for fast modular exponentiation," *Advances in Cryptology - EUROCRYPT '96*, p. 166. Springer-Verlag, Berlin, 1996.

Ohta, K.

- Koyama, K. and Ohta, K., "Identity based conference key distribution systems," *Advances in Cryptology - CRYPTO '87*, p. 175. Springer-Verlag, Berlin, 1987.
- Koyama, K. and Ohta, K., "Security of improved identity-based conference key distribution systems," *Advances in Cryptology - EUROCRYPT '88*, p. 11. Springer-Verlag, Berlin, 1988.
- Ohta, K. and Okamoto, T., "A modification of the Fiat-Shamir scheme," *Advances in Cryptology - CRYPTO '88*, p. 232. Springer-Verlag, Berlin, 1989.
- Okamoto, T. and Ohta, K., "Divertible zero knowledge interactive proofs and commutative random self-reducibility," *Advances in Cryptology - EUROCRYPT '89*, p. 134. Springer-Verlag, Berlin, 1989.
- Okamoto, T. and Ohta, K., "Disposable zero-knowledge authentications and their applications to untraceable electronic cash," *Advances in Cryptology - CRYPTO '89*, p. 481. Springer-Verlag, Berlin, 1989.
- Miyaguchi, S., Ohta, K. and Iwata, M., "Confirmation that some hash functions are not collision free," *Advances in Cryptology - EUROCRYPT '90*, p. 326. Springer-Verlag, Berlin, 1990.
- Ohta, K., Okamoto, T. and Koyama, K., "Membership authentication for hierarchical multigroups using the extended Fiat-Shamir scheme," *Advances in Cryptology - EUROCRYPT '90*, p. 446. Springer-Verlag, Berlin, 1990.
- Okamoto, T. and Ohta, K., "How to utilize the randomness of zero-knowledge proofs (Extended abstract)," *Advances in Cryptology - CRYPTO '90*, p. 456. Springer-Verlag, Berlin, 1990.
- Okamoto, T., Chaum, D. and Ohta, K., "Direct zero knowledge proofs of computational power in five rounds," *Advances in Cryptology - EUROCRYPT '91*, p. 96. Springer-Verlag, Berlin, 1991.
- Fujioka, A., Okamoto, T. and Ohta, K., "Interactive bi-proof systems and undeniable signature schemes," *Advances in Cryptology - EUROCRYPT '91*, p. 243. Springer-Verlag, Berlin, 1991.
- Morita, H., Ohta, K. and Miyaguchi, S., "A switching closure test to analyze cryptosystems (Extended abstract)," *Advances in Cryptology - CRYPTO '91*, p. 183. Springer-Verlag, Berlin, 1991.
- Okamoto, T. and Ohta, K., "Universal electronic cash," *Advances in Cryptology - CRYPTO '91*, p. 324. Springer-Verlag, Berlin, 1991.
- Ohta, K., Okamoto, T. and Fujioka, A., "Secure bit commitment function against divertibility," *Advances in Cryptology - EUROCRYPT '92*, p. 324. Springer-Verlag, Berlin, 1992.

Okamoto, T.

- Ohta, K. and Okamoto, T., "A modification of the Fiat-Shamir scheme," *Advances in Cryptology - CRYPTO '88*, p. 232. Springer-Verlag, Berlin, 1989.
- Okamoto, T. and Ohta, K., "Divertible zero knowledge interactive proofs and commutative random self-reducibility," *Advances in Cryptology - EUROCRYPT '89*, p. 134. Springer-Verlag, Berlin, 1989.
- Okamoto, T. and Ohta, K., "Disposable zero-knowledge authentications and their applications to untraceable electronic cash," *Advances in Cryptology - CRYPTO '89*, p. 481. Springer-Verlag, Berlin, 1989.
- Ohta, K., Okamoto, T. and Koyama, K., "Membership authentication for hierarchical multigroups using the extended Fiat-Shamir scheme," *Advances in Cryptology - EUROCRYPT '90*, p. 446. Springer-Verlag, Berlin, 1990.
- Okamoto, T. and Ohta, K., "How to utilize the randomness of zero-knowledge proofs (Extended abstract)," *Advances in Cryptology - CRYPTO '90*, p. 456. Springer-Verlag, Berlin, 1990.
- Okamoto, T., Chaum, D. and Ohta, K., "Direct zero knowledge proofs of computational power in five rounds," *Advances in Cryptology - EUROCRYPT '91*, p. 96. Springer-Verlag, Berlin, 1991.
- Fujioka, A., Okamoto, T. and Ohta, K., "Interactive bi-proof systems and undeniable signature schemes," *Advances in Cryptology - EUROCRYPT '91*, p. 243. Springer-Verlag, Berlin, 1991.
- Fujioka, A., Okamoto, T. and Miyaguchi, S., "ESIGN: An efficient digital signature implementation for smart cards," *Advances in Cryptology - EUROCRYPT '91*, p. 446. Springer-Verlag, Berlin, 1991.
- Koyama, K., Maurer, U. M., Okamoto, T. and Vanstone, S. A., "New public-key schemes based on elliptic curves over the ring Z_n," *Advances in Cryptology - CRYPTO '91*, p. 252. Springer-Verlag, Berlin, 1991.
- Okamoto, T. and Sakurai, K., "Efficient algorithms for the construction of hyperelliptic cryptosystems," *Advances in Cryptology - CRYPTO '91*, p. 267. Springer-Verlag, Berlin, 1991.
- Okamoto, T. and Ohta, K., "Universal electronic cash," *Advances in Cryptology - CRYPTO '91*, p. 324. Springer-Verlag, Berlin, 1991.
- Ohta, K., Okamoto, T. and Fujioka, A., "Secure bit commitment function against divertibility," *Advances in Cryptology - EUROCRYPT '92*, p. 324. Springer-Verlag, Berlin, 1992.
- Okamoto, T., Sakurai, K. and Shizuya, H., "How intractable is the discrete logarithm for a general finite group?," *Advances in Cryptology - EUROCRYPT '92*, p. 420. Springer-Verlag, Berlin, 1992.
- Okamoto, T., "Provably secure and practical identification schemes and corresponding signature schemes," *Advances in Cryptology - CRYPTO '92*, p. 31. Springer-Verlag, Berlin, 1992.

378

Orton, G. A.

- Orton, G. A., Roy, M. P., Scott, P. A., Peppard, L. E. and Tavares, S. E., "VLSI implementation of public-key encryption algorithms," *Advances in Cryptology - CRYPTO '86*, p. 277. Springer-Verlag, Berlin, 1986.
- Orton, G. A., "A multiple-iterated trapdoor for dense compact knapsacks," *Advances in Cryptology - EUROCRYPT '94*, p. 112. Springer-Verlag, Berlin, 1995.

Orup, H.

- Orup, H., Svendsen, E. and Andreasen, E., "VICTOR - an efficient RSA hardware implementation," *Advances in Cryptology - EUROCRYPT '90*, p. 245. Springer-Verlag, Berlin, 1990.

Ostrovsky, R.

- Kilian, J., Micali, S. and Ostrovsky, R., "Minimum resource zero-knowledge proofs (extended abstracts)," *Advances in Cryptology - CRYPTO '89*, p. 545. Springer-Verlag, Berlin, 1989.
- Ostrovsky, R., "An efficient software protection scheme," *Advances in Cryptology - CRYPTO '89*, p. 610. Springer-Verlag, Berlin, 1989.
- Naor, M., Ostrovsky, R., Venkatesan, R. and Yung, M., "Perfect zero-knowledge arguments for NP can be based on general complexity assumptions," *Advances in Cryptology - CRYPTO '92*, p. 196. Springer-Verlag, Berlin, 1992.
- Goldwasser, S. and Ostrovsky, R., "Invariant signatures and non-interactive zero-knowledge proofs are equivalent," *Advances in Cryptology - CRYPTO '92*, p. 228. Springer-Verlag, Berlin, 1992.
- Ostrovsky, R., Venkatesan, R. and Yung, M., "Interactive hashing simplifies zero-knowledge protocol design," *Advances in Cryptology - EUROCRYPT '93*, p. 267. Springer-Verlag, Berlin, 1993.
- Canetti, R., Dwork, C., Naor, M. and Ostrovsky, R., "Deniable Encryption," *Advances in Cryptology - CRYPTO '97*, p. 90. Springer-Verlag, Berlin, 1997.
- Juels, A., Luby, M. and Ostrovsky, R., "Security of Blind Digital Signatures," *Advances in Cryptology - CRYPTO '97*, p. 150. Springer-Verlag, Berlin, 1997.
- Dolev, S. and Ostrovsky, R., "Efficient Anonymous Multicast and Reception," *Advances in Cryptology - CRYPTO '97*, p. 395. Springer-Verlag, Berlin, 1997.

Oswald, A.

- Mueller, W. B. and Oswald, A., "Dickson pseudoprimes and primality testing," *Advances in Cryptology - EUROCRYPT '91*, p. 512. Springer-Verlag, Berlin, 1991.

Parkin, G. I. P.

- Davies, D. W. and Parkin, G. I. P., "The average cycle size of the key-stream in output feedback encipherment," *Cryptography - Proceedings of the Workshop on Cryptography, Burg Feuerstein, Germany*, p. 263. Springer-Verlag, Berlin, 1983.
- Davies, D. W. and Parkin, G. I. P., "The average cycle size of the key stream in output feedback encipherment (Abstract)," *Advances in Cryptology: Proceedings of CRYPTO '82*, p. 97. Plenum Publishing, New York, USA, 1982.

Patarin, J.

- Camion, P. and Patarin, J., "The knapsack hash function proposed at Crypto'89 can be broken," *Advances in Cryptology - EUROCRYPT '91*, p. 39. Springer-Verlag, Berlin, 1991.
- Patarin, J., "New results on pseudorandom permutation generators based on the DES scheme," *Advances in Cryptology - CRYPTO '91*, p. 301. Springer-Verlag, Berlin, 1991.
- Patarin, J., "How to construct pseudorandom and super pseudorandom permutations from one single pseudorandom function," *Advances in Cryptology - EUROCRYPT '92*, p. 256. Springer-Verlag, Berlin, 1992.
- Patarin, J., "How to find and avoid collisions for the knapsack hash function," *Advances in Cryptology - EUROCRYPT '93*, p. 305. Springer-Verlag, Berlin, 1993.
- Patarin, J. and Chauvaud, P., "Improved algorithms for the permuted kernel problem," *Advances in Cryptology - CRYPTO '93*, p. 391. Springer-Verlag, Berlin, 1993.
- Patarin, J., "Cryptanalysis of the Matsumoto and Imai Public Key Scheme of Eurocrypt '88," *Advances in Cryptology - CRYPTO '95*, p. 248. Springer-Verlag, Berlin, 1995.
- Coppersmith, D., Franklin, M. K., Patarin, J. and Reiter, M. K., "Low-exponent RSA with related messages," *Advances in Cryptology - EUROCRYPT '96*, p. 1. Springer-Verlag, Berlin, 1996.
- Patarin, J., "Hidden fields equations (HFE) and isomorphisms of polynomials (IP): two new families of asymmetric algorithms," *Advances in Cryptology - EUROCRYPT '96*, p. 33. Springer-Verlag, Berlin, 1996.
- Patarin, J., "Asymmetric Cryptography with a Hidden Monomial," *Advances in Cryptology - CRYPTO '96*, p. 45. Springer-Verlag, Berlin, 1996.

Paulus, S.

- Buchmann, J. A. and Paulus, S., "A One Way Function Based on Ideal Arithmetic in Number Fields," *Advances in Cryptology - CRYPTO '97*, p. 385. Springer-Verlag, Berlin, 1997.

Pedersen, T. P.

- Brandt, J., Damgård, I. B., Landrock, P. and Pedersen, T. P., "Zero-knowledge authentication scheme with secret key exchange," *Advances in Cryptology - CRYPTO '88*, p. 583. Springer-Verlag, Berlin, 1989.
- Boyar, J., Chaum, D., Damgård, I. B. and Pedersen, T. P., "Convertible undeniable signatures," *Advances in Cryptology - CRYPTO '90*, p. 189. Springer-Verlag, Berlin, 1990.
- Pedersen, T. P., "Distributed provers with applications to undeniable signatures," *Advances in Cryptology - EUROCRYPT '91*, p. 221. Springer-Verlag, Berlin, 1991.
- Pedersen, T. P., "A threshold cryptosystem without a trusted party (Extended abstract)," *Advances in Cryptology - EUROCRYPT '91*, p. 522. Springer-Verlag, Berlin, 1991.
- Pedersen, T. P., "Non-interactive and information-theoretic secure verifiable secret sharing," *Advances in Cryptology - CRYPTO '91*, p. 129. Springer-Verlag, Berlin, 1991.
- Heyst, E. van and Pedersen, T. P., "How to make efficient fail-stop signatures," *Advances in Cryptology - EUROCRYPT '92*, p. 366. Springer-Verlag, Berlin, 1992.
- Chaum, D. and Pedersen, T. P., "Transferred cash grows in size," *Advances in Cryptology - EUROCRYPT '92*, p. 390. Springer-Verlag, Berlin, 1992.
- van Heijst, E., Pedersen, T. P. and Pfitzmann, B., "New constructions of fail-stop signatures and lower bounds," *Advances in Cryptology - CRYPTO '92*, p. 15. Springer-Verlag, Berlin, 1992.
- Chaum, D. and Pedersen, T. P., "Wallet databases with observers," *Advances in Cryptology - CRYPTO '92*, p. 89. Springer-Verlag, Berlin, 1992.
- Cramer, R. and Pedersen, T. P., "Improved privacy in wallets with observers," *Advances in Cryptology - EUROCRYPT '93*, p. 329. Springer-Verlag, Berlin, 1993.
- Damgård, I. B., Pedersen, T. P. and Pfitzmann, B., "On the existence of statistically hiding bit commitment schemes and fail-stop signatures," *Advances in Cryptology - CRYPTO '93*, p. 250. Springer-Verlag, Berlin, 1993.
- Chen, L., Damgård, I. B. and Pedersen, T. P., "Parallel divertibility of proofs of knowledge," *Advances in Cryptology - EUROCRYPT '94*, p. 140. Springer-Verlag, Berlin, 1995.
- Chen, L. and Pedersen, T. P., "New group signature schemes," *Advances in Cryptology - EUROCRYPT '94*, p. 171. Springer-Verlag, Berlin, 1995.
- Chen, L. and Pedersen, T. P., "On the efficiency of group signatures providing information-theoretic anonymity," *Advances in Cryptology - EUROCRYPT '95*, p. 39. Springer-Verlag, Berlin, 1995.
- Knudsen, L. R. and Pedersen, T. P., "On the difficulty of software key escrow," *Advances in Cryptology - EUROCRYPT '96*, p. 237. Springer-Verlag, Berlin, 1996.

- Damgård, I. B. and Pedersen, T. P., "New convertible undeniable signature schemes," *Advances in Cryptology - EUROCRYPT '96*, p. 372. Springer-Verlag, Berlin, 1996.

Peppard, L. E.

- Orton, G. A., Roy, M. P., Scott, P. A., Peppard, L. E. and Tavares, S. E., "VLSI implementation of public-key encryption algorithms," *Advances in Cryptology - CRYPTO '86*, p. 277. Springer-Verlag, Berlin, 1986.
- Sivabalan, M., Tavares, S. E. and Peppard, L. E., "On the design of SP networks from an information theoretic point of view," *Advances in Cryptology - CRYPTO '92*, p. 260. Springer-Verlag, Berlin, 1992.

Peralta, R.

- Berger, R., Peralta, R. and Tedrick, T., "A provably secure oblivious transfer protocol," *Advances in Cryptology: Proceedings of EUROCRYPT '84*, p. 379. Springer-Verlag, Berlin, 1984.
- Peralta, R., "Simultaneous security of bits in the discrete log.," *Advances in Cryptology - EUROCRYPT '85*, p. 62. Springer-Verlag, Berlin, 1985.
- Berger, R., Kannan, S. and Peralta, R., "A framework for the study of cryptographic protocols," *Advances in Cryptology - CRYPTO '85*, p. 87. Springer-Verlag, Berlin, 1986.
- Peralta, R. and van de Graaf, J., "A Simple an Fast Probabilistic Algorithm for Computing Square Roots Modulo a Prime Number," *Abstracts of Papers: EUROCRYPT '86*, p. 15. Department of Electrical Engineering, University of Linköping, Linkoping, Sweden, 1986.
- Chaum, D., Evertse, J. H., van de Graaf, J. and Peralta, R., "Demonstrating possession of a discrete logarithm without revealing it," *Advances in Cryptology - CRYPTO '86*, p. 200. Springer-Verlag, Berlin, 1986.
- van de Graaf, J. and Peralta, R., "A simple and secure way to show the validity of your public key," *Advances in Cryptology - CRYPTO '87*, p. 128. Springer-Verlag, Berlin, 1987.
- Davida, G. I., Desmedt, Y. and Peralta, R., "A key distribution system based on any one-way function (extended abstract)," *Advances in Cryptology - EUROCRYPT '89*, p. 75. Springer-Verlag, Berlin, 1989.
- Boyar, J. and Peralta, R., "On the concrete complexity of zero-knowledge proofs," *Advances in Cryptology - CRYPTO '89*, p. 507. Springer-Verlag, Berlin, 1989.
- Davida, G. I., Desmedt, Y. and Peralta, R., "On the importance of memory resources in the security of key exchange protocols (extended abstract)," *Advances in Cryptology - EUROCRYPT '90*, p. 11. Springer-Verlag, Berlin, 1990.
- Peralta, R., "A quadratic sieve on the n-dimensional cube," *Advances in Cryptology - CRYPTO '92*, p. 324. Springer-Verlag, Berlin, 1992.
- Boyar, J. and Peralta, R., "Short discreet proofs," *Advances in Cryptology - EUROCRYPT '96*, p. 131. Springer-Verlag, Berlin, 1996.

Persiano, G.

- De Santis, A., Micali, S. and Persiano, G., "Noninteractive zero-knowledge proof systems," *Advances in Cryptology - CRYPTO '87*, p. 52. Springer-Verlag, Berlin, 1987.
- De Santis, A., Micali, S. and Persiano, G., "Non-interactive zero-knowledge with preprocessing," *Advances in Cryptology - CRYPTO '88*, p. 269. Springer-Verlag, Berlin, 1989.
- De Santis, A. and Persiano, G., "Public-randomness in public-key cryptography (extended abstract)," *Advances in Cryptology - EUROCRYPT '90*, p. 46. Springer-Verlag, Berlin, 1990.
- De Santis, A., Di Crescenzo, G. and Persiano, G., "Secret sharing and perfect zero-knowledge," *Advances in Cryptology - CRYPTO '93*, p. 73. Springer-Verlag, Berlin, 1993.

Pessoa, F.

- Dial, G. and Pessoa, F., "Sharma-Mittal Entropy and Shannon's Random Cipher Result," *Abstracts of Papers: EUROCRYPT '86*, p. 28. Department of Electrical Engineering, University of Linköping, Linkoping, Sweden, 1986.

Peterson, C. G.

- Hughes, R. J., Luther, G. G., Morgan, G. L., Peterson, C. G. and Simmons, C., "Quantum Cryptography over Underground Optical Fibers," *Advances in Cryptology - CRYPTO '96*, p. 329. Springer-Verlag, Berlin, 1996.

Petrovic, S. V.

- Golic, J. D. and Petrovic, S. V., "A generalized correlation attack with a probabilistic constrained edit distance," *Advances in Cryptology - EUROCRYPT '92*, p. 472. Springer-Verlag, Berlin, 1992.

Pfitzmann, A.

- Pfitzmann, A. and Waidner, M., "Networks without user observability–design options.," *Advances in Cryptology - EUROCRYPT '85*, p. 245. Springer-Verlag, Berlin, 1985.
- Pfitzmann, B. and Pfitzmann, A., "How to break the direct RSA-implementation of MIXes," *Advances in Cryptology - EUROCRYPT '89*, p. 373. Springer-Verlag, Berlin, 1989.

Pfitzmann, B.

- Pfitzmann, B. and Pfitzmann, A., "How to break the direct RSA-implementation of MIXes," *Advances in Cryptology - EUROCRYPT '89*, p. 373. Springer-Verlag, Berlin, 1989.
- Waidner, M. and Pfitzmann, B., "The dining cryptographers in the disco: unconditional sender and recipient untraceability with computationally secure serviceability," *Advances in Cryptology - EUROCRYPT '89*, p. 690. Springer-Verlag, Berlin, 1989.
- Bleumer, G., Pfitzmann, B. and Waidner, M., "A remark on signature scheme where forgery can be proved," *Advances in Cryptology - EUROCRYPT '90*, p. 441. Springer-Verlag, Berlin, 1990.
- Pfitzmann, B. and Waidner, M., "How to break and repair a "provably secure" untraceable payment system," *Advances in Cryptology - CRYPTO '91*, p. 338. Springer-Verlag, Berlin, 1991.
- Chaum, D., van Heijst, E. and Pfitzmann, B., "Cryptographically strong undeniable signatures, unconditionally secure for the signer," *Advances in Cryptology - CRYPTO '91*, p. 470. Springer-Verlag, Berlin, 1991.
- Pfitzmann, B. and Waidner, M., "Attacks on protocols for server-aided RSA computation," *Advances in Cryptology - EUROCRYPT '92*, p. 153. Springer-Verlag, Berlin, 1992.
- van Heijst, E., Pedersen, T. P. and Pfitzmann, B., "New constructions of fail-stop signatures and lower bounds," *Advances in Cryptology - CRYPTO '92*, p. 15. Springer-Verlag, Berlin, 1992.
- Damgård, I. B., Pedersen, T. P. and Pfitzmann, B., "On the existence of statistically hiding bit commitment schemes and fail-stop signatures," *Advances in Cryptology - CRYPTO '93*, p. 250. Springer-Verlag, Berlin, 1993.
- Pfitzmann, B., "Breaking an efficient anonymous channel," *Advances in Cryptology - EUROCRYPT '94*, p. 332. Springer-Verlag, Berlin, 1995.
- Pfitzmann, B., Schunter, M. and Waidner, M., "How to break another "provably secure" payment system," *Advances in Cryptology - EUROCRYPT '95*, p. 121. Springer-Verlag, Berlin, 1995.
- Pfitzmann, B. and Schunter, M., "Asymmetric fingerprinting," *Advances in Cryptology - EUROCRYPT '96*, p. 84. Springer-Verlag, Berlin, 1996.
- Pfitzmann, B. and Waidner, M., "Anonymous Fingerprinting," *Advances in Cryptology - EUROCRYPT '97*, p. 88. Springer-Verlag, Berlin, 1997.
- Baric, N. and Pfitzmann, B., "Collision-Free Accumulators and Fail-Stop Signature Schemes Without Trees," *Advances in Cryptology - EUROCRYPT '97*, p. 480. Springer-Verlag, Berlin, 1997.

Pichler, F.

- Pichler, F., "Analog scrambling by the general fast fourier transform," *Cryptography - Proceedings of the Workshop on Cryptography, Burg Feuerstein, Germany*, p. 173. Springer-Verlag, Berlin, 1983.

- Pichler, F., "On the Walsh-Fourier Analysis of Correlation-Immune Switching Functions," *Abstracts of Papers: EUROCRYPT '86*, p. 43. Department of Electrical Engineering, University of Linköping, Linkoping, Sweden, 1986.
- Pichler, F., "Finite state machine modelling of cryptographic systems in LOOPS," *Advances in Cryptology - EUROCRYPT '87*, p. 65. Springer-Verlag, Berlin, 1987.

Pieprzyk, J.

- Pieprzyk, J., "Algebraical structures of cryptographic transformations," *Advances in Cryptology: Proceedings of EUROCRYPT '84*, p. 16. Springer-Verlag, Berlin, 1984.
- Pieprzyk, J., "On public-key cryptosystems built using polynomial rings.," *Advances in Cryptology - EUROCRYPT '85*, p. 73. Springer-Verlag, Berlin, 1985.
- Pieprzyk, J., "Non-linearity of exponent permutations," *Advances in Cryptology - EUROCRYPT '89*, p. 80. Springer-Verlag, Berlin, 1989.
- Pieprzyk, J., "How to construct pseudorandom permutations from single pseudorandom functions," *Advances in Cryptology - EUROCRYPT '90*, p. 140. Springer-Verlag, Berlin, 1990.
- Sadeghiyan, B. and Pieprzyk, J., "A construction for one-way hash functions and pseudorandom bit generators," *Advances in Cryptology - EUROCRYPT '91*, p. 431. Springer-Verlag, Berlin, 1991.
- Pieprzyk, J. and Safavi-Naini, R., "Randomized authentication systems," *Advances in Cryptology - EUROCRYPT '91*, p. 472. Springer-Verlag, Berlin, 1991.
- Pieprzyk, J., "Probabilistic analysis of elementary randomizers," *Advances in Cryptology - EUROCRYPT '91*, p. 542. Springer-Verlag, Berlin, 1991.
- Sadeghiyan, B. and Pieprzyk, J., "A construction of super pseudorandom permutations from a single pseudorandom function," *Advances in Cryptology - EUROCRYPT '92*, p. 267. Springer-Verlag, Berlin, 1992.
- Charnes, C., O'Connor, L., Pieprzyk, J., Safavi-Naini, R. and Zheng, Y., "Comments on Soviet encryption algorithm," *Advances in Cryptology - EUROCRYPT '94*, p. 433. Springer-Verlag, Berlin, 1995.

Piller, E.

- Schaumueller, I. and Piller, E., "A method of protection based on the use of smart cards and cryptographic techniques," *Advances in Cryptology: Proceedings of EUROCRYPT '84*, p. 446. Springer-Verlag, Berlin, 1984.

Pinkas, B.

- McInnes, J. L. and Pinkas, B., "On the impossibility of private key cryptography with weakly random keys," *Advances in Cryptology - CRYPTO '90*, p. 421. Springer-Verlag, Berlin, 1990.
- Naor, M. and Pinkas, B., "Visual Authentication and Identification," *Advances in Cryptology - CRYPTO '97*, p. 322. Springer-Verlag, Berlin, 1997.

Pinkas, D.

- Pinkas, D., "The Need for a Standarized Compression Algorithm for Digital Signatures," *Abstracts of Papers: EUROCRYPT '86*, p. 7. Department of Electrical Engineering, University of Linköping, Linkoping, Sweden, 1986.

Pinter, S.

- Herzberg, A. and Pinter, S., "Public protection of software," *Advances in Cryptology - CRYPTO '85*, p. 158. Springer-Verlag, Berlin, 1986.

Piper, F.

- Piper, F., "Stream ciphers," *Cryptography - Proceedings of the Workshop on Cryptography, Burg Feuerstein, Germany*, p. 181. Springer-Verlag, Berlin, 1983.
- Beth, T. and Piper, F., "The stop-and-go generator," *Advances in Cryptology: Proceedings of EUROCRYPT '84*, p. 88. Springer-Verlag, Berlin, 1984.
- Burmester, M. V. D., Desmedt, Y., Piper, F. and Walker, M., "A general zero-knowledge scheme," *Advances in Cryptology - EUROCRYPT '89*, p. 122. Springer-Verlag, Berlin, 1989.

Piret, P.

- Davio, M., Desmedt, Y., Fosseprez, M., Govaerts, R., Hulsbosch, J., Neutjens, P., Piret, P., Quisquater, J. J., Vandewalle, J. and Wouters, P., "Analytical characteristics of the DES," *Advances in Cryptology: Proceedings of CRYPTO '83*, p. 171. Plenum Publishing, New York, USA, 1984.
- Desmedt, Y., Delsarte, P., Odlyzko, A. M. and Piret, P., "Fast cryptanalysis of the Matsumoto-Imai public key scheme," *Advances in Cryptology: Proceedings of EUROCRYPT '84*, p. 142. Springer-Verlag, Berlin, 1984.

Piveteau, J. M.

- Camenisch, J. L., Piveteau, J. M. and Stadler, M. A., "Blind signatures based on the discrete logarithm problem," *Advances in Cryptology - EUROCRYPT '94*, p. 428. Springer-Verlag, Berlin, 1995.
- Stadler, M. A., Piveteau, J. M. and Camenisch, J. L., "Fair blind signatures," *Advances in Cryptology - EUROCRYPT '95*, p. 209. Springer-Verlag, Berlin, 1995.

Plany, J

- Fairfield, R. C., Matusevich, A and Plany, J, "An LSI digital encryption processor (DEP)," *Advances in Cryptology: Proceedings of CRYPTO '84*, p. 115. Springer-Verlag, Berlin, 1985.

Plotkin, G.

- Abadi, M., Burrows, M., Lampson, B. and Plotkin, G., "A calculus for access control in distributed systems," *Advances in Cryptology - CRYPTO '91*, p. 1. Springer-Verlag, Berlin, 1991.

Plumstead, J. B.

- Plumstead, J. B., "Inferring a sequence produced by a linear congruence (Abstract)," *Advances in Cryptology: Proceedings of CRYPTO '82*, p. 317. Plenum Publishing, New York, USA, 1982.

Pointcheval, D.

- Pointcheval, D., "A new identification scheme based on the perceptrons problem," *Advances in Cryptology - EUROCRYPT '95*, p. 319. Springer-Verlag, Berlin, 1995.
- Pointcheval, D. and Stern, J., "Security proofs for signature schemes," *Advances in Cryptology - EUROCRYPT '96*, p. 387. Springer-Verlag, Berlin, 1996.

Pomerance, C.

- Pomerance, C., Smith, J. W. and Wagstaff, S. S. Jr., "New ideas for factoring large integers," *Advances in Cryptology: Proceedings of CRYPTO '83*, p. 81. Plenum Publishing, New York, USA, 1984.
- Pomerance, C., "The quadratic sieve factoring algorithm," *Advances in Cryptology: Proceedings of EUROCRYPT '84*, p. 169. Springer-Verlag, Berlin, 1984.

Porter, S.

- Porter, S., "A Password Extension for Improved Human Factors," *Advances in Cryptography*, p. 81. University of California, Santa Barbara, Santa Barbara, California, USA, 1982.

Porto, A. di

- Naccache, D., M'raihi, D., Wolfowicz, W. and Porto, A. di, "Are crypto-accelerators really inevitable? 20 bit zero-knowledge in less than a second on simple 8-bit microcontrollers," *Advances in Cryptology - EUROCRYPT '95*, p. 404. Springer-Verlag, Berlin, 1995.

Portz, M.

- Portz, M., "On the use of interconnection networks in cryptography," *Advances in Cryptology - EUROCRYPT '91*, p. 302. Springer-Verlag, Berlin, 1991.

Poullet, Y.

- Antoine, M., Brakeland, Jean-Franc, Eloy, M. and Poullet, Y., "Legal requirements facing new signature technology (invited)," *Advances in Cryptology - EUROCRYPT '89*, p. 273. Springer-Verlag, Berlin, 1989.

Preneel, B.

- Preneel, B., Bosselaers, A., Govaerts, R. and Vandewalle, J., "A chosen text attack on the modified cryptographic checksum algorithm of Cohen and Huang," *Advances in Cryptology - CRYPTO '89*, p. 154. Springer-Verlag, Berlin, 1989.
- Preneel, B., Van Leekwijck, W., Van Linden, L., Govaerts, R. and Vandewalle, J., "Propagation characteristics of Boolean functions," *Advances in Cryptology - EUROCRYPT '90*, p. 161. Springer-Verlag, Berlin, 1990.
- Preneel, B., Govaerts, R. and Vandewalle, J., "Boolean functions satisfying higher order propagation criteria," *Advances in Cryptology - EURO-CRYPT '91*, p. 141. Springer-Verlag, Berlin, 1991.
- Preneel, B., Chaum, D., Fumy, W., Jansen, C. J. A., Landrock, P. and Roelofsen, G., "Race Integrity Primitives Evaluation," *Advances in Cryptology - EUROCRYPT '91*, p. 547. Springer-Verlag, Berlin, 1991.
- Preneel, B., Nuttin, M., Rijmen, V. and Buelens, J., "Cryptanalysis of the CFB mode of the DES with a reduced number of rounds," *Advances in Cryptology - CRYPTO '93*, p. 212. Springer-Verlag, Berlin, 1993.
- Preneel, B., Govaerts, R. and Vandewalle, J., "Hashfunctions based on block ciphers: a synthetic approach," *Advances in Cryptology - CRYPTO '93*, p. 368. Springer-Verlag, Berlin, 1993.
- Preneel, B. and van Oorschot, P. C., "MDx-MAC and Building Fast MACs from Hash Functions," *Advances in Cryptology - CRYPTO '95*, p. 1. Springer-Verlag, Berlin, 1995.
- Preneel, B. and van Oorschot, P. C., "On the security of two MAC algorithms," *Advances in Cryptology - EUROCRYPT '96*, p. 19. Springer-Verlag, Berlin, 1996.
- Knudsen, L. R. and Preneel, B., "Fast and Secure Hashing Based on Codes," *Advances in Cryptology - CRYPTO '97*, p. 485. Springer-Verlag, Berlin, 1997.

Presttun, K.

- Presttun, K., "Integrating cryptography in ISDN," *Advances in Cryptology - CRYPTO '87*, p. 9. Springer-Verlag, Berlin, 1987.

Price, W. L.

- Davies, D. W. and Price, W. L., "Engineering secure information systems.," *Advances in Cryptology - EUROCRYPT '85*, p. 191. Springer-Verlag, Berlin, 1985.
- Price, W. L., "The NPL Intelligent Token and its Application," *Abstracts of Papers: EUROCRYPT '86*, p. 10. Department of Electrical Engineering, University of Linköping, Linkoping, Sweden, 1986.
- Price, W. L., "Standards for data security a change of direction," *Advances in Cryptology - CRYPTO '87*, p. 3. Springer-Verlag, Berlin, 1987.
- Price, W. L., "Progress in data security standardisation," *Advances in Cryptology - CRYPTO '89*, p. 620. Springer-Verlag, Berlin, 1989.

Proctor, N.

- Proctor, N., "A self-synchronizing cascaded cipher system with dynamic control of error propagation," *Advances in Cryptology: Proceedings of CRYPTO '84*, p. 174. Springer-Verlag, Berlin, 1985.

Purdy, G. B.

- Purdy, G. B., Simmons, G. J. and Studies, J., "Software Protection Using "Communal Key Cryptosystems"," *Advances in Cryptography*, p. 79. University of California, Santa Barbara, Santa Barbara, California, USA, 1982.
- Blakley, G. R., Meadows, C. and Purdy, G. B., "Fingerprinting long forgiving messages," *Advances in Cryptology - CRYPTO '85*, p. 180. Springer-Verlag, Berlin, 1986.
- Simmons, G. J. and Purdy, G. B., "Zero-knowledge proofs of identity and veracity of transaction receipts," *Advances in Cryptology - EUROCRYPT '88*, p. 35. Springer-Verlag, Berlin, 1988.

Purtill, M. R.

- Brickell, E. F., Moore, J. H. and Purtill, M. R., "Structure in the S-boxes of the DES," *Advances in Cryptology - CRYPTO '86*, p. 3. Springer-Verlag, Berlin, 1986.

Putter, P. S.

- Wagner, N. R., Putter, P. S. and Cain, M. R., "Using algorithms as keys in stream ciphers.," *Advances in Cryptology - EUROCRYPT '85*, p. 149. Springer-Verlag, Berlin, 1985.
- Wagner, N. R., Putter, P. S. and Cain, M. R., "Large-scale randomization techniques," *Advances in Cryptology - CRYPTO '86*, p. 393. Springer-Verlag, Berlin, 1986.

Quang A, N.

- Quang A, N., "Elementary Proof of Rueppel's Linear Complexity Conjecture," *Abstracts of Papers: EUROCRYPT '86*, p. 34. Department of Electrical Engineering, University of Linköping, Linkoping, Sweden, 1986.

390

Quisquater, J. J.

- Davio, M., Goethals, J. M. and Quisquater, J. J., "Authentication procedures," *Cryptography - Proceedings of the Workshop on Cryptography, Burg Feuerstein, Germany*, p. 283. Springer-Verlag, Berlin, 1983.
- Davio, M., Desmedt, Y., Fosseprez, M., Govaerts, R., Hulsbosch, J., Neutjens, P., Piret, P., Quisquater, J. J., Vandewalle, J. and Wouters, P., "Analytical characteristics of the DES," *Advances in Cryptology: Proceedings of CRYPTO '83*, p. 171. Plenum Publishing, New York, USA, 1984.
- Davio, M., Desmedt, Y. and Quisquater, J. J., "Propagation characteristics of the DES," *Advances in Cryptology: Proceedings of EUROCRYPT '84*, p. 62. Springer-Verlag, Berlin, 1984.
- Davio, M., Desmedt, Y., Goubert, J., Hoornaert, F. and Quisquater, J. J., "Efficient hardware and software implementations for the DES," *Advances in Cryptology: Proceedings of CRYPTO '84*, p. 144. Springer-Verlag, Berlin, 1985.
- Desmedt, Y., Quisquater, J. J. and Davio, M., "Dependence of output on input in DES: small avalanche characteristics," *Advances in Cryptology: Proceedings of CRYPTO '84*, p. 359. Springer-Verlag, Berlin, 1985.
- Quisquater, J. J., Desmedt, Y. and Davio, M., "The importance of "good" key scheduling schemes (how to make a secure DES scheme with < 48 bits keys?)," *Advances in Cryptology - CRYPTO '85*, p. 537. Springer-Verlag, Berlin, 1986.
- Desmedt, Y., Hoornaert, F. and Quisquater, J. J., "Several Exhaustive Key Search Machines and DES," *Abstracts of Papers: EUROCRYPT '86*, p. 17. Department of Electrical Engineering, University of Linköping, Linkoping, Sweden, 1986.
- Desmedt, Y. and Quisquater, J. J., "Public-key systems based on the difficulty of tampering (Is there a difference between DES and RSA?)," *Advances in Cryptology - CRYPTO '86*, p. 111. Springer-Verlag, Berlin, 1986.
- Quisquater, J. J., "Secret distribution of keys for public key systems," *Advances in Cryptology - CRYPTO '87*, p. 203. Springer-Verlag, Berlin, 1987.
- Guillou, L. C. and Quisquater, J. J., "Efficient digital publickey signatures with shadow," *Advances in Cryptology - CRYPTO '87*, p. 223. Springer-Verlag, Berlin, 1987.
- Quisquater, J. J. and Delescaille, J. P., "Other cycling tests for DES," *Advances in Cryptology - CRYPTO '87*, p. 255. Springer-Verlag, Berlin, 1987.
- Guillou, L. C. and Quisquater, J. J., "A practical zero-knowledge protocol fitted to security microprocessor minimizing both transmission and memory," *Advances in Cryptology - EUROCRYPT '88*, p. 123. Springer-Verlag, Berlin, 1988.

- Guillou, L. C. and Quisquater, J. J., "A "paradoxical" identity-based signature scheme resulting from zero-knowledge," *Advances in Cryptology - CRYPTO '88*, p. 216. Springer-Verlag, Berlin, 1989.
- Quisquater, J. J. and Girault, M., "2n-BIT hash-functions using n-BIT symmetric block cipher algorithms," *Advances in Cryptology - EUROCRYPT '89*, p. 102. Springer-Verlag, Berlin, 1989.
- Quisquater, J. J. and Delescaille, J. P., "How easy is collision search? Application to DES," *Advances in Cryptology - EUROCRYPT '89*, p. 429. Springer-Verlag, Berlin, 1989.
- Quisquater, J. J. and Bouckaert, A., "Zero-knowledge procedures for confidential access to medical records," *Advances in Cryptology - EUROCRYPT '89*, p. 662. Springer-Verlag, Berlin, 1989.
- De Soete, M., Quisquater, J. J. and Vedder, K., "A signature with shared verification scheme," *Advances in Cryptology - CRYPTO '89*, p. 253. Springer-Verlag, Berlin, 1989.
- Quisquater, J. J. and Delescaille, J. P., "How easy is collision search. New results and applications to DES," *Advances in Cryptology - CRYPTO '89*, p. 408. Springer-Verlag, Berlin, 1989.
- Quisquater, J. J., Guillou, L. C., Annick, M. and Berson, T. A., "How to explain zero-knowledge protocols to your children," *Advances in Cryptology - CRYPTO '89*, p. 628. Springer-Verlag, Berlin, 1989.
- Guillou, L. C., Quisquater, J. J., Walker, M., Landrock, P. and Shaer, C., "Precautions taken against various potential attacks in ISO/IEC DIS 9796," *Advances in Cryptology - EUROCRYPT '90*, p. 465. Springer-Verlag, Berlin, 1990.
- De Waleffe, D. and Quisquater, J. J., "CORSAIR: A smart card for public key cryptosystems," *Advances in Cryptology - CRYPTO '90*, p. 502. Springer-Verlag, Berlin, 1990.
- Delos, O. and Quisquater, J. J., "An identity-based signature scheme with bounded life-span," *Advances in Cryptology - CRYPTO '94*, p. 83. Springer-Verlag, Berlin, 1994.
- Beguin, P. and Quisquater, J. J., "Fast Server-Aided RSA Signatures Secure Against Active Attacks," *Advances in Cryptology - CRYPTO '95*, p. 57. Springer-Verlag, Berlin, 1995.

Rabin, T.

- Micali, S. and Rabin, T., "Collective coin tossing without assumptions nor broadcasting," *Advances in Cryptology - CRYPTO '90*, p. 253. Springer-Verlag, Berlin, 1990.
- Gennaro, R., Jarecki, S., Krawczyk, H. and Rabin, T., "Robust threshold DSS signatures," *Advances in Cryptology - EUROCRYPT '96*, p. 354. Springer-Verlag, Berlin, 1996.
- Gennaro, R., Jarecki, S., Krawczyk, H. and Rabin, T., "Robust and Efficient Sharing of RSA Functions," *Advances in Cryptology - CRYPTO '96*, p. 157. Springer-Verlag, Berlin, 1996.

- Gennaro, R., Krawczyk, H. and Rabin, T., "RSA-Based Undeniable Signatures," *Advances in Cryptology - CRYPTO '97*, p. 132. Springer-Verlag, Berlin, 1997.

Rackoff, C.

- Luby, M. and Rackoff, C., "How to construct pseudo-random permutations from pseudo-random functions," *Advances in Cryptology - CRYPTO '85*, p. 447. Springer-Verlag, Berlin, 1986.
- Micali, S., Rackoff, C. and Sloan, B., "The notion of security for probabilistic cryptosystems," *Advances in Cryptology - CRYPTO '86*, p. 381. Springer-Verlag, Berlin, 1986.
- Luby, M. and Rackoff, C., "A study of password security," *Advances in Cryptology - CRYPTO '87*, p. 392. Springer-Verlag, Berlin, 1987.
- Rackoff, C., "A basic theory of public and private cryptosystems (invited talk)," *Advances in Cryptology - CRYPTO '88*, p. 249. Springer-Verlag, Berlin, 1989.
- Rackoff, C. and Simon, D. R., "Non-interactive zero-knowledge proof of knowledge and chosen ciphertext attack," *Advances in Cryptology - CRYPTO '91*, p. 433. Springer-Verlag, Berlin, 1991.

Rankine, G.

- Rankine, G., "THOMAS–A complete single chip RSA device," *Advances in Cryptology - CRYPTO '86*, p. 480. Springer-Verlag, Berlin, 1986.

Rao, T. R. N.

- Rao, T. R. N. and Nam, K. H., "Private-key algebraic-coded cryptosystems," *Advances in Cryptology - CRYPTO '86*, p. 35. Springer-Verlag, Berlin, 1986.
- Rao, T. R. N., "On Struik-Tilburg cryptanalysis of Rao-Nam scheme," *Advances in Cryptology - CRYPTO '87*, p. 458. Springer-Verlag, Berlin, 1987.
- Hwang, T. and Rao, T. R. N., "Secret error-correcting codes (SECC)," *Advances in Cryptology - CRYPTO '88*, p. 540. Springer-Verlag, Berlin, 1989.
- Hwang, T. and Rao, T. R. N., "Private-key algebraic-code cryptosystems with high information rates," *Advances in Cryptology - EUROCRYPT '89*, p. 657. Springer-Verlag, Berlin, 1989.
- Zeng, K., Yang, C. H. and Rao, T. R. N., "On the linear consistency test (LCT) in cryptanalysis with applications," *Advances in Cryptology - CRYPTO '89*, p. 164. Springer-Verlag, Berlin, 1989.
- Zeng, K., Yang, C. H. and Rao, T. R. N., "An improved linear syndrome algorithm in cryptanalysis with applications," *Advances in Cryptology - CRYPTO '90*, p. 34. Springer-Verlag, Berlin, 1990.

Raphaeli, D.
- Naccache, D., M'raihi, D., Vaudenay, S. and Raphaeli, D., "Can D. S. A. be improved? Complexity trade-offs with the digital signature standard," *Advances in Cryptology - EUROCRYPT '94*, p. 77. Springer-Verlag, Berlin, 1995.

Reeds, J. A.
- Reeds, J. A. and Sloane, N. J. A., "Shift register synthesis (modulo m).," *Advances in Cryptology: Proceedings of CRYPTO '83*, p. 249. Plenum Publishing, New York, USA, 1984.
- Reeds, J. A. and Manferdelli, J. L., "DES has no per round linear factors," *Advances in Cryptology: Proceedings of CRYPTO '84*, p. 377. Springer-Verlag, Berlin, 1985.

Reif, J. H.
- Reif, J. H. and Tygar, J. D., "Efficient parallel pseudo-random number generation," *Advances in Cryptology - CRYPTO '85*, p. 433. Springer-Verlag, Berlin, 1986.

Reiter, M. K.
- Franklin, M. K. and Reiter, M. K., "Verifiable signature sharing," *Advances in Cryptology - EUROCRYPT '95*, p. 50. Springer-Verlag, Berlin, 1995.
- Coppersmith, D., Franklin, M. K., Patarin, J. and Reiter, M. K., "Low-exponent RSA with related messages," *Advances in Cryptology - EUROCRYPT '96*, p. 1. Springer-Verlag, Berlin, 1996.

Retkin, H.
- Gordon, J. A. and Retkin, H., "Are big S-boxes best?," *Cryptography - Proceedings of the Workshop on Cryptography, Burg Feuerstein, Germany*, p. 257. Springer-Verlag, Berlin, 1983.

Reyneri, J. M.
- Hellman, M. E., Karnin, E. and Reyneri, J. M., "On the Necessity or Exhaustive Search for System-Invariant Cryptanalysis," *Advances in Cryptography*, p. 2. University of California, Santa Barbara, Santa Barbara, California, USA, 1982.
- Amirazizi, H., Karnin, E. and Reyneri, J. M., "Compact Knapsacks are Polynomially Solvable," *Advances in Cryptography*, p. 17. University of California, Santa Barbara, Santa Barbara, California, USA, 1982.
- Hellman, M. E. and Reyneri, J. M., "Fast computation of discrete logarithms in GF(q)," *Advances in Cryptology: Proceedings of CRYPTO '82*, p. 3. Plenum Publishing, New York, USA, 1982.
- Hellman, M. E. and Reyneri, J. M., "Drainage and the DES," *Advances in Cryptology: Proceedings of CRYPTO '82*, p. 129. Plenum Publishing, New York, USA, 1982.

Rijmen, V.

- Preneel, B., Nuttin, M., Rijmen, V. and Buelens, J., "Cryptanalysis of the CFB mode of the DES with a reduced number of rounds," *Advances in Cryptology - CRYPTO '93*, p. 212. Springer-Verlag, Berlin, 1993.
- Borst, J., Knudsen, L. R. and Rijmen, V., "Two Attacks on Reduced IDEA (Extended Abstract)," *Advances in Cryptology - EUROCRYPT '97*, p. 1. Springer-Verlag, Berlin, 1997.

Rimensberger, U.

- Rimensberger, U., "Encryption: needs, requirements and solutions in banking networks.," *Advances in Cryptology - EUROCRYPT '85*, p. 208. Springer-Verlag, Berlin, 1985.

Rivest, R. L.

- Rivest, R. L. and Sherman, A. T., "Randomized encryption techniques," *Advances in Cryptology: Proceedings of CRYPTO '82*, p. 145. Plenum Publishing, New York, USA, 1982.
- Rivest, R. L., "A short report on the RSA chip," *Advances in Cryptology: Proceedings of CRYPTO '82*, p. 327. Plenum Publishing, New York, USA, 1982.
- Rivest, R. L., "RSA chips (past/present/future)," *Advances in Cryptology: Proceedings of EUROCRYPT '84*, p. 159. Springer-Verlag, Berlin, 1984.
- Chor, B. and Rivest, R. L., "A knapsack type public key cryptosystem based on arithmetic in finite fields," *Advances in Cryptology: Proceedings of CRYPTO '84*, p. 54. Springer-Verlag, Berlin, 1985.
- Rivest, R. L. and Shamir, A., "Efficient factoring based on partial information.," *Advances in Cryptology - EUROCRYPT '85*, p. 31. Springer-Verlag, Berlin, 1985.
- Kaliski, B. S., Rivest, R. L. and Sherman, A. T., "Is the data encryption standard a group?.," *Advances in Cryptology - EUROCRYPT '85*, p. 81. Springer-Verlag, Berlin, 1985.
- Kaliski, B. S., Rivest, R. L. and Sherman, A. T., "Is DES a pure cipher? (Results of more cycling experiments on DES)," *Advances in Cryptology - CRYPTO '85*, p. 212. Springer-Verlag, Berlin, 1986.
- Rivest, R. L., "The MD4 message digest algorithm," *Advances in Cryptology - CRYPTO '90*, p. 303. Springer-Verlag, Berlin, 1990.
- Rivest, R. L., "Finding four million large random primes," *Advances in Cryptology - CRYPTO '90*, p. 625. Springer-Verlag, Berlin, 1990.

Robert, J. M.

- Bennett, C. H., Brassard, G. and Robert, J. M., "How to reduce your enemy's information," *Advances in Cryptology - CRYPTO '85*, p. 468. Springer-Verlag, Berlin, 1986.
- Brassard, G., Crépeau, C. and Robert, J. M., "All-or-nothing disclosure of secrets," *Advances in Cryptology - CRYPTO '86*, p. 234. Springer-Verlag, Berlin, 1986.

Robshaw, M. J. B.

- Kaliski, B. S. and Robshaw, M. J. B., "Linear cryptanalysis using multiple approximations," *Advances in Cryptology - CRYPTO '94*, p. 26. Springer-Verlag, Berlin, 1994.
- Knudsen, L. R. and Robshaw, M. J. B., "Non-linear approximations in linear cryptanalysis," *Advances in Cryptology - EUROCRYPT '96*, p. 224. Springer-Verlag, Berlin, 1996.

Roe, M.

- Anderson, R. and Roe, M., "The GCHQ Protocol and Its Problems," *Advances in Cryptology - EUROCRYPT '97*, p. 134. Springer-Verlag, Berlin, 1997.

Roelofsen, G.

- Vandewalle, J., Chaum, D., Fumy, W., Jansen, C. J. A., Landrock, P. and Roelofsen, G., "A European call for cryptographic algorithms: RIPE; Race Integrity Primitives Evaluation," *Advances in Cryptology - EUROCRYPT '89*, p. 267. Springer-Verlag, Berlin, 1989.
- Preneel, B., Chaum, D., Fumy, W., Jansen, C. J. A., Landrock, P. and Roelofsen, G., "Race Integrity Primitives Evaluation," *Advances in Cryptology - EUROCRYPT '91*, p. 547. Springer-Verlag, Berlin, 1991.

Rogaway, P.

- Ben-Or, M., Goldreich, O., Goldwasser, S., Hastad, J., Kilian, J., Micali, S. and Rogaway, P., "Everything provable is provable in zero-knowledge," *Advances in Cryptology - CRYPTO '88*, p. 37. Springer-Verlag, Berlin, 1989.
- Beaver, D., Feigenbaum, J., Kilian, J. and Rogaway, P., "Security with low communication overhead (Extended abstract)," *Advances in Cryptology - CRYPTO '90*, p. 62. Springer-Verlag, Berlin, 1990.
- Micali, S. and Rogaway, P., "Secure computation," *Advances in Cryptology - CRYPTO '91*, p. 392. Springer-Verlag, Berlin, 1991.
- Bellare, M. and Rogaway, P., "Entity authentication and key distribution," *Advances in Cryptology - CRYPTO '93*, p. 232. Springer-Verlag, Berlin, 1993.
- Bellare, M. and Rogaway, P., "Optimal asymmetric encryption," *Advances in Cryptology - EUROCRYPT '94*, p. 92. Springer-Verlag, Berlin, 1995.
- Bellare, M., Kilian, J. and Rogaway, P., "The security of cipher block chaining," *Advances in Cryptology - CRYPTO '94*, p. 341. Springer-Verlag, Berlin, 1994.
- Bellare, M., Guerin, R. and Rogaway, P., "XOR MACs: New Methods for Message Authentication Using Finite Pseudorandom Functions," *Advances in Cryptology - CRYPTO '95*, p. 15. Springer-Verlag, Berlin, 1995.
- Rogaway, P., "Bucket Hashing and its Application to Fast Message Authentication," *Advances in Cryptology - CRYPTO '95*, p. 29. Springer-Verlag, Berlin, 1995.

- Bellare, M. and Rogaway, P., "The exact security of digital signatures how to sign with RSA and Rabin," *Advances in Cryptology - EUROCRYPT '96*, p. 399. Springer-Verlag, Berlin, 1996.
- Kilian, J. and Rogaway, P., "How to Protect DES Against Exhaustive Key Search," *Advances in Cryptology - CRYPTO '96*, p. 252. Springer-Verlag, Berlin, 1996.
- Bellare, M. and Rogaway, P., "Collision-Resistant Hashing: Towards Making UOWHFs Practical," *Advances in Cryptology - CRYPTO '97*, p. 470. Springer-Verlag, Berlin, 1997.

Roggeman, Y.

- Roggeman, Y., "Varying feedback shift registers," *Advances in Cryptology - EUROCRYPT '89*, p. 670. Springer-Verlag, Berlin, 1989.

Rohatgi, P.

- Gennaro, R. and Rohatgi, P., "How to Sign Digital Streams," *Advances in Cryptology - CRYPTO '97*, p. 180. Springer-Verlag, Berlin, 1997.

Roijakkers, Sandra

- Chaum, D. and Roijakkers, Sandra, "Unconditionally Secure Digital Signatures," *Advances in Cryptology - CRYPTO '90*, p. 206. Springer-Verlag, Berlin, 1990.

Rooij, P. de

- Rooij, P. de, "On the security of the Schnorr scheme using preprocessing," *Advances in Cryptology - EUROCRYPT '91*, p. 71. Springer-Verlag, Berlin, 1991.
- Rooij, P. de, "On Schnorr's preprocessing for digital signature schemes," *Advances in Cryptology - EUROCRYPT '93*, p. 435. Springer-Verlag, Berlin, 1993.
- Rooij, P. de, "Efficient exponentiation using precomputation and vector addition chains," *Advances in Cryptology - EUROCRYPT '94*, p. 389. Springer-Verlag, Berlin, 1995.

Rosen, A.

- Kushilevitz, E. and Rosen, A., "A randomness-rounds tradeoff in private computation," *Advances in Cryptology - CRYPTO '94*, p. 397. Springer-Verlag, Berlin, 1994.

Rosenbaum, U.

- Beutelspacher, A. and Rosenbaum, U., "Essentially l-fold secure authentication systems," *Advances in Cryptology - EUROCRYPT '90*, p. 294. Springer-Verlag, Berlin, 1990.

Roy, M. P.

- Orton, G. A., Roy, M. P., Scott, P. A., Peppard, L. E. and Tavares, S. E., "VLSI implementation of public-key encryption algorithms," *Advances in Cryptology - CRYPTO '86*, p. 277. Springer-Verlag, Berlin, 1986.

Royer, J. S.

- Kurtz, S. A., Mahaney, S. R. and Royer, J. S., "On the power of 1-way functions," *Advances in Cryptology - CRYPTO '88*, p. 578. Springer-Verlag, Berlin, 1989.

Rubin, A.

- Shoup, V. and Rubin, A., "Session key distribution using smart cards," *Advances in Cryptology - EUROCRYPT '96*, p. 321. Springer-Verlag, Berlin, 1996.

Rubinfeld, R.

- Kilian, J. and Rubinfeld, R., "Interactive proofs with space bounded provers," *Advances in Cryptology - CRYPTO '91*, p. 225. Springer-Verlag, Berlin, 1991.

Rudich, S.

- Impagliazzo, R. and Rudich, S., "Limits on the provable consequences of one-way permutations (invited talk)," *Advances in Cryptology - CRYPTO '88*, p. 8. Springer-Verlag, Berlin, 1989.
- Rudich, S., "The use of interaction in public cryptosystems (Extended abstract)," *Advances in Cryptology - CRYPTO '91*, p. 242. Springer-Verlag, Berlin, 1991.

Rueppel, R. A.

- Massey, J. L. and Rueppel, R. A., "Linear ciphers and random sequence generators with multiple clocks," *Advances in Cryptology: Proceedings of EUROCRYPT '84*, p. 74. Springer-Verlag, Berlin, 1984.
- Rueppel, R. A., "Linear complexity and random sequences.," *Advances in Cryptology - EUROCRYPT '85*, p. 167. Springer-Verlag, Berlin, 1985.
- Rueppel, R. A., "Correlation immunity and the summation generator," *Advances in Cryptology - CRYPTO '85*, p. 260. Springer-Verlag, Berlin, 1986.
- Rueppel, R. A. and Staffelbach, O., "Products of Linear Recurring Sequence with Maximum Complexity," *Abstracts of Papers: EUROCRYPT '86*, p. 30. Department of Electrical Engineering, University of Linköping, Linkoping, Sweden, 1986.
- Rueppel, R. A., "When shift registers clock themselves," *Advances in Cryptology - EUROCRYPT '87*, p. 53. Springer-Verlag, Berlin, 1987.
- Rueppel, R. A., "Key agreements based on function composition," *Advances in Cryptology - EUROCRYPT '88*, p. 3. Springer-Verlag, Berlin, 1988.
- Rueppel, R. A., "On the security of Schnorr's pseudo random generator," *Advances in Cryptology - EUROCRYPT '89*, p. 423. Springer-Verlag, Berlin, 1989.
- Rueppel, R. A., "A formal approach to security architectures," *Advances in Cryptology - EUROCRYPT '91*, p. 387. Springer-Verlag, Berlin, 1991.
- Desmedt, Y., Landrock, P., Lenstra, A. K., McCurley, K. S., Odlyzko, A. M., Rueppel, R. A. and Smid, M. E., "The Eurocrypt '92 Controversial Issue: Trapdoor Primes and Moduli," *Advances in Cryptology - EUROCRYPT '92*, p. 194. Springer-Verlag, Berlin, 1992.
- Nyberg, K. and Rueppel, R. A., "Message recovery for signature schemes based on the discrete logarithm problem," *Advances in Cryptology - EUROCRYPT '94*, p. 182. Springer-Verlag, Berlin, 1995.

Ruggiu, G.

- Ruggiu, G., "Cryptology and complexity theories," *Advances in Cryptology: Proceedings of EUROCRYPT '84*, p. 3. Springer-Verlag, Berlin, 1984.

Rundell, W.

- Blakley, G. R. and Rundell, W., "Cryptosystems based on an analog of heat flow," *Advances in Cryptology - CRYPTO '87*, p. 306. Springer-Verlag, Berlin, 1987.

Rushanan, J. J.

- Games, R. A. and Rushanan, J. J., "Blind synchronization of m-sequences with even span," *Advances in Cryptology - EUROCRYPT '93*, p. 168. Springer-Verlag, Berlin, 1993.

Sako, K.

- Sako, K. and Kilian, J., "Secure voting using partially compatible homomorphisms," *Advances in Cryptology - CRYPTO '94*, p. 411. Springer-Verlag, Berlin, 1994.
- Sako, K. and Kilian, J., "Receipt-free mix-type voting scheme A practical solution to the implementation of a voting booth," *Advances in Cryptology - EUROCRYPT '95*, p. 393. Springer-Verlag, Berlin, 1995.
- Jakobsson, M., Sako, K. and Impagliazzo, R., "Designated verifier proofs and their applications," *Advances in Cryptology - EUROCRYPT '96*, p. 143. Springer-Verlag, Berlin, 1996.

Sakurai, K.

- Okamoto, T. and Sakurai, K., "Efficient algorithms for the construction of hyperelliptic cryptosystems," *Advances in Cryptology - CRYPTO '91*, p. 267. Springer-Verlag, Berlin, 1991.
- Okamoto, T., Sakurai, K. and Shizuya, H., "How intractable is the discrete logarithm for a general finite group?," *Advances in Cryptology - EUROCRYPT '92*, p. 420. Springer-Verlag, Berlin, 1992.
- Sakurai, K. and Itoh, T., "On the discrepancy between serial and parallel of zero-knowledge protocols," *Advances in Cryptology - CRYPTO '92*, p. 246. Springer-Verlag, Berlin, 1992.
- Sakurai, K. and Shizuya, H., "Relationships among the computational powers of breaking discrete log cryptosystems," *Advances in Cryptology - EUROCRYPT '95*, p. 341. Springer-Verlag, Berlin, 1995.

Salvail, L.

- Bennett, C. H., Bessette, F., Brassard, G., Salvail, L. and Smolin, J., "Experimental quantum cryptography," *Advances in Cryptology - EUROCRYPT '90*, p. 253. Springer-Verlag, Berlin, 1990.
- Brassard, G. and Salvail, L., "Secret key reconciliation by public discussion," *Advances in Cryptology - EUROCRYPT '93*, p. 410. Springer-Verlag, Berlin, 1993.
- Crépeau, C. and Salvail, L., "Quantum oblivious mutual identification," *Advances in Cryptology - EUROCRYPT '95*, p. 133. Springer-Verlag, Berlin, 1995.

Santha, M.

- Crépeau, C. and Santha, M., "On the reversibility of oblivious transfer," *Advances in Cryptology - EUROCRYPT '91*, p. 106. Springer-Verlag, Berlin, 1991.

Sasase, Iwao

- Habutsu, T., Nishio, Y., Sasase, Iwao and Mori, S., "A secret key cryptosystem by iterating a chaotic map," *Advances in Cryptology - EUROCRYPT '91*, p. 127. Springer-Verlag, Berlin, 1991.

Satoh, T.

- Kurosawa, K. and Satoh, T., "Design of SAC/PC(1) of Order k Boolean Functions and Three Other Cryptographic Criteria," *Advances in Cryptology - EUROCRYPT '97*, p. 434. Springer-Verlag, Berlin, 1997.

Sattler, J.

- Sattler, J. and Schnorr, C. P., "Ein Effizienzvergleich der Factorisierungsverfahren von Morrison-Brillhart und Schroeppel (An efficient comparison of the factorization procedures of Morrison-Brillhart and Schroeppel)," *Cryptography - Proceedings of the Workshop on Cryptography, Burg Feuerstein, Germany*, p. 331. Springer-Verlag, Berlin, 1983.

Sauerbrey, J.

- Sauerbrey, J. and Dietel, A., "Resource requirements for the application of addition chains in modulo exponentiation," *Advances in Cryptology - EUROCRYPT '92*, p. 174. Springer-Verlag, Berlin, 1992.

Schaefer, F.

- Beth, T. and Schaefer, F., "Non supersingular elliptic curves for public key cryptosystems," *Advances in Cryptology - EUROCRYPT '91*, p. 316. Springer-Verlag, Berlin, 1991.

Schaumueller, I.

- Schaumueller, I. and Piller, E., "A method of protection based on the use of smart cards and cryptographic techniques," *Advances in Cryptology: Proceedings of EUROCRYPT '84*, p. 446. Springer-Verlag, Berlin, 1984.

Schaumueller-Bichl, I.

- Schaumueller-Bichl, I., "Cryptonalysis of the data encryption standard by the method of formal coding," *Cryptography - Proceedings of the Workshop on Cryptography, Burg Feuerstein, Germany*, p. 235. Springer-Verlag, Berlin, 1983.
- Schaumueller-Bichl, I., "ICcards in high-security applications," *Advances in Cryptology - EUROCRYPT '87*, p. 177. Springer-Verlag, Berlin, 1987.

Scheidler, R.

- Scheidler, R., Buchmann, J. A. and Williams, H. C., "Implementation of a key exchange protocol using real quadratic fields (extended abstract)," *Advances in Cryptology - EUROCRYPT '90*, p. 98. Springer-Verlag, Berlin, 1990.

Schneier, B.

- Kelsey, J., Schneier, B. and Wagner, D., "Key-Schedule Cryptanalysis of IDEA, G-DES, GOST, SAFER, and Triple-DES," *Advances in Cryptology - CRYPTO '96*, p. 237. Springer-Verlag, Berlin, 1996.
- Wagner, D., Schneier, B. and Kelsey, J., "Cryptanalysis of the Cellular Message Encryption Algorithm," *Advances in Cryptology - CRYPTO '97*, p. 526. Springer-Verlag, Berlin, 1997.

Schnorr, C. P.

- Schnorr, C. P., "Is the RSA scheme safe?," *Cryptography - Proceedings of the Workshop on Cryptography, Burg Feuerstein, Germany*, p. 325. Springer-Verlag, Berlin, 1983.
- Sattler, J. and Schnorr, C. P., "Ein Effizienzvergleich der Factorisierungsverfahren von Morrison-Brillhart und Schroeppel (An efficient comparison of the factorization procedures of Morrison-Brillhart and Schroeppel)," *Cryptography - Proceedings of the Workshop on Cryptography, Burg Feuerstein, Germany*, p. 331. Springer-Verlag, Berlin, 1983.
- Ong, H. and Schnorr, C. P., "Signatures through approximate representations by quadratic forms," *Advances in Cryptology: Proceedings of CRYPTO '83*, p. 117. Plenum Publishing, New York, USA, 1984.
- Schnorr, C. P. and Alexi, W., "RSA-bits are 0.5 + epsilon secure," *Advances in Cryptology: Proceedings of EUROCRYPT '84*, p. 113. Springer-Verlag, Berlin, 1984.
- Ong, H., Schnorr, C. P. and Shamir, A., "Efficient signature schemes based on polynomial equations," *Advances in Cryptology: Proceedings of CRYPTO '84*, p. 37. Springer-Verlag, Berlin, 1985.
- Schnorr, C. P., "On the construction of a random number generator and random function generators," *Advances in Cryptology - EUROCRYPT '88*, p. 225. Springer-Verlag, Berlin, 1988.
- Micali, S. and Schnorr, C. P., "Efficient, perfect random number generators," *Advances in Cryptology - CRYPTO '88*, p. 173. Springer-Verlag, Berlin, 1989.
- Schnorr, C. P., "Efficient identification and signatures for smart cards," *Advances in Cryptology - EUROCRYPT '89*, p. 688. Springer-Verlag, Berlin, 1989.
- Schnorr, C. P., "Efficient identification and signatures for smart cards," *Advances in Cryptology - CRYPTO '89*, p. 239. Springer-Verlag, Berlin, 1989.
- Ong, H. and Schnorr, C. P., "Fast signature generation with a Fiat Shamir - like scheme," *Advances in Cryptology - EUROCRYPT '90*, p. 432. Springer-Verlag, Berlin, 1990.
- Coster, M. J., LaMacchia, B. A., Odlyzko, A. M. and Schnorr, C. P., "An improved low-density subset sum algorithm," *Advances in Cryptology - EUROCRYPT '91*, p. 54. Springer-Verlag, Berlin, 1991.

- Schnorr, C. P., "Factoring integers and computing discrete logarithms via diophantine approximation," *Advances in Cryptology - EUROCRYPT '91*, p. 281. Springer-Verlag, Berlin, 1991.
- Schnorr, C. P., "FFT-hash II, efficient cryptographic hashing," *Advances in Cryptology - EUROCRYPT '92*, p. 45. Springer-Verlag, Berlin, 1992.
- Niederreiter, H. and Schnorr, C. P., "Local randomness in candidate one-way functions," *Advances in Cryptology - EUROCRYPT '92*, p. 408. Springer-Verlag, Berlin, 1992.
- Schnorr, C. P. and Vaudenay, S., "Black box cryptanalysis of hash networks based on multipermutations," *Advances in Cryptology - EUROCRYPT '94*, p. 47. Springer-Verlag, Berlin, 1995.
- Schnorr, C. P. and Hoerner, H. H., "Attacking the Chor-Rivest cryptosystem by improved lattice reduction," *Advances in Cryptology - EUROCRYPT '95*, p. 1. Springer-Verlag, Berlin, 1995.
- Schnorr, C. P., "Security of 2^t-Root Identification and Signatures," *Advances in Cryptology - CRYPTO '96*, p. 143. Springer-Verlag, Berlin, 1996.
- Fischlin, R. and Schnorr, C. P., "Stronger Security Proofs for RSA and Rabin Bits," *Advances in Cryptology - EUROCRYPT '97*, p. 267. Springer-Verlag, Berlin, 1997.

Schoebi, P.

- Schoebi, P. and Massey, J. L., "Fast authentication in a trapdoor - knapsack public key cryptosystem," *Cryptography - Proceedings of the Workshop on Cryptography, Burg Feuerstein, Germany*, p. 289. Springer-Verlag, Berlin, 1983.
- Schoebi, P., "Perfect Authentication Systems for Data Sources with Arbitrary Statistics," *Abstracts of Papers: EUROCRYPT '86*, p. 1. Department of Electrical Engineering, University of Linköping, Linkoping, Sweden, 1986.

Schoenmakers, B.

- Cramer, R., Damgård, I. B. and Schoenmakers, B., "Proofs of partial knowledge and simplified design of witness hiding protocols," *Advances in Cryptology - CRYPTO '94*, p. 174. Springer-Verlag, Berlin, 1994.
- Cramer, R., Franklin, M. K., Schoenmakers, B. and Yung, M., "Multi-authority secret-ballot elections with linear work," *Advances in Cryptology - EUROCRYPT '96*, p. 72. Springer-Verlag, Berlin, 1996.
- Cramer, R., Gennaro, R. and Schoenmakers, B., "A Secure and Optimally Efficient Multi-Authority Election Scheme," *Advances in Cryptology - EUROCRYPT '97*, p. 103. Springer-Verlag, Berlin, 1997.

Schrift, A. W.

- Schrift, A. W. and Shamir, A., "On the universality of the next bit test," *Advances in Cryptology - CRYPTO '90*, p. 394. Springer-Verlag, Berlin, 1990.

Schroeppel, R.

- Schroeppel, R., Orman, H., O'Malley, S. and Spatscheck, O., "Fast Key Exchange with Elliptic Curve Systems," *Advances in Cryptology - CRYPTO '95*, p. 43. Springer-Verlag, Berlin, 1995.

Schuchmann, H. R.

- Schuchmann, H. R., "Enigma variations," *Cryptography - Proceedings of the Workshop on Cryptography, Burg Feuerstein, Germany*, p. 65. Springer-Verlag, Berlin, 1983.

Schunter, M.

- Pfitzmann, B., Schunter, M. and Waidner, M., "How to break another "provably secure" payment system," *Advances in Cryptology - EUROCRYPT '95*, p. 121. Springer-Verlag, Berlin, 1995.
- Pfitzmann, B. and Schunter, M., "Asymmetric fingerprinting," *Advances in Cryptology - EUROCRYPT '96*, p. 84. Springer-Verlag, Berlin, 1996.

Schwenk, J.

- Schwenk, J. and Eisfeld, J., "Public key encryption and signature schemes based on polynominals over Z_n," *Advances in Cryptology - EUROCRYPT '96*, p. 60. Springer-Verlag, Berlin, 1996.

Scnanning, B. P.

- Scnanning, B. P. and Kowalchuk, J., "MEMO: A Hybrid Approach to Encrypted Electronic Mail," *Advances in Cryptography*, p. 64. University of California, Santa Barbara, Santa Barbara, California, USA, 1982.

Scott, P. A.

- Orton, G. A., Roy, M. P., Scott, P. A., Peppard, L. E. and Tavares, S. E., "VLSI implementation of public-key encryption algorithms," *Advances in Cryptology - CRYPTO '86*, p. 277. Springer-Verlag, Berlin, 1986.

Seberry, J.

- Khoo, D. S. P., Bird, G. J. and Seberry, J., "Encryption Exponent 3 and the Security of RSA," *Abstracts of Papers: EUROCRYPT '86*, p. 55. Department of Electrical Engineering, University of Linköping, Linkoping, Sweden, 1986.
- Gyoery, R. and Seberry, J., "Electronic funds transfer point of sale in Australia," *Advances in Cryptology - CRYPTO '86*, p. 347. Springer-Verlag, Berlin, 1986.
- Brown, L. and Seberry, J., "On the design of permutation P in DES type cryptosystems," *Advances in Cryptology - EUROCRYPT '89*, p. 696. Springer-Verlag, Berlin, 1989.
- Zheng, Y. and Seberry, J., "Practical approaches to attaining security against adaptively chosen ciphertext attacks (extended abstract)," *Advances in Cryptology - CRYPTO '92*, p. 292. Springer-Verlag, Berlin, 1992.
- Seberry, J., Zhang, X. M. and Zheng, Y., "On constructions and nonlinearity of correlation immune functions," *Advances in Cryptology - EUROCRYPT '93*, p. 181. Springer-Verlag, Berlin, 1993.
- Seberry, J., Zhang, X. M. and Zheng, Y., "Nonlinearly balanced boolean functions and their propagation characteristics," *Advances in Cryptology - CRYPTO '93*, p. 49. Springer-Verlag, Berlin, 1993.
- Seberry, J., Zhang, X. M. and Zheng, Y., "Relationships among nonlinearity criteria," *Advances in Cryptology - EUROCRYPT '94*, p. 376. Springer-Verlag, Berlin, 1995.
- Seberry, J., Zhang, X. M. and Zheng, Y., "Pitfalls in designing substitution boxes," *Advances in Cryptology - CRYPTO '94*, p. 383. Springer-Verlag, Berlin, 1994.

Sedlak, H.

- Sedlak, H., "The RSA cryptography processor," *Advances in Cryptology - EUROCRYPT '87*, p. 95. Springer-Verlag, Berlin, 1987.

Seifert, F. J.

- Kowatsch, M., Eichinger, B. O. and Seifert, F. J., "Message protection by spread spectrum modulation in a packet voice radio link.," *Advances in Cryptology - EUROCRYPT '85*, p. 273. Springer-Verlag, Berlin, 1985.

Selmer, E.

- Selmer, E., "From the memoirs of a Norwegian cryptologist," *Advances in Cryptology - EUROCRYPT '93*, p. 142. Springer-Verlag, Berlin, 1993.

Sendrier, N.

- Camion, P., Carlet, C., Charpin, P. and Sendrier, N., "On correlation-immune functions," *Advances in Cryptology - CRYPTO '91*, p. 86. Springer-Verlag, Berlin, 1991.

Serconek, S.

- Massey, J. L. and Serconek, S., "A Fourier transform approach to the linear complexity of nonlinearly filtered sequences," *Advances in Cryptology - CRYPTO '94*, p. 332. Springer-Verlag, Berlin, 1994.
- Massey, J. L. and Serconek, S., "Linear Complexity of Periodic Sequences: A General Theory," *Advances in Cryptology - CRYPTO '96*, p. 358. Springer-Verlag, Berlin, 1996.

Serpell, S. C.

- Serpell, S. C. and Brookson, C. B., "Encryption and key management for the ECS satellite service," *Advances in Cryptology: Proceedings of EURO-CRYPT '84*, p. 426. Springer-Verlag, Berlin, 1984.
- Serpell, S. C., Brookson, C. B. and Clark, B. L., "A prototype encryption system using public key," *Advances in Cryptology: Proceedings of CRYPTO '84*, p. 3. Springer-Verlag, Berlin, 1985.

Sgarro, A.

- Sgarro, A., "Equivocations for homophonic ciphers," *Advances in Cryptology: Proceedings of EUROCRYPT '84*, p. 51. Springer-Verlag, Berlin, 1984.
- Sgarro, A., "A measure of semiequivocation," *Advances in Cryptology - EUROCRYPT '88*, p. 375. Springer-Verlag, Berlin, 1988.
- Sgarro, A., "Informational divergence bounds for authentication codes," *Advances in Cryptology - EUROCRYPT '89*, p. 93. Springer-Verlag, Berlin, 1989.
- Sgarro, A., "Lower bounds for authentication codes with splitting," *Advances in Cryptology - EUROCRYPT '90*, p. 283. Springer-Verlag, Berlin, 1990.
- Sgarro, A., "Information-theoretic bounds for authentication frauds," *Advances in Cryptology - EUROCRYPT '92*, p. 467. Springer-Verlag, Berlin, 1992.

Shaer, C.

- Guillou, L. C., Quisquater, J. J., Walker, M., Landrock, P. and Shaer, C., "Precautions taken against various potential attacks in ISO/IEC DIS 9796," *Advances in Cryptology - EUROCRYPT '90*, p. 465. Springer-Verlag, Berlin, 1990.

Shafi Goldwasser

- Shafi Goldwasser, "A "Paradoxical" Solution to the Signature Problem," *Advances in Cryptology: Proceedings of CRYPTO '84*, p. 467. Springer-Verlag, Berlin, 1985.

Shamir, A.

- Shamir, A., "The Generation or Cryptographically Strong Pseudo-Random Sequences," *Advances in Cryptography*, p. 1. University of California, Santa Barbara, Santa Barbara, California, USA, 1982.
- Shamir, A., "A polynomial time algorithm for breaking the basic Merkle-Hellman cryptosystem (Extended abstract)," *Advances in Cryptology: Proceedings of CRYPTO '82*, p. 279. Plenum Publishing, New York, USA, 1982.
- Ong, H., Schnorr, C. P. and Shamir, A., "Efficient signature schemes based on polynomial equations," *Advances in Cryptology: Proceedings of CRYPTO '84*, p. 37. Springer-Verlag, Berlin, 1985.
- Shamir, A., "Identity-based cryptosystems and signature schemes," *Advances in Cryptology: Proceedings of CRYPTO '84*, p. 47. Springer-Verlag, Berlin, 1985.
- Rivest, R. L. and Shamir, A., "Efficient factoring based on partial information.," *Advances in Cryptology - EUROCRYPT '85*, p. 31. Springer-Verlag, Berlin, 1985.
- Even, S., Goldreich, O. and Shamir, A., "On the security of ping-pong protocols when implemented using the RSA," *Advances in Cryptology - CRYPTO '85*, p. 58. Springer-Verlag, Berlin, 1986.
- Shamir, A., "On the security of DES," *Advances in Cryptology - CRYPTO '85*, p. 280. Springer-Verlag, Berlin, 1986.
- Fiat, A. and Shamir, A., "How to prove yourself: practical solutions to identification and signature problems," *Advances in Cryptology - CRYPTO '86*, p. 186. Springer-Verlag, Berlin, 1986.
- Matias, Y. and Shamir, A., "A video scrambling technique based on space filling curves," *Advances in Cryptology - CRYPTO '87*, p. 398. Springer-Verlag, Berlin, 1987.
- Micali, S. and Shamir, A., "An improvement of the Fiat-Shamir identification and signature scheme," *Advances in Cryptology - CRYPTO '88*, p. 244. Springer-Verlag, Berlin, 1989.
- Feige, U., Shamir, A. and Tennenholtz, M., "The noisy oracle problem," *Advances in Cryptology - CRYPTO '88*, p. 284. Springer-Verlag, Berlin, 1989.
- Feige, U. and Shamir, A., "Zero knowledge proofs of knowledge in two rounds," *Advances in Cryptology - CRYPTO '89*, p. 526. Springer-Verlag, Berlin, 1989.
- Shamir, A., "An efficient identification scheme based on permuted kernels (extended abstract)," *Advances in Cryptology - CRYPTO '89*, p. 606. Springer-Verlag, Berlin, 1989.
- Biham, E. and Shamir, A., "Differential cryptanalysis of DES-like cryptosystems (Extended abstract)," *Advances in Cryptology - CRYPTO '90*, p. 2. Springer-Verlag, Berlin, 1990.

- Lapidot, D. and Shamir, A., "Publicly verifiable non-interactive zero-knowledge proofs," *Advances in Cryptology - CRYPTO '90*, p. 353. Springer-Verlag, Berlin, 1990.
- Schrift, A. W. and Shamir, A., "On the universality of the next bit test," *Advances in Cryptology - CRYPTO '90*, p. 394. Springer-Verlag, Berlin, 1990.
- Biham, E. and Shamir, A., "Differential cryptanalysis of Feal and N-Hash," *Advances in Cryptology - EUROCRYPT '91*, p. 1. Springer-Verlag, Berlin, 1991.
- Biham, E. and Shamir, A., "Differential cryptanalysis of Snefru, Khafre, REDOC-II, LOKI and Lucifer (Extended abstract)," *Advances in Cryptology - CRYPTO '91*, p. 156. Springer-Verlag, Berlin, 1991.
- Lapidot, D. and Shamir, A., "A one-round, two-prover, zero-knowledge protocol for NP," *Advances in Cryptology - CRYPTO '91*, p. 213. Springer-Verlag, Berlin, 1991.
- Biham, E. and Shamir, A., "Differential cryptanalysis of the full 16-round DES," *Advances in Cryptology - CRYPTO '92*, p. 487. Springer-Verlag, Berlin, 1992.
- Shamir, A., "Efficient signature schemes based on birational permutations," *Advances in Cryptology - CRYPTO '93*, p. 1. Springer-Verlag, Berlin, 1993.
- Naor, M. and Shamir, A., "Visual cryptography," *Advances in Cryptology - EUROCRYPT '94*, p. 1. Springer-Verlag, Berlin, 1995.
- Shamir, A., "Memory efficient variants of public-key schemes for smart card applications," *Advances in Cryptology - EUROCRYPT '94*, p. 445. Springer-Verlag, Berlin, 1995.
- Coppersmith, D. and Shamir, A., "Lattice Attacks on NTRU," *Advances in Cryptology - EUROCRYPT '97*, p. 52. Springer-Verlag, Berlin, 1997.
- Biham, E. and Shamir, A., "Differential Fault Analysis of Secret Key Cryptosystems," *Advances in Cryptology - CRYPTO '97*, p. 513. Springer-Verlag, Berlin, 1997.

Shaw, J.

- Boneh, D. and Shaw, J., "Collusion-Secure Fingerprinting for Digital Data," *Advances in Cryptology - CRYPTO '95*, p. 452. Springer-Verlag, Berlin, 1995.

Sherman, A. T.

- Rivest, R. L. and Sherman, A. T., "Randomized encryption techniques," *Advances in Cryptology: Proceedings of CRYPTO '82*, p. 145. Plenum Publishing, New York, USA, 1982.
- Kaliski, B. S., Rivest, R. L. and Sherman, A. T., "Is the data encryption standard a group?.," *Advances in Cryptology - EUROCRYPT '85*, p. 81. Springer-Verlag, Berlin, 1985.

- Kaliski, B. S., Rivest, R. L. and Sherman, A. T., "Is DES a pure cipher? (Results of more cycling experiments on DES)," *Advances in Cryptology - CRYPTO '85*, p. 212. Springer-Verlag, Berlin, 1986.

Sherwood, J. R.

- Sherwood, J. R. and Gallo, V. A., "The application of smart cards for RSA digital signatures in a network comprising both interactive and store-and-forward facilities," *Advances in Cryptology - CRYPTO '88*, p. 484. Springer-Verlag, Berlin, 1989.

Shimizu, A.

- Shimizu, A. and Miyaguchi, S., "Fast data encipherment algorithm FEAL," *Advances in Cryptology - EUROCRYPT '87*, p. 267. Springer-Verlag, Berlin, 1987.

Shinozaki, S.

- Shinozaki, S., Itoh, T., Fujioka, A. and Tsujii, S., "Provably secure key-updating schemes in identity-based systems," *Advances in Cryptology - EUROCRYPT '90*, p. 16. Springer-Verlag, Berlin, 1990.

Shizuya, H.

- Shizuya, H., "On the complexity of hyperelliptic discrete logarithm problem," *Advances in Cryptology - EUROCRYPT '91*, p. 337. Springer-Verlag, Berlin, 1991.
- Okamoto, T., Sakurai, K. and Shizuya, H., "How intractable is the discrete logarithm for a general finite group?," *Advances in Cryptology - EURO-CRYPT '92*, p. 420. Springer-Verlag, Berlin, 1992.
- Itoh, T., Ohta, Y. and Shizuya, H., "Language dependent secure bit commitment," *Advances in Cryptology - CRYPTO '94*, p. 188. Springer-Verlag, Berlin, 1994.
- Sakurai, K. and Shizuya, H., "Relationships among the computational powers of breaking discrete log cryptosystems," *Advances in Cryptology - EUROCRYPT '95*, p. 341. Springer-Verlag, Berlin, 1995.

Shmuely, Z.

- Yacobi, Y. and Shmuely, Z., "On key distribution systems," *Advances in Cryptology - CRYPTO '89*, p. 344. Springer-Verlag, Berlin, 1989.

410

Shoup, V.

- Beaver, D., Feigenbaum, J. and Shoup, V., "Hiding instances in zero-knowledge proof systems (Extended abstract)," *Advances in Cryptology - CRYPTO '90*, p. 326. Springer-Verlag, Berlin, 1990.
- Shoup, V. and Rubin, A., "Session key distribution using smart cards," *Advances in Cryptology - EUROCRYPT '96*, p. 321. Springer-Verlag, Berlin, 1996.
- Shoup, V., "On the security of a practical identification scheme," *Advances in Cryptology - EUROCRYPT '96*, p. 344. Springer-Verlag, Berlin, 1996.
- Shoup, V., "On Fast and Provably Secure Message Authentication Based on Universal Hashing," *Advances in Cryptology - CRYPTO '96*, p. 313. Springer-Verlag, Berlin, 1996.
- Shoup, V., "Lower Bounds for Discrete Logarithms and Related Problems," *Advances in Cryptology - EUROCRYPT '97*, p. 256. Springer-Verlag, Berlin, 1997.

Shub, M.

- Blum, L., Blum, M. and Shub, M., "Comparison of two pseudo-random number generators," *Advances in Cryptology: Proceedings of CRYPTO '82*, p. 61. Plenum Publishing, New York, USA, 1982.

Sidney, R.

- Micali, S. and Sidney, R., "A Simple Method for Generating and Sharing Pseudo-Random Functions, with Applications to Clipper-like Key Escrow Systems," *Advances in Cryptology - CRYPTO '95*, p. 185. Springer-Verlag, Berlin, 1995.

Siegenthaler, T.

- Siegenthaler, T., "Cryptanalysts representation of nonlinearly filtered ML-sequences.," *Advances in Cryptology - EUROCRYPT '85*, p. 103. Springer-Verlag, Berlin, 1985.
- Siegenthaler, T., "Design of combiners to prevent divide and conquer attacks," *Advances in Cryptology - CRYPTO '85*, p. 273. Springer-Verlag, Berlin, 1986.
- Siegenthaler, T., "Correlation-Immune Polynomials over Finite Fields," *Abstracts of Papers: EUROCRYPT '86*, p. 42. Department of Electrical Engineering, University of Linköping, Linkoping, Sweden, 1986.
- Siegenthaler, T., Kleiner, A. W. and Forre, R., "Generation of binary sequences with controllable complexity and ideal r-tuple distribution," *Advances in Cryptology - EUROCRYPT '87*, p. 15. Springer-Verlag, Berlin, 1987.

Simmons, C.

- Hughes, R. J., Luther, G. G., Morgan, G. L., Peterson, C. G. and Simmons, C., "Quantum Cryptography over Underground Optical Fibers," *Advances in Cryptology - CRYPTO '96*, p. 329. Springer-Verlag, Berlin, 1996.

Simmons, G. J.

- Simmons, G. J., "A System for Point-of-Sale or Access User Authentication and Identification," *Advances in Cryptography*, p. 31. University of California, Santa Barbara, Santa Barbara, California, USA, 1982.
- Purdy, G. B., Simmons, G. J. and Studies, J., "Software Protection Using "Communal Key Cryptosystems"," *Advances in Cryptography*, p. 79. University of California, Santa Barbara, Santa Barbara, California, USA, 1982.
- Brickell, E. F., Davis, J. A. and Simmons, G. J., "A preliminary report on the cryptanalysis of Merkle-Hellman knapsack cryptosystems," *Advances in Cryptology: Proceedings of CRYPTO '82*, p. 289. Plenum Publishing, New York, USA, 1982.
- Simmons, G. J., "The prisoner's problem and the subliminal channel," *Advances in Cryptology: Proceedings of CRYPTO '83*, p. 51. Plenum Publishing, New York, USA, 1984.
- Davis, J. A., Holdridge, D. B. and Simmons, G. J., "Status report on factoring (at the Sandia National Labs)," *Advances in Cryptology: Proceedings of EUROCRYPT '84*, p. 183. Springer-Verlag, Berlin, 1984.
- Simmons, G. J., "The subliminal channel and digital signatures," *Advances in Cryptology: Proceedings of EUROCRYPT '84*, p. 364. Springer-Verlag, Berlin, 1984.
- Simmons, G. J., "Authentication theory/coding theory," *Advances in Cryptology: Proceedings of CRYPTO '84*, p. 411. Springer-Verlag, Berlin, 1985.
- Simmons, G. J., "The practice of authentication.," *Advances in Cryptology - EUROCRYPT '85*, p. 261. Springer-Verlag, Berlin, 1985.
- Simmons, G. J., "A secure subliminal channel (?)," *Advances in Cryptology - CRYPTO '85*, p. 33. Springer-Verlag, Berlin, 1986.
- Moore, J. H. and Simmons, G. J., "Cycle Structure of the Weak and Semi-Weak DES Keys," *Abstracts of Papers: EUROCRYPT '86*, p. 16. Department of Electrical Engineering, University of Linköping, Linkoping, Sweden, 1986.
- Moore, J. H. and Simmons, G. J., "Cycle structure of the DES with weak and semi-weak keys," *Advances in Cryptology - CRYPTO '86*, p. 9. Springer-Verlag, Berlin, 1986.
- Simmons, G. J., "Message authentication with arbitration of transmitter/receiver disputes," *Advances in Cryptology - EUROCRYPT '87*, p. 151. Springer-Verlag, Berlin, 1987.
- Simmons, G. J., "An impersonation proof identity verification scheme," *Advances in Cryptology - CRYPTO '87*, p. 211. Springer-Verlag, Berlin, 1987.
- Simmons, G. J., "A natural taxonomy for digital information authentication schemes," *Advances in Cryptology - CRYPTO '87*, p. 269. Springer-Verlag, Berlin, 1987.

- Simmons, G. J. and Purdy, G. B., "Zero-knowledge proofs of identity and veracity of transaction receipts," *Advances in Cryptology - EUROCRYPT '88*, p. 35. Springer-Verlag, Berlin, 1988.
- Simmons, G. J., "How to (really) share a secret," *Advances in Cryptology - CRYPTO '88*, p. 390. Springer-Verlag, Berlin, 1989.
- Simmons, G. J., "Prepositioned shared secret and/or shared control schemes (invited)," *Advances in Cryptology - EUROCRYPT '89*, p. 436. Springer-Verlag, Berlin, 1989.
- Ingemarsson, I. and Simmons, G. J., "A protocol to set up shared secret schemes without the assistance of mutually trusted party," *Advances in Cryptology - EUROCRYPT '90*, p. 266. Springer-Verlag, Berlin, 1990.
- Simmons, G. J., "Geometric shared secret and/or shared control schemes," *Advances in Cryptology - CRYPTO '90*, p. 216. Springer-Verlag, Berlin, 1990.
- Simmons, G. J., "Subliminal communication is easy using the DSA," *Advances in Cryptology - EUROCRYPT '93*, p. 218. Springer-Verlag, Berlin, 1993.
- Simmons, G. J., "The consequences of trust in shared secret schemes," *Advances in Cryptology - EUROCRYPT '93*, p. 448. Springer-Verlag, Berlin, 1993.

Simon, D. R.

- Rackoff, C. and Simon, D. R., "Non-interactive zero-knowledge proof of knowledge and chosen ciphertext attack," *Advances in Cryptology - CRYPTO '91*, p. 433. Springer-Verlag, Berlin, 1991.
- Simon, D. R., "Anonymous Communication and Anonymous Cash," *Advances in Cryptology - CRYPTO '96*, p. 61. Springer-Verlag, Berlin, 1996.

Siuda, C.

- Siuda, C., "Security in open distributed processing," *Advances in Cryptology - EUROCRYPT '89*, p. 249. Springer-Verlag, Berlin, 1989.

Sivabalan, M.

- Sivabalan, M., Tavares, S. E. and Peppard, L. E., "On the design of SP networks from an information theoretic point of view," *Advances in Cryptology - CRYPTO '92*, p. 260. Springer-Verlag, Berlin, 1992.

Skubiszewska, M. H.

- Bennett, C. H., Brassard, G., Crépeau, C. and Skubiszewska, M. H., "Practical quantum oblivious transfer," *Advances in Cryptology - CRYPTO '91*, p. 351. Springer-Verlag, Berlin, 1991.

Sloan, B.

- Micali, S., Rackoff, C. and Sloan, B., "The notion of security for probabilistic cryptosystems," *Advances in Cryptology - CRYPTO '86*, p. 381. Springer-Verlag, Berlin, 1986.

Sloane, N. J. A.

- Sloane, N. J. A., "Encrypting by random rotations," *Cryptography - Proceedings of the Workshop on Cryptography, Burg Feuerstein, Germany*, p. 71. Springer-Verlag, Berlin, 1983.
- Reeds, J. A. and Sloane, N. J. A., "Shift register synthesis (modulo m).," *Advances in Cryptology: Proceedings of CRYPTO '83*, p. 249. Plenum Publishing, New York, USA, 1984.

Smeets, B.

- Smeets, B., "On the use of the binary multiplying channel in a private communication system," *Advances in Cryptology: Proceedings of EUROCRYPT '84*, p. 339. Springer-Verlag, Berlin, 1984.
- Smeets, B., "A comment on Neiderreiter's public key cryptosystem.," *Advances in Cryptology - EUROCRYPT '85*, p. 40. Springer-Verlag, Berlin, 1985.
- Smeets, B., "A note on sequences generated by clock controlled shift registers.," *Advances in Cryptology - EUROCRYPT '85*, p. 142. Springer-Verlag, Berlin, 1985.
- Smeets, B., "Some Properties of Sequences Generated by a Windmill Machine," *Abstracts of Papers: EUROCRYPT '86*, p. 37. Department of Electrical Engineering, University of Linköping, Linkoping, Sweden, 1986.
- Smeets, B. and Chambers, W. G., "Windmill generators: A generalization and an observation of how many there are," *Advances in Cryptology - EUROCRYPT '88*, p. 325. Springer-Verlag, Berlin, 1988.
- Smeets, B., Vanroose, P. and Wan, Z., "On the construction of authentication codes with secrecy and codes withstanding spoofing attacks of order $L_i=2$," *Advances in Cryptology - EUROCRYPT '90*, p. 306. Springer-Verlag, Berlin, 1990.
- Chepyzhov, V. and Smeets, B., "On a fast correlation attack on certain stream ciphers," *Advances in Cryptology - EUROCRYPT '91*, p. 176. Springer-Verlag, Berlin, 1991.
- Johansson, T., Kabatianski, G. A. and Smeets, B., "On the relation between A-codes and codes correcting independent errors," *Advances in Cryptology - EUROCRYPT '93*, p. 1. Springer-Verlag, Berlin, 1993.
- Bierbrauer, J., Johansson, T., Kabatianski, G. A. and Smeets, B., "On families of hash functions via geometric codes and concatenation," *Advances in Cryptology - CRYPTO '93*, p. 331. Springer-Verlag, Berlin, 1993.
- Johansson, T. and Smeets, B., "On A2-codes including arbiter's attacks," *Advances in Cryptology - EUROCRYPT '94*, p. 456. Springer-Verlag, Berlin, 1995.

Smid, M. E.

- Smid, M. E., "DES '81: An Update," *Advances in Cryptography*, p. 39. University of California, Santa Barbara, Santa Barbara, California, USA, 1982.
- Desmedt, Y., Landrock, P., Lenstra, A. K., McCurley, K. S., Odlyzko, A. M., Rueppel, R. A. and Smid, M. E., "The Eurocrypt '92 Controversial Issue: Trapdoor Primes and Moduli," *Advances in Cryptology - EURO-CRYPT '92*, p. 194. Springer-Verlag, Berlin, 1992.
- Smid, M. E. and Branstad, D. K., "Response to comments on the NIST proposed Digital Signature Standard," *Advances in Cryptology - CRYPTO '92*, p. 76. Springer-Verlag, Berlin, 1992.

Smith, D.

- Diffie, W., Klein, M., Dertouzos, M. L., Gleason, A. and Smith, D., "Panel Discussion: National Security and Commercial Security: Division of Responsibility," *Advances in Cryptography*, p. 154. University of California, Santa Barbara, Santa Barbara, California, USA, 1982.

Smith, J. M.

- Smith, J. M., "Practical problems with a cryptographic protection scheme (invited)," *Advances in Cryptology - CRYPTO '89*, p. 64. Springer-Verlag, Berlin, 1989.
- Broscius, A. G. and Smith, J. M., "Exploiting parallelism in hardware implementation of the DES," *Advances in Cryptology - CRYPTO '91*, p. 367. Springer-Verlag, Berlin, 1991.

Smith, J. W.

- Pomerance, C., Smith, J. W. and Wagstaff, S. S. Jr., "New ideas for factoring large integers," *Advances in Cryptology: Proceedings of CRYPTO '83*, p. 81. Plenum Publishing, New York, USA, 1984.

Smolin, J.

- Bennett, C. H., Bessette, F., Brassard, G., Salvail, L. and Smolin, J., "Experimental quantum cryptography," *Advances in Cryptology - EURO-CRYPT '90*, p. 253. Springer-Verlag, Berlin, 1990.

Snider, T.

- O'Connor, L. and Snider, T., "Suffix trees and string complexity," *Advances in Cryptology - EUROCRYPT '92*, p. 138. Springer-Verlag, Berlin, 1992.

So, N.

- Beaver, D. and So, N., "Global, unpredictable bit generation without broadcast," *Advances in Cryptology - EUROCRYPT '93*, p. 424. Springer-Verlag, Berlin, 1993.

Staffelbach, O.

- Rueppel, R. A. and Staffelbach, O., "Products of Linear Recurring Sequence with Maximum Complexity," *Abstracts of Papers: EUROCRYPT '86*, p. 30. Department of Electrical Engineering, University of Linköping, Linkoping, Sweden, 1986.
- Meier, W. and Staffelbach, O., "Fast correlation attacks on stream ciphers," *Advances in Cryptology - EUROCRYPT '88*, p. 301. Springer-Verlag, Berlin, 1988.
- Meier, W. and Staffelbach, O., "Nonlinearity criteria for cryptographic functions," *Advances in Cryptology - EUROCRYPT '89*, p. 549. Springer-Verlag, Berlin, 1989.
- Meier, W. and Staffelbach, O., "Correlation properties of combiners with memory in stream ciphers (extended abstract)," *Advances in Cryptology - EUROCRYPT '90*, p. 204. Springer-Verlag, Berlin, 1990.
- Staffelbach, O. and Meier, W., "Cryptographic significance of the carry for ciphers based on integer addition," *Advances in Cryptology - CRYPTO '90*, p. 601. Springer-Verlag, Berlin, 1990.
- Meier, W. and Staffelbach, O., "Analysis of pseudo random sequences generated by cellular automata," *Advances in Cryptology - EUROCRYPT '91*, p. 186. Springer-Verlag, Berlin, 1991.
- Meier, W. and Staffelbach, O., "Efficient multiplication on certain nonsupersingular elliptic curves," *Advances in Cryptology - CRYPTO '92*, p. 333. Springer-Verlag, Berlin, 1992.
- Meier, W. and Staffelbach, O., "The self-shrinking generator," *Advances in Cryptology - EUROCRYPT '94*, p. 205. Springer-Verlag, Berlin, 1995.

Steenbeek, A.

- Chaum, D., den Boer, B., van Heyst, E., Mjoelsnes, S. F. and Steenbeek, A., "Efficient offline electronic checks (extended abstract)," *Advances in Cryptology - EUROCRYPT '89*, p. 294. Springer-Verlag, Berlin, 1989.

Steer, D. G.

- Steer, D. G., Strawczynski, L., Diffie, W. and Wiener, M. J., "A secure audio teleconference system," *Advances in Cryptology - CRYPTO '88*, p. 520. Springer-Verlag, Berlin, 1989.

Stephan, W.

- Hornauer, G., Stephan, W. and Wernsdorf, R., "Markov ciphers and alternating groups," *Advances in Cryptology - EUROCRYPT '93*, p. 453. Springer-Verlag, Berlin, 1993.

Stephens, N. M.

- Stephens, N. M., "Lenstra's factorisation method based on elliptic curves," *Advances in Cryptology - CRYPTO '85*, p. 409. Springer-Verlag, Berlin, 1986.

Stern, J.

- Stern, J., "An alternative to the Fiat-Shamir protocol," *Advances in Cryptology - EUROCRYPT '89*, p. 173. Springer-Verlag, Berlin, 1989.
- Stern, J. and Toffin, P., "Cryptanalysis of a public-key cryptosystem based on approximations by rational numbers," *Advances in Cryptology - EUROCRYPT '90*, p. 313. Springer-Verlag, Berlin, 1990.
- Chee, Y. Meng, Joux, A. and Stern, J., "The cryptanalysis of a new public-key cryptosystem based on modular knapsacks," *Advances in Cryptology - CRYPTO '91*, p. 204. Springer-Verlag, Berlin, 1991.
- Blackburn, S. R., Murphy, S. and Stern, J., "Weaknesses of a public-key cryptosystem based on factorizations of finite groups," *Advances in Cryptology - EUROCRYPT '93*, p. 50. Springer-Verlag, Berlin, 1993.
- Stern, J., "A new identification scheme based on syndrome decoding," *Advances in Cryptology - CRYPTO '93*, p. 13. Springer-Verlag, Berlin, 1993.
- Coppersmith, D., Stern, J. and Vaudenay, S., "Attacks on the birational permutation signature schemes," *Advances in Cryptology - CRYPTO '93*, p. 435. Springer-Verlag, Berlin, 1993.
- Stern, J., "Designing identification schemes with keys of short size," *Advances in Cryptology - CRYPTO '94*, p. 164. Springer-Verlag, Berlin, 1994.
- Girault, M. and Stern, J., "On the length of cryptographic hash-values used in identification schemes," *Advances in Cryptology - CRYPTO '94*, p. 202. Springer-Verlag, Berlin, 1994.
- Fischer, J. B. and Stern, J., "An efficient pseudo-random generator provably as secure as syndrome decoding," *Advances in Cryptology - EUROCRYPT '96*, p. 245. Springer-Verlag, Berlin, 1996.
- Pointcheval, D. and Stern, J., "Security proofs for signature schemes," *Advances in Cryptology - EUROCRYPT '96*, p. 387. Springer-Verlag, Berlin, 1996.
- Naccache, D. and Stern, J., "A New Public-Key Cryptosystem," *Advances in Cryptology - EUROCRYPT '97*, p. 27. Springer-Verlag, Berlin, 1997.
- Nguyen, P. and Stern, J., "Merkle-Hellman Revisited: A Cryptanalysis of the Qu-Vanstone Cryptosystem Based on Group Factorizations," *Advances in Cryptology - CRYPTO '97*, p. 198. Springer-Verlag, Berlin, 1997.

Stinson, D. R.

- Stinson, D. R., "Some constructions and bounds for authentication codes," *Advances in Cryptology - CRYPTO '86*, p. 418. Springer-Verlag, Berlin, 1986.
- Stinson, D. R. and Vanstone, S. A., "A combinatorial approach to threshold schemes," *Advances in Cryptology - CRYPTO '87*, p. 330. Springer-Verlag, Berlin, 1987.
- Stinson, D. R., "A construction for authentication/secrecy codes from certain combinatorial designs," *Advances in Cryptology - CRYPTO '87*, p. 355. Springer-Verlag, Berlin, 1987.

- Brickell, E. F. and Stinson, D. R., "Authentication codes with multiple arbiters," *Advances in Cryptology - EUROCRYPT '88*, p. 51. Springer-Verlag, Berlin, 1988.
- Brickell, E. F. and Stinson, D. R., "The detection of cheaters in threshold schemes," *Advances in Cryptology - CRYPTO '88*, p. 564. Springer-Verlag, Berlin, 1989.
- Brickell, E. F. and Stinson, D. R., "Some improved bounds on the information rate of perfect secret sharing schemes (Extended abstract)," *Advances in Cryptology - CRYPTO '90*, p. 242. Springer-Verlag, Berlin, 1990.
- Stinson, D. R., "Combinatorial characterizations of authentication codes," *Advances in Cryptology - CRYPTO '91*, p. 62. Springer-Verlag, Berlin, 1991.
- Stinson, D. R., "Universal hashing and authentication codes," *Advances in Cryptology - CRYPTO '91*, p. 74. Springer-Verlag, Berlin, 1991.
- Blundo, C., De Santis, A., Stinson, D. R. and Vaccaro, U., "Graph decompositions and secret sharing schemes," *Advances in Cryptology - EUROCRYPT '92*, p. 1. Springer-Verlag, Berlin, 1992.
- Stinson, D. R., "New general lower bounds on the information rate of secret sharing schemes," *Advances in Cryptology - CRYPTO '92*, p. 168. Springer-Verlag, Berlin, 1992.
- Blundo, C., Giorgio Gaggia, A. and Stinson, D. R., "On the dealer's randomness required in secret sharing schemes," *Advances in Cryptology - EUROCRYPT '94*, p. 35. Springer-Verlag, Berlin, 1995.
- Bierbrauer, J., Gopalakrishnan, K. and Stinson, D. R., "Bounds for resilient functions and orthogonal arrays," *Advances in Cryptology - CRYPTO '94*, p. 247. Springer-Verlag, Berlin, 1994.
- Atici, M. and Stinson, D. R., "Universal Hashing and Multiple Authentication," *Advances in Cryptology - CRYPTO '96*, p. 16. Springer-Verlag, Berlin, 1996.
- Blundo, C., Mattos, L. A. F. and Stinson, D. R., "Trade-offs Between Communication and Storage in Unconditionally Secure Schemes for Broadcast Encryption and Interactive Key Distribution," *Advances in Cryptology - CRYPTO '96*, p. 387. Springer-Verlag, Berlin, 1996.
- Kurosawa, K., Johansson, T. and Stinson, D. R., "Almost k-wise Independent Sample Spaces and Their Cryptologic Applications," *Advances in Cryptology - EUROCRYPT '97*, p. 409. Springer-Verlag, Berlin, 1997.

Stockmeyer, L.
- Dwork, C. and Stockmeyer, L., "Zero-knowledge with finite state verifiers (invited talk)," *Advances in Cryptology - CRYPTO '88*, p. 71. Springer-Verlag, Berlin, 1989.

Stornetta, W. Scott
- Haber, S. and Stornetta, W. Scott, "How to time-stamp a digital document," *Advances in Cryptology - CRYPTO '90*, p. 437. Springer-Verlag, Berlin, 1990.

Strawczynski, L.
- Steer, D. G., Strawczynski, L., Diffie, W. and Wiener, M. J., "A secure audio teleconference system," *Advances in Cryptology - CRYPTO '88*, p. 520. Springer-Verlag, Berlin, 1989.

Struik, R.
- Struik, R. and van Tilburg, J., "The Rao-Nam scheme is insecure against a chosen-plaintext attack," *Advances in Cryptology - CRYPTO '87*, p. 445. Springer-Verlag, Berlin, 1987.

Studies, J.
- Purdy, G. B., Simmons, G. J. and Studies, J., "Software Protection Using "Communal Key Cryptosystems"," *Advances in Cryptography*, p. 79. University of California, Santa Barbara, Santa Barbara, California, USA, 1982.

Svendsen, E.
- Orup, H., Svendsen, E. and Andreasen, E., "VICTOR - an efficient RSA hardware implementation," *Advances in Cryptology - EUROCRYPT '90*, p. 245. Springer-Verlag, Berlin, 1990.

Swanson, L.
- Blakley, G. R. and Swanson, L., "Infinite structures in information theory," *Advances in Cryptology: Proceedings of CRYPTO '82*, p. 39. Plenum Publishing, New York, USA, 1982.

Syverson, P.
- Syverson, P. and Meadows, C., "Formal requirements for key distribution protocols," *Advances in Cryptology - EUROCRYPT '94*, p. 320. Springer-Verlag, Berlin, 1995.

Takagi, T.
- Takagi, T., "Fast RSA-Type Cryptosystems Using n-adic Expansion," *Advances in Cryptology - CRYPTO '97*, p. 372. Springer-Verlag, Berlin, 1997.

Tanada, K.
- Chao, J., Tanada, K. and Tsujii, S., "Design of elliptic curves with controllable lower boundary of extension degree for reduction attacks," *Advances in Cryptology - CRYPTO '94*, p. 50. Springer-Verlag, Berlin, 1994.

Tanaka, H.
- Tanaka, H., "A realization scheme for the identity based cryptosystem," *Advances in Cryptology - CRYPTO '87*, p. 340. Springer-Verlag, Berlin, 1987.

Tapp, A.

- Crépeau, C., Graaf, J. van de and Tapp, A., "Committed Oblivious Transfer and Private Multi-Party Computation," *Advances in Cryptology - CRYPTO '95*, p. 110. Springer-Verlag, Berlin, 1995.

Tardy-Corfdir, A.

- Tardy-Corfdir, A. and Gilbert, H., "A known plaintext attack of FEAL and FEAL-6," *Advances in Cryptology - CRYPTO '91*, p. 172. Springer-Verlag, Berlin, 1991.

Tatebayashi, M.

- Tatebayashi, M., Matsuzaki, N. and Newman, D. B. Jr., "Key distribution protocol for digital mobile communication systems," *Advances in Cryptology - CRYPTO '89*, p. 324. Springer-Verlag, Berlin, 1989.

Tavares, S. E.

- Avis, G. M. and Tavares, S. E., "Using data uncertainty to increase the crypto-complexity of simple private key enciphering schemes," *Advances in Cryptology: Proceedings of CRYPTO '82*, p. 139. Plenum Publishing, New York, USA, 1982.
- Spencer, M. E. and Tavares, S. E., "A layered broadcast cryptographic system," *Advances in Cryptology: Proceedings of CRYPTO '83*, p. 157. Plenum Publishing, New York, USA, 1984.
- Leung, A. K. and Tavares, S. E., "Sequence complexity as a test for cryptographic systems," *Advances in Cryptology: Proceedings of CRYPTO '84*, p. 468. Springer-Verlag, Berlin, 1985.
- Moore, T. E. and Tavares, S. E., "A layered approach to the design of private key cryptosystems," *Advances in Cryptology - CRYPTO '85*, p. 227. Springer-Verlag, Berlin, 1986.
- Webster, A. F. and Tavares, S. E., "On the design of S-boxes," *Advances in Cryptology - CRYPTO '85*, p. 523. Springer-Verlag, Berlin, 1986.
- Orton, G. A., Roy, M. P., Scott, P. A., Peppard, L. E. and Tavares, S. E., "VLSI implementation of public-key encryption algorithms," *Advances in Cryptology - CRYPTO '86*, p. 277. Springer-Verlag, Berlin, 1986.
- Chick, G. C. and Tavares, S. E., "Flexible access control with master keys," *Advances in Cryptology - CRYPTO '89*, p. 316. Springer-Verlag, Berlin, 1989.
- Adams, C. M. and Tavares, S. E., "Good S-boxes are easy to find," *Advances in Cryptology - CRYPTO '89*, p. 612. Springer-Verlag, Berlin, 1989.
- Dawson, M. H. and Tavares, S. E., "An expanded set of S-box design criteria based on information theory and its relation to differential-like attacks," *Advances in Cryptology - EUROCRYPT '91*, p. 352. Springer-Verlag, Berlin, 1991.
- Sivabalan, M., Tavares, S. E. and Peppard, L. E., "On the design of SP networks from an information theoretic point of view," *Advances in Cryptology - CRYPTO '92*, p. 260. Springer-Verlag, Berlin, 1992.

Taylor, P. D.

- Akl, S. G. and Taylor, P. D., "Cryptographic solution to a multilevel security problem," *Advances in Cryptology: Proceedings of CRYPTO '82*, p. 237. Plenum Publishing, New York, USA, 1982.

Taylor, R.

- Taylor, R., "An integrity check value algorithm for stream ciphers," *Advances in Cryptology - CRYPTO '93*, p. 40. Springer-Verlag, Berlin, 1993.
- Taylor, R., "Near optimal unconditionally secure authentication," *Advances in Cryptology - EUROCRYPT '94*, p. 244. Springer-Verlag, Berlin, 1995.

Tedrick, T.

- Tedrick, T., "How to exchange half a bit," *Advances in Cryptology: Proceedings of CRYPTO '83*, p. 147. Plenum Publishing, New York, USA, 1984.
- Berger, R., Peralta, R. and Tedrick, T., "A provably secure oblivious transfer protocol," *Advances in Cryptology: Proceedings of EUROCRYPT '84*, p. 379. Springer-Verlag, Berlin, 1984.
- Tedrick, T., "Fair exchange of secrets," *Advances in Cryptology: Proceedings of CRYPTO '84*, p. 434. Springer-Verlag, Berlin, 1985.
- Tedrick, T., "On the history of cryptography during WW2, and possible new directions for cryptographic research.," *Advances in Cryptology - EUROCRYPT '85*, p. 18. Springer-Verlag, Berlin, 1985.

Teng, S. H.

- Huang, M. and Teng, S. H., "A universal problem in secure and verifiable distributed computation," *Advances in Cryptology - CRYPTO '88*, p. 336. Springer-Verlag, Berlin, 1989.
- Teng, S. H., "Functional inversion and communication complexity," *Advances in Cryptology - CRYPTO '91*, p. 232. Springer-Verlag, Berlin, 1991.

Tennenholtz, M.

- Feige, U., Shamir, A. and Tennenholtz, M., "The noisy oracle problem," *Advances in Cryptology - CRYPTO '88*, p. 284. Springer-Verlag, Berlin, 1989.

Terada, R.

- Koyama, K. and Terada, R., "Nonlinear parity circuits and their cryptographic applications," *Advances in Cryptology - CRYPTO '90*, p. 582. Springer-Verlag, Berlin, 1990.

Tezuks, S.

- Tezuks, S., "A new class of nonlinear functions for running-key generators," *Advances in Cryptology - EUROCRYPT '88*, p. 317. Springer-Verlag, Berlin, 1988.

422

Theobald, T.

- Theobald, T., "How to Break Shamir's Asymmetric Basis," *Advances in Cryptology - CRYPTO '95*, p. 136. Springer-Verlag, Berlin, 1995.

Thiel, C.

- Biehl, I., Buchmann, J. A., Meyer, B., Thiel, C. and Thiel, C., "Tools for proving zero knowledge," *Advances in Cryptology - EUROCRYPT '92*, p. 356. Springer-Verlag, Berlin, 1992.
- Biehl, I., Buchmann, J. A., Meyer, B., Thiel, C. and Thiel, C., "Tools for proving zero knowledge," *Advances in Cryptology - EUROCRYPT '92*, p. 356. Springer-Verlag, Berlin, 1992.
- Biehl, I., Buchmann, J. A. and Thiel, C., "Cryptographic protocols based on discrete logarithms in real-quadratic orders," *Advances in Cryptology - CRYPTO '94*, p. 56. Springer-Verlag, Berlin, 1994.

Tillich, Jean-Pierre

- Tillich, Jean-Pierre and Zemor, G., "Hashing with SL_2," *Advances in Cryptology - CRYPTO '94*, p. 40. Springer-Verlag, Berlin, 1994.

Timmann, K. P.

- Timmann, K. P., "The rating of understanding in secure voice communication systems," *Cryptography - Proceedings of the Workshop on Cryptography, Burg Feuerstein, Germany*, p. 157. Springer-Verlag, Berlin, 1983.

Toffin, P.

- Vallee, B., Girault, M. and Toffin, P., "How to break Okamoto's cryptosystem by reducing lattice bases," *Advances in Cryptology - EUROCRYPT '88*, p. 281. Springer-Verlag, Berlin, 1988.
- Girault, M., Toffin, P. and Vallee, B., "Computation of approximate L-th roots modulo n and application to cryptography," *Advances in Cryptology - CRYPTO '88*, p. 100. Springer-Verlag, Berlin, 1989.
- Stern, J. and Toffin, P., "Cryptanalysis of a public-key cryptosystem based on approximations by rational numbers," *Advances in Cryptology - EUROCRYPT '90*, p. 313. Springer-Verlag, Berlin, 1990.

Tombak, L.

- Safavi-Naini, R. and Tombak, L., "Optimal authentication systems," *Advances in Cryptology - EUROCRYPT '93*, p. 12. Springer-Verlag, Berlin, 1993.
- Safavi-Naini, R. and Tombak, L., "Authentication codes in plaintext and chosen-content attacks," *Advances in Cryptology - EUROCRYPT '94*, p. 254. Springer-Verlag, Berlin, 1995.

Tompa, M.

- Tompa, M. and Woll, H., "How to share a secret with cheaters," *Advances in Cryptology - CRYPTO '86*, p. 261. Springer-Verlag, Berlin, 1986.

Tsuruoka, Y.

- Koyama, K. and Tsuruoka, Y., "Speeding up elliptic cryptosystems by using a signed binary window method," *Advances in Cryptology - CRYPTO '92*, p. 345. Springer-Verlag, Berlin, 1992.

Turbat, A.

- Turbat, A., "Smart cards," *Advances in Cryptology: Proceedings of EURO-CRYPT '84*, p. 457. Springer-Verlag, Berlin, 1984.

Turkin, Andrey I.

- Korzhik, Valery I. and Turkin, Andrey I., "Cryptanalysis of McEliece's Public-Key Cryptosystem," *Advances in Cryptology - EUROCRYPT '91*, p. 68. Springer-Verlag, Berlin, 1991.

Tygar, J. D.

- Reif, J. H. and Tygar, J. D., "Efficient parallel pseudo-random number generation," *Advances in Cryptology - CRYPTO '85*, p. 433. Springer-Verlag, Berlin, 1986.
- Herlihy, M. P. and Tygar, J. D., "How to make replicated data secure," *Advances in Cryptology - CRYPTO '87*, p. 379. Springer-Verlag, Berlin, 1987.

Ugon, M.

- Guillou, L. C. and Ugon, M., "Smart card, a highly reliable and portable security device," *Advances in Cryptology - CRYPTO '86*, p. 464. Springer-Verlag, Berlin, 1986.

Uyematsu, T.

- Tsunoo, Y., Okamoto, E. and Uyematsu, T., "Ciphertext only attack for one-way function of the MAP using one ciphertext," *Advances in Cryptology - CRYPTO '94*, p. 369. Springer-Verlag, Berlin, 1994.

Vaccaro, U.

- Capocelli, R. M., De Santis, A., Gargano, L. and Vaccaro, U., "On the size of shares for secret sharing schemes," *Advances in Cryptology - CRYPTO '91*, p. 101. Springer-Verlag, Berlin, 1991.
- Blundo, C., De Santis, A., Stinson, D. R. and Vaccaro, U., "Graph decompositions and secret sharing schemes," *Advances in Cryptology - EURO-CRYPT '92*, p. 1. Springer-Verlag, Berlin, 1992.
- Blundo, C., De Santis, A., Gargano, L. and Vaccaro, U., "On the information rate of secret sharing schemes," *Advances in Cryptology - CRYPTO '92*, p. 148. Springer-Verlag, Berlin, 1992.
- Blundo, C., De Santis, A., Herzberg, A., Kutten, S., Vaccaro, U. and Yung, M., "Perfectly-secure key distribution for dynamic conferences," *Advances in Cryptology - CRYPTO '92*, p. 471. Springer-Verlag, Berlin, 1992.
- Carpentieri, M., De Santis, A. and Vaccaro, U., "Size of shares and probability of cheating in threshold schemes," *Advances in Cryptology - EURO-CRYPT '93*, p. 118. Springer-Verlag, Berlin, 1993.
- Blundo, C., Cresti, A., De Santis, A. and Vaccaro, U., "Fully dynamic secret sharing schemes," *Advances in Cryptology - CRYPTO '93*, p. 110. Springer-Verlag, Berlin, 1993.
- Blundo, C., De Santis, A., Di Crescenzo, G., Gaggia, A. Giorgio and Vaccaro, U., "Multi-secret sharing schemes," *Advances in Cryptology - CRYPTO '94*, p. 150. Springer-Verlag, Berlin, 1994.

Vainish, R.

- Goldreich, O. and Vainish, R., "How to solve any protocol probleman efficiency improvement," *Advances in Cryptology - CRYPTO '87*, p. 73. Springer-Verlag, Berlin, 1987.

Vallee, B.

- Vallee, B., Girault, M. and Toffin, P., "How to break Okamoto's cryptosystem by reducing lattice bases," *Advances in Cryptology - EUROCRYPT '88*, p. 281. Springer-Verlag, Berlin, 1988.
- Girault, M., Toffin, P. and Vallee, B., "Computation of approximate L-th roots modulo n and application to cryptography," *Advances in Cryptology - CRYPTO '88*, p. 100. Springer-Verlag, Berlin, 1989.

van Antwerpen, H.

- Chaum, D. and van Antwerpen, H., "Undeniable signatures," *Advances in Cryptology - CRYPTO '89*, p. 212. Springer-Verlag, Berlin, 1989.

Van Auseloos, J.

- Van Auseloos, J., "Technical security: The starting point," *Advances in Cryptology - EUROCRYPT '89*, p. 243. Springer-Verlag, Berlin, 1989.

van de Graaf, J.

- Peralta, R. and van de Graaf, J., "A Simple an Fast Probabilistic Algorithm for Computing Square Roots Modulo a Prime Number," *Abstracts of Papers: EUROCRYPT '86*, p. 15. Department of Electrical Engineering, University of Linköping, Linkoping, Sweden, 1986.
- Chaum, D., Evertse, J. H., van de Graaf, J. and Peralta, R., "Demonstrating possession of a discrete logarithm without revealing it," *Advances in Cryptology - CRYPTO '86*, p. 200. Springer-Verlag, Berlin, 1986.
- Chaum, D., Evertse, J. H. and van de Graaf, J., "An improved protocol for demonstrating possession of discrete logarithms and some generalizations," *Advances in Cryptology - EUROCRYPT '87*, p. 127. Springer-Verlag, Berlin, 1987.
- Chaum, D., Damgård, I. B. and van de Graaf, J., "Multiparty computations ensuring privacy of each party's input and correctness of the result," *Advances in Cryptology - CRYPTO '87*, p. 87. Springer-Verlag, Berlin, 1987.
- van de Graaf, J. and Peralta, R., "A simple and secure way to show the validity of your public key," *Advances in Cryptology - CRYPTO '87*, p. 128. Springer-Verlag, Berlin, 1987.
- Brickell, E. F., Chaum, D., Damgård, I. B. and van de Graaf, J., "Gradual and verifiable release of a secret," *Advances in Cryptology - CRYPTO '87*, p. 156. Springer-Verlag, Berlin, 1987.

van der Hulst, M. P.

- Bosma, W. and van der Hulst, M. P., "Faster primality testing (extended abstract)," *Advances in Cryptology - EUROCRYPT '89*, p. 652. Springer-Verlag, Berlin, 1989.

van Heijst, E.

- Chaum, D., van Heijst, E. and Pfitzmann, B., "Cryptographically strong undeniable signatures, unconditionally secure for the signer," *Advances in Cryptology - CRYPTO '91*, p. 470. Springer-Verlag, Berlin, 1991.
- van Heijst, E., Pedersen, T. P. and Pfitzmann, B., "New constructions of fail-stop signatures and lower bounds," *Advances in Cryptology - CRYPTO '92*, p. 15. Springer-Verlag, Berlin, 1992.

van Heyst, E.

- Chaum, D., den Boer, B., van Heyst, E., Mjoelsnes, S. F. and Steenbeek, A., "Efficient offline electronic checks (extended abstract)," *Advances in Cryptology - EUROCRYPT '89*, p. 294. Springer-Verlag, Berlin, 1989.
- Evertse, J. H. and van Heyst, E., "Which new RSA signatures can be computed from some given RSA signatures? (extended abstract)," *Advances in Cryptology - EUROCRYPT '90*, p. 83. Springer-Verlag, Berlin, 1990.

van Trung, T.

- Horvath, T., Magliveras, S. S. and van Trung, T., "A parallel permutation multiplier for a PGM crypto-chip," *Advances in Cryptology - CRYPTO '94*, p. 108. Springer-Verlag, Berlin, 1994.

Vandemeulebroecke, A.

- Vandemeulebroecke, A., Vanzieleghem, E., Jespers, P. G. A. and Denayer, T., "A single chip 1024 bits RSA processor," *Advances in Cryptology - EUROCRYPT '89*, p. 219. Springer-Verlag, Berlin, 1989.

Vandewalle, J.

- Davio, M., Desmedt, Y., Fosseprez, M., Govaerts, R., Hulsbosch, J., Neutjens, P., Piret, P., Quisquater, J. J., Vandewalle, J. and Wouters, P., "Analytical characteristics of the DES," *Advances in Cryptology: Proceedings of CRYPTO '83*, p. 171. Plenum Publishing, New York, USA, 1984.
- Vandewalle, J., Govaerts, R., De Becker, W., Decroos, M. and Speybrouck, G., "Implementation study of public key cryptography protection in an existing electronic mail and document handling system.," *Advances in Cryptology - EUROCRYPT '85*, p. 43. Springer-Verlag, Berlin, 1985.
- Cloetens, H., Bierens, L., Vandewalle, J. and Govaerts, R., "Additional Properties in the S-Boxes of the DES," *Abstracts of Papers: EUROCRYPT '86*, p. 20. Department of Electrical Engineering, University of Linköping, Linkoping, Sweden, 1986.
- Jorissen, F., Vandewalle, J. and Govaerts, R., "Extension of Brickell's algorithm for breaking high density knapsacks," *Advances in Cryptology - EUROCRYPT '87*, p. 109. Springer-Verlag, Berlin, 1987.
- Verbauwhede, I., Hoornaert, F., Vandewalle, J. and De Man, H., "Security considerations in the design and implementation of a new DES chip," *Advances in Cryptology - EUROCRYPT '87*, p. 287. Springer-Verlag, Berlin, 1987.
- Hoornaert, F., Decroos, M., Vandewalle, J. and Govaerts, R., "Fast RSA-hardware: dream or reality," *Advances in Cryptology - EUROCRYPT '88*, p. 257. Springer-Verlag, Berlin, 1988.
- Vandewalle, J., Chaum, D., Fumy, W., Jansen, C. J. A., Landrock, P. and Roelofsen, G., "A European call for cryptographic algorithms: RIPE; Race Integrity Primitives Evaluation," *Advances in Cryptology - EUROCRYPT '89*, p. 267. Springer-Verlag, Berlin, 1989.
- Preneel, B., Bosselaers, A., Govaerts, R. and Vandewalle, J., "A chosen text attack on the modified cryptographic checksum algorithm of Cohen and Huang," *Advances in Cryptology - CRYPTO '89*, p. 154. Springer-Verlag, Berlin, 1989.
- Preneel, B., Van Leekwijck, W., Van Linden, L., Govaerts, R. and Vandewalle, J., "Propagation characteristics of Boolean functions," *Advances in Cryptology - EUROCRYPT '90*, p. 161. Springer-Verlag, Berlin, 1990.

- Preneel, B., Govaerts, R. and Vandewalle, J., "Boolean functions satisfying higher order propagation criteria," *Advances in Cryptology - EUROCRYPT '91*, p. 141. Springer-Verlag, Berlin, 1991.
- Daemen, J., Govaerts, R. and Vandewalle, J., "Resynchronization weaknesses in synchronous stream ciphers," *Advances in Cryptology - EUROCRYPT '93*, p. 159. Springer-Verlag, Berlin, 1993.
- Bosselaers, A., Govaerts, R. and Vandewalle, J., "Comparison of three modular reduction functions," *Advances in Cryptology - CRYPTO '93*, p. 175. Springer-Verlag, Berlin, 1993.
- Daemen, J., Govaerts, R. and Vandewalle, J., "Weak keys for IDEA," *Advances in Cryptology - CRYPTO '93*, p. 224. Springer-Verlag, Berlin, 1993.
- Preneel, B., Govaerts, R. and Vandewalle, J., "Hashfunctions based on block ciphers: a synthetic approach," *Advances in Cryptology - CRYPTO '93*, p. 368. Springer-Verlag, Berlin, 1993.
- Bosselaers, A., Govaerts, R. and Vandewalle, J., "Fast Hashing on the Pentium," *Advances in Cryptology - CRYPTO '96*, p. 298. Springer-Verlag, Berlin, 1996.
- Bosselaers, A., Govaerts, R. and Vandewalle, J., "SHA: A Design for Parallel Architectures?," *Advances in Cryptology - EUROCRYPT '97*, p. 348. Springer-Verlag, Berlin, 1997.

Vanroose, P.
- Smeets, B., Vanroose, P. and Wan, Z., "On the construction of authentication codes with secrecy and codes withstanding spoofing attacks of order $L_\lambda=2$," *Advances in Cryptology - EUROCRYPT '90*, p. 306. Springer-Verlag, Berlin, 1990.

Vanstone, S. A.
- Blake, I. F., Mullin, R. C. and Vanstone, S. A., "Computing logarithms in $GF(2^n)$," *Advances in Cryptology: Proceedings of CRYPTO '84*, p. 73. Springer-Verlag, Berlin, 1985.
- Stinson, D. R. and Vanstone, S. A., "A combinatorial approach to threshold schemes," *Advances in Cryptology - CRYPTO '87*, p. 330. Springer-Verlag, Berlin, 1987.
- Agnew, G. B., Mullin, R. C. and Vanstone, S. A., "An interactive data exchange protocol based on discrete exponentiation," *Advances in Cryptology - EUROCRYPT '88*, p. 159. Springer-Verlag, Berlin, 1988.
- Agnew, G. B., Mullin, R. C. and Vanstone, S. A., "Fast exponentiation in $GF(2^n)$," *Advances in Cryptology - EUROCRYPT '88*, p. 251. Springer-Verlag, Berlin, 1988.
- Agnew, G. B., Mullin, R. C. and Vanstone, S. A., "A fast elliptic curve cryptosystem," *Advances in Cryptology - EUROCRYPT '89*, p. 706. Springer-Verlag, Berlin, 1989.

- Koyama, K., Maurer, U. M., Okamoto, T. and Vanstone, S. A., "New public-key schemes based on elliptic curves over the ring Z_n," *Advances in Cryptology - CRYPTO '91*, p. 252. Springer-Verlag, Berlin, 1991.
- Harper, G., Menezes, A. and Vanstone, S. A., "Public-key cryptosystems with very small key lengths," *Advances in Cryptology - EUROCRYPT '92*, p. 163. Springer-Verlag, Berlin, 1992.
- Agnew, G. B., Mullin, R. C. and Vanstone, S. A., "On the development of a fast elliptic curve cryptosystem," *Advances in Cryptology - EUROCRYPT '92*, p. 482. Springer-Verlag, Berlin, 1992.

Vanzieleghem, E.

- Vandemeulebroecke, A., Vanzieleghem, E., Jespers, P. G. A. and Denayer, T., "A single chip 1024 bits RSA processor," *Advances in Cryptology - EUROCRYPT '89*, p. 219. Springer-Verlag, Berlin, 1989.

Varadharajan, V.

- Varadharajan, V., "Trapdoor rings and their use in cryptography," *Advances in Cryptology - CRYPTO '85*, p. 369. Springer-Verlag, Berlin, 1986.

Vasek, J. T.

- Lang, A. L. and Vasek, J. T., "Evaluating Relative Security or Commercial ComSec Devices," *Advances in Cryptography*, p. 124. University of California, Santa Barbara, Santa Barbara, California, USA, 1982.

Vaudenay, S.

- Vaudenay, S., "FFT-Hash-II is not yet collision-free," *Advances in Cryptology - CRYPTO '92*, p. 587. Springer-Verlag, Berlin, 1992.
- Coppersmith, D., Stern, J. and Vaudenay, S., "Attacks on the birational permutation signature schemes," *Advances in Cryptology - CRYPTO '93*, p. 435. Springer-Verlag, Berlin, 1993.
- Schnorr, C. P. and Vaudenay, S., "Black box cryptanalysis of hash networks based on multipermutations," *Advances in Cryptology - EUROCRYPT '94*, p. 47. Springer-Verlag, Berlin, 1995.
- Naccache, D., M'raihi, D., Vaudenay, S. and Raphaeli, D., "Can D. S. A. be improved? Complexity trade-offs with the digital signature standard," *Advances in Cryptology - EUROCRYPT '94*, p. 77. Springer-Verlag, Berlin, 1995.
- Chabaud, F. and Vaudenay, S., "Links between differential and linear cryptanalysis," *Advances in Cryptology - EUROCRYPT '94*, p. 356. Springer-Verlag, Berlin, 1995.
- Vaudenay, S., "Hidden Collisions on DSS," *Advances in Cryptology - CRYPTO '96*, p. 83. Springer-Verlag, Berlin, 1996.

Venkatesan, R.

- Naor, M., Ostrovsky, R., Venkatesan, R. and Yung, M., "Perfect zero-knowledge arguments for NP can be based on general complexity assumptions," *Advances in Cryptology - CRYPTO '92*, p. 196. Springer-Verlag, Berlin, 1992.
- Ostrovsky, R., Venkatesan, R. and Yung, M., "Interactive hashing simplifies zero-knowledge protocol design," *Advances in Cryptology - EUROCRYPT '93*, p. 267. Springer-Verlag, Berlin, 1993.
- Aiello, W. and Venkatesan, R., "Foiling birthday attacks in length-doubling transformations," *Advances in Cryptology - EUROCRYPT '96*, p. 307. Springer-Verlag, Berlin, 1996.
- Boneh, D. and Venkatesan, R., "Hardness of Computing the Most Significant Bits of Secret Keys in Diffie-Hellman and Related Schemes," *Advances in Cryptology - CRYPTO '96*, p. 129. Springer-Verlag, Berlin, 1996.

Verbauwhede, I.

- Verbauwhede, I., Hoornaert, F., Vandewalle, J. and De Man, H., "Security considerations in the design and implementation of a new DES chip," *Advances in Cryptology - EUROCRYPT '87*, p. 287. Springer-Verlag, Berlin, 1987.

Verheul, E. R.

- Verheul, E. R. and van Tilborg, H. C. A., "Binding ElGamal: A Fraud-Detectable Alternative to Key-Escrow Proposals," *Advances in Cryptology - EUROCRYPT '97*, p. 119. Springer-Verlag, Berlin, 1997.

Vienna, G.

- Jaburek, W. J. and Vienna, G., "A generalization of ElGamal's public key cryptosystem," *Advances in Cryptology - EUROCRYPT '89*, p. 23. Springer-Verlag, Berlin, 1989.

Vogel, R.

- Vogel, R., "On the linear complexity of cascaded sequences," *Advances in Cryptology: Proceedings of EUROCRYPT '84*, p. 99. Springer-Verlag, Berlin, 1984.

Wagner, D.

- Kelsey, J., Schneier, B. and Wagner, D., "Key-Schedule Cryptanalysis of IDEA, G-DES, GOST, SAFER, and Triple-DES," *Advances in Cryptology - CRYPTO '96*, p. 237. Springer-Verlag, Berlin, 1996.
- Wagner, D., Schneier, B. and Kelsey, J., "Cryptanalysis of the Cellular Message Encryption Algorithm," *Advances in Cryptology - CRYPTO '97*, p. 526. Springer-Verlag, Berlin, 1997.

Wagner, N. R.

- Mueller-Schloer, C. and Wagner, N. R., "Cryptographic protection of personal data cards," *Advances in Cryptology: Proceedings of CRYPTO '82*, p. 219. Plenum Publishing, New York, USA, 1982.
- Wagner, N. R. and Magyarik, M. R., "A public key cryptosystem based on the word problem," *Advances in Cryptology: Proceedings of CRYPTO '84*, p. 19. Springer-Verlag, Berlin, 1985.
- Wagner, N. R., Putter, P. S. and Cain, M. R., "Using algorithms as keys in stream ciphers.," *Advances in Cryptology - EUROCRYPT '85*, p. 149. Springer-Verlag, Berlin, 1985.
- Wagner, N. R., Putter, P. S. and Cain, M. R., "Large-scale randomization techniques," *Advances in Cryptology - CRYPTO '86*, p. 393. Springer-Verlag, Berlin, 1986.

Wagstaff, S. S. Jr.

- Pomerance, C., Smith, J. W. and Wagstaff, S. S. Jr., "New ideas for factoring large integers," *Advances in Cryptology: Proceedings of CRYPTO '83*, p. 81. Plenum Publishing, New York, USA, 1984.

Waidner, M.

- Pfitzmann, A. and Waidner, M., "Networks without user observability–design options.," *Advances in Cryptology - EUROCRYPT '85*, p. 245. Springer-Verlag, Berlin, 1985.
- Waidner, M., "Unconditional sender and recipient untraceability in spite of active attacks," *Advances in Cryptology - EUROCRYPT '89*, p. 302. Springer-Verlag, Berlin, 1989.
- Waidner, M. and Pfitzmann, B., "The dining cryptographers in the disco: unconditional sender and recipient untraceability with computationally secure serviceability," *Advances in Cryptology - EUROCRYPT '89*, p. 690. Springer-Verlag, Berlin, 1989.
- Bleumer, G., Pfitzmann, B. and Waidner, M., "A remark on signature scheme where forgery can be proved," *Advances in Cryptology - EUROCRYPT '90*, p. 441. Springer-Verlag, Berlin, 1990.
- Pfitzmann, B. and Waidner, M., "How to break and repair a "provably secure" untraceable payment system," *Advances in Cryptology - CRYPTO '91*, p. 338. Springer-Verlag, Berlin, 1991.
- Pfitzmann, B. and Waidner, M., "Attacks on protocols for server-aided RSA computation," *Advances in Cryptology - EUROCRYPT '92*, p. 153. Springer-Verlag, Berlin, 1992.
- Pfitzmann, B., Schunter, M. and Waidner, M., "How to break another "provably secure" payment system," *Advances in Cryptology - EUROCRYPT '95*, p. 121. Springer-Verlag, Berlin, 1995.
- Pfitzmann, B. and Waidner, M., "Anonymous Fingerprinting," *Advances in Cryptology - EUROCRYPT '97*, p. 88. Springer-Verlag, Berlin, 1997.

Waldvogel, C.

- Hohl, W., Lai, X., Meier, T. and Waldvogel, C., "Security of iterated hash functions based on block ciphers," *Advances in Cryptology - CRYPTO '93*, p. 379. Springer-Verlag, Berlin, 1993.

Walker, M.

- Beker, H. J. and Walker, M., "Key management for secure electronic funds transfer in a retail environment," *Advances in Cryptology: Proceedings of CRYPTO '84*, p. 401. Springer-Verlag, Berlin, 1985.
- Burmester, M. V. D., Desmedt, Y., Piper, F. and Walker, M., "A general zero-knowledge scheme," *Advances in Cryptology - EUROCRYPT '89*, p. 122. Springer-Verlag, Berlin, 1989.
- De Soete, M., Vedder, K. and Walker, M., "Cartesian authentication schemes," *Advances in Cryptology - EUROCRYPT '89*, p. 476. Springer-Verlag, Berlin, 1989.
- Guillou, L. C., Quisquater, J. J., Walker, M., Landrock, P. and Shaer, C., "Precautions taken against various potential attacks in ISO/IEC DIS 9796," *Advances in Cryptology - EUROCRYPT '90*, p. 465. Springer-Verlag, Berlin, 1990.

Walter, C. D.

- Walter, C. D., "Faster modular multiplication by operand scaling," *Advances in Cryptology - CRYPTO '91*, p. 313. Springer-Verlag, Berlin, 1991.

Walter, G. G.

- Davida, G. I. and Walter, G. G., "A public key analog cryptosystem," *Advances in Cryptology - EUROCRYPT '87*, p. 143. Springer-Verlag, Berlin, 1987.

Wambach, G.

- Damm, F., Heider, F. P. and Wambach, G., "MIMD-factorisation on hypercubes," *Advances in Cryptology - EUROCRYPT '94*, p. 400. Springer-Verlag, Berlin, 1995.

Wan, Z.

- Liu, M. and Wan, Z., "Generalized multiplexed sequences.," *Advances in Cryptology - EUROCRYPT '85*, p. 135. Springer-Verlag, Berlin, 1985.
- Smeets, B., Vanroose, P. and Wan, Z., "On the construction of authentication codes with secrecy and codes withstanding spoofing attacks of order $L_{\dot{\iota}}=2$," *Advances in Cryptology - EUROCRYPT '90*, p. 306. Springer-Verlag, Berlin, 1990.

Wang, C. H.

- Wang, C. H., Hwang, T. and Tsai, J. J., "On the Matsumoto and Imai's human identification scheme," *Advances in Cryptology - EUROCRYPT '95*, p. 382. Springer-Verlag, Berlin, 1995.

Wang, M.

- Wang, M. and Massey, J. L., "The Characterization of All Binary Sequences with Perfect Linear Complexity Profiles," *Abstracts of Papers: EUROCRYPT '86*, p. 35. Department of Electrical Engineering, University of Linköping, Linkoping, Sweden, 1986.
- Massey, J. L., Maurer, U. M. and Wang, M., "Nonexpanding, key-minimal, robustly-perfect, linear and bilinear ciphers," *Advances in Cryptology - EUROCRYPT '87*, p. 237. Springer-Verlag, Berlin, 1987.
- Wang, M., "Linear complexity profiles and continued fractions," *Advances in Cryptology - EUROCRYPT '89*, p. 571. Springer-Verlag, Berlin, 1989.

Wayner, P. C.

- Wayner, P. C., "Content-addressable search engines and DES-like systems," *Advances in Cryptology - CRYPTO '92*, p. 575. Springer-Verlag, Berlin, 1992.

Weber, D.

- Weber, D., "An implementation of the general number field sieve to compute discrete logarithms mod p," *Advances in Cryptology - EUROCRYPT '95*, p. 95. Springer-Verlag, Berlin, 1995.

Webster, A. F.

- Webster, A. F. and Tavares, S. E., "On the design of S-boxes," *Advances in Cryptology - CRYPTO '85*, p. 523. Springer-Verlag, Berlin, 1986.

Weidenman, P.

- Frank, O. and Weidenman, P., "Controlling Individual Information in Statistics by Coding," *Abstracts of Papers: EUROCRYPT '86*, p. 49. Department of Electrical Engineering, University of Linköping, Linkoping, Sweden, 1986.

Weinstein, S. B.

- Weinstein, S. B., "Security Mechanisms in Electronic Cards," *Advances in Cryptography*, p. 109. University of California, Santa Barbara, Santa Barbara, California, USA, 1982.

Welschenbach, M.

- Heider, F. P., Kraus, D. and Welschenbach, M., "Some Preliminary Remarks on the Decimal, Shift an Add-Algorithm (DSA)," *Abstracts of Papers: EUROCRYPT '86*, p. 3. Department of Electrical Engineering, University of Linköping, Linkoping, Sweden, 1986.

436

Wernsdorf, R.

- Wernsdorf, R., "The one-round functions of the DES generate the alternating group," *Advances in Cryptology - EUROCRYPT '92*, p. 99. Springer-Verlag, Berlin, 1992.
- Hornauer, G., Stephan, W. and Wernsdorf, R., "Markov ciphers and alternating groups," *Advances in Cryptology - EUROCRYPT '93*, p. 453. Springer-Verlag, Berlin, 1993.

White, S. R.

- White, S. R., "Convert distributed processing with computer viruses," *Advances in Cryptology - CRYPTO '89*, p. 616. Springer-Verlag, Berlin, 1989.

Whitfield, D.

- Whitfield, D., "Cryptography, the next Two Decades," *Advances in Cryptography*, p. 84. University of California, Santa Barbara, Santa Barbara, California, USA, 1982.

Wichmann, P.

- Wichmann, P., "Cryptanalysis of a modified rotor machine," *Advances in Cryptology - EUROCRYPT '89*, p. 395. Springer-Verlag, Berlin, 1989.
- Bauspiess, F., Knobloch, H.-J. and Wichmann, P., "Inverting the pseudo exponentiation," *Advances in Cryptology - EUROCRYPT '90*, p. 344. Springer-Verlag, Berlin, 1990.

Wiener, M. J.

- Steer, D. G., Strawczynski, L., Diffie, W. and Wiener, M. J., "A secure audio teleconference system," *Advances in Cryptology - CRYPTO '88*, p. 520. Springer-Verlag, Berlin, 1989.
- Wiener, M. J., "Cryptanalysis of short RSA secret exponents," *Advances in Cryptology - EUROCRYPT '89*, p. 372. Springer-Verlag, Berlin, 1989.
- van Oorschot, P. C. and Wiener, M. J., "A known-plaintext attack on two-key triple encryption," *Advances in Cryptology - EUROCRYPT '90*, p. 318. Springer-Verlag, Berlin, 1990.
- Campbell, K. W. and Wiener, M. J., "DES is not a group," *Advances in Cryptology - CRYPTO '92*, p. 512. Springer-Verlag, Berlin, 1992.
- van Oorschot, P. C. and Wiener, M. J., "On Diffie-Hellman key agreement with short exponents," *Advances in Cryptology - EUROCRYPT '96*, p. 332. Springer-Verlag, Berlin, 1996.
- van Oorschot, P. C. and Wiener, M. J., "Improving Implementable Meet-in-the-Middle Attacks by Orders of Magnitude," *Advances in Cryptology - CRYPTO '96*, p. 229. Springer-Verlag, Berlin, 1996.

438

Wilson, D. B.

- Brickell, E. F., Gordon, D. M., McCurley, K. S. and Wilson, D. B., "Fast exponentiation with precomputation (Extended abstract)," *Advances in Cryptology - EUROCRYPT '92*, p. 200. Springer-Verlag, Berlin, 1992.

Winkler, P.

- Lenstra, A. K., Winkler, P. and Yacobi, Y., "A Key Escrow System with Warrant Bounds," *Advances in Cryptology - CRYPTO '95*, p. 197. Springer-Verlag, Berlin, 1995.

Winternitz, R. S.

- Winternitz, R. S., "Security of a keystream cipher with secret initial value (Abstract)," *Advances in Cryptology: Proceedings of CRYPTO '82*, p. 133. Plenum Publishing, New York, USA, 1982.
- Winternitz, R. S., "Producing a oneway hash function from DES," *Advances in Cryptology: Proceedings of CRYPTO '83*, p. 203. Plenum Publishing, New York, USA, 1984.

Wirl, K.

- Hess, P. and Wirl, K., "A voice scrambling system for testing and demonstration," *Cryptography - Proceedings of the Workshop on Cryptography, Burg Feuerstein, Germany*, p. 147. Springer-Verlag, Berlin, 1983.

Wolf, S.

- Maurer, U. M. and Wolf, S., "Diffie-Hellman Oracles," *Advances in Cryptology - CRYPTO '96*, p. 268. Springer-Verlag, Berlin, 1996.
- Maurer, U. M. and Wolf, S., "Privacy Amplification Secure Against Active Adversaries," *Advances in Cryptology - CRYPTO '97*, p. 307. Springer-Verlag, Berlin, 1997.

Wolfowicz, W.

- Wolfowicz, W., Brugia, O. and Improta, S., "An encryption and authentication procedure for tele-surveillance systems," *Advances in Cryptology: Proceedings of EUROCRYPT '84*, p. 437. Springer-Verlag, Berlin, 1984.
- Naccache, D., M'raihi, D., Wolfowicz, W. and Porto, A. di, "Are crypto-accelerators really inevitable? 20 bit zero-knowledge in less than a second on simple 8-bit microcontrollers," *Advances in Cryptology - EUROCRYPT '95*, p. 404. Springer-Verlag, Berlin, 1995.

Wolfram, S.

- Wolfram, S., "Cryptography with cellular automata," *Advances in Cryptology - CRYPTO '85*, p. 429. Springer-Verlag, Berlin, 1986.

Woll, H.

- Tompa, M. and Woll, H., "How to share a secret with cheaters," *Advances in Cryptology - CRYPTO '86*, p. 261. Springer-Verlag, Berlin, 1986.

Yacobi, Y.

- Brickell, E. F. and Yacobi, Y., "On privacy homomorphisms," *Advances in Cryptology - EUROCRYPT '87*, p. 117. Springer-Verlag, Berlin, 1987.
- Brickell, E. F., Lee, P. J. and Yacobi, Y., "Secure audio teleconference," *Advances in Cryptology - CRYPTO '87*, p. 418. Springer-Verlag, Berlin, 1987.
- Yacobi, Y., "Attack on the KoyamaOhta identity based key distribution scheme," *Advances in Cryptology - CRYPTO '87*, p. 429. Springer-Verlag, Berlin, 1987.
- Yacobi, Y. and Shmuely, Z., "On key distribution systems," *Advances in Cryptology - CRYPTO '89*, p. 344. Springer-Verlag, Berlin, 1989.
- Yacobi, Y., "Exponentiating faster with addition chains," *Advances in Cryptology - EUROCRYPT '90*, p. 222. Springer-Verlag, Berlin, 1990.
- Yacobi, Y., "A key distribution "paradox"," *Advances in Cryptology - CRYPTO '90*, p. 268. Springer-Verlag, Berlin, 1990.
- Yacobi, Y., "Discrete-log with compressible exponents," *Advances in Cryptology - CRYPTO '90*, p. 639. Springer-Verlag, Berlin, 1990.
- Maurer, U. M. and Yacobi, Y., "Non-interative public-key cryptography," *Advances in Cryptology - EUROCRYPT '91*, p. 498. Springer-Verlag, Berlin, 1991.
- Beller, M. J. and Yacobi, Y., "Batch Diffie-Hellman key agreement systems and their application to portable communications," *Advances in Cryptology - EUROCRYPT '92*, p. 208. Springer-Verlag, Berlin, 1992.
- Maurer, U. M. and Yacobi, Y., "A remark on a non-interactive public-key distribution system," *Advances in Cryptology - EUROCRYPT '92*, p. 458. Springer-Verlag, Berlin, 1992.
- Lenstra, A. K., Winkler, P. and Yacobi, Y., "A Key Escrow System with Warrant Bounds," *Advances in Cryptology - CRYPTO '95*, p. 197. Springer-Verlag, Berlin, 1995.

Yamagishi, A.

- Matsui, M. and Yamagishi, A., "A new method for known plaintext attack of FEAL cipher," *Advances in Cryptology - EUROCRYPT '92*, p. 81. Springer-Verlag, Berlin, 1992.

Yang, C. H.

- Zeng, K., Yang, C. H. and Rao, T. R. N., "On the linear consistency test (LCT) in cryptanalysis with applications," *Advances in Cryptology - CRYPTO '89*, p. 164. Springer-Verlag, Berlin, 1989.
- Zeng, K., Yang, C. H. and Rao, T. R. N., "An improved linear syndrome algorithm in cryptanalysis with applications," *Advances in Cryptology - CRYPTO '90*, p. 34. Springer-Verlag, Berlin, 1990.

Yang, J.-H.

- Zeng, K., Yang, J.-H. and Dai, Z., "Patterns of entropy drop of the key in an S-box of the DES," *Advances in Cryptology - CRYPTO '87*, p. 438. Springer-Verlag, Berlin, 1987.
- Dai, Z. and Yang, J.-H., "Linear complexity of periodically repeated random sequences," *Advances in Cryptology - EUROCRYPT '91*, p. 168. Springer-Verlag, Berlin, 1991.

Yao, A.

- Goldwasser, S., Micali, S. and Yao, A., "On signatures and authentication," *Advances in Cryptology: Proceedings of CRYPTO '82*, p. 211. Plenum Publishing, New York, USA, 1982.

Yeh, Y. S.

- Davida, G. I. and Yeh, Y. S., "Multilevel Cryptosecure Relational Database," *Abstracts of Papers: EUROCRYPT '86*, p. 50. Department of Electrical Engineering, University of Linköping, Linkoping, Sweden, 1986.

Yin, Y. L.

- Kaliski, B. S. and Yin, Y. L., "On Differential and Linear Cryptanalysis of the RC-5 Encryption Algorithm," *Advances in Cryptology - CRYPTO '95*, p. 171. Springer-Verlag, Berlin, 1995.

Yoon, H.

- Hong, S. M., Oh, S. Y. and Yoon, H., "New modular multiplication algorithms for fast modular exponentiation," *Advances in Cryptology - EUROCRYPT '96*, p. 166. Springer-Verlag, Berlin, 1996.

Young, A.

- Young, A. and Yung, M., "The Dark Side of "Black-Box" Cryptography, or: Should We Trust Capstone?," *Advances in Cryptology - CRYPTO '96*, p. 89. Springer-Verlag, Berlin, 1996.
- Young, A. and Yung, M., "Kleptography: Using Cryptography Against Cryptography," *Advances in Cryptology - EUROCRYPT '97*, p. 62. Springer-Verlag, Berlin, 1997.
- Young, A. and Yung, M., "The Prevalence of KIeptographic Attacks on Discrete-Log Based Cryptosystems," *Advances in Cryptology - CRYPTO '97*, p. 264. Springer-Verlag, Berlin, 1997.

Yung, M.

- Yung, M., "Cryptoprotocols: Subscription to a public key, the secret blocking and the multi-player mental poker game," *Advances in Cryptology: Proceedings of CRYPTO '84*, p. 439. Springer-Verlag, Berlin, 1985.
- Galil, Z., Haber, S. and Yung, M., "Symmetric public-key encryption," *Advances in Cryptology - CRYPTO '85*, p. 128. Springer-Verlag, Berlin, 1986.
- Impagliazzo, R. and Yung, M., "Direct minimum knowledge computations," *Advances in Cryptology - CRYPTO '87*, p. 40. Springer-Verlag, Berlin, 1987.
- Galil, Z., Haber, S. and Yung, M., "Cryptographic computation: secure fault tolerant protocols and the publickey model," *Advances in Cryptology - CRYPTO '87*, p. 135. Springer-Verlag, Berlin, 1987.
- Galil, Z., Haber, S. and Yung, M., "A secure public-key authentication scheme," *Advances in Cryptology - EUROCRYPT '89*, p. 3. Springer-Verlag, Berlin, 1989.
- Brassard, G., Crépeau, C. and Yung, M., "Everything in NP can be argued in perfect zero-knowledge in a bounded number of rounds (extended abstract)," *Advances in Cryptology - EUROCRYPT '89*, p. 192. Springer-Verlag, Berlin, 1989.
- Yung, M., "Zero-knowledge proofs of computational power (extended summary)," *Advances in Cryptology - EUROCRYPT '89*, p. 196. Springer-Verlag, Berlin, 1989.
- De Santis, A. and Yung, M., "On the design of provably-secure cryptographic hash functions," *Advances in Cryptology - EUROCRYPT '90*, p. 412. Springer-Verlag, Berlin, 1990.
- Brassard, G. and Yung, M., "One-way group actions," *Advances in Cryptology - CRYPTO '90*, p. 94. Springer-Verlag, Berlin, 1990.
- Desmedt, Y. and Yung, M., "Arbitrated unconditionally secure authentication can be unconditionally protected against arbiter's attacks (Extended abstract)," *Advances in Cryptology - CRYPTO '90*, p. 177. Springer-Verlag, Berlin, 1990.
- De Santis, A. and Yung, M., "Cryptographic applications of the non-interactive metaproof and many-prover systems (Preliminary version)," *Advances in Cryptology - CRYPTO '90*, p. 366. Springer-Verlag, Berlin, 1990.
- Desmedt, Y. and Yung, M., "Weaknesses of undeniable signature schemes," *Advances in Cryptology - EUROCRYPT '91*, p. 205. Springer-Verlag, Berlin, 1991.
- Bird, R., Gopal, I., Herzberg, A., Janson, P., Kutten, S., Molva, R. and Yung, M., "Systematic design of two-party authentication protocols," *Advances in Cryptology - CRYPTO '91*, p. 44. Springer-Verlag, Berlin, 1991.
- Naor, M., Ostrovsky, R., Venkatesan, R. and Yung, M., "Perfect zero-knowledge arguments for NP can be based on general complexity assump-

tions," *Advances in Cryptology - CRYPTO '92*, p. 196. Springer-Verlag, Berlin, 1992.

- Bellare, M. and Yung, M., "Certifying cryptographic tools: The case of trapdoor permutations," *Advances in Cryptology - CRYPTO '92*, p. 442. Springer-Verlag, Berlin, 1992.
- Blundo, C., De Santis, A., Herzberg, A., Kutten, S., Vaccaro, U. and Yung, M., "Perfectly-secure key distribution for dynamic conferences," *Advances in Cryptology - CRYPTO '92*, p. 471. Springer-Verlag, Berlin, 1992.
- Ostrovsky, R., Venkatesan, R. and Yung, M., "Interactive hashing simplifies zero-knowledge protocol design," *Advances in Cryptology - EUROCRYPT '93*, p. 267. Springer-Verlag, Berlin, 1993.
- Franklin, M. K. and Yung, M., "The blinding of weak signatures," *Advances in Cryptology - EUROCRYPT '94*, p. 67. Springer-Verlag, Berlin, 1995.
- Frankel, Y. and Yung, M., "Escrow Encryption Systems Visited: Attacks, Analysis and Designs," *Advances in Cryptology - CRYPTO '95*, p. 222. Springer-Verlag, Berlin, 1995.
- Frankel, Y. and Yung, M., "Cryptanalysis of the Immunized LL Public Key Systems," *Advances in Cryptology - CRYPTO '95*, p. 287. Springer-Verlag, Berlin, 1995.
- Herzberg, A., Jarecki, S., Krawczyk, H. and Yung, M., "Proactive Secret Sharing Or: How to Cope With Perpetual Leakage," *Advances in Cryptology - CRYPTO '95*, p. 339. Springer-Verlag, Berlin, 1995.
- Cramer, R., Franklin, M. K., Schoenmakers, B. and Yung, M., "Multi-authority secret-ballot elections with linear work," *Advances in Cryptology - EUROCRYPT '96*, p. 72. Springer-Verlag, Berlin, 1996.
- Young, A. and Yung, M., "The Dark Side of "Black-Box" Cryptography, or: Should We Trust Capstone?," *Advances in Cryptology - CRYPTO '96*, p. 89. Springer-Verlag, Berlin, 1996.
- Jakobsson, M. and Yung, M., "Proving Without Knowing: On Oblivious, Agnostic and Blindfolded Provers," *Advances in Cryptology - CRYPTO '96*, p. 186. Springer-Verlag, Berlin, 1996.
- Young, A. and Yung, M., "Kleptography: Using Cryptography Against Cryptography," *Advances in Cryptology - EUROCRYPT '97*, p. 62. Springer-Verlag, Berlin, 1997.
- Bellare, M., Jakobsson, M. and Yung, M., "Round-Optimal Zero-Knowledge Arguments Based on Any One-Way Function," *Advances in Cryptology - EUROCRYPT '97*, p. 280. Springer-Verlag, Berlin, 1997.
- Jakobsson, M. and Yung, M., "Distributed "Magic Ink" Signatures," *Advances in Cryptology - EUROCRYPT '97*, p. 450. Springer-Verlag, Berlin, 1997.
- Di Crescenzo, G., Okamoto, T. and Yung, M., "Keeping the SZK-Verifier Honest Unconditionally," *Advances in Cryptology - CRYPTO '97*, p. 31. Springer-Verlag, Berlin, 1997.

- Young, A. and Yung, M., "The Prevalence of KIeptographic Attacks on Discrete-Log Based Cryptosystems," *Advances in Cryptology - CRYPTO '97*, p. 264. Springer-Verlag, Berlin, 1997.
- Frankel, Y., Gemmell, P., MacKenzie, P. D. and Yung, M., "Proactive RSA," *Advances in Cryptology - CRYPTO '97*, p. 440. Springer-Verlag, Berlin, 1997.

Zayer, J.

- Buchmann, J. A., Loho, J. and Zayer, J., "An implementation of the general number field sieve," *Advances in Cryptology - CRYPTO '93*, p. 159. Springer-Verlag, Berlin, 1993.

Zemor, G.

- Zemor, G., "Hash functions and graphs with large girths," *Advances in Cryptology - EUROCRYPT '91*, p. 508. Springer-Verlag, Berlin, 1991.
- Tillich, Jean-Pierre and Zemor, G., "Hashing with SL_2," *Advances in Cryptology - CRYPTO '94*, p. 40. Springer-Verlag, Berlin, 1994.

Zeng, K.

- Zeng, K., Yang, J.-H. and Dai, Z., "Patterns of entropy drop of the key in an S-box of the DES," *Advances in Cryptology - CRYPTO '87*, p. 438. Springer-Verlag, Berlin, 1987.
- Zeng, K. and Huang, M., "On the linear syndrome method in cryptoanalysis," *Advances in Cryptology - CRYPTO '88*, p. 469. Springer-Verlag, Berlin, 1989.
- Dai, Z. and Zeng, K., "Feedforward functions defined by de Brujin sequences," *Advances in Cryptology - EUROCRYPT '89*, p. 544. Springer-Verlag, Berlin, 1989.
- Zeng, K., Yang, C. H. and Rao, T. R. N., "On the linear consistency test (LCT) in cryptanalysis with applications," *Advances in Cryptology - CRYPTO '89*, p. 164. Springer-Verlag, Berlin, 1989.
- Zeng, K., Yang, C. H. and Rao, T. R. N., "An improved linear syndrome algorithm in cryptanalysis with applications," *Advances in Cryptology - CRYPTO '90*, p. 34. Springer-Verlag, Berlin, 1990.

- Seberry, J., Zhang, X. M. and Zheng, Y., "Relationships among nonlinearity criteria," *Advances in Cryptology - EUROCRYPT '94*, p. 376. Springer-Verlag, Berlin, 1995.
- Charnes, C., O'Connor, L., Pieprzyk, J., Safavi-Naini, R. and Zheng, Y., "Comments on Soviet encryption algorithm," *Advances in Cryptology - EUROCRYPT '94*, p. 433. Springer-Verlag, Berlin, 1995.
- Seberry, J., Zhang, X. M. and Zheng, Y., "Pitfalls in designing substitution boxes," *Advances in Cryptology - CRYPTO '94*, p. 383. Springer-Verlag, Berlin, 1994.
- Zhang, X. M. and Zheng, Y., "On nonlinear resilient functions," *Advances in Cryptology - EUROCRYPT '95*, p. 274. Springer-Verlag, Berlin, 1995.
- Zhang, X. M. and Zheng, Y., "Auto-correlations and new bounds on the nonlinearity of boolean functions," *Advances in Cryptology - EUROCRYPT '96*, p. 294. Springer-Verlag, Berlin, 1996.
- Zheng, Y., "Digital Signcryption or How to Achieve Cost (Signature & Encryption << Cost (Signature) + Cost (Encryption)," *Advances in Cryptology - CRYPTO '97*, p. 165. Springer-Verlag, Berlin, 1997.

Zieschang, T.

- Zieschang, T., "Combinatorial Properties of Basic Encryption Operations," *Advances in Cryptology - EUROCRYPT '97*, p. 14. Springer-Verlag, Berlin, 1997.

Keyword Index

A reference of the form c90-323 refers to a paper in CRYPTO '90 starting on page 323. A reference e91-14 refers to a paper in EUROCRYPT '91 starting on page 14.

A5 algorithm e97-239

access control c81-31, e84-480, c89-316, e90-446, c91-1

algebraic number fields c85-369, c97-385

alternating step generator e87-5, c97-499

analog cryptosystems c81-59, c81-115, c81-120, e82-130, e82-147, e82-157, e82-173, c84-83, c84-95, e87-143

anonymity c81-138, c84-432, e85-241, e89-302, e89-320, e89-373, e89-690, e93-248, e94-332, e95-39, c96-61, e97-88, c97-395

approximation attacks e96-268

arbitrated signature schemes (see also digital signatures) c81-65, c87-216

arthur-merlin games c88-580, c97-31

asymmetric encryption (see public key cryptosystems)

audio teleconference c87-418, c89-324

authentication codes c84-411, e85-261, c85-42, e86-1, c86-418, e87-167, e87-171, c87-269, c87-355, e88-57, c88-311, e90-283, e90-294, e90-306, c90-169, c90-177, e91-472, c91-62, e92-467, e93-1, e93-12, e94-244, e94-254, e94-456, c94-140, e95-289, c96-16, c96-31, e97-149, e97-409
 − arbitration e87-151, e88-51, c93-343
 − interactive authentication c93-355, c94-121, e95-158
 − perfect e89-476
 − universal hashing c82-79, c91-74, c91-74, e95-311

avalanche criterion (see also DES S-box design) c81-53, c84-359, c84-468, c85-523, c88-450, e89-63, c89-612, e90-174, c90-564, e93-102, e94-376, e97-434

BAN logic e93-240, e93-443

banking networks c81-31, c81-38, c82-187, c84-393, c84-401, e85-208, c86-347

batch operations
 − Diffie-Hellman e92-208
 − RSA c89-175

Benes network e96-307

bent functions e90-151, c92-280, e93-77, e94-356, c94-383, e97-422

Berlekamp-Massey algorithm (see also linear complexity) c83-249, c86-405, e88-345, c89-90, e96-256, e94-215, c95-262

452

Springer
and the
environment

At Springer we firmly believe that an international science publisher has a special obligation to the environment, and our corporate policies consistently reflect this conviction.

We also expect our business partners – paper mills, printers, packaging manufacturers, etc. – to commit themselves to using materials and production processes that do not harm the environment. The paper in this book is made from low- or no-chlorine pulp and is acid free, in conformance with international standards for paper permanency.

 Springer

Lecture Notes in Computer Science

For information about Vols. 1–1512
please contact your bookseller or Springer-Verlag

Vol. 1549: M. Pettersson, Compiling Natural Semantics. XVII, 240 pages. 1999.

Vol. 1550: B. Christianson, B. Crispo, W.S. Harbison, M. Roe (Eds.), Security Protocols. Proceedings, 1998. VIII, 241 pages. 1999.

Vol. 1551: G. Gupta (Ed.), Practical Aspects of Declarative Languages. Proceedings, 1999. VIII, 367 pgages. 1999.

Vol. 1552: Y. Kambayashi, D.L. Lee, E.-P. Lim, M.K. Mohania, Y. Masunaga (Eds.), Advances in Database Technologies. Proceedings, 1998. XIX, 592 pages. 1999.

Vol. 1553: S.F. Andler, J. Hansson (Eds.), Active, Real-Time, and Temporal Database Systems. Proceedings, 1997. VIII, 245 pages. 1998.

Vol. 1554: S. Nishio, F. Kishino (Eds.), Advanced Multimedia Content Processing. Proceedings, 1998. XIV, 454 pages. 1999.

Vol. 1555: J.P. Müller, M.P. Singh, A.S. Rao (Eds.), Intelligent Agents V. Proceedings, 1998. XXIV, 455 pages. 1999. (Subseries LNAI).

Vol. 1556: S. Tavares, H. Meijer (Eds.), Selected Areas in Cryptography. Proceedings, 1998. IX, 377 pages. 1999.

Vol. 1557: P. Zinterhof, M. Vajteršic, A. Uhl (Eds.), Parallel Computation. Proceedings, 1999. XV, 604 pages. 1999.

Vol. 1558: H. J.v.d. Herik, H. Iida (Eds.), Computers and Games. Proceedings, 1998. XVIII, 337 pages. 1999.

Vol. 1559: P. Flener (Ed.), Logic-Based Program Synthesis and Transformation. Proceedings, 1998. X, 331 pages. 1999.

Vol. 1560: K. Imai, Y. Zheng (Eds.), Public Key Cryptography. Proceedings, 1999. IX, 327 pages. 1999.

Vol. 1561: I. Damgård (Ed.), Lectures on Data Security. VII, 250 pages. 1999.

Vol. 1562: C.L. Nehaniv (Ed.), Computation for Metaphors, Analogy, and Agents. X, 389 pages. 1999. (Subseries LNAI).

Vol. 1563: Ch. Meinel, S. Tison (Eds.), STACS 99. Proceedings, 1999. XIV, 582 pages. 1999.

Vol. 1565: P. Chen, J. Akoka, H. Kangassalo, B. Thalheim (Eds.), Conceptual Modeling. XXIV, 303 pages. 1999.

Vol. 1567: P. Antsaklis, W. Kohn, M. Lemmon, A. Nerode, S. Sastry (Eds.), Hybrid Systems V. X, 445 pages. 1999.

Vol. 1568: G. Bertrand, M. Couprie, L. Perroton (Eds.), Discrete Geometry for Computer Imagery. Proceedings, 1999. XI, 459 pages. 1999.

Vol. 1569: F.W. Vaandrager, J.H. van Schuppen (Eds.), Hybrid Systems: Computation and Control. Proceedings, 1999. X, 271 pages. 1999.

Vol. 1570: F. Puppe (Ed.), XPS-99: Knowledge-Based Systems. VIII, 227 pages. 1999. (Subseries LNAI).

Vol. 1571: P. Noriega, C. Sierra (Eds.), Agent Mediated Electronic Commerce. Proceedings, 1998. IX, 207 pages. 1999. (Subseries LNAI).

Vol. 1572: P. Fischer, H.U. Simon (Eds.), Computational Learning Theory. Proceedings, 1999. X, 301 pages. 1999. (Subseries LNAI).

Vol. 1574: N. Zhong, L. Zhou (Eds.), Methodologies for Knowledge Discovery and Data Mining. Proceedings, 1999. XV, 533 pages. 1999. (Subseries LNAI).

Vol. 1575: S. Jähnichen (Ed.), Compiler Construction. Proceedings, 1999. X, 301 pages. 1999.

Vol. 1576: S.D. Swierstra (Ed.), Programming Languages and Systems. Proceedings, 1999. X, 307 pages. 1999.

Vol. 1577: J.-P. Finance (Ed.), Fundamental Approaches to Software Engineering. Proceedings, 1999. X, 245 pages. 1999.

Vol. 1578: W. Thomas (Ed.), Foundations of Software Science and Computation Structures. Proceedings, 1999. X, 323 pages. 1999.

Vol. 1579: W.R. Cleaveland (Ed.), Tools and Algorithms for the Construction and Analysis of Systems. Proceedings, 1999. XI, 445 pages. 1999.

Vol. 1580: A. Včkovski, K.E. Brassel, H.-J. Schek (Eds.), Interoperating Geographic Information Systems. Proceedings, 1999. XI, 329 pages. 1999.

Vol. 1581: J.-Y. Girard (Ed.), Typed Lambda Calculi and Applications. Proceedings, 1999. VIII, 397 pages. 1999.

Vol. 1582: A. Lecomte, F. Lamarche, G. Perrier (Eds.), Logical Aspects of Computational Linguistics. Proceedings, 1997. XI, 251 pages. 1999. (Subseries LNAI).

Vol. 1584: G. Gottlob, E. Grandjean, K. Seyr (Eds.), Computer Science Logic. Proceedings, 1998. X, 431 pages. 1999.

Vol. 1586: J. Rolim et al. (Eds.), Parallel and Distributed Processing. Proceedings, 1999. XVII, 1443 pages. 1999.

Vol. 1587: J. Pieprzyk, R. Safavi-Naini, J. Seberry (Eds.), Information Security and Privacy. Proceedings, 1999. XI, 327 pages. 1999.

Vol. 1590: P. Atzeni, A. Mendelzon, G. Mecca (Eds.), The World Wide Web and Databases. Proceedings, 1998. VIII, 213 pages. 1999.

Vol. 1592: J. Stern (Ed.), Advances in Cryptology – EUROCRYPT '99. Proceedings, 1999. XII, 475 pages. 1999.

Vol. 1593: P. Sloot, M. Bubak, A. Hoekstra, B. Hertzberger (Eds.), High-Performance Computing and Networking. Proceedings, 1999. XXIII, 1318 pages. 1999.

Vol. 1594: P. Ciancarini, A.L. Wolf (Eds.), Coordination Languages and Models. Proceedings, 1999. IX, 420 pages. 1999.

Vol. 1596: R. Poli, H.-M. Voigt, S. Cagnoni, D. Corne, G.D. Smith, T.C. Fogarty (Eds.), Evolutionary Image Analysis, Signal Processing and Telecommunications. Proceedings, 1999. X, 225 pages. 1999.

Vol. 1597: H. Zuidweg, M. Campolargo, J. Delgado, A. Mullery (Eds.), Intelligence in Services and Networks. Proceedings, 1999. XII, 552 pages. 1999.

Vol. 1602: A. Sivasubramaniam, M. Lauria (Eds.), Network-Based Parallel Computing. Proceedings, 1999. VIII, 225 pages. 1999.

Vol. 1605: J. Billington, M. Diaz, G. Rozenberg (Eds.), Application of Petri Nets to Communication Networks. IX, 303 pages. 1999.

Vol. 1609: Z. W. Raś, A. Skowron (Eds.), Foundations of Intelligent Systems. Proceedings, 1999. XII, 676 pages. 1999. (Subseries LNAI).